Yamaha XJ6 & FZ6R
Service and Repair Manual

by Matthew Coombs

Models covered – Europe   *(5889-272)*
XJ6-N/NA. 599.8cc. 2009 to 2015
XJ6-SP. 599.8cc. 2013 to 2015
XJ6-S/SA Diversion. 599.8cc. 2009 to 2015
XJ6-F/FA Diversion. 599.8cc. 2010 to 2015

Models covered – US
FZ6R. 599.8cc. 2009 to 2015

© Haynes Publishing 2015

ABCDE
FGHIJ
KLMNO
PQRST

A book in the Haynes Service and Repair Manual Series

ISBN: 978 0 85733 889 1

British Library Cataloguing in Publication Data
A catalogue record for this book is available from the British Library.

Library of Congress Catalog Card Number 2014958876

Printed in the USA

Haynes Publishing
Sparkford, Yeovil, Somerset BA22 7JJ, England

Haynes North America, Inc
861 Lawrence Drive, Newbury Park, California 91320, USA

Haynes Publishing Nordiska AB
Box 1504, 751 45 Uppsala, Sweden

Contents

LIVING WITH YOUR YAMAHA

Introduction

Pre-ride checks

MAINTENANCE

Routine maintenance and servicing

Contents

REPAIRS AND OVERHAUL

Engine, transmission and associated systems

Chassis components

Electrical system

Wiring diagrams

REFERENCE

Index

Yamaha
Musical instruments to motorcycles

**The FS1E -
first bike of many sixteen year olds in the UK**

The Yamaha Motor Company

The Yamaha name can be traced back to 1889, when Torakusu Yamaha founded the Yamaha Organ Manufacturing Company. Such was the success of the company, that in 1897 it became Nippon Gakki Limited and manufactured a wide range of reed organs and pianos.

During World War II, Nippon Gakki's manufacturing base was utilised by the Japanese authorities to produce propellers and fuel tanks for their aviation industry. The end of the war brought about a huge public demand for low cost transport and many firms decided to utilise their obsolete aircraft tooling for the production of motorcycles. Nippon Gakki's first motorcycle went on sale in February 1955 and was named the 125 YA-1 Red Dragonfly. This machine was a copy of the German DKW RT125 motorcycle, featuring a single cylinder two-stroke engine with a four-speed gearbox. Due to the outstanding success of this model the motorcycle operation was separated from Nippon Gakki in July 1955 and the Yamaha Motor Company was formed.

The YA-1 also received acclaim by winning two of Japan's biggest road races, the Mount Fuji Climbing race and the Asama Volcano race. The high level of public demand for the YA-1 led to the development of a whole series of two-stroke singles and twins.

Having made a large impact on their home market, Yamahas were exported to the USA in 1958 and to the UK in 1962. In the UK the signing of an Anglo-Japanese trade agreement during 1962 enabled the sale of Japanese lightweight motorcycles and scooters in Britain. At that time, competition between the many motorcycle producers in Japan had reduced numbers significantly and by the end of the sixties, only the big-four which are familiar with today remained.

Yamaha Europe was founded in 1968 and based in Holland. Although originally set up to market marine products, the Dutch base is now the official European Headquarters and distribution centre. Yamaha motorcycles are built at factories in Holland, Denmark, Norway, Italy, France, Spain and Portugal. Yamahas are imported into the UK by Yamaha Motor UK Ltd, formerly Mitsui Machinery Sales (UK) Ltd. Mitsui and Co. were originally a trading house, handling the shipping, distribution and marketing of Japanese products into western countries. Ultimately Mitsui Machinery Sales was formed to handle Yamaha motorcycles and outboard motors.

Based on the technology derived from its motorcycle operation, Yamaha have produced many other products, such as automobile and lightweight aircraft engines, marine engines and boats, generators, pumps, ATVs, snowmobiles, golf cars, industrial robots, lawnmowers, swimming pools and archery equipment.

Two-strokes first

Part of Yamaha's success was a whole string of innovations in the two-stroke world. Autolube engine lubrication, torque induction, multi-ported engines, reed valves and power valves kept their two-strokes at the forefront of technology. Many advances were achieved with the use of racing as a development laboratory. They went to the USA in the late 1950s with an air-cooled 250cc twin but didn't hit the GPs until the early 1960s when Fumio Ito scored a hat-trick of sixth places in the Isle of Man TT, the Dutch TT and the Belgian GP. This experiment gave rise to the idea of the over-the-counter racer, an idea that became reality in the TD1, the first in an unmatched series of two-stroke racers that were the standard issue for privateers at national and international level for years and helped Yamaha develop their road engines. While privateers raced the twins, Yamaha built the outrageously complicated vee-four 250 for Phil Read and followed it with a vee-four 125 that Bill Ivy lapped the Isle of Man on at over 100mph! When the FIM regulations were changed to limit the smaller GP classes to two cylinders, these exotic bikes died but set the scene for an unparalleled dynasty of mass-produced racers based on the same technology as the road bikes.

In the 1960s and 70s the two-stroke engined YAS3 125, YDS1 to YDS7 250 and YR5 350 formed the core of Yamaha's range. By the mid-70s they had been superseded by the RD (Race-Developed) 125, 250, and 350 range of two-stroke twins, featuring improved 7-port engines with reed valve induction. Braking

was improved by the use of an hydraulic brake on the front wheel of DX models, instead of the drum arrangement used previously, and cast alloy wheels were available as an option on later RD models. The RD350 was replaced by the RD400 in 1976.

Running parallel with the RD twins was a range of single-cylinder two-strokes. Used in a variety of chassis types, the engine was used in the popular 50 cc FS1-E moped, the V50 to 90 step-thrus, RS100 and 125, YB100 and the DT trail range.

The TD racers got water-cooling in 1973 to become the TZs, the most successful and numerous over-the-counter racers ever built. That same year, Jarno Saarinen became the first rider to win a 500cc GP on a four-cylinder two-stroke on the new in-line four which was effectively a pair of TZs side-by-side. TZs won everywhere – including the Daytona 200 and 500 races when overbored to 351cc. A 700cc TZ also appeared, one year later taken out to 750cc. Steve Baker won the first Formula 750 world title – one of the precursors of Superbike – on one in 1977. The following year Kenny Roberts won Yamaha's first world 500 title and would be succeeded by Wayne Rainey and Eddie Lawson before Mick Doohan and the NSR500 took over.

The air-cooled single and twin cylinder RD

road bikes were eventually replaced by the LC series in 1980, featuring liquid-cooled engines, radical new styling, spiral pattern cast wheels and cantilever rear suspension (Yamaha's Monoshock). Of all the LC models, the RD350LC, or RD350R as it was later known, has made the most impact in the market. Later models had YPVS (Yamaha Power Valve System) engines, another first for Yamaha – this was essentially a valve located in the exhaust ports which was electronically operated to alter port timing to achieve maximum power output. The RD500LC was the largest two-stroke made by Yamaha and differed from the other LCs by the use of its vee-four cylinder engine.

With the exception of the RD350R, now manufactured in Brazil, the LC range has been discontinued. Two-stroke engined models have given way to environmental pressure, and thus with a few exceptions, such as the TZR125 and TZR250, are used only in scooters and small capacity bikes.

The Four-strokes

Yamaha concentrated solely on two-stroke models until 1970 when the XS1 was produced, their first four-stroke motorcycle. It was perhaps Yamaha's success with two-strokes that postponed an earlier

The distinctive paintwork and trim of the RD models

move into the four-stroke motorcycle market, although their work with Toyota during the 1960s had given them a sound base in four-stroke technology.

The XS1 had a 650 cc twin-cylinder SOHC engine and was later to become known as the XS650, appearing also in the popular SE custom form. Yamaha introduced a three cylinder 750 cc engine in 1976, fitted in a sport-tourer frame and called the XS750, TX750 in the USA . The XS750 established itself well in the sport tourer class and remained in production with very few changes until uprated to 850 cc in 1980.

Other four-strokes followed in 1976, with the introduction of the XS250/360/400 series twins. The XS range was strengthened in 1978 by the four-cylinder XS1100.

The 1980s saw a new family of four-strokes, the XJ550, 650, 750 and 900 Fours. Improvements over the XS range amounted to a slimmer DOHC engine unit due to the relocation of the alternator behind the cylinders, electronic ignition and uprated braking and suspension systems. Models were available mainly in standard trim, although custom-styled Maxims were produced especially for the US market. The XJ650T was the first model from Yamaha to have a turbo-charged engine. Although these early XJ models have now been discontinued, their roots live on in the XJ600S and XJ900S Diversion (Seca II) models.

The FZR prefix encompasses the pure

The XS650 led the way for Yamaha's four-stroke range

sports Yamaha models. With the exception of the 16-valve FZR400 and FZR600 models, the FZ/FZR750 and FZR1000 used 20-valve engines, two exhaust valves and three inlet valves per cylinder. This concept was called Genesis and gave improved gas flow to the combustion chambers. Other features of the new engine were the use of down-draught carburetors and the engine's inclined angle in the frame, plus the change to liquid-cooling. Lightweight Deltabox design aluminium frames and uprated suspension improved the bikes's handling. The Genesis engine lives on in the YZF750 and 1000 models.

Yamaha's XS750 was produced from 1976 to 1982 and then uprated to 850 cc

The Genesis concept was the basis of Yamaha's foray into four-stroke racing, first with a bike known simply as 'The Genesis', an FZ750 motor in a TT Formula 1 bike with which the factory attempted to steal the Honda RVF750's thunder at important events like the Suzuka 8 Hours and the Bol d'Or although they never fielded it for a whole World Championship season. That had to wait for the advent of the World Superbike Championship, although there was no full works team until 1995, instead it was left to individual importers to support teams. It was the Australian Dealer Team Yamaha which scored the factory's first World Superbike win in the series debut year of 1988. The rider? Mick Doohan. Slightly, embarrassingly, it was the steel framed FZ750 rather than the FZR homologation special that won races. The OW01 was a race winner, mainly in the hands of Fabrizio Pirovano, the factory's most successful Superbike racer with ten victories, but national success in the UK, Japan, and in the Daytona 200 has not been translated into World Championships for any of Yamaha's 750s.

The vee-twin engine has been the mainstay of the XV Virago range. Since 1981 XVs have been produced in 535, 700, 750, 920, 1000 and 1100 engine sizes, all using the same basic air-cooled sohc vee-twin engine. Other uses of vee engines have been in the XZ550 of the early 1980s, the XVZ12 Venture and the mighty VMX-12 V-Max.

Yamaha has always been a sporting-orientated company whose motto could be 'Racing Improves the Breed', so it's no surprise that the latest generation of lightweight sportsters are at the cutting edge of performance on and off the track. The R6 won more races than any other machine in the inaugural year of the World Supersports Championship, the R7 won a race in its debut year in World Superbike in the hands

A new family of four-strokes was released in 1980 with the introduction of the XJ range

of the mercurial Noriyuki Haga, and the mighty 1000cc R1 ended Honda's domination of the Isle of Man F1 TT when David Jefferies won three races in a week in 1999.

XJ trilogy

Yamaha have a long history of building 600cc across-the-frame fours that caught the mood of the times very nicely. The factory could even claim to have invented the class as they were first with a 600-4, the XJ600 of 1984 that stayed in

production into the 1990s. It was derived from 400cc home-market models and found a new market segment by the clever trick of being the same size and weight as most of the 550cc fours around but delivering 750cc-style performance. This was right at the time when motorcycles were rapidly going through the change from air-cooled two-valve motors into four-valve water-cooled power plants and the classes, or market sectors, were not as clearly defined as they would become.

It turned out Yamaha had got it right and despite the emergence of more sporting 600s from Kawasaki and Honda the XJ was a popular, affordable machine with just enough credibility to be a critical and commercial success. It was also around for a comparatively long time which tells you much about the bike. Owners liked it and demand for secondhand examples was always high.

The XJ remained a middle of the road option but the motor was wrapped in sporting clothes to produce the FZ600 in 1986, not to be confused with the FZR which got a new, water-cooled four-valves-per-cylinder motor in a Deltabox frame and was in the range for ten years from 1989 onwards.

The true spirit of the XJ range was revisited in 1991 with the launch of the Diversion, known as the Seca in the USA and Australia. The original two-valves-per-cylinder engine was retained and given more midrange at the expense of top end. It was wrapped in tubular steel chassis but given a smart half fairing and three-spoke wheels. This was as basic a motorcycle as you could find at the end of the 20th Century and start of the 21st, but like the original XJ it was a very long-lived model thanks to low prices and minimal running costs. It did exactly what you thought

The XJ6-N

The XJ6-SP

The XJ6-S

The XJ6-F

it would do and no more. The Diversion was an extremely popular base for a police bike, which tells you a lot about the model's costs and reliability. It sold over 160,000 units worldwide.

Yamaha were of course offering a sporty 600-4 option with the FZR and six years into the Diversion's model life they launched a true race replica in the shape of the R6. The first-generation 16v R6 motor was then used in the FZ6 Fazer, a more sporty all-rounder and that is the motor that found its way to the reborn XJ6 in 2009 and its close relative the Diversion, which had a half-fairing and nothing else to differentiate it from the N model. One of the original Diversion's major selling points was its price. It was very, very cheap. It also had a pleasantly retro feel and charm well before such things became fashionable. The current line-up of XJ6, Diversion and the fully-faired Diversion F all comply wiith the UK's A2 licence requirements.

Acknowledgements

Our thanks are due to Bransons Motorcycles of Yeovil and Bridge Motorcycles of Exeter, who supplied the machines featured in the illustrations throughout this manual. We would also like to thank NGK Spark Plugs (UK) Ltd for supplying the colour spark plug condition photographs, the Avon Rubber Company for supplying information on tyre fitting and Draper Tools Ltd for some of the workshop tools shown.

Thanks are also due to Yamaha Motor (UK) Ltd who supplied model photographs, and to Julian Ryder who wrote the introduction 'Musical Instruments to Motorcycles'.

About this Manual

The aim of this manual is to help you get the best value from your motorcycle. It can do so in several ways. It can help you decide what work must be done, even if you choose to have it done by a dealer; it provides information and procedures for routine maintenance and servicing; and it offers diagnostic and repair procedures to follow when trouble occurs.

We hope you use the manual to tackle the work yourself. For many simpler jobs, doing it yourself may be quicker than arranging an appointment to get the motorcycle into a dealer and making the trips to leave it and pick it up. More importantly, a lot of money can be saved by avoiding the expense the shop must pass on to you to cover its labour and overhead costs. An added benefit is the sense of satisfaction and accomplishment that you feel after doing the job yourself.

References to the left or right side of the motorcycle assume you are sitting on the seat, facing forward.

We take great pride in the accuracy of information given in this manual, but motorcycle manufacturers make alterations and design changes during the production run of a particular motorcycle of which they do not inform us. No liability can be accepted by the authors or publishers for loss, damage or injury caused by any errors in, or omissions from, the information given.

Illegal copying

EUROPE MODELS

Model	Code	Year
XJ6-N	20S1, 20S2	2009
XJ6-N	20S5, 20SA	2010
XJ6-N	20SB	2011
XJ6-N	20SF, 20SJ	2013
XJ6-N	20SR, 20ST	2014
XJ6-N	B611, B612	2015
XJ6-SP	20SL, 20SM	2013
XJ6-SP	20SU, 20SV	2014
XJ6-NA	36B1	2009
XJ6-NA	36B2, 36B3	2010
XJ6-NA	36B4	2011
XJ6-NA	36B5, 36B6,	2013
XJ6-NA	36B9, 36BA	2014
XJ6-NA	36BD, 36BE	2015
XJ6-SPA	36B7, 36B8	2013
XJ6-SPA	36BB, 36BC	2014
XJ6-S	36C1	2009
XJ6-S	36C4	2010
XJ6-S	36C6	2011
XJ6-S	36C9, 36CB	2013
XJ6-S	36CC, 36CE	2014
XJ6-S	36CF, 36CH	2015
XJ6-SA	36D1	2009
XJ6-SA	36D2	2010
XJ6-SA	36D3	2011
XJ6-SA	36D5, 36D7	2013
XJ6-SA	36D8, 36DA	2014
XJ6-SA	36DB, 36DD	2015
XJ6-F	1CW1, 1CW4	2010
XJ6-F	1CW8	2011
XJ6-F	1CWG, 1CWJ	2013
XJ6-F	1CWN, 1CWP	2014
XJ6-F	1CWV, 1CWW	2015
XJ6-FA	1DG1	2010
XJ6-FA	1DG2	2011
XJ6-FA	1DG3, 1DG4	2013
XJ6-FA	1DG5, 1DG6	2014
XJ6-FA	1DG7, 1DG8	2015

The frame number is stamped into the right-hand side of the steering head and is also on the sticker on the side of the frame (arrowed)

The engine number (arrowed) is stamped into the back of the crankcase

Frame and engine numbers

The frame serial number is stamped into the right-hand side of the steering head and is repeated on a sticker on the right-hand side of the frame. The engine number is stamped into the rear of the crankcase. The model code label is on the rear sub-frame under the seat. These numbers should be recorded and kept in a safe place so they can be given to the police in the event of a theft.

The frame serial number, engine serial number, and model code should also be kept in a handy place (such as with your driver's licence) so that they are always available when ordering parts for your machine.

The procedures in this manual identify the bikes by model (e.g. XJ6-N or XJ6-S), and if necessary (where changes have been made over the model life) by model code and/or year (e.g. 2013 XJ6-N 20SJ).

US MODELS

Model	Code	Year
FZ6R	Y	2009
FZ6R	Z	2010
FZ6R	A	2011
FZ6R	B	2012
FZ6R	D	2013
FZ6R	E	2014
FZ6R	F	2015
Note: FZ6RC indicates California market		

Buying spare parts

Once you have found all the identification numbers, record them for reference when buying parts. Since the manufacturers change specifications, parts and vendors (companies that manufacture various components on the machine), providing the ID numbers is the only way to be reasonably sure that you are buying the correct parts.

Whenever possible, take the worn part to the dealer so direct comparison with the new component can be made. Along the trail from the manufacturer to the parts shelf, there are numerous places that the part can end up with the wrong number or be listed incorrectly.

The two places to purchase new parts for your motorcycle – the accessory store and the franchised dealer – differ in the type of parts they carry. While dealers can obtain virtually every part for your motorcycle, the accessory dealer is usually limited to normal high wear items such as spark plugs, chains, sprockets, brake pads, etc.

Used parts can be obtained for roughly half the price of new ones, but you can't always be sure of what you're getting. Once again, take your worn part to the breaker's yard for direct comparison.

Whether buying new, used or rebuilt parts, the best course is to deal directly with someone who specialises in parts for your particular make.

XJ6-N, XJ6-NA and XJ6-SP

The XJ6-N was launched in 2009, and the N model is the 'naked' version.

The engine, a liquid-cooled, in-line four cylinder with two chain driven overhead camshafts actuating on four valves per cylinder, is based on that originally used in the Yamaha R6, and then in de-tuned form in the FZ-6 Fazer. The camshafts and valve duration and lift have been revised from those of the Fazer, and smaller 32 mm throttle bodies and narrower exhaust header pipes are fitted, all giving more torque low down in the rev range, and more power in the mid-range. The gearchange mechanism and clutch have also been revised to give a smoother gearchange.

The exhaust system is an under-slung one-piece unit, incorporating a catalytic converter and oxygen sensor. Yamaha's air induction system (AIS) feeds filtered air into the exhaust ports to improve exhaust end-gas burning.

The clutch is a conventional cable-operated, wet, multi-plate unit and the gearbox has 6-speeds. Drive to the rear wheel is by chain and sprockets.

The engine is housed in an all-new tubular steel frame that uses the engine as a stressed member. The front suspension has conventional oil-damped 41 mm forks, which are non-adjustable. The rear suspension has a single shock absorber acting directly on a box-section swingarm.

Seventeen-inch, five-spoke cast aluminium wheels are fitted front and rear, with twin, two-piston sliding caliper disc brakes at the front and a single-piston, sliding caliper disc brake at the rear. The NA model has an anti-lock brake system (ABS).

The XJ6-SP was launched in 2013, and is the same as the standard N except with different graphics and a two-piece seat.

There have been no major changes since the model was launched.

The XJ6-S and XJ6-SA

The XJ6-S was launched in 2009, and is a half-faired version of XJ6-N. The only differences are in the headlight, instrument and front turn signal mounts and the mirrors.

There have been no major changessince the model was launched.

The XJ6-F, XJ6-FA and FZ6R

The XJ6-F was launched in 2010, and is a fully-faired version of XJ6-N. The only differences are as for the S models,and are in the headlight, instrument and front turn signal mounts and the mirrors, but the belly pan is replaced by the lower sections of the fairing. The FZ6R is the US version of the XJ6-F, with the only difference being a two-piece seat.

There have been no major changes since the model was launched.

Height

Seat height

Wheelbase

Length

Dimensions and weights

Overall length
- XJ6-N/NA .... 2115 mm
- XJ6-S/SA, XJ6-F/FA and FZ6R .... 2120 mm

Overall width. .... 770 mm

Overall height
- XJ6-N/NA .... 1085 mm
- XJ6-S/SA .... 1210 mm
- XJ6-F/FA and FZ6R .... 1185 mm

Wheelbase .... 1440 mm

Seat height .... 785 mm

Wet weight (with all fluids and full fuel tank)
- XJ6-N .... 205 kg
- XJ6-NA .... 210 kg
- XJ6-S .... 211 kg
- XJ6-SA .... 216 kg
- XJ6-F .... 215 kg
- XJ6-FA .... 220 kg
- FZ6R .... 212 kg (467 lb)
- FZ6RC .... 213 kg (470 lb)

Engine

Type	Four-stroke 16V in-line four
Capacity	599.8 cc
Bore	65.5 mm
Stroke	44.5 mm
Compression ratio	12.2 to 1
Cooling system.	Liquid cooled
Clutch	Wet multi-plate
Transmission.	Six-speed constant mesh
Final drive.	Chain and sprockets
Camshafts	DOHC, chain-driven
Throttle bodies	Mikuni 32EIDW-B1/1
Ignition system	Digital electronic CDI

Chassis

Frame type.	Tubular steel
Rake and trail.	26°, 103.5 mm
Fuel tank capacity (including reserve)	17.3 litres
Reserve capacity (with fuel light on).	3.2 litres

Front suspension
- Type .... 41 mm oil-damped conventional telescopic forks
- Travel .... 130 mm
- Adjustment .... None

Rear suspension
- Type .... Single shock absorber, box-section steel swingarm
- Travel .... 42.0 mm at shock, 130 mm at wheel
- Adjustment .... Spring pre-load

Wheels .... 17 inch 5-spoke alloys

Tyres
- Front .... 120/70-ZR17 M/C (58W) tubeless
- Rear .... 160/60-ZR17 M/C (69W) tubeless

Front brake. .... Twin 298 mm discs with 2-piston sliding calipers

Rear brake .... Single 245 mm disc with single piston sliding caliper

Professional mechanics are trained in safe working procedures. However enthusiastic you may be about getting on with the job at hand, take the time to ensure that your safety is not put at risk. A moment's lack of attention can result in an accident, as can failure to observe simple precautions.

There will always be new ways of having accidents, and the following is not a comprehensive list of all dangers; it is intended rather to make you aware of the risks and to encourage a safe approach to all work you carry out on your bike.

Asbestos

● Certain friction, insulating, sealing and other products - such as brake pads, clutch linings, gaskets, etc. - contain asbestos. Extreme care must be taken to avoid inhalation of dust from such products since it is hazardous to health. If in doubt, assume that they do contain asbestos.

Fire

● Remember at all times that petrol is highly flammable. Never smoke or have any kind of naked flame around, when working on the vehicle. But the risk does not end there - a spark caused by an electrical short-circuit, by two metal surfaces contacting each other, by careless use of tools, or even by static electricity built up in your body under certain conditions, can ignite petrol vapour, which in a confined space is highly explosive. Never use petrol as a cleaning solvent. Use an approved safety solvent.

● Always disconnect the battery earth terminal before working on any part of the fuel or electrical system, and never risk spilling fuel on to a hot engine or exhaust.

● It is recommended that a fire extinguisher of a type suitable for fuel and electrical fires is kept handy in the garage or workplace at all times. Never try to extinguish a fuel or electrical fire with water.

Fumes

● Certain fumes are highly toxic and can quickly cause unconsciousness and even death if inhaled to any extent. Petrol vapour comes into this category, as do the vapours from certain solvents such as trichloro-ethylene. Any draining or pouring of such volatile fluids should be done in a well ventilated area.

● When using cleaning fluids and solvents, read the instructions carefully. Never use materials from unmarked containers - they may give off poisonous vapours.

● Never run the engine of a motor vehicle in an enclosed space such as a garage. Exhaust fumes contain carbon monoxide which is extremely poisonous; if you need to run the engine, always do so in the open air or at least have the rear of the vehicle outside the workplace.

The battery

● Never cause a spark, or allow a naked light near the vehicle's battery. It will normally be giving off a certain amount of hydrogen gas, which is highly explosive.

● Always disconnect the battery ground (earth) terminal before working on the fuel or electrical systems (except where noted).

● If possible, loosen the filler plugs or cover when charging the battery from an external source. Do not charge at an excessive rate or the battery may burst.

● Take care when topping up, cleaning or carrying the battery. The acid electrolyte, evenwhen diluted, is very corrosive and should not be allowed to contact the eyes or skin. Always wear rubber gloves and goggles or a face shield. If you ever need to prepare electrolyte yourself, always add the acid slowly to the water; never add the water to the acid.

Electricity

● When using an electric power tool, inspection light etc., always ensure that the appliance is correctly connected to its plug and that, where necessary, it is properly grounded (earthed). Do not use such appliances in damp conditions and, again, beware of creating a spark or applying excessive heat in the vicinity of fuel or fuel vapour. Also ensure that the appliances meet national safety standards.

● A severe electric shock can result from touching certain parts of the electrical system, such as the spark plug wires (HT leads), when the engine is running or being cranked, particularly if components are damp or the insulation is defective. Where an electronic ignition system is used, the secondary (HT) voltage is much higher and could prove fatal.

Remember...

✗ **Don't** start the engine without first ascer-taining that the transmission is in neutral.

✗ **Don't** suddenly remove the pressure cap from a hot cooling system - cover it with a cloth and release the pressure gradually first, or you may get scalded by escaping coolant.

✗ **Don't** attempt to drain oil until you are sure it has cooled sufficiently to avoid scalding you.

✗ **Don't** grasp any part of the engine or exhaust system without first ascertaining that it is cool enough not to burn you.

✗ **Don't** allow brake fluid or antifreeze to contact the machine's paintwork or plastic components.

✗ **Don't** siphon toxic liquids such as fuel, hydraulic fluid or antifreeze by mouth, or allow them to remain on your skin.

✗ **Don't** inhale dust - it may be injurious to health (see Asbestos heading).

✗ **Don't** allow any spilled oil or grease to remain on the floor - wipe it up right away, before someone slips on it.

✗ **Don't** use ill-fitting spanners or other tools which may slip and cause injury.

✗ **Don't** lift a heavy component which may be beyond your capability - get assistance.

✗ **Don't** rush to finish a job or take unverified short cuts.

✗ **Don't** allow children or animals in or around an unattended vehicle.

✗ **Don't** inflate a tyre above the recommended pressure. Apart from overstressing the carcass, in extreme cases the tyre may blow off forcibly.

✔ **Do** ensure that the machine is supported securely at all times. This is especially important when the machine is blocked up to aid wheel or fork removal.

✔ **Do** take care when attempting to loosen a stubborn nut or bolt. It is generally better to pull on a spanner, rather than push, so that if you slip, you fall away from the machine rather than onto it.

✔ **Do** wear eye protection when using power tools such as drill, sander, bench grinder etc.

✔ **Do** use a barrier cream on your hands prior to undertaking dirty jobs - it will protect your skin from infection as well as making the dirt easier to remove afterwards; but make sure your hands aren't left slippery. Note that long-term contact with used engine oil can be a health hazard.

✔ **Do** keep loose clothing (cuffs, ties etc. and long hair) well out of the way of moving mechanical parts.

✔ **Do** remove rings, wristwatch etc., before working on the vehicle - especially the electrical system.

✔ **Do** keep your work area tidy - it is only too easy to fall over articles left lying around.

✔ **Do** exercise caution when compressing springs for removal or installation. Ensure that the tension is applied and released in a controlled manner, using suitable tools which preclude the possibility of the spring escaping violently.

✔ **Do** ensure that any lifting tackle used has a safe working load rating adequate for the job.

✔ **Do** get someone to check periodically that all is well, when working alone on the vehicle.

✔ **Do** carry out work in a logical sequence and check that everything is correctly assembled and tightened afterwards.

✔ **Do** remember that your vehicle's safety affects that of yourself and others. If in doubt on any point, get professional advice.

● If in spite of following these precautions, you are unfortunate enough to injure yourself, seek medical attention as soon as possible.

Engine oil level

Before you start:
✔ Support the motorcycle upright on level ground.
✔ Start the engine and let it idle for several minutes to allow it to reach normal operating temperature. *Caution: Do not run the engine in an enclosed space such as a garage or workshop.*
✔ Leave the motorcycle undisturbed for a few minutes to allow the oil level to stabilise.

Bike care:
● If you have to add oil frequently, you should check whether you have any oil leaks. If there is no sign of oil leakage from the joints and gaskets the engine could be burning oil (see *Fault Finding*).

The correct oil:
● Modern, high-revving engines place great demands on their oil. It is very important that the correct oil for your bike is used – do not use car engine oils.
● Always top up with a good quality motorcycle oil of the specified type and viscosity and do not overfill the engine.

Oil type	API grade SG or higher, JASO grade MA
Oil viscosity	SAE 10W30, 10W40, 10W50, 15W40, 20W40 or 20W50

1 Unscrew the dipstick (arrowed) from the right-hand side of the crankcase...

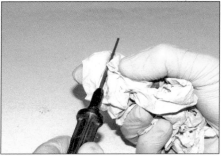

2 ...and use clean rag or a paper towel to wipe off all the oil.

3 Insert the clean dipstick back into the engine, but do not screw it in.

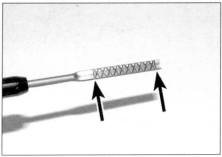

4 Remove the dipstick and check the level of the oil, which should be somewhere between the upper and lower level lines (arrowed).

5 If the level is below the lower line, unscrew the filler cap from the top of the clutch cover.

6 Add the recommended grade and type of oil, to bring the level almost up to the upper line on the dipstick. Do not overfill.

7 Check the filler cap and dipstick O-rings (arrowed) are in place, then screw the cap and dipstick in. Run the engine, switch it off and wait a few minutes, then check the level again.

Suspension, steering and drive chain

Suspension and Steering:
● Check that the front and rear suspension operates smoothly without binding.
● Check that the rear shock pre-load is adjusted as required.
● Check that the steering moves smoothly from lock-to-lock.

Final drive:
● Check that the drive chain slack isn't excessive, and adjust it if necessary (see Chapter 1).
● If the chain looks dry, lubricate it (see Chapter 1).

Coolant level

Before you start:

✔ Make sure you have a supply of coolant available – either a pre-mix coolant as sold for motorcycle engines, or prepare a mixture of 50% distilled water and 50% corrosion inhibited ethylene glycol anti-freeze. Note: *Yamaha specify that soft tap water can be used if necessary, but NOT hard water. If in doubt, boil the water first or use only distilled water.*
✔ Always check the coolant level when the engine is cold.
✔ Support the motorcycle upright on level ground.

⚠ **Warning: DO NOT remove the radiator pressure cap to add coolant. Topping up is done via the coolant reservoir tank filler. DO NOT leave open containers of coolant about, as it is poisonous.**

✔ On XJ6-F/FA models and FZ6R models remove the centre section of the lower fairing (see Chapter 7).

Bike care:

● Use only the specified coolant mixture. It is important that anti-freeze is used in the system all year round, and not just in the winter. Do not top the system up using only water, as the system will become too diluted.

● Do not overfill the reservoir. If the coolant is significantly above the FULL level line at any time, the surplus should be siphoned or drained off to prevent the possibility of it being expelled out of the overflow hose.
● If the coolant level falls steadily, check the system for leaks (see Chapter 1). If no leaks are found and the level continues to fall, it is recommended that the machine be taken to a Yamaha dealer for a pressure test.

1 The reservoir is mounted in front of the engine. The coolant level must be between the FULL and LOW level lines (arrowed) marked on the reservoir.

2 If the coolant level does not lie between the FULL and LOW level lines, open the reservoir filler cap.

3 Top the coolant level up with the recommended coolant mixture, then fit the cap.

Brake fluid levels

⚠ **Warning: Brake hydraulic fluid can harm your eyes and damage painted surfaces, so use extreme caution when handling and pouring it and cover surrounding surfaces with rag. Do not use fluid that has been standing open for some time, as it absorbs moisture from the air which can cause a dangerous loss of braking effectiveness.**

Before you start:

✔ The front brake fluid reservoir is on the right-hand handlebar. The rear brake fluid reservoir is located behind the right-hand side panel – remove the panel for access (see Chapter 7).
✔ Make sure you have a supply of DOT 4 hydraulic fluid.
✔ Wrap a rag around the reservoir being worked on to ensure that any spillage does not come into contact with painted surfaces.
✔ Support the bike upright on level ground.

Bike care:

● The fluid in the front and rear brake master cylinder reservoirs will drop very gradually as the brake pads wear down.

FRONT BRAKE

● If either fluid reservoir requires repeated topping-up there could be a leak somewhere in the system, which must be investigated immediately.

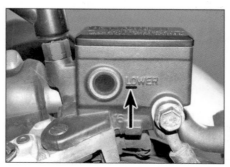

1 The front brake fluid level is visible through the window in the reservoir body – it must be above the LOWER level line (arrowed).

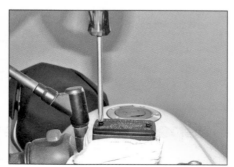

2 If the level is below the LOWER level line undo the reservoir cover screws and remove the cover, the diaphragm plate and the diaphragm.

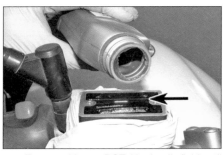

3 Top-up with new DOT 4 hydraulic fluid until the level is just below the UPPER level line (arrowed) cast on the inside of the reservoir. Take care to avoid spills (see **Warning**) and do not overfill.

4 Wipe any moisture out of the diaphragm using a clean lint-free cloth.

5 Make sure the diaphragm is correctly seated before fitting the plate and cover.

REAR BRAKE

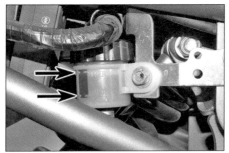

1 The rear brake fluid level is visible through the reservoir body – it must be between the UPPER and LOWER level lines (arrowed).

2 If the level is below the LOWER level line unscrew the mounting bolt (arrowed) and draw the reservoir out from behind the frame tube so the top is accessible.

3 Hold the reservoir, unscrew the cap and remove the plate and the diaphragm.

4 Top-up with new DOT 4 hydraulic fluid until the level is between the level lines. Take care to avoid spills (see **Warning**) and do not overfill.

5 Wipe any moisture out of the diaphragm using a clean lint-free cloth.

6 Make sure the diaphragm is correctly seated before fitting the plate and cap. Fit the reservoir and tighten the bolt.

Legal and safety

Lighting and signalling:
● Take a minute to check that the headlight, tail light, brake light, instrument lights and turn signals all work correctly.
● Check that the horn sounds when the switch is operated.
● A working speedometer graduated in mph is a statutory requirement in the UK.

Safety:
● Check that the throttle grip rotates smoothly and snaps shut when released, in all steering positions. Also check for the correct amount of freeplay (see Chapter 1).
● Check that the steering moves freely from lock-to-lock.
● Check that the brake lever and pedal, clutch lever and gearchange lever operate smoothly. Lubricate them at the specified intervals or when necessary (see Chapter 1).
● Check that the engine shuts off when the kill switch is operated.

● Check that the sidestand and centrestand (where fitted) return springs hold the stands up securely when they are retracted.

Fuel:
● This may seem obvious, but check that you have enough fuel to complete your journey. If you notice signs of fuel leakage – rectify the cause immediately.
● Make sure you use the correct grade fuel – see Chapter 4 Specifications.

Tyres

Tyre tread depth:

● At the time of writing UK law requires that the tread depth must be at least 1 mm over the entire tread breadth all the way around the tyre, with no bald patches. Many riders, however, consider 2 mm tread depth minimum to be a safer limit. Yamaha recommend a minimum of 1.6 mm.

● Many tyres now incorporate wear indicators in the tread. Identify the triangular pointer or TWI mark on the tyre sidewall to locate the indicator bar and fit a new tyre if the tread has worn down to the bar.

The correct pressures:

● The tyre pressures must be checked when

cold, not immediately after riding. Note that low tyre pressures will cause abnormal tread wear and unsafe handling, and may cause the tyre to slip on the rim or come off. High tyre pressures will cause abnormal tread wear and unsafe handling.

● Use an accurate pressure gauge. Many garage forecourt gauges are wildly inaccurate. If you buy your own, spend as much as you can justify on a quality gauge.

● Correct air pressure will increase tyre life and provide maximum stability, handling capability and ride comfort. Tyre pressures are printed on a label stuck to the swingarm.

Tyre care:

● Check the tyres carefully for cuts, tears, embedded nails or other sharp objects and excessive wear. Operation of the motorcycle with excessively worn tyres is extremely hazardous, as traction and handling are directly affected.

● Check the condition of the tyre valve and make sure a dust cap is fitted.

● Pick out any stones or nails which may have become embedded in the tyre tread. If left, they will eventually penetrate through the casing and cause a puncture.

● If tyre damage is apparent, or unexplained loss of pressure is experienced, seek the advice of a tyre fitting specialist without delay.

Loading*/speed	Front	Rear
Up to 90 kg (198 lb) load	33 psi (2.25 Bar)	36 psi (2.5 Bar)
90 kg (198 lb) up to max. load	36 psi (2.5 Bar)	42 psi (2.9 Bar)
High speed riding	33 psi (2.25 Bar)	36 psi (2.5 Bar)
*Load is the total weight of the rider, passenger, luggage and any accessories.		

Recommended max. load	
XJ6-N	195 kg (430 lb)
XJ6-NA	190 kg (419 lb)
XJ6-S	189 kg (417 lb)
XJ6-SA	184 kg (406 lb)
XJ6-F	185 kg (408 lb)
XJ6-FA	180 kg (397 lb)
FZ6R	188 kg (414 lb)
FZ6RC	187 kg (412 lb)

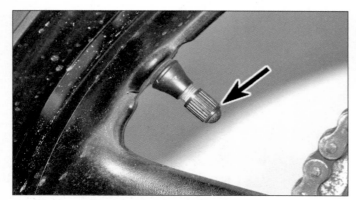

1 Remove the cap (arrowed) from the valve – if it's missing, fit a new one.

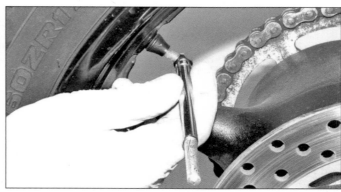

2 Check the tyre pressures when the tyres are cold and keep them properly inflated. Fit the cap on completion.

3 Measure tread depth at the centre of the tyre using a tread depth gauge.

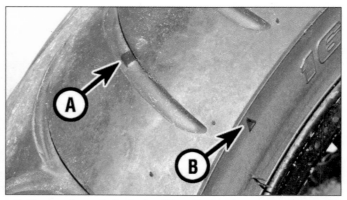

4 Tyre tread wear indicator bar (A) and its location marking (B) (usually either an arrow, a triangle or the letters TWI) on the sidewall.

Chapter 1
Routine maintenance and Servicing

Contents

Degrees of difficulty

| **Easy,** suitable for novice with little experience | | **Fairly easy,** suitable for beginner with some experience | | **Fairly difficult,** suitable for competent DIY mechanic | | **Difficult,** suitable for experienced DIY mechanic | 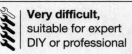 | **Very difficult,** suitable for expert DIY or professional | |

Engine

Spark plugs	
Type	NGK CR9E
Electrode gap	0.6 to 0.7 mm
Engine idle speed	1250 to 1350 rpm
Cylinder identification	numbered 1 to 4 from left to right
Throttle body synchronisation – intake vacuum at idle	238 mmHg
Throttle body synchronisation – max. difference between bodies	10 mmHg
Valve clearances (COLD engine)	
Intake valves	0.13 to 0.20 mm
Exhaust valves	0.23 to 0.30 mm

Cycle parts

Drive chain slack	45 to 55 mm
Rear brake pedal position	46.5 mm (see text)
Throttle cable freeplay	3 to 5 mm
Clutch cable freeplay (at lever ball end)	10 to 15 mm
Tyre pressures (cold)	see *Pre-ride checks*

Lubricants and fluids

Fuel	see Chapter 4
Engine oil type	API grade SG or higher, JASO grade MA, SAE 10W30, 10W40, 10W50, 15W40, 20W40 or 20W50
Engine oil capacity	
Oil change	2.5 litres
Oil and filter change	2.8 litres
Following engine overhaul – dry engine, new filter	3.4 litres
Coolant type	Pre-mixed coolant for motorcycle engines, or a mixture of 50% distilled water and 50% ethylene glycol anti-freeze with corrosion inhibitors for aluminium engines. *Note that Yamaha specify that soft tap water can be used, but NOT hard water. If in doubt, boil the water first or use only distilled water.*
Coolant capacity	
Radiator	2.0 litres
Reservoir	0.25 litre
Brake fluid	DOT 4
Drive chain	Aerosol chain lubricant suitable for O-ring chains
Steering head bearings	Lithium-based multi-purpose grease
Shock absorber bush, collars and seals	Molybdenum disulphide grease
Swingarm pivot bolt and seals	Molybdenum disulphide grease
Swingarm bearings	Lithium-based multi-purpose grease
Wheel bearing seals	Lithium-based multi-purpose grease
Gearchange lever, clutch lever, front brake lever, rear brake pedal, stand pivots	Lithium-based multi-purpose grease
Cables	Aerosol cable lubricant
Throttle twistgrip	Lithium-based multi-purpose grease

Torque wrench settings

Cooling system drain bolt	10 Nm
Frame bracket bolts	30 Nm
Fork clamp bolts (top yoke)	20 Nm
Oil drain plug	43 Nm
Oil filter	17 Nm
Rear axle nut	90 Nm
Spark plugs	13 Nm
Steering head bearing adjuster nut – using Yamaha tool	
Initial setting	52 Nm
Final setting	18 Nm
Steering stem nut	110 Nm
Timing rotor cover bolts	10 Nm

Pre-ride
- ☐ See *Pre-ride checks* at the beginning of this manual.

After the initial 600 miles (1000 km)
Note: *This check is usually performed by a Yamaha dealer after the first 600 miles (1000 km) from new. Thereafter, maintenance is carried out according to the following intervals of the schedule.*

Every 500 miles (800 km)
- ☐ Check, adjust, clean and lubricate the drive chain (Section 1)

Every 6000 miles (10,000 km)
- ☐ Check and adjust the spark plugs (Section 2)
- ☐ Check and adjust the idle speed (Section 3)
- ☐ Check/adjust throttle body synchronisation (Section 4)
- ☐ Check the fuel system and the air induction system (AIS) (Section 5)
- ☐ Check and adjust the throttle cables (Section 6)
- ☐ Check and adjust the clutch cable (Section 7)
- ☐ Lubricate the clutch/gearchange/brake lever/brake pedal/stand pivots and cables (Section 8)
- ☐ Check the cooling system (Section 9)
- ☐ Change the engine oil (Section 10)
- ☐ Check the brake system (Section 11)
- ☐ Check the condition of the wheels, wheel bearings and tyres (Section 12)
- ☐ Check the front and rear suspension (Section 13)
- ☐ Check and adjust the steering head bearings (Section 14)
- ☐ Check the sidestand and starter safety circuit (Section 15)
- ☐ Check the tightness of all nuts, bolts and fasteners (Section 16)
- ☐ Check the battery (Section 17)

Every 12,000 miles (20,000 km)
Carry out all the items under the previous interval, plus the following:
- ☐ Fit new spark plugs (see Section 2)
- ☐ Fit a new engine oil filter (Section 10)
- ☐ Re-grease the steering head bearings (see Chapter 5)

Every 25,000 miles (40,000 km)
- ☐ Fit a new air filter and clean the filter housing (Section 18)
- ☐ Check and adjust the valve clearances (Section 19)

Every 30,000 miles (50,000 km)
- ☐ Re-grease the swingarm bearings (Chapter 5)

Every two years
- ☐ Fit new master cylinder and caliper seals (Chapter 6)
- ☐ Change the brake fluid (Chapter 6)

Every three years
- ☐ Change the coolant (see Chapter 3)

Every four years
- ☐ Fit new brake hoses (see Chapter 6)

Non-scheduled maintenance
- ☐ Fit new fuel hoses (Section 5)
- ☐ Change the front fork oil (see Chapter 5)

Pre-ride
☐ See *Pre-ride checks* at the beginning of this manual.

After the initial 600 miles (1000 km)
Note: *This check is usually performed by a Yamaha dealer after the first 600 miles (1000 km) from new. Thereafter, maintenance is carried out according to the following intervals of the schedule.*

Every 500 miles (800 km)
☐ Check, adjust, clean and lubricate the drive chain (Section 1)

Every 4000 miles (7000 km)
☐ Check and adjust the spark plugs (Section 2)
☐ Check and adjust the idle speed (Section 3)
☐ Check/adjust throttle body synchronisation (Section 4)
☐ Check the fuel system (Section 5)
☐ Check the crankcase breather hose (Section 18)
☐ Check the exhaust system for leaks (Section 16)
☐ Check and adjust the throttle cables (Section 6)
☐ Check and adjust the clutch cable (Section 7)
☐ Lubricate the clutch/gearchange/brake lever/brake pedal/sidestand pivots and cables (Section 8)
☐ Check the cooling system (Section 9)
☐ Change the engine oil (Section 10)
☐ Check the brake system (Section 11)
☐ Check the condition of the wheels, wheel bearings and tyres (Section 12)
☐ Check the front and rear suspension (Section 13)
☐ Check and adjust the steering head bearings (Section 14)
☐ Check the sidestand and starter safety circuit (Section 15)
☐ Check the tightness of all nuts, bolts and fasteners (Section 16)
☐ Check the battery (Section 17)

Every 8000 miles (13,000 km)
Carry out all the items under the previous interval, plus the following:
☐ Fit new spark plugs (Section 2)
☐ Fit a new engine oil filter (Section 10)

Every 12,000 miles (20,000 km)
☐ Check the air induction system (AIS) and the EVAP system (Section 5)
☐ Re-grease the steering head bearings (Chapter 5)

Every 24,000 miles (38,000 km)
☐ Fit a new air filter and clean the air filter housing (Section 18)

Every 26,000 miles (42,000 km)
☐ Check and adjust the valve clearances (Section 19)

Every 30,000 miles (50,000 km)
☐ Re-grease the swingarm bearings (Chapter 5)

Every two years
☐ Fit new master cylinder and caliper seals (Chapter 6)
☐ Change the brake fluid (Chapter 6)
☐ Change the coolant (Chapter 3)

Every four years
☐ Fit new brake hoses (Chapter 6)

Non-scheduled maintenance
☐ Fit new fuel hoses (Section 5)
☐ Change the front fork oil (Chapter 5)

Component locations on the right side

1 Rear shock pre-load adjuster
2 Rear brake fluid reservoir
3 Engine oil filler
4 Throttle cable upper adjuster
5 Front brake fluid reservoir
6 Frame number and VIN label
7 Fork seal
8 Radiator pressure cap
9 Coolant level reservoir
10 Coolant drain bolt
11 Engine oil dipstick
12 Rear brake light switch
13 Rear brake pedal height adjuster
14 Drive chain adjuster

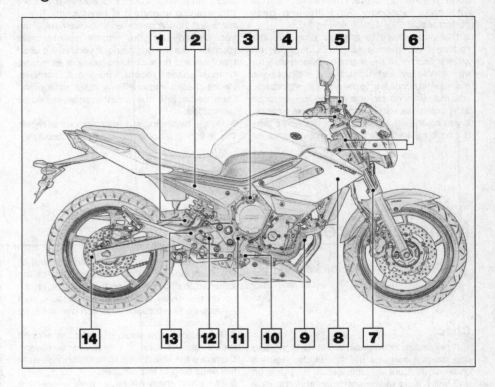

Component locations on the left side

1 Steering head bearing adjuster
2 Clutch cable upper adjuster
3 Clutch cable in-line adjuster
4 Air filter
5 Throttle cable lower adjuster
6 Idle speed adjuster
7 Battery
8 Drive chain adjuster
9 Engine number
10 Oil filter
11 Engine oil drain plug
12 Fork seal

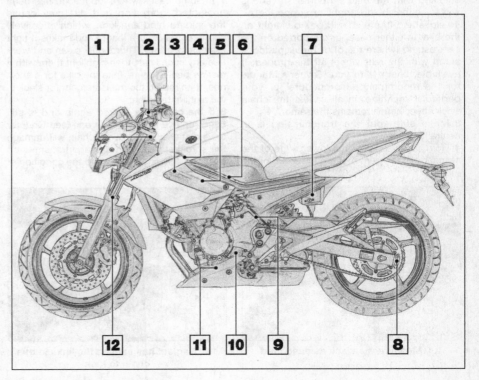

1 This Chapter is designed to help the home mechanic maintain his/her motorcycle for safety, economy, long life and peak performance.

2 Deciding where to start or plug into the routine maintenance schedule depends on several factors. If the warranty period on your motorcycle has just expired, and if it has been maintained according to the warranty standards, you may want to pick up routine maintenance as it coincides with the next mileage interval. If you have owned the machine for some time but have never performed any maintenance on it, then you may want to start at the beginning and include all frequent procedures to ensure that nothing important is overlooked. If you have just had a major engine overhaul, then you should start the engine maintenance routines from the beginning. If you have a used machine and have no knowledge of its history or maintenance record, you should combine all the checks into one large initial service and then settle into the maintenance schedule prescribed.

3 Before beginning any maintenance or repair, the machine should be cleaned thoroughly, especially around the oil filter, drain plugs and valve cover. Cleaning will help ensure that dirt does not contaminate the engine and will allow you to detect wear and damage that could otherwise easily go unnoticed.

4 Certain maintenance information is sometimes printed on decals attached to the motorcycle. If any information on the decals differs from that included here, use the information on the decal.

⚠ *Warning: Read the Safety first! section of this manual carefully before starting work.*

Maintenance procedures

1 Drive chain and sprockets

Check

1 A neglected drive chain won't last long and can quickly damage the sprockets. Routine chain adjustment and lubrication isn't difficult and will ensure maximum chain and sprocket life.

Caution: Riding the bike with excess slack in the chain could lead to damage.

2 Yamaha specify that the chain can be checked with the bike supported in various ways – either held upright or supported on its sidestand (there should be no weight on the bike in either case) or supported on the centrestand (where fitted) or a rear paddock stand with the rear wheel off the ground. If available, check with your Owner's Manual for the recommended procedure for your particular machine. In all cases, the chain slack specification remains the same.

3 Make sure that the transmission is in neutral.

4 Hold a ruler against the lower edge of the swingarm in the centre of the lower run of the chain. Push down on the chain to take out all the slack and note the measurement of the lower edge of the chain on the ruler, then push up on the chain and note the measurement again **(see illustration)** – don't move the ruler during these checks.

5 To calculate the slack, subtract the second measurement from the first measurement. Compare the result with specification given at the beginning of this Chapter.

6 Since the chain will rarely wear evenly, roll the bike forward (or rotate the wheel) so that another section of chain can be checked; do this several times to check the entire length of chain, and mark the tightest spot.

7 In some cases where lubrication has been neglected, corrosion and dirt may cause the links to bind and kink, which effectively shortens the chain's length and makes it tight **(see illustration)**. Thoroughly clean and work free any such links, then highlight them with a marker pen or paint. Take the bike for a short ride, then repeat the measurement for slack in the highlighted area.

8 If the chain has kinked again and is still tight, replace it with a new one (see Chapter 6). A rusty, kinked or worn chain will damage the sprockets and can damage transmission bearings. If in any doubt as to the condition of a chain, it is far better to fit a new one than risk damage to other components and possibly yourself.

9 Check the entire length of the chain for worn or damaged rollers and sideplates, loose links and pins, and missing O-rings and replace it with a new one if necessary. From time to time, and particularly if the chain is old and most of the adjustment has been taken up, or if the sprockets are wearing, refer to Chapter six and check the amount of chain stretch.

Caution: Never fit a new chain onto old sprockets, and never use the old chain if you fit new sprockets – replace the chain and sprockets as a set – see Chapter 6.

Adjustment

10 Rotate the rear wheel until the chain is positioned with the tightest spot at the centre of its bottom run (see Step 6). Support the bike as before.

11 Loosen the rear wheel axle nut **(see illustration)**.

12 Loosen the locknut on the adjuster on both sides of the swingarm, then turn the adjuster nuts evenly and a small amount at a time, clockwise to reduce slack and anti-clockwise to increase it, keeping some forward pressure on the wheel to make sure the adjuster

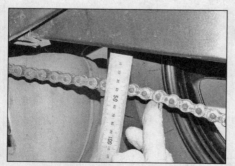

1.4 Measure the slack as described

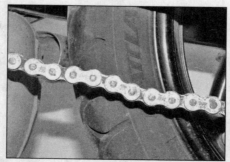

1.7 Neglect has caused the links in this chain to kink

1.11 Slacken the rear axle nut (arrowed)

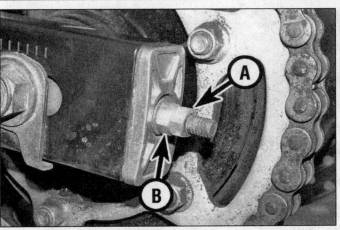

1.12a Slacken the locknut (A) on each side and turn the adjuster nuts (B) as required

1.12b Axle alignment marks and marker plate notch (arrowed) – models with adjustment marker plate

nuts and plates remain butted against the swingarm ends, until the amount of slack is within the specified range **(see illustration)**. Now check that the axle alignment marks on both sides of the swingarm are equal – if not, the rear wheel will be out of alignment with the front **(see illustrations)**.

13 If there is a discrepancy in the position of the alignment marks, correct it with the adjusters and then check the chain tension again as described above.

14 Push the wheel forwards and tighten the axle nut to the torque setting specified at the beginning of this Chapter, then tighten the adjuster locknuts securely. Recheck the adjustment.

15 If the chain is difficult to adjust satisfactorily, or if it is close to the end of available adjustment, check the chain stretch as described in Chapter 6.

Cleaning and lubrication

16 The best time to lubricate the chain is after the motorcycle has been ridden. When the chain is warm, the lubricant will penetrate the joints between the sideplates better than when cold.

17 If required, wash the chain using a dedicated aerosol cleaner or in paraffin (kerosene), then wipe it off and allow it to dry, using compressed air if available **(see illustration)**. If the chain is excessively dirty, remove the rear wheel (see Chapter 6) and soak the chain in paraffin.

Caution: Don't use petrol (gasoline), solvent or other cleaning fluids which might damage the internal sealing properties of the chain. Don't use high-pressure water. The entire process shouldn't take longer than five to six minutes – if it does, the O-rings in the chain rollers could be damaged.

18 Apply the lubricant to the area where the sideplates overlap – not the middle of the rollers. Protect the tyre from overspray with a rag or piece of cardboard **(see illustration)**.

Note: Use an aerosol chain lube that is specifically for O-ring chains. Engine oil can be used but it will not stick to the chain as well as dedicated chain lube and therefore not provide long lasting lubrication.

⚠ *Warning: Take care not to get any lubricant on the tyres or brake system components. If any of the lubricant inadvertently contacts them, clean it off thoroughly using a suitable solvent or dedicated brake cleaner before riding the machine.*

Sprocket wear check

19 If the drive chain is worn or damaged, it is likely that the sprockets will also be worn.

1.12c Axle alignment marks – models without adjustment marker plate

20 Remove the front sprocket cover (see Chapter 6). Check the teeth on the front and rear sprockets for wear **(see illustration)**. If the sprocket teeth are worn excessively, follow the procedure in Chapter 6 and replace the chain and both sprockets with a new set.

21 Check the front and rear sprocket nuts are tight (refer to *Specifications* in Chapter 6 for torque settings).

22 Inspect the drive chain slider on the front of the swingarm for excessive wear and damage and replace it with a new one if necessary (see Chapter 5).

1.17 Specially shaped chain cleaning brushes are available from good suppliers

1.18 Apply the lubricant to the overlap between the sideplates

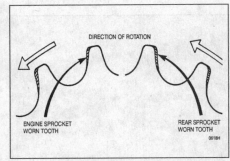

1.20 Check the sprockets in the areas indicated to see if they are worn excessively

2.2a Release the two cable-ties (arrowed) on the left-hand side...

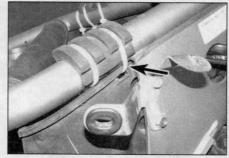

2.2b ...and the single cable-tie (arrowed) on the right...

2.2c ...and note how the shield locates before removing it

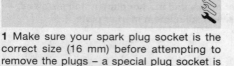

2 Spark plugs

1 Make sure your spark plug socket is the correct size (16 mm) before attempting to remove the plugs – a special plug socket is supplied in the motorcycle's tool kit, which is stored under the seat.

2 Remove the fuel tank, the air filter housing, and the AIS air cut-off valve and hoses (see Chapter 4). Release the cable-ties and remove the rubber heat shield, noting how it fits **(see illustrations)**.

3 Clean the area around each spark plug cap to prevent any dirt falling into the spark plug wells. Check that the cylinder location is marked on each HT lead (numbered 1 to 4 from the left-hand side), then pull the cap off each spark plug **(see illustration)**.

4 Using either the Yamaha plug socket or a deep socket type wrench, unscrew the plugs from the cylinder head **(see illustration)**. Lay each plug out in relation to its cylinder so that if any plug shows up a problem, it will be easy to identify the troublesome cylinder.

5 Inspect the electrodes for wear. Both the centre and side electrodes should have square edges and the side electrodes should be of uniform thickness. Look for excessive deposits and evidence of a cracked or chipped insulator around the centre electrode. Compare your spark plugs to the colour spark plug reading chart at the end of this manual. Check the threads, the washer and the ceramic insulator body for cracks and other damage.

6 If the electrodes are not excessively worn, and if the deposits can be easily removed with a wire brush, and there are no cracks or chips visible in the insulator, the plugs can be

re-gapped and re-used. If in doubt concerning the condition of the plugs, replace them with new ones, as the expense is minimal. Note that new spark plugs should be fitted at every second service interval.

7 Before installing the plugs, make sure they are the correct type and heat range and check the gap between the side (earth) electrodes and the centre electrode **(see illustrations)**. Compare the gap to that specified and adjust as necessary. If the gap must be adjusted, bend the side electrodes only and be very careful not to chip or crack the insulator nose **(see illustration)**. Make sure the sealing washer is in place on the plug before installing it.

8 Carefully thread the plugs into the head turning the tool shaft by hand, making sure they do not cross-thread – if they become prematurely tight remove them and start again, do not force them or you will damage the cylinder head **(see illustration)**. Once the

2.3 Pull the cap off the spark plug

2.4 Unscrew and remove the plug

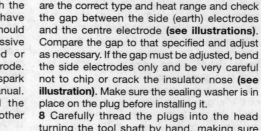
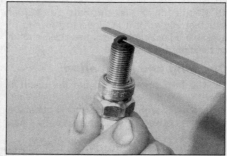

2.7a Using a feeler gauge to measure the spark plug electrode gap

2.7b Using a wire type gauge to measure the spark plug electrode gap

2.7c Adjust the electrode gap by bending the side electrode only

2.8 Thread the plugs in by hand initially

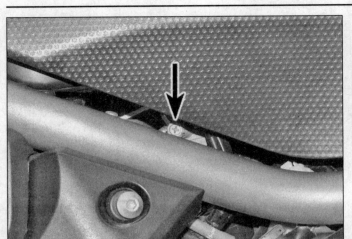
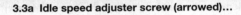

3.3a Idle speed adjuster screw (arrowed)…

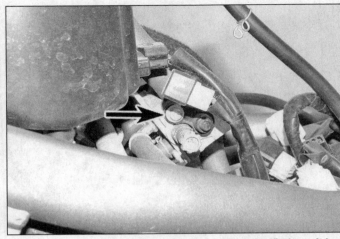

3.3b …do not turn the screw (arrowed – tank raised) above it by mistake

plugs are finger-tight, the job can be finished with the tool handle or a socket wrench. If a torque wrench is available, tighten the spark plugs to the torque setting specified at the beginning of this Chapter. Otherwise tighten them by 1/4 to 1/2 turn after they have been fully hand tightened and have seated. Do not over-tighten them.

9 Fit the plug caps, pushing them all the way onto the plugs **(see illustration 2.3)**. Make sure that the caps are connected to the correct cylinder – each HT lead should be marked with its cylinder number (see Step 3).

10 Fit the rubber heat shield and secure it with the cable-ties **(see illustrations 2.2c, b and a)**. Install the AIS components, air filter housing and fuel tank (see Chapter 4).

3 Idle speed

1 Check and adjust the idle speed before and after the throttle bodies are synchronised (balanced), after checking the valve clearances, and when it is obviously too high or too low. Before adjusting the idle speed, make sure the valve clearances were checked and a new air filter was fitted at the previous prescribed interval, and that the spark plugs are clean and their gaps are correct. Also, with the engine running turn the handlebars back-and-forth and see if the idle speed changes - if it does, the throttle cables may not be adjusted or routed correctly, or may be worn out. This is a dangerous condition that can cause loss of control of the bike. Be sure to correct this problem before proceeding.

2 Run the engine up to normal operating temperature.

3 The idle speed adjuster is located on the left-hand side of the machine between the lower edge of the fuel tank and the frame **(see illustration)** – do not mistake the idle speed adjuster for the screw on the throttle bodies

that is just above it **(see illustration)**. With the engine idling, turn the adjuster until the speed listed in this Chapter's Specifications is obtained. Turn the knob clockwise to increase idle speed, and anti-clockwise to decrease it.

4 Snap the throttle open and shut a few times, then recheck the idle speed. If necessary, repeat the adjustment procedure.

5 If a smooth, steady idle cannot be achieved, the throttle bodies may need synchronising (see Section 4). Also check the intake ducts for loose clamps or bolts and cracks, which will cause an air leak, resulting in a weak mixture, and then if necessary check the operation of the fast idle unit (see Chapter 4).

4 Throttle body synchronisation

⚠️ *Warning: Petrol (gasoline) is extremely flammable, so take extra precautions when you work on any part of the fuel system. Don't smoke or allow open flames or bare light bulbs near the work area, and don't work in a garage where a natural gas-type appliance is present. If you spill any fuel on your skin, rinse it off immediately with soap and water. When you perform any kind of work on the fuel system, wear safety glasses and have a fire extinguisher suitable for a Class B type fire (flammable liquids) on hand.*

⚠️ *Warning: Do not allow exhaust gases to build up in the work area; either perform the check outside or use an exhaust gas extraction system.*
Special tool: *A set of vacuum gauges or a manometer is necessary for this job.*

1 Throttle body synchronisation ensures each throttle body passes the same amount of fuel/air mixture to each cylinder. This is done by measuring the vacuum produced in each cylinder. Throttle bodies that are out of

synchronisation will result in increased fuel consumption, higher engine temperature, less than ideal throttle response and higher vibration levels. Before synchronising the throttle bodies, and if not already done, refer to Section 3 and check the idle speed is properly adjusted, and that the other maintenance procedures mentioned have been carried out according to schedule .

2 To synchronise the throttle bodies you will need a set of vacuum gauges or a manometer **(see illustration)**. These instruments measure engine vacuum, and can be obtained from motorcycle dealers or mail order parts suppliers. The equipment used should be suitable for a four cylinder engine and come complete with the necessary adapters and hoses to fit the take-off points.

3 Start the engine and let it run until it reaches normal operating temperature, then shut it off. Support the motorcycle upright on level ground using the centrestand (where fitted) or an auxiliary stand. Raise the fuel tank (see Chapter 4).

4 Locate the synchronising hoses on the left and right-hand sides of the throttle body assembly - the hoses for Nos. 1 and 2 cylinders are on the left-hand side and for Nos. 3 and 4 cylinders are on the right-hand side, and the hoses for cylinders 1 and 4

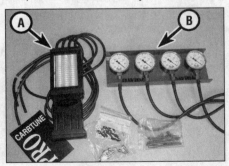

4.2 Manometer (A) and vacuum gauges (B)

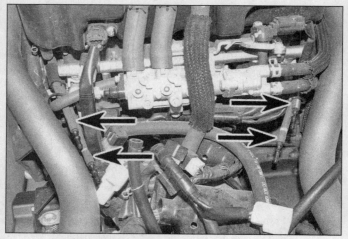

4.4 Throttle body synchronising hoses (arrowed)

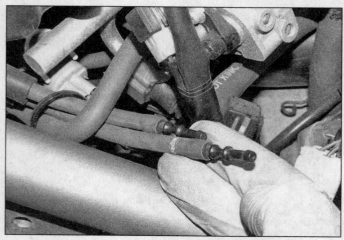

4.5 Remove the blanking plug from the end of each hose

extend further rearwards than those for 2 and 3, and are marked red **(see illustration)**. If in doubt trace each hose to the front of the throttle body assembly to check which throttle body it is connected to.

5 Remove the blanking plug from each hose and connect it to the appropriate vacuum gauge or manometer hose with the adapter **(see illustration)**. Make sure the No. 1 gauge is attached to the hose from the No. 1 (left-hand) throttle body, and so on.

6 Start the engine and let it idle, making sure the speed is still correct. If the gauges are fitted with damping adjustment, set this so that the needle flutter is just eliminated but so that they can still respond to small changes in pressure.

7 Use the No. 1 cylinder as the base to which all the others are matched. The vacuum readings for the Nos. 2, 3 and 4 cylinders should be the same as the No. 1 cylinder,

or at least within the maximum difference specified at the beginning of this Chapter **(see illustration)**.

8 If the vacuum readings vary, turn the appropriate adjuster screw(s) until the readings are all the same **(see illustration)**. After each adjustment, open and close the throttle quickly to settle the setting and check the reading on the gauges again. **Note:** *If an adjuster screw is inadvertently unscrewed, screw it in ¾ of a turn, then make any fine adjustment to its setting according to the gauge readings.*

9 When all the throttle bodies are synchronised, open and close the throttle quickly to settle the settings, and recheck the gauge readings, readjusting if necessary.

10 Remove the gauges and fit the blanking plugs **(see illustration 4.5)**.

11 Lower the fuel tank (see Chapter 4).

12 Check and adjust the idle speed (see Section 3).

5 Fuel system, air induction system (AIS) and EVAP system

⚠️ **Warning:** *Petrol (gasoline) is extremely flammable, so take extra precautions when you work on any part of the fuel system. Don't smoke or allow open flames or bare light bulbs near the work area, and don't work in a garage where a natural gas-type appliance is present. If you spill any fuel on your skin, rinse it off immediately with soap and water. When you perform any kind of work on the fuel system, wear safety glasses and have a fire extinguisher suitable for a Class B type fire (flammable liquids) on hand.*

Fuel system

1 Raise the fuel tank (see Chapter 4) and

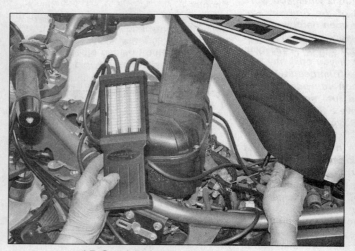

4.7 Synchronise the throttle bodies...

4.8 ...using the adjuster screws (arrowed) – numbers correspond to cylinders

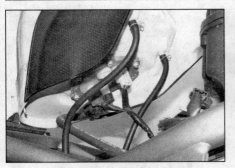

5.1 Check the tank and hoses as described

5.4 Synchronising/fast idle unit hoses (arrowed)

5.6 Air filter housing clamp screws (arrowed) – Nos. 1 and 2 cylinders

check the underside of the tank, the fuel supply hose and its union, and the tank overflow and breather hoses for signs of leaks, cracking, hardening or damage **(see illustration)**. Replace any hose that has deteriorated with a new one (see Chapter 4). Check the lower ends of the overflow and breather hoses for blockages.

2 If the joint between the fuel pump mounting plate and the tank is leaking, check the mounting bolts are tightened to the specified torque setting (see Chapter 4); if the leak persists, remove the pump and fit a new gasket (see Chapter 4).

3 Remove the tank and the air filter housing (see Chapter 4).

4 Inspect the hoses connected to the synchronising/fast idle unit for signs of cracking, hardening or damage **(see illustration)**. Check that the hoses are held securely by the spring clips. Replace any clips that are corroded or sprained.

5 Inspect the joints between the fuel rail, the injectors and the throttle bodies. If there are any fuel leaks, remove the fuel rail and fit new seals and O-rings to the injectors (see Chapter 4).

6 Make sure the joints between the air filter housing and the throttle bodies are in good condition and that the clamp screws are tight **(see illustration)**.

7 Check that the clamp screws on the intake ducts between the throttle bodies and the cylinder head are tight **(see illustration)** – you need a long screwdriver inserted from the opposite side.

Air induction system (AIS)

8 To reduce the amount of unburned hydrocarbons released in the exhaust gases, an air induction system (AIS) is fitted. The system consists of the air cut-off valve (mounted above the valve cover), the reed valves (fitted in the valve cover) and the hoses linking them **(see illustration)**. The cut-off valve is actuated electronically by the ECU.

9 The system is not adjustable and requires little maintenance. To gain access for inspection, remove the air filter housing (see Chapter 4).

10 Note that carbon deposits inside the air filter housing, particularly on the right-hand side around the union for the AIS hose, indicate a fault with the reed valves (see Section 18 and Chapter 4).

11 Check that the AIS hoses are not kinked or pinched, are in good condition and are securely connected at each end. Replace any hoses that are cracked, split or generally deteriorated with new ones. Replace any spring clips that are corroded or sprained.

12 If the valve clearances are all correct and the throttle bodies have been synchronised and have no other faults, but the idle speed cannot be set properly, it is possible that the AIS is faulty. Refer to Chapter 4 for further information on the system and for checks if it is believed to be faulty.

EVAP system (California models)

13 Raise the fuel tank (see Chapter 4). Visually inspect all the system hoses between the fuel tank, the roll-over valve and the canister for kinks and splits and any other damage or deterioration. Make sure that the hoses are securely connected with a clamp on each end. Replace any hoses that are damaged or deteriorated with new ones.

14 Refer to your dealer for further information and tests on the system.

6 Throttle cables

1 Make sure the throttle twistgrip rotates easily from fully closed to fully open with the front wheel turned at various angles. The twistgrip should return automatically from fully open to fully closed when released.

2 If the throttle sticks, this is probably due to a cable fault. Remove the cables (see Chapter 4) and lubricate them (see Section 8). If the inner cables still do not run smoothly in the outer cables, replace the cables with new ones.

3 With the cables removed, check that the twistgrip turns smoothly around the handlebar – dirt combined with a lack of lubrication can cause the action to be stiff. If necessary, unscrew the handlebar end-weight with a suitable Allen key and slide the twistgrip off the handlebar **(see illustration)**. Clean any old grease from

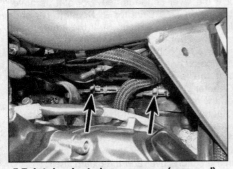

5.7 Intake duct clamp screws (arrowed) – Nos. 3 and 4 cylinders

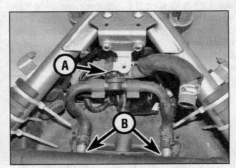

5.8 AIS cut-off valve (A) and hoses, and reed valves (B)

6.3 Handlebar end-weight screw (arrowed)

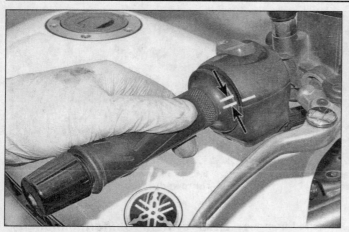

6.4 Check for the specified amount of free rotation in the twistgrip

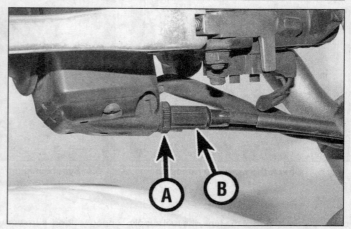

6.5 Throttle cable adjuster lockring (A) and adjuster (B)

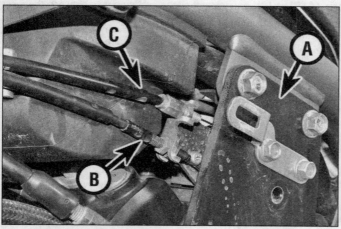

6.8 Remove the bracket (A) if required. Throttle opening cable (B) and closing cable (C)

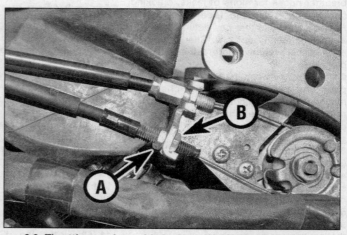

6.9 Throttle opening cable locknut (A) and adjuster nut (B)

the bar and the inside of the tube. Smear some new grease of the specified type onto the bar, then refit the twistgrip and end-weight. Install the lubricated or new cables, making sure they are correctly routed (see Chapter 4). If this fails to improve the operation of the throttle, the fault could lie in the throttle bodies. Remove them and check the action of the throttle linkage and butterflies (see Chapter 4).

4 With the throttle operating smoothly, check for a small amount of freeplay in the opening cable, measured in terms of the amount of twistgrip rotation before the throttle opens, and compare the amount to that listed in this Chapter's Specifications (see illustration). If it is incorrect, adjust the cables as follows:

5 Initially adjust freeplay using the adjuster in the throttle opening cable where it leaves the housing on the handlebar. Loosen the lock ring and turn the adjuster until the specified amount of freeplay is obtained, then retighten the lock ring (see illustration). Turn the adjuster in to increase freeplay and out to reduce it.

6 If the adjuster has reached its limit of adjustment, reset it so that the freeplay is at a maximum, then adjust the cable at the throttle body end as follows:

7 On XJ6-N models remove the left-hand side cover, on XJ6-S models remove the left-hand fairing side panels, and on XJ6-F and FZ6R models remove the left-hand lower fairing panel (see Chapter 7).

8 For best access remove the frame bracket to access the throttle cable adjusters (see illustration). The lower cable in the bracket on the throttle bodies is the opening cable, and the upper cable is the closing cable.

9 Loosen the locknut on the opening cable adjuster and turn the adjuster nut until the specified amount of twistgrip freeplay is obtained, then tighten the locknut (see illustration). Further adjustments can now be made at the handlebar end (see Step 5). If the cables cannot be adjusted as specified, replace them with new ones (see Chapter 4).

 Warning: Turn the handlebars all the way through their travel with the engine idling. Idle speed should not change. If it does, the cables may be routed incorrectly. Correct this condition before riding the motorcycle.

10 Check that the throttle twistgrip operates smoothly and snaps shut when released. Fit

the frame bracket and tighten the bolts to the torque setting specified at the beginning of the Chapter. Install the body panels.

7 Clutch cable

1 Check that the clutch lever operates smoothly and easily.

2 If the lever action is heavy or stiff, remove the cable (see Chapter 2, Section 12) and lubricate it (see Section 8). If the inner cable still does not run smoothly in the outer cable, replace the cable with a new one. Install the lubricated or new cable (see Chapter 2).

3 If the lever itself is stiff, remove it (see Chapter 5) and check for damage or distortion, or any other cause, and remedy as necessary. Clean and lubricate the pivot and contact areas (see Section 8).

4 If the lever and cable are good, refer to Chapter 2 and check the release mechanism in the clutch cover and the clutch itself.

5 With the clutch operating smoothly, check that the clutch lever is correctly adjusted.

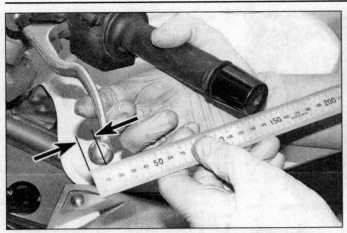

7.5 Clutch cable freeplay is measured at the ball end of the lever

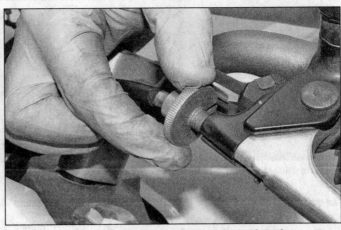

7.6 Turn the adjuster to set the correct freeplay

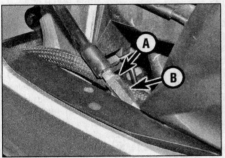

7.8 Clutch cable adjuster locknut (A) and adjuster (B) – XJ6-N model shown with side cover in place

Periodic adjustment is necessary to compensate for wear in the clutch plates and stretch of the cable. Check that the amount of freeplay at the clutch lever end is within the specifications listed at the beginning of this Chapter **(see illustration)**.

6 If adjustment is required, thread the adjuster in or out of the handlebar bracket until the required amount of freeplay is obtained **(see illustration)**. To increase freeplay, turn the adjuster clockwise (into the lever bracket). To reduce freeplay, turn the adjuster anti-clockwise (out of the lever bracket). Make sure the cable removal slot in the adjuster does not align with the slot in the lever bracket.

7 If all the adjustment has been taken up at the lever, reset the adjuster to give the maximum amount of freeplay, then set the correct amount of freeplay using the adjuster in the cable on the left-hand side of the engine – to access it, on XJ6-N models for best access remove the left-hand side cover, on XJ6-S models remove the left-hand fairing side panels, and on XJ6-F and FZ6R models remove the left-hand lower fairing panel (see Chapter 7).

8 Slacken the adjuster locknut, then turn the adjuster as required to obtain the correct freeplay **(see illustration)**. When the correct amount of freeplay has been achieved, hold the adjuster to prevent it rotating and tighten the locknut.

9 Install the body panels.

8 Stand, lever pivots and cable lubrication

Pivot points

1 Since the controls, cables and various other components of a motorcycle are exposed to the elements, they should be checked and lubricated periodically to ensure safe and trouble-free operation.

2 The clutch and brake lever pivots, footrest pivots, brake pedal and gearchange lever pivots and linkage, and stand pivots should be lubricated frequently. In order for the lubricant to be applied where it will do the most good, the component should be disassembled (see Chapter 5).

3 The lubricant recommended by Yamaha for each application is listed at the beginning of the Chapter. If an aerosol lubricant is being used, it can be applied to the pivot joint gaps and will usually work its way into the areas where friction occurs, so less disassembly of the component is needed (however it is always better to do so and clean off all corrosion, dirt and old lubricant first).

4 If grease is used, apply it sparingly as it may attract dirt (which could cause the controls to bind or wear at an accelerated rate). **Note:** *An alternative lubricant for the control lever pivots is a dry-film lubricant (available from many sources by different names).*

Cables

Special tool: *A cable lubricating adapter is necessary for this procedure.*

5 To lubricate the cables, disconnect the relevant cable at its upper end, then lubricate it with a pressure adapter and aerosol cable lubricant **(see illustrations)**. See Chapter 4 for throttle cable removal procedures, and Chapter 2 for the clutch cable.

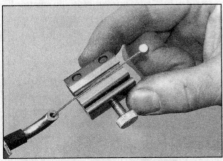

8.5a Fit the cable into the adapter...

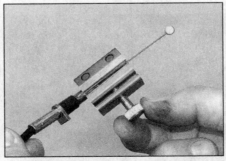

8.5b ...and tighten the screw to seal it in...

8.5c ...then apply the lubricant using the nozzle provided inserted in the hole in the adapter

8.6a Sidestand springs (arrowed)

8.6b Centrestand springs (arrowed)

Stands

6 The stand return springs must be capable of retracting the stand fully and holding it retracted when the motorcycle is in use. If a spring has sagged or broken, it must be replaced with a new one **(see illustrations)**.

7 If necessary, refer to the procedure in Chapter 5 to remove the stand.

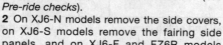

9 Cooling system

Check

 Warning: The engine must be cool before beginning this procedure.

1 Check the coolant level in the reservoir (see *Pre-ride checks*).

2 On XJ6-N models remove the side covers, on XJ6-S models remove the fairing side panels, and on XJ6-F and FZ6R models remove the lower fairing panels (see Chapter 7). Check the entire cooling system for evidence of leaks.

3 Examine each coolant hose along its entire length **(see illustration)**. Look for cracks, splits, abrasions and other signs of deterioration. Squeeze each hose at various points. They should feel firm, yet pliable, and return to their original shape when released. If they are cracked or hard, replace them with new ones. If necessary, tighten the hose clips carefully to prevent future leaks.

4 Examine the oil cooler inlet and outlet hoses on the front of the engine for damage and signs of deterioration **(see illustration)**.

Check that the hose clips are secure and that there are no signs of either coolant or oil leaks at the oil cooler-to-crankcase joint. If there is, refer to Chapter 2 – if coolant is leaking from the body replace the cooler with a new one, and if oil is leaking first make sure the cooler bolt is tightened to the specified torque, and if it is, or if leaks persists, remove the cooler and replace the O-ring with a new one.

5 Check for leaks around the pump on the right-hand side of the engine **(see illustration)**. If it is leaking around the cover, check that the bolts are tight. If they are, remove the cover and replace the O-ring with a new one (see Chapter 3). If it is leaking around the crankcase, remove the pump and replace the body O-ring with a new one (see Chapter 3).

6 To prevent water leaking from the cooling system to the lubrication system and vice versa, two seals are fitted on the water pump shaft. If either seal fails, a drain hole in the underside of the pump body allows the coolant or oil to escape and prevents them mixing. Look for tell-tale signs of leaks where the water pump body enters the crankcase **(see illustration)**.

7 The water seal is of the mechanical type and bears on the inner face of the pump impeller. The oil seal is of the normal feathered lip type. If there are signs of coolant leaking, remove the pump and replace the mechanical seal with a new one. If it is oil that is leaking, or if the leaks are white with the texture of emulsion, replace both seals with new ones (the mechanical seal has to be removed in order to remove the oil seal, and it cannot be reused). Refer to Chapter 3 for seal replacement.

8 Check the radiator for leaks and other damage. Leaks in the radiator leave tell-tale scale deposits or coolant stains on the outside of the core below the leak. If leaks are noted, remove the radiator (see Chapter 3) and have it repaired by a specialist. *Caution: Do not use a liquid leak stopping compound to try to repair leaks.*

9 Check the radiator fins for mud, dirt and insects, which may impede the flow of air through the radiator. If the fins are dirty, remove the radiator (see Chapter 3) and clean it, using water or low pressure compressed air directed through the fins from the back. If the fins are bent or distorted, straighten them carefully with a screwdriver **(see illustration)**.

9.3 Squeeze the hoses to check for cracks, deterioration and hardening. Make sure all clamps (arrowed) are tight

9.4 Oil cooler (arrowed) and hoses

9.5 Water pump (arrowed) and hoses

9.6 Check the drainage hole on the underside (arrowed) for signs of leakage

9.9 Check the radiator fins for blockages and carefully straighten any bent ones

Bent or damaged fins will restrict the airflow and impair the efficiency of the radiator causing the engine to overheat. Where there is substantial damage to the radiator's surface area, replace the radiator with a new one.

10 On XJ6-N and XJ6-S models unscrew the radiator pressure cap lock bolt and remove the lock plate, noting how it fits (**see illustration**). On all models undo the cap by turning it anti-clockwise until it reaches a stop (**see illustration**). If you hear a hissing sound (indicating that there is still pressure in the system), wait until it stops. Now press down on the cap and continue turning until it can be removed. Note the location of the locking tab.

11 Check the condition of the coolant in the system. If it is rust-coloured or if accumulations of scale are visible, drain and flush the system and refill with new coolant (see below). Check the antifreeze content of the coolant with an antifreeze hydrometer – a 50% content should give a reading of 1.084 at 5°C to 1.074 at 25°C, varying accordingly in between. The system must have the correct coolant mixture (see Specifications) – if the coolant is too weak (i.e. too little anti-freeze giving a low reading – anything below 1.07 when cold and 1.06 when hot) there will not be adequate protection against freezing and corrosion, and if it is too strong the ability to cool the engine is reduced. If the hydrometer indicates an incorrect mixture, drain and refill the system (see below).

12 The function of the pressure cap is crucial to the correct running of the cooling system. Check the cap seal for cracks and other damage (**see illustration 9.10b**). If the coolant level consistently drops and/or the bike overheats, and no evidence of leaks can be found, have the cap pressure checked by a Yamaha dealer, or just fit a new one – they are not expensive.

13 Fit the cap by turning it clockwise until it reaches the first stop then push down on the cap and continue turning until it will turn no further. On XJ6-N and XJ6-S models fit the lock plate and bolt (**see illustration 9.10a**).

14 Start the engine and let it reach normal operating temperature, then check for leaks again. As the coolant temperature increases beyond normal, the fan should come on automatically and the temperature should

9.10a Remove the locking bolt and plate (where fitted)

9.10b Remove the pressure cap as described

begin to drop. If it does not, refer to Chapter 3 and check the fan switch, fan motor and fan circuit carefully.

15 If the coolant level is consistently low, and no evidence of leaks can be found, and you have fitted a new pressure cap to the radiator (see Step 12), have the entire system pressure-checked by a Yamaha dealer.

Change the coolant

 Warning: Allow the engine to cool completely before performing this maintenance operation. Also, don't allow antifreeze to come into contact with your skin or the painted surfaces of the motorcycle. Rinse off spills immediately with plenty of water. Antifreeze is highly toxic if ingested. Never leave antifreeze lying around in an open container or in puddles on the floor; children and pets are attracted by its sweet smell and may drink it. Check with local authorities (councils) about disposing of antifreeze. Many communities have collection centres where antifreeze can be disposed of safely. Antifreeze is also combustible, so don't store it near open flames.

Draining

16 Support the motorcycle upright on level ground. On XJ6-N models remove the right-hand side cover and the belly-pan, on XJ6-S models remove the right-hand fairing

side panel and the belly-pan, and on XJ6-F and FZ6R models remove the right-hand lower fairing panel (see Chapter 7).

17 Remove the coolant reservoir (see Chapter 3). Empty the contents of the reservoir into a suitable container, rinse the inside with clean water and refit it.

18 Remove the radiator pressure cap (see Step 10).

19 Position a suitable container beneath the drain bolt on the water pump. Unscrew the bolt, noting that the coolant will spurt out (so hold the container up to it) and allow the coolant to completely drain from the system (**see illustrations**). Note that a new drain bolt sealing washer must be used.

Flushing

20 Flush the system with clean tap water by inserting a garden hose in the radiator filler neck. Allow the water to run through the system until it is clear when it flows out of the drain hole. If there is a lot of rust in the water, remove the radiator (see Chapter 3) and have it professionally cleaned. If the drain hole appears to be clogged with sediment, remove the water pump cover and clean the inside of the pump (see Chapter 3).

Refilling

21 Fit a new sealing washer onto the drain bolt and tighten it to the torque setting specified at the beginning of this Chapter (**see illustration**).

22 Fill the system via the radiator with the specified coolant mixture (see this Chapter's

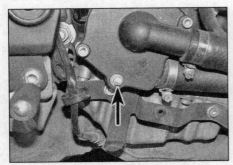

9.19a Unscrew the drain bolt (arrowed)...

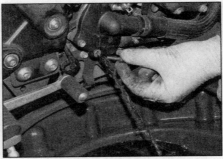

9.19b ...and allow the coolant to drain

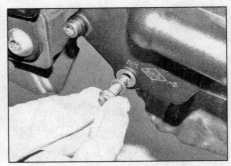

9.21 Always use a new sealing washer

9.22 Fill the system as described

9.23a Fill the reservoir...

9.23b ...to the F line (arrowed)

Specifications) **(see illustration)**. **Note:** *Pour the coolant in slowly to minimise the amount of air entering the system.* When the system appears full, move the bike off its stand then squeeze the hoses and shake the bike slightly to dislodge any air bubbles and dissipate the coolant, then place the bike back on the stand and top the system up.

23 When the system is full (all the way up to the top of the radiator filler neck), fit the pressure cap (do not yet fit the lock plate on N and S models). Now fill the coolant reservoir to the FULL mark and fit the cap **(see illustrations)**.

24 Start the engine and allow it to run for several minutes. Flick the throttle open 3 or 4 times, so that the engine speed rises to approximately 4000 – 5000 rpm, then stop the engine. Any air trapped in the system should bleed back to the top of the radiator, and the level will drop.

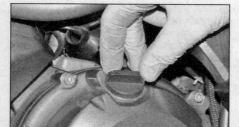

10.3 Unscrew the oil filler cap

25 Wait a few minutes for the coolant to settle, then remove the pressure cap and check the coolant level in both the radiator and the coolant reservoir. If necessary, top up the radiator to the base of the filler neck, then fit the pressure cap, and on XJ6-N and XJ6-S models fit the lock plate and bolt **(see illustrations 9.10b and a)**. Also top up the coolant reservoir to the FULL mark.

26 Check the system for leaks.

27 Do not dispose of the old coolant by pouring it down the drain. Instead pour it into a heavy plastic container, cap it tightly and take it into an authorised disposal site or service station – see **Warning** on page 1•15.

28 Install the body panels.

10 Engine oil and filter

⚠ ***Warning: Be careful when draining the oil, as the exhaust pipes, the engine, and the oil itself can cause severe burns.***

Engine oil

1 Regular oil changes are the single most important maintenance procedure you can perform on a motorcycle. The oil not only lubricates the internal parts of the engine, transmission and clutch, but it also acts as a coolant, a cleaner, a sealant, and a protector. Because of these demands, the oil takes a terrific amount of abuse and should be replaced often with new oil of the recommended grade and

type and marked as suitable for motorcycles. Saving a little money on the difference in cost between a good oil and a cheap oil won't pay off if the engine is damaged. The oil filter should be changed with every second oil change (see Steps 10 and 11).

2 Before changing the oil, warm up the engine so the oil will drain easily. On XJ6-N and XJ6-S models remove the belly pan, and on XJ6-F and FZ6R models remove the left-hand lower fairing panel (see Chapter 7).

3 Support the motorcycle upright on level ground and place a clean drain tray below the left-hand side of the engine. Unscrew the oil filler cap from the clutch cover to vent the engine unit and to act as a reminder that there is no oil in the engine **(see illustration)**.

4 Unscrew the oil drain plug from the left-hand side of the sump and allow the oil to flow into the drain tray **(see illustrations)**. Remove the sealing washer from the plug **(see illustration 10.5)** – a new one must be used. If you are changing the oil filter, do so now (Steps 9 to 11).

5 When the oil has completely drained, fit the plug with its new washer and tighten it to the torque setting specified at the beginning of this Chapter **(see illustration)**. Avoid overtightening, as you will damage the sump.

6 Refill the engine using the recommended type and amount of oil so the level lies between the maximum and minimum level lines on the dipstick (see *Pre-ride checks)*. Start the engine and let it run for two or three minutes. Stop the engine, wait a few minutes, then check the oil level. If necessary, add more oil to bring the level almost up to the

10.4a Unscrew the oil drain plug (arrowed)...

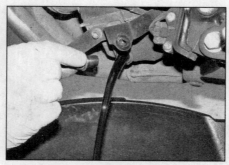

10.4b ...and allow the oil to drain

10.5 Always use a new sealing washer

Note: *It is illegal and anti-social to dump oil down the drain. To find the location of your local oil recycling bank in the UK, call 03708 506 506 or visit www.oilbankline.org.uk*

In the US note that any oil supplier must accept used oil for recycling.

maximum level line on the dipstick. Check that there are no leaks around the drain plug and filter. Install the body panels.

7 The old oil drained from the engine cannot be re-used and must be disposed of properly. Check with your local refuse disposal company, disposal facility or environmental agency to see whether they will accept the used oil for recycling – most will. Don't pour used oil into drains or onto the ground.

Oil filter

Special tool: *A filter removing tool is necessary for this job (see illustration 10.11a).*

8 Drain the engine oil as described in Steps 2 to 4.

9 The oil filter is located on the lower left-hand side of the engine. Place the drain tray below it. Clean the crankcase around the filter. When removing and installing the filter hold the sidestand switch wiring aside so it does not get in the way.

10 Unscrew the filter using a filter removal tool **(see illustrations)**. **Note:** *Make sure you purchase the correct size of oil filter tool to fit the Yamaha filter cartridge – many sizes are available.* A filter tool that can be used with a socket wrench is the best as it allows the new filter to be tightened to the specified torque. Tip any residual oil into the drain tray.

11 Clean the sealing surface on the crankcase carefully with a suitable solvent. Remove any protective packaging from the new filter **(see illustration)**. Smear clean engine oil onto the seal, then screw the filter onto the engine until the seal just seats **(see illustration)**. If a suitable oil filter tool is being used, tighten the filter to the torque setting specified at the beginning of this Chapter. Otherwise, tighten the filter as tight as possible by hand, or by the number of turns specified on the filter or its packaging. **Note:** *Do*

10.10a Unscrew the filter using a filter removal adapter...

10.11a Remove any packaging and smear some clean oil onto the seal...

10.10b ...and drain its oil into the tray

10.11b ...then thread the filter onto the engine and tighten it as described

not use a strap or chain wrench to tighten the filter as you will damage it.

12 Refill the engine to the specified level (see Steps 5 and 6).

13 Remember to drain all the old oil from the filter into the drain tray. Note that the old filter should be taken to the oil disposal facility rather than disposed of with the household rubbish.

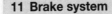

11 Brake system

Brake system check

1 A routine check of the brake system will ensure that any problems are discovered and remedied before the rider's safety is jeopardised.

2 Check the brake lever and pedal for

looseness, rough action, excessive play, bends, and other damage. Replace any damaged parts with new ones (see Chapter 5). Clean and lubricate the lever and pedal pivots if their action is stiff or rough (see Section 8).

3 Make sure all brake fasteners are tight. Check the fluid level in the reservoirs (see *Pre-ride checks*). Inspect the brake pads for wear (see Steps 11 to 13).

4 If the lever or pedal action is spongy, bleed the brakes (see Chapter 7). Change the brake fluid at the specified service interval.

5 Look for leaks at the hose connections and check for cracks in the hoses themselves **(see illustration)**. The hoses should be replaced with new ones at the specified service interval – or sooner if they show signs of damage or deterioration (see Steps 15 and 16).

6 Check the brake master cylinder and caliper seals for signs of leaking fluid (see Steps 17 and 18).

7 Make sure the brake light operates when the front brake lever is pulled in. The front brake light switch, mounted on the underside of the master cylinder, is not adjustable. If it fails to operate properly, check it (see Chapter 8).

8 Make sure the brake light is activated just before the rear brake takes effect. The switch is mounted behind the rider's right-hand footrest bracket. If adjustment is necessary, hold the switch and turn the adjuster nut on the switch body until the brake light is activated when required **(see illustration)**. If the brake light comes on too late, turn the nut clockwise. If the brake light comes on too soon or is permanently on, turn the nut anti-

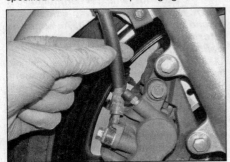

11.5 Check the hoses as described

11.8 Rear brake light switch adjuster nut (arrowed)

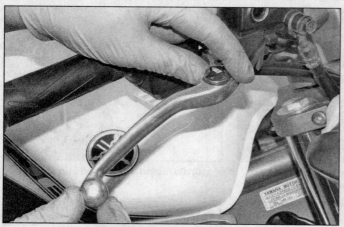

11.9a Pull the lever forwards and turn the adjuster...

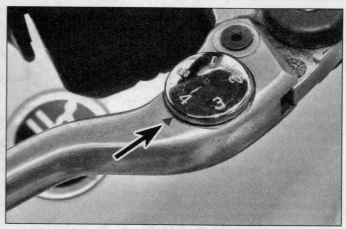

11.9b ...aligning the required setting with the mark (arrowed)

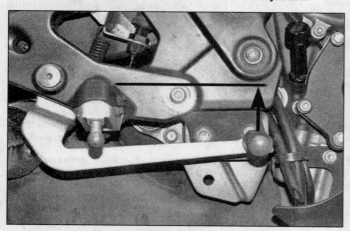

11.10a Check the height of the pedal...

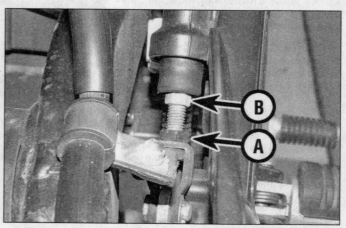

11.10b ...and adjust if necessary by slackening the locknut (A) and turning the pushrod hex (B)

clockwise. If the switch doesn't operate the brake light, check it (see Chapter 8).

9 The front brake lever has a span adjuster that alters the distance of the lever from the handlebar. Each setting is identified by a number on the adjuster, which must align with the arrow on the lever **(see illustrations)**. Pull the lever away from the handlebar and turn the adjuster until the setting that best suits the rider is obtained. There are five settings – setting 1 gives the largest span, and setting 5 the smallest. Make sure the

selected setting number aligns exactly with the arrow mark to ensure correct engagement of the adjuster setting.

10 Check the position of the brake pedal. Measure the vertical distance between the top of the brake pedal and the upper edge of the footrest **(see illustration)**. Compare the result with the specification at the beginning of this Chapter. If the pedal height is incorrect, or if the rider's preference is different, loosen the locknut on the top of the clevis on the master cylinder pushrod, then turn the pushrod using a spanner

on the hex at the top of the rod until the pedal is at the correct or desired height **(see illustration)**. After adjustment check that some of the bottom of the pushrod end is still visible below the nut under the clevis. On completion tighten the locknut. Adjust the rear brake light switch after adjusting the pedal position (see Step 8).

Brake pad wear check

⚠️ *Warning: The dust created by the brake system may contain asbestos, which is harmful to your health. Never blow it out with compressed air and don't inhale any of it. An approved filtering mask should be worn when working on the brakes.*

11 The front brake pads can be checked from the front of the caliper **(see illustration)**. However, if the pads are dirty or if you are in doubt as to the amount of friction material remaining, it is advisable to follow the procedure in Chapter 6 and displace the calipers – the pads can then be lifted off the caliper brackets and inspected individually.

12 The rear brake pads on all models can be checked from the rear of the caliper **(see illustration)**. However, if the pads are dirty or

11.11 Front brake pad wear indicator (arrowed)

11.12 Rear brake pad wear indicator (arrowed)

if you are in doubt as to the amount of friction material remaining, it is advisable to follow the procedure in Chapter 6 and remove the pads so that they can be inspected individually.

13 The brake pads have wear indicator grooves – if the friction material is worn to the bottom of the groove, i.e. the groove is only just or is no longer visible, new pads must be fitted. There are also minimum thicknesses for the friction material (see Chapter 6 Specifications). **Note:** *Some after-market pads may use different wear indicators; always check with your supplier before fitting.* **Note:** *It is not possible to degrease the friction material; if the pads are contaminated in any way they must be replaced with new ones.*

Brake fluid change

14 The brake fluid should be changed at the specified service interval or whenever a master cylinder or caliper overhaul is carried out. Refer to Chapter 6 for details. Ensure that all the old fluid is pumped from the system. Check the level in the fluid reservoir and test the brakes before riding the motorcycle.

Brake hoses

15 The hoses will deteriorate with age and even if they appear to be in good condition they should be replaced with new ones at the specified service interval (see Chapter 6).

16 Always replace the banjo union sealing washers with new ones when fitting new hoses. Refill the system with new brake fluid and bleed the system as described in Chapter 6.

Brake caliper and master cylinder seals

17 Brake system seals will deteriorate over a period of time and lose their effectiveness. Old master cylinder seals will cause sticky operation of the brake lever or pedal; old caliper seals will cause the pistons to stick or fluid leak out. The seals should be replaced with new ones at the specified service interval or sooner if defects are evident.

18 Replace all the seals in each caliper as a set – a rebuild kit for each caliper is available. Front and rear master cylinder seals are supplied as a kit along with a new piston and spring assembly (see Chapter 6).

13.2 Pump the forks to check their action

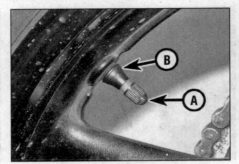

12.2 Make sure a cap (A) is fitted, and check the rubber seal (B)

12 Wheels, wheel bearings and tyres

Wheels

1 Cast wheels are virtually maintenance free, but they should be kept clean and checked periodically for cracks and other damage. Also check the wheel runout and alignment (see Chapter 6). Never attempt to repair damaged cast wheels; they must be replaced with new ones.

2 Make sure the valve cap is in place and tight **(see illustration)**. Check the tyre valve rubber for signs of damage or deterioration and have it replaced with a new one if necessary. Check that any wheel balance weights are fixed firmly to the wheel rim. If the weights have fallen off, have the wheel rebalanced by a motorcycle tyre specialist.

Wheel bearings

Note: *Avoid using a high pressure cleaner around the wheel hubs. Water may penetrate the wheel bearing seals and wash out the grease, leading to corrosion and premature bearing failure.*

3 Wheel bearings will wear over a period of time and result in handling problems.

4 Support the motorcycle upright using the centrestand. Check for any play in the bearings by pushing and pulling each wheel against the hub **(see illustration)**. Also rotate the wheels

13.3 Check the fork inner tube (arrowed) above the dust seal for leaks, pitting and corrosion

12.4 Checking for play in the wheel bearings

and check that they spin smoothly and quietly, but do not mistake brake pad-to-disc noise for noisy bearings.

5 If any play is detected in the hub, or if the wheel does not rotate smoothly (and this is not due to brake or chain drag), the wheel must be removed for thorough inspection of the bearings (see Chapter 6).

Tyres

6 Check the tyre condition and tread depth thoroughly (see *Pre-ride checks*).

13 Suspension

1 The suspension components must be maintained in top operating condition to ensure rider safety. Loose, worn or damaged suspension parts decrease the motorcycle's stability and control.

Front suspension check

2 While standing alongside the motorcycle, apply the front brake and push on the handlebars to compress the forks several times **(see illustration)**. Check that they move up and down smoothly without binding. If binding is felt, the forks should be disassembled and inspected (see Chapter 5).

3 Inspect the fork inner tubes for signs of scratches, corrosion and pitting, and oil leaks **(see illustration)**. Displace the stone guard from the top of the fork outer tube, then carefully lever the dust seals out using a flat-bladed screwdriver and inspect the area around the fork seals (see Chapter 5). Any scratches, corrosion and pitting will cause premature seal failure. If the damage is excessive, new tubes should be installed (see Chapter 5).

4 If oil is leaking, new seals must be fitted (see Chapter 5). If there is evidence of corrosion between the seal retaining ring and its groove in the fork outer tube spray the area with a penetrative lubricant, otherwise the ring will be difficult to remove if needed. Press the dust seal back into place on completion.

5 Check the tightness of all suspension nuts and bolts to be sure none have worked loose, referring to the torque settings specified at the beginning of Chapter 5.

13.6 Check the rod (arrowed) for signs of oil

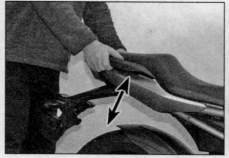

13.7 Pump the rear suspension to check its action

13.8 Checking for play in the swingarm bearings

Rear suspension check

Note: *Avoid using a high pressure cleaner around the swingarm pivots and the lower shock absorber mounting. Water may penetrate the bearing seals and wash out the grease, leading to corrosion and premature bearing failure.*

6 Inspect the rear shock for fluid leaks and loose mountings **(see illustration)**. If the shock is leaking, a new one should be installed (see Chapter 5).

7 With the aid of an assistant to support the bike, compress the rear suspension several times **(see illustration)**. It should move up and down freely without binding. If any binding is felt, the worn or faulty component must be identified and checked. The problem could be due to either the shock absorber, the suspension linkage components or the swingarm components (see Chapter 5).

8 Support the motorcycle so that the rear wheel is off the ground. Grasp the swingarm and rock it from side to side – there should be no discernible movement at the ends of the swingarm (Yamaha specify a maximum of 1 mm sideplay) **(see illustration)**. If there is a little movement or a slight clicking can be heard, inspect the tightness of all the rear suspension mounting bolts and nuts, referring to the torque settings specified at the beginning of Chapter 5, and re-check for movement.

9 Next, grasp the top of the rear wheel and pull it upwards – there should be no discernible freeplay before the shock absorber begins to compress **(see illustration)**. Any freeplay felt in either check indicates worn bearings in the

swingarm, or worn shock absorber mountings. The worn components must be identified and checked (see Chapter 6).

10 To make an accurate assessment of the swingarm bearings it is necessary to remove the rear wheel (see Chapter 6), and detach the shock absorber from the swingarm (see Chapter 5). Grasp the rear of the swingarm with one hand and place your other hand at the junction of the swingarm and the frame. Try to move the rear of the swingarm from side-to-side. Any wear (play) in the bearings should be felt as movement between the swingarm and the frame at the front. If there is any play, the swingarm will be felt to move forward and backward at the front (not from side-to-side).

11 Next, move the swingarm up and down through its full travel – it should move freely, without any binding or rough spots. If any play in the swingarm is noted, or if the swingarm does not move freely, remove the swingarm for inspection of the bearings (see Chapter 5).

Front fork oil change

12 Although there is no set interval for changing the fork oil, note that the oil will degrade over a period of time and lose its damping qualities. Refer to Chapter 5 for details of front fork removal, oil draining and refilling. The forks do not need to be completely disassembled to change the oil.

Rear suspension bearing lubrication

13 Over a period of time the grease in the swingarm bearings will be washed out (especially if pressure washers are used) or

will harden allowing the ingress of dirt and water.

14 The swingarm should be removed at the specified service interval and the bearings cleaned and re-greased as necessary (see Chapter 5).

14 Steering head bearings

Freeplay check and adjustment

1 Steering head bearings can become dented, rough or loose during normal use of the machine. In extreme cases, worn or loose steering head bearings can cause steering wobble – a condition that is potentially dangerous.

Check

2 Support the motorcycle in an upright position using the centrestand where fitted, or an auxiliary stand, and raise the front wheel off the ground by placing a support under the engine, or if you have a centrestand by having an assistant push down on the rear.

3 Point the front wheel straight-ahead, and slowly turn the handlebars from side to side. Any dents or roughness in the bearing races will be felt and if the bearings are too tight the bars will not move smoothly and freely. If the bearings are damaged or the action is rough, they should be replaced with new ones (see Chapter 5). If the bearings are too tight they should be adjusted as described below.

4 Again point the wheel straight-ahead, and tap the front of the wheel to one side. The wheel should 'fall' under its own weight to the limit of its lock, indicating that the bearings are not too tight (take into account the restriction that cables and wiring may have). Check for similar movement to the other side.

5 Next, grasp the forks and try to pull and push them forwards and backwards **(see illustration)**. Any looseness in the steering head bearings will be felt as front-to-rear movement of the forks. If play is felt in the bearings, adjust them as follows.

Adjustment

Special tool: *Either the Yamaha service tool described in Step 10 or a suitably sized*

13.9 Checking for play in the suspension bearings and shock mounts

14.5 Checking for play in the steering head bearings

14.7a Slacken the clamp bolt (arrowed) on each side

14.7b Remove both instrument bracket bolts

14.8a Unscrew the nut...

14.8b ...and displace the yoke/handlebar assembly

14.9a Remove the lockwasher...

14.9b ...then slacken the locknut

C-spanner is required for this procedure (see illustration 14.11a).

6 Remove the fuel tank (see Chapter 4). On XJ6-S, XJ6-F and FZ6R models remove the fairing (see Chapter 7). **Note:** *Although it is not strictly necessary to remove the fuel tank and fairing, doing so will prevent the possibility of damage, should a tool slip.*

7 Slacken the fork clamp bolts in the top yoke **(see illustration)**. On XJ6-N models unscrew the instrument bracket bolts from the underside of the top yoke **(see illustration)**.

8 Unscrew the steering stem nut and remove it along with its washer, then ease the top yoke up and off the fork tubes and support or tie it as required, using some rag as a cushion **(see illustrations)**.

9 Remove the tabbed lockwasher, noting how it fits, then slacken the locknut, using a C-spanner if required, though it should only be finger-tight **(see illustrations)**. If you have the tools described in Step 10 unscrew and remove the locknut, then remove the rubber washer **(see illustrations)**. If you do not have the tools and are following Step 11 the locknut can be left loose on the stem and the rubber washer can stay in place.

10 To adjust the bearings as specified by Yamaha, a special service tool (Pt. No. 90890-01403 for Europe, or YU-33975 for US) and a torque wrench are required. If the tool is available, first slacken the adjuster nut slightly to take pressure off the bearing, then tighten the nut to the initial torque setting specified at the beginning of this Chapter. Make sure the torque wrench handle is at

14.9c Remove the locknut...

right-angles (90°) to the centre line between the adjuster nut and the service tool wrench socket **(see illustration)**. Now slacken the nut, then tighten it to the final torque setting specified.

11 If the Yamaha tool is not available use a C-spanner to slacken the adjuster nut

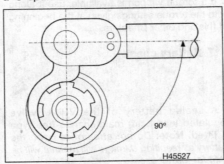

14.10 Make sure the tool and torque wrench are correctly positioned

14.9d ...and the rubber washer if required

slightly to take pressure off the bearing then tighten the nut until all freeplay is removed **(see illustration)**. Now tighten the nut a little more to pre-load the bearings. Now slacken the nut and retighten it, setting it so that all freeplay is just removed from the bearings,

14.11 Using a C-spanner to adjust the steering head bearings

yet the steering is able to move freely from side to side. Tighten the nut only a little at a time, and after each adjustment repeat the checks outlined in Steps 3 to 5, with the bike supported as in Step 2.

12 Turn the steering from lock to lock five times to settle the bearings, then recheck the adjustment or the torque setting depending on your method used. The object is to set the adjuster nut so that the bearings are under a very light loading, just enough to remove any freeplay.

Caution: Take great care not to apply excessive pressure because this will cause premature failure of the bearings.

13 With the bearings correctly adjusted, fit the rubber washer and the locknut if removed, making sure the flat side of the nut faces down onto the washer (the upper side has a slight ridged section) **(see illustrations 14.9d and c)**. Tighten the locknut finger-tight, then tighten it further until its notches align with those in the adjuster nut, making sure the adjuster nut does not turn as well. Fit the tabbed lockwasher so that the tabs locate into the notches in both the locknut and adjuster nut **(see illustration 14.9a)**.

14 Fit the top yoke onto the steering stem and forks **(see illustration 14.8b)**. Fit the washer and steering stem nut and tighten it to the torque setting specified at the beginning of this Chapter **(see illustrations)**. Now tighten the fork clamp bolts in the top yoke to the specified torque **(see illustration 14.7a)**. On XJ6-N models fit the instrument bracket bolts into the underside of the top yoke **(see illustration 14.7b)**.

15 Recheck the bearing adjustment as described in Steps 3 to 5.

Lubrication

16 Over a considerable time the grease in the bearings will be dispersed or will harden allowing the ingress of dirt and water.

17 At the specified interval the steering head should be disassembled and the bearings cleaned and re-greased (see Chapter 5, Section 10).

15 Sidestand and starter safety circuit

1 The sidestand switch prevents the motorcycle being started if the transmission is in gear and the stand is down, and cuts the engine if the stand is put down while the engine is running and in gear.

2 Check the operation of the safety circuit (which incorporates the sidestand, clutch and neutral switches, and the starter circuit cut-off relay) by shifting the transmission into neutral, retracting the stand and starting the engine. Pull in the clutch lever and select a gear. Extend the sidestand. The engine should stop as the sidestand is extended.

3 Also make sure that the engine cannot be

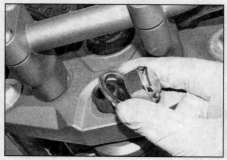
14.14a Fit the washer and stem nut...

started while in gear unless the stand is up and the clutch lever is pulled in. If the circuit does not operate as described, check the individual components of the safety circuit (see Chapter 8).

16 Nuts, bolts and fasteners

1 Since vibration of the machine tends to loosen fasteners, all nuts, bolts, screws, etc. should be periodically checked for tightness.

2 Pay particular attention to the following:
  Brake caliper and master cylinder mounting bolts
  Brake hose banjo bolts and caliper bleed valves
  Brake disc bolts
  Exhaust system bolts/nuts
  Engine oil drain plug
  Engine mounting bolts
  Spark plugs
  Lever and pedal bolts
  Handlebar clamp bolts
  Footrest, centrestand (where fitted) and sidestand bolts
  Shock absorber mounting bolts
  Swingarm pivot bolt
  Front fork clamp bolts (top and bottom yoke) and fork top bolts
  Steering stem nut
  Front axle and axle clamp bolt
  Rear axle nut
  Front and rear sprocket nuts
  Chain adjuster locknuts

3 If a torque wrench is available, use it along with the torque settings given at the beginning of this and other Chapters.

17 Battery check

1 A sealed battery of the VRLA (valve regulated lead acid) maintenance-free type is fitted. **Note:** *Do not attempt to open the battery as resulting damage will mean it will be unfit for further use.*

2 All that should be done is to check that the terminals are clean and tight and that

14.14b ...and tighten to the specified torque

the casing is not damaged or leaking. See Chapter 8 for further details.

Caution: Be extremely careful when handling or working around the battery. The electrolyte gel is very caustic and an explosive gas (hydrogen) is given off when the battery is charging.

3 If the machine is not in regular use, disconnect the battery and give it a refresher charge every month to six weeks (see Chapter 8, Section 4).

18 Air filter

Note: *If the machine is continually ridden in dusty conditions, replace the filter more frequently than specified.*

Note: *All models are fitted with a disposable oil-impregnated paper element that cannot be cleaned. Replace the filter with a new one at the specified service interval.*

1 Remove the fuel tank (see Chapter 4).

2 Undo the air filter housing cover screws and displace the cover **(see illustration)**.

3 Lift the filter out of the housing, noting which way round it fits **(see illustration)**.

4 Clean out any dirt from the filter housing and cover. Check the housing drain in the bottom left-hand corner **(see illustration)**. If necessary, release the clip and drain off any accumulated fluid.

5 Check for carbon deposits inside the housing, particularly on the right-hand side around the union for the AIS hose. Carbon deposits indicate a fault with the AIS reed valves in the engine valve cover (see Chapter 4).

18.2 Undo the screws all round...

6 Check the condition of the rubber seals, one in the groove in the rim of the cover, the other in the housing, and replace them with new ones if necessary **(see illustration)**. Make sure the seals are fully seated in their grooves.

7 Fit the new filter into the housing, making sure it is the correct way round **(see illustration 18.3)**.

8 Fit the cover and check that it is seated all the way round. Fit and tighten the screws.

9 Check the crankcase breather hose between the engine and the rear of the air filter housing for loose connections, cracks and deterioration, and replace it with a new one if necessary **(see illustration)**.

10 Install the fuel tank (see Chapter 4).

19 Valve clearances

1 The engine must be completely cool for this maintenance procedure, so let the machine sit overnight before beginning.

2 Remove the fuel tank, air filter housing, throttle bodies and AIS assembly (see Chapter 4).

3 Remove the spark plugs (see Section 2).

4 Remove the valve cover (see Chapter 2).

5 Remove the timing rotor cover (see Chapter 2, Section 8).

6 The cylinders are numbered 1 to 4 from left to right, viewed as normally seated on the bike. Make a chart or sketch of all valve positions so that a note of each clearance can be made against the relevant valve.

7 Using a spanner on the timing rotor bolt and rotating in a clockwise direction only, turn the engine until the 'T' mark on the ignition rotor faces to the rear and aligns with the crankcase mating surfaces and the camshaft lobes for the No. 1 (left-hand) cylinder face away from each other **(see illustrations)**. If the cam lobes are facing towards each other, turn the engine clockwise 360° (one full turn) so that the 'T' mark again aligns with the crankcase mating surfaces. The camshaft lobes will now be facing away from each other and the No. 1 cylinder will be at TDC (top dead centre) on the compression stroke.

8 Check the clearances on the No. 1 cylinder intake and exhaust valves. Insert a feeler

18.3 ...then displace the cover and lift the filter out

18.6 Check the seals (arrowed) are in good condition and correctly seated

19.7a Turn the engine clockwise...

19.7c ...and the No. 1 cylinder cam lobes (arrowed) point away from each other

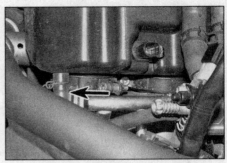
18.4 Check the drain (arrowed)

18.9 Crankcase breather hose (arrowed)

19.7b ... until the T mark aligns with the crankcase joint...

gauge of the same thickness as the correct valve clearance (see Specifications) between the camshaft lobe and follower of each valve and check that it is a firm sliding fit **(see illustrations)** – you should feel a slight drag when the you pull the gauge out. If not, use the feeler gauges to measure the exact clearance. Record the measured clearance on your chart.

9 Now turn the engine clockwise 180° (half a turn) so that the camshaft lobes for the No. 2 cylinder are facing away from each

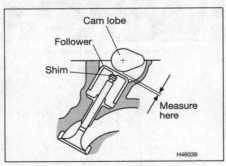
19.8a Measure the valve clearance ...

Cam lobe
Follower
Shim
Measure here
H46039

19.8b ... using a feeler gauge

19.14a Lift out the cam follower...

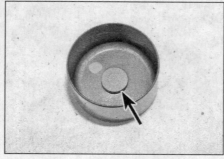

19.14b ...and retrieve the shim (arrowed)

19.15 Measure the shim using a micrometer to confirm its size

other. The No. 2 cylinder is now at TDC on the compression stroke. Measure the clearances of the No. 2 cylinder valves using the method described in Step 8.

10 Now turn the engine clockwise 180° (half a turn) so that the camshaft lobes for the No. 4 cylinder are facing away from each other. The No. 4 cylinder is now at TDC on the compression stroke. Measure the clearances of the No. 4 cylinder valves using the method described in Step 8.

11 Now turn the engine clockwise 180° (half a turn) so that the camshaft lobes for the No. 3 cylinder are facing away from each other. The No. 3 cylinder is now at TDC on the compression stroke. Measure the clearances of the No. 3 cylinder valves using the method described in Step 8.

12 When all clearances have been measured and recorded, identify whether the clearance on any valve falls outside that specified. If it does, the shim between the cam follower and the valve must be replaced with one of a thickness that will restore the correct clearance.

13 Shim replacement requires removal of

the camshafts (see Chapter 2). There is no need to remove both camshafts if shims from only one need replacing. Place rags over the spark plug holes and the cam chain tunnel to prevent a shim from dropping into the engine on removal.

14 With the camshaft removed, remove the cam follower of the valve in question, then retrieve the shim from inside the follower **(see illustrations)**. If it is not in the follower, pick it out of the top of the valve using either a magnet, a small screwdriver with a dab of grease on it (the shim will stick to the grease), or a screwdriver and a pair of pliers. Do not allow the shim to fall into the engine.

15 Measure the thickness of the shim using a micrometer. A size should be marked on the upper face of the shim (though it could have rubbed off) – a shim marked 175 is 1.75 mm thick, but the shim should measured anyway to allow for wear **(see illustration)**.

16 Calculate the required replacement shim by using the formula $a = (b - c) + d$, where a is the required replacement shim size, b is the measured valve clearance, c is the specified

valve clearance, and d is the existing shim thickness. For example:

The measured clearance of an exhaust valve is 0.35 mm, so b = 0.35
The specified clearance range for an exhaust valve is 0.23 to 0.30 mm, the mid-point being 0.26 mm, so c = 0.26
The thickness of the existing shim is 1.80 mm, so d = 1.8
Therefore, the required replacement shim a = 0.35 -0.26 +1.8 (a = 1.89 mm). Round this to the nearest available shim size, which is 190.

Note: *If the existing shim is marked with a number not ending in 0 or 5, round it up or down as appropriate to the nearest number ending in 0 or 5. Shims are available in 0.05 mm increments from 1.20 mm to 2.40 mm.*

17 Obtain the replacement shim, then lubricate it with molybdenum disulphide grease and fit it into its recess in the top of the valve, with the size marking facing up **(see illustration)**. Check that the shim is correctly seated, then lubricate the follower with molybdenum disulphide oil (a 50/50 mixture of molybdenum disulphide grease and engine oil) and fit it onto the valve **(see illustration)**. Repeat the process for any other valves until the clearances are correct, then install the camshafts (see Chapter 2).

18 Rotate the crankshaft clockwise several turns to seat the new shim(s), then check the clearances again.

19 Install the valve cover (see Chapter 2).

20 Install the timing rotor cover (see Chapter 2, Section 8).

21 Install all remaining components in the reverse order of removal. On completion, check the engine oil level (see *Pre-ride* checks). Check and adjust the idle speed (see Section 3).

19.17a Fit the shim into its recess...

19.17b ...then fit the follower

Chapter 2
Engine, clutch and transmission

Contents

Degrees of difficulty

Easy, suitable for novice with little experience | **Fairly easy,** suitable for beginner with some experience | **Fairly difficult,** suitable for competent DIY mechanic | **Difficult,** suitable for experienced DIY mechanic | **Very difficult,** suitable for expert DIY or professional

Specifications

General

Type	Four-stroke in-line four
Capacity	599.8 cc
Bore	65.5 mm
Stroke	44.5 mm
Compression ratio	12.2 to 1
Cylinder numbering	1 to 4 from left to right
Cooling system	Liquid cooled
Clutch	Wet multi-plate
Transmission	Six-speed constant mesh
Final drive	Chain

Cylinder head
Warpage (max) . . . . 0.05 mm

Camshafts

Lobe height	
Standard	31.85 to 13.95 mm
Service limit (min)	31.8 mm
Journal diameter	22.967 to 22.980 mm
Holder diameter	23.008 to 23.029 mm
Journal oil clearance	0.028 to 0.062 mm
Service limit (all models)	0.08 mm
Runout (max)	0.06 mm

Valves, guides and springs

Valve clearances	see Chapter 1
Intake valve	
Stem diameter	
Standard	3.975 to 3.990 mm
Service limit (min)	3.945 mm
Guide bore diameter	
XJ6-N, XJ6-S and FZ6R models	
Standard	4.000 to 4.012 mm
Service limit (max)	4.042 mm
XJ6-F models	
Standard	4.005 to 4.015 mm
Service limit (max)	4.053 mm
Stem-to-guide clearance	
XJ6-N, XJ6-S and FZ6R models	
Standard	0.010 to 0.037 mm
Service limit (max)	0.08 mm
XJ6-F models	
Standard	0.015 to 0.040 mm
Service limit (max)	0.08 mm
Stem runout	0.04 mm
Head diameter	24.9 to 25.1 mm
Face width	1.21 to 2.49 mm
Seat width	
Standard	0.9 to 1.1 mm
Service limit (max)	1.6 mm
Margin thickness	
Standard	0.6 to 0.8 mm
Service limit (min)	0.5 mm
Exhaust valve	
Stem diameter	
Standard	3.960 to 3.975 mm
Service limit (min)	3.930 mm
Guide bore diameter	
XJ6-N, XJ6-S and FZ6R models	
Standard	4.000 to 4.012 mm
Service limit (max)	4.042 mm
XJ6-F models	
Standard	4.005 to 4.015 mm
Service limit (max)	4.053 mm
Stem-to-guide clearance	
XJ6-N, XJ6-S and FZ6R models	
Standard	0.025 to 0.052 mm
Service limit (max)	0.10 mm
XJ6-F models	
Standard	0.030 to 0.055 mm
Service limit (max)	0.10 mm
Stem runout	0.04 mm
Head diameter	21.9 to 22.1 mm
Face width	1.21 to 2.49 mm
Seat width	
Standard	0.9 to 1.1 mm
Service limit (max)	1.6 mm
Margin thickness	
Standard	0.6 to 0.8 mm
Service limit (min)	0.5 mm
Valve spring free length	
Standard	39.08 mm
Service limit (min)	37.13 mm
Valve spring bend (max)	1.7 mm

Clutch
Friction plates
Quantity
Outer plate 1
Centre plates 6
Inner plate 1
Thickness
Outer and centre plates
Standard .... 2.92 to 3.08 mm
Service limit (min) .... 2.82 mm
Inner plate
Standard .... 2.94 to 3.06 mm
Service limit (min) .... 2.84 mm
Plain plates
Quantity 7
Thickness .... 1.9 to 2.1 mm
Warpage (max) .... 0.1 mm
Clutch springs
Free length .... 55.0 mm
Service limit .... 52.25 mm

Lubrication system
Engine oil pressure (at 96°C) .... 34.5 psi (2.4 Bar) @ 6600 rpm
Relief valve opening pressure .... 71.05 to 82.65 psi (4.9 to 5.7 Bar)
Oil pump
Inner rotor tip-to-outer rotor clearance
Standard .... less than 0.12 mm
Service limit (max) .... 0.20 mm
Outer rotor-to-housing clearance
Standard .... 0.09 to 0.15 mm
Service limit (max) .... 0.22 mm

Cylinder bores
Bore .... 65.50 to 65.51 mm
Ovality (max) .... 0.05 mm
Taper (max) .... 0.05 mm
Cylinder compression @ 400 rpm
Standard .... 220.5 psi (15.5 Bar)
Maximum .... 235 psi (16.5 Bar)
Minimum .... 185 psi (13.0 Bar)
Max. difference between cylinders .... 14 psi (1.0 Bar)
Piston-to-bore clearance *
Standard .... 0.010 to 0.035 mm
Service limit .... 0.055 mm

Pistons
Piston diameter (measured 5 mm up from skirt, at 90° to piston
pin axis) .... 65.475 to 65.490 mm
Piston-to-bore clearance
Standard .... 0.010 to 0.035 mm
Service limit .... 0.055 mm
Piston pin diameter
Standard .... 15.990 to 15.995 mm
Service limit (min) .... 15.970 mm
Piston pin bore diameter in piston
Standard .... 16.002 to 16.013 mm
Service limit (max) .... 16.043 mm
Piston pin-to-piston pin bore clearance
Standard .... 0.007 to 0.023 mm
Service limit .... 0.073 mm

Crankshaft and bearings
Main bearing oil clearance
Standard .... 0.016 to 0.040 mm
Service limit (max) .... 0.10 mm
Runout (max) .... 0.03 mm

Piston rings

Top compression ring

Type	Barrel
Ring width..	2.45 mm
Ring thickness	0.9 mm
Ring end gap (installed)	
Standard..	0.25 to 0.35 mm
Service limit (max)..................................	0.60 mm
Piston ring-to-groove clearance	
Standard..	0.030 to 0.065 mm
Service limit (max)..................................	0.115 mm

2nd compression ring

Type	Taper
Ring width..	2.5 mm
Ring thickness	0.8 mm
Ring end gap (installed)	
Standard..	0.70 to 0.80 mm
Service limit (max)..................................	1.15 mm
Piston ring-to-groove clearance	
Standard..	0.030 to 0.065 mm
Service limit (max)..................................	0.125 mm

Oil ring

Ring width..	2.0 mm
Ring thickness	1.5 mm
Side-rail end gap (installed)	0.10 to 0.35 mm

Connecting rods

Piston pin-to-small-end bore clearance........................	0.32 to 0.50 mm
Big-end side clearance..	0.160 to 0.262 mm
Big-end oil clearance	
Standard..	0.038 to 0.062 mm
Service limit (max)	0.08 mm

Transmission

Gear ratios (no. of teeth)

Primary reduction	1.955 to 1 (86/44)
Final reduction	2.875 to 1 (46/16)
1st gear...	2.846 to 1 (37/13)
2nd gear...	1.947 to 1 (37/19)
3rd gear...	1.555 to 1 (28/18)
4th gear...	1.333 to 1 (32/24)
5th gear...	1.190 to 1 (25/21)
6th gear...	1.083 to 1 (26/24)
Shaft runout (max)	0.02 mm

Gearchange mechanism

Selector fork shaft runout (max).............................	0.05 mm
Selector fork end thickness	
Standard..	5.76 to 5.89 mm
Service limit (max)	5.5 mm

Torque wrench settings

Alternator cover bolts..	10 Nm
Breather plate bolts	12 Nm
Cam chain tensioner mounting bolts	12 Nm
Camshaft holder bolts	10 Nm
Camshaft sprocket bolts	20 Nm
Clutch nut..	95 Nm
Clutch cover bolts	10 Nm
Clutch release mechanism shaft housing bolts	10 Nm
Clutch spring bolts	8 Nm
Connecting rod cap bolts	
Initial setting	15 Nm
Final setting (see Section 21)	+ 120°

Torque wrench settings (continued)

Crankcase bolts (see Section 19)
  8 mm bolts
    Nos. 1 to 7 and 10
      1st stage . . . .   20 Nm
      2nd stage . . . .   12 Nm
      3rd stage . . . .   + 55°
    Nos. 8 and 9
      1st stage . . . .   20 Nm
      2nd stage . . . .   12 Nm
      3rd stage . . . .   + 80°
    Nos. 11 and 12 . . . .   24 Nm
  6 mm bolts
    Nos. 13 and 14 . . . .   12 Nm
    Nos. 15 to 27 . . . .   10 Nm
Crankcase breather cover bolts . . . .   10 Nm
Cylinder head bolts (see Section 10)
  10 mm bolts
    1st stage . . . .   19 Nm
    2nd stage . . . .   50 Nm
    3rd stage . . . .   12 Nm
    Final stage . . . .   120°
  6 mm bolts . . . .   12 Nm
Engine mounting bolts/nuts . . . .   55 Nm
Gearchange shaft centralising spring locating pin . . . .   22 Nm
Oil cooler bolt . . . .   63 Nm
Oil filter boss . . . .   70 Nm
Oil pipe (U-shaped) bolts . . . .   12 Nm
Oil pump drive chain guide bolts . . . .   12 Nm
Oil pump housing bolts . . . .   12 Nm
Oil pump mounting bolts . . . .   12 Nm
Oil sump bolts . . . .   10 Nm
Selector fork shaft retaining plate bolts . . . .   10 Nm
Starter clutch bolts . . . .   32 Nm
Swingarm pivot bolt nut . . . .   110 Nm
Timing rotor bolt . . . .   35 Nm
Timing rotor cover bolts . . . .   10 Nm
Transmission input shaft bearing housing Torx screws . . . .   12 Nm
Valve cover bolts . . . .   12 Nm

1 General information

The engine is a liquid-cooled in-line four, with four valves per cylinder. The valves are operated by double overhead camshafts that are driven by chain off the right-hand end of the crankshaft. The engine assembly is constructed from aluminium alloy. The crankcase is divided horizontally.

The crankcase incorporates a wet sump, pressure-fed lubrication system, which uses a chain-driven, dual-rotor oil pump, an oil filter, a relief valve and an oil level switch – there is no oil pressure switch. The pump chain runs off the clutch housing. The oil is circulated through a cooler located on the front of the crankcases.

The alternator is on the left-hand end of the crankshaft, and the starter clutch is on the back of the alternator.

Power from the crankshaft is routed to the transmission via the clutch. The clutch is a wet, multi-plate type and is gear-driven off the crankshaft. The transmission is a six-speed constant-mesh unit. Final drive to the rear wheel is by chain and sprockets.

Read the *Safety first!* section of this manual carefully before starting work.

2 Component access

Operations possible with the engine in the frame

The components and assemblies listed below can be removed without having to remove the engine assembly from the frame. If however, a number of areas require attention at the same time, removal of the engine is recommended.

Valve cover
Camshafts
Cam chain
Cylinder head
Water pump and thermostat
Clutch and starter clutch
Gearchange mechanism
Alternator
Starter motor
Crankshaft position (CKP) sensor
Oil filter and cooler
Oil sump, oil strainer and oil pressure
  relief valve
Oil pump

Operations requiring engine removal

It is necessary to remove the engine from the frame to gain access to the following components.

Crankshaft and bearings
Connecting rods and bearings
Cylinder bores, pistons and piston rings
Transmission shafts
Selector drum and forks

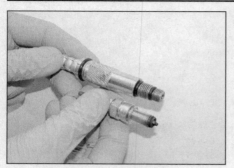

3.5 Select the correct adapter

3.7 Thread the adapter into the cylinder head

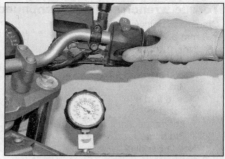

3.8 Measuring cylinder compression

3 Engine wear assessment

⚠ **Warning: Be careful when working on the hot engine – the exhaust pipes, the engine and engine components can cause severe burns.**

1 Poor engine performance may be caused by leaking valves, incorrect valve clearances, a leaking head gasket, or worn pistons, piston rings or cylinders. A cylinder compression check will highlight these conditions and can also indicate the presence of excessive carbon deposits in the cylinder head, and a leakdown test (for which special equipment is needed – consult a Yamaha dealer) will pinpoint the actual cause(s) of the problem.

Cylinder compression test

Special tools: *A compression gauge with an adapter that matches the spark plug threads is necessary for this procedure. Yamaha can provide a gauge (part no. 90890-03081 in Europe, YU-33223 in the US) and gauge adapter (part no. 90890-04136) for this purpose.*

2 Among other things, poor starting and engine performance may be caused by leaking valves, a leaking head gasket or worn pistons, rings and/or cylinder walls. A cylinder compression check will help pinpoint these conditions.

3 Before carrying out the test, check that the valve clearances are correct (see Chapter 1).

4 Run the engine until it reaches normal operating temperature, then turn the ignition OFF.

5 Refer to Chapter 1, Section 2, and remove the spark plugs. Select the correct gauge adapter to match the spark plug thread size (16 mm) and fit it onto the end of the gauge hose **(see illustration)**.

6 Fit the plugs back into their caps and arrange the plugs so that their metal bodies are earthed against the engine or frame.

7 Working on the first cylinder to be tested, thread the gauge adapter into the spark plug hole **(see illustration)**.

8 Open the throttle fully and crank the engine over on the starter motor until the gauge reading has built up to a maximum figure and then remains stable **(see illustration)**. Make a note of the pressure reading and then repeat the procedure on the other cylinders. Turn the ignition OFF when the test has been completed.

9 Compare the results with the specifications at the beginning of this Chapter (see *Cylinder bores*). If they are all within the specified range and the maximum difference between any cylinders is less than specified, the engine is in good condition.

10 If there is a marked difference between the readings, or if the readings are lower than specified, it is likely components in the engine top-end are worn. Pour a small quantity of clean engine oil through the spark plug hole of the cylinder being checked, then test for compression again. An increase in pressure indicates worn or broken piston rings. No change in the pressure indicates a problem with the valves or cylinder head gasket.

11 Readings that are higher than specified are unlikely, but if found indicate excessive carbon build-up in the combustion chamber and on the top of the piston. If this is the case, remove the cylinder head and clean the carbon deposits off.

12 When the test is complete, refer to Chapter 1 and install the spark plugs.

Leak-down (cylinder leakage) test

13 A leak down or 'cylinder leakage' test is similar to a compression test in that it tells you how well a cylinder is sealing, but it does so by testing how much pressure is lost through leakage, as opposed to how much pressure is created through compression. Many professionals prefer a leak test to a compression test as it more accurately pin-points the cause of the problem before any disassembly is done, as it is easy to tell where the leakage is occurring. Generally however the required equipment is more expensive than for a compression test and a source of compressed air is essential. If you think a test is needed take the bike to a suitably equipped dealer or workshop. If you decide to purchase your own equipment follow the manufacturer's instructions.

14 A leakage test can also be used in conjunction with a compression test to diagnose other kinds of problems, such as a faulty valve train component, incorrect valve timing, faulty ignition or fuel delivery problems.

Engine oil pressure check

Special tools: *An oil pressure gauge with a 16 mm threaded adapter is necessary for this procedure. Yamaha provide a gauge (part no. 90890-03153 in Europe, YU-03153 in the US) and gauge adapter (part no. 90890-03139) for this purpose.*

15 If there is any doubt about the performance of the engine lubrication system an oil pressure check must be carried out. The check provides useful information about the state of wear of the engine. **Note:** *This engine is fitted with an oil level sensor and low level warning light, not an oil pressure switch and low pressure warning light. The function of the circuit is described in Chapter 8.*

16 Check the engine oil level and top up if necessary (see *Pre-ride checks*).

17 Run the engine until it reaches normal operating temperature, then turn the ignition OFF. Support the machine upright.

18 Place a drain tray under the alternator cover. Unscrew the oil gallery plug below the alternator cover, then quickly screw the adapter into the threads. Connect the pressure gauge to the adapter **(see illustration)**.

⚠ **Warning: Take great care not to burn your hand on the hot engine unit, exhaust pipe or with engine oil when accessing the gauge take-off point on the crankcase. Do not allow exhaust gases to build up in the work area; either perform the check outside or use an exhaust gas extraction system.**

3.18 Oil gallery plug (arrowed)

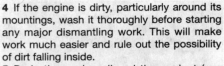

19 Start the engine and increase the engine speed to 6600 rpm whilst watching the pressure gauge reading. Make a note of the reading. The oil pressure should be similar to that given in the specifications at the beginning of this Chapter.

20 Stop the engine.

21 Fit a new O-ring onto the oil gallery bolt and lubricate it with clean engine oil.

22 Unscrew the gauge and adapter from the crankcase, then install the oil gallery bolt and tighten it to the specified torque setting. Check the engine oil level (see *Pre-ride checks*).

23 If the pressure is significantly lower than the standard, either the pressure relief valve is stuck open, the oil pump is faulty, the oil strainer or filter is blocked, or there is considerable engine wear. Begin diagnosis by checking the oil filter, strainer and relief valve, then the oil pump (see Sections 17 and 18). If those items check out okay, the engine bearing oil clearances are likely to be excessive and the engine needs to be overhauled.

24 If the pressure is too high, either an oil passage is clogged, the relief valve is stuck closed or the wrong grade of oil is being used.

25 Refer to the appropriate Sections within this Chapter and rectify any problems before running the engine again.

4 Engine removal and installation

Caution: The engine is very heavy. Engine removal and installation should be carried out with the aid of at least one assistant. Personal injury or damage could occur if the engine falls or is dropped. An hydraulic or mechanical floor jack should be used to support and lower or raise the engine, if possible.

Removal

Note: If you intend to remove the alternator, timing rotor or clutch with the engine removed from the frame, it is best to slacken the rotor bolts and clutch nut while the engine is still in the frame – they are tight and the engine needs to be held securely while they are undone. Refer to Chapter 8 for the alternator, Section 9 for the timing rotor and Section 13 for the clutch.

1 Support the motorcycle securely in an upright position, on the centrestand if fitted, or using an auxiliary stand or stands – you cannot support the bike on its sidestand as it needs to be removed. Tie the front brake lever to the handlebar so the bike can't move. Work can be made easier by raising the machine to a suitable working height on an hydraulic ramp or a suitable platform. Make sure the motorcycle is secure and will not topple over (see Section 1 of *Tools and Workshop Tips* in the *Reference* section). When disconnecting any wiring, cables and hoses, it is advisable to mark or tag them as a reminder of where they connect, and make a note of any ties and guides that secure them and how they are routed.

2 Remove the seat and the side panels (see Chapter 7). Disconnect the battery (see Chapter 8).

3 On XJ6-N models remove the side covers and the belly-pan, on XJ6-S models remove the fairing side panels and the belly-pan, and on XJ6-F and FZ6R models remove the lower fairing panels and brackets (see Chapter 7). Remove the lower fairing brackets or belly-pan brackets, according to model **(see illustration)**.

4 If the engine is dirty, particularly around its mountings, wash it thoroughly before starting any major dismantling work. This will make work much easier and rule out the possibility of dirt falling inside.

5 Drain the engine oil and the coolant (see Chapter 1).

6 Remove the fuel tank, the air filter housing and the throttle bodies (see Chapter 4). Plug the intake manifolds with clean rag.

7 Remove the radiator, disconnecting the hoses from the engine and removing them along with the radiator (see Chapter 3).

8 Remove the exhaust system (see Chapter 4).

9 Remove the coolant reservoir and the radiator mounting bracket on the front of the engine, noting how it fits (see Chapter 3).

10 Remove the AIS control valve along with the hoses (see Chapter 4).

11 Release the cable-ties and remove the rubber heat shield, noting how it fits **(see illustrations)**. Clean the area around each spark plug cap to prevent any dirt falling into the spark plug wells. Check that the cylinder location is marked on each HT lead (numbered 1 to 4 from the left-hand side), then pull the cap off each spark plug **(see illustration)**.

12 Detach the clutch cable from the release mechanism arm (see Section 12).

13 Disconnect the wiring connectors for the alternator, sidestand switch, crankshaft

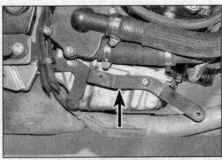
4.3 Remove the bracket (arrowed) from each side – XJ6-N shown

4.11a Release the two cable-ties (arrowed) on the left-hand side...

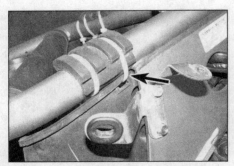
4.11b ...and the single cable-tie (arrowed) on the right...

4.11c ...and note how the shield locates before removing it

4.11d Pull the cap off the spark plug

4.13a The various wiring connectors are inside the rubber boots (arrowed)

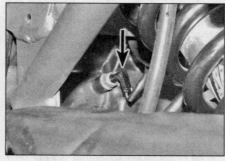

4.13b Neutral switch wiring connector (arrowed)

4.14 Unscrew the nut (arrowed) and detach the starter lead

position sensor, oil level sensor, and speed sensor **(see illustration)**. Disconnect the wiring connector from the neutral switch **(see illustration)**. Feed the sidestand switch wire down to the switch, noting its routing.

14 Peel back the boot on the starter motor terminal, then unscrew the starter motor terminal nut and detach the lead **(see illustration)**. Secure the lead clear of the engine.

15 Unscrew the bolt securing the engine earth (ground) lead and detach the lead **(see illustration)**. Secure the lead clear of the engine.

16 Note the alignment of the punch mark on the gearchange linkage arm with the line across the end of the shaft, then unscrew the

bolt, slide the arm off, and position it clear **(see illustrations)**.

17 Remove the front sprocket and slip the chain off the transmission output shaft (see Chapter 6).

18 Unscrew the swingarm pivot bolt nut **(see illustration)**. Unscrew the swingarm pivot bracket bolts and remove the complete pivot/footrest/sidestand bracket assembly **(see illustrations)**.

19 At this point, position an hydraulic or mechanical jack under the engine with a block of wood between the jack head and sump. Make sure the jack is centrally positioned so the engine will not topple in any direction when the last mounting bolt is removed and the engine is supported only by the jack.

Take the weight of the engine on the jack, but make sure the bike is not being lifted. If a centrestand is being used it is also advisable to place a block of wood between the rear wheel and the ground in case the bike tilts back onto the rear wheel when the engine is removed.

20 Check around the engine and frame to make sure that all the necessary wiring, cables and hoses have been disconnected, and that any that remain connected to the engine are not retained by any clips, guides or brackets on the frame, and that any staying behind are not held to the engine. When removing the engine mounting bolts note which fits where as there are different lengths and sizes.

21 Unscrew and remove the two front

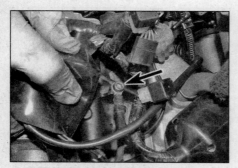

4.15 Unscrew the bolt (arrowed) and detach the earth lead

4.16a Note the alignment of the arm on the shaft...

4.16b ...then unscrew the bolt and slide the gearchange arm off

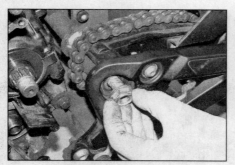

4.18a Unscrew the nut...

4.18b ...and the two bracket bolts...

4.18c ...and remove the bracket assembly

mounting bolts and washers on the right-hand side **(see illustration)**.

22 Unscrew and remove the two front mounting bolts and washers on the left-hand side **(see illustration)**.

23 Unscrew the nuts and remove the washers from the right-hand ends of the upper and lower rear mounting bolts, but do not withdraw the bolts **(see illustration)**. Make sure the engine is properly supported on the jack, and have an assistant support it as well, then withdraw the mounting bolts **(see illustration)**.

24 Carefully lower the engine and bring it forward, then manoeuvre it out of the frame from the right-hand side.

Installation

25 Installation is the reverse of removal, noting the following points:

● With the aid of an assistant, place the engine unit onto the jack and block of wood and carefully raise it into position so that the mounting bolt holes align. Make sure no wires, cables or hoses become trapped between the engine and the frame.

● Lubricate the threads of the upper and lower rear mounting bolts with engine oil and slide them into place **(see illustration 4.23b)**. Fit the washers and nuts and tighten them finger-tight only at this stage **(see illustration)**.

● Fit the front mounting bolts with their washers and tighten them finger-tight only at this stage **(see illustrations 4.21 and 4.22)**.

● Counter-hold the lower rear mounting bolt and tighten the nut to the torque setting specified at the beginning of this Chapter. Repeat for the upper rear mounting bolt.

● Tighten the front mounting bolts on the left-hand side to the specified torque, then tighten the mounting bolts on the right-hand side to the specified torque.

● Clean the threads of the left-hand swingarm pivot plate bolts, then apply some fresh threadlock and tighten them securely **(see illustration 4.18b)**. Tighten the swingarm pivot bolt nut to the specified torque **(see illustration 4.18a)**.

● Make sure all wires, cables and hoses are correctly routed and connected, and secured by any clips or ties.

4.21 Unscrew the two front bolts on the right-hand side...

4.22 ...and on the left-hand side

● Refill the engine with oil and coolant to the correct levels (see Chapter 1 and *Pre-ride checks*).

● Check the throttle and clutch cable freeplay (see Chapter 1).

● Adjust the drive chain tension (see Chapter 1).

● Start the engine and check that there are no oil or coolant leaks.

● Adjust the engine idle speed (see Chapter 1).

5 Engine overhaul general information

1 Before beginning the engine overhaul, read through the related procedures to familiarise yourself with the scope and requirements of the job. Overhauling an engine is not all that difficult, but it is time consuming. Check on the availability of parts and make sure that any necessary special tools are obtained in advance.

2 Most work can be done with a decent set of typical workshop hand tools, although a number of precision measuring tools are required for inspecting parts to determine if they are worn.

3 To ensure maximum life and minimum trouble from a rebuilt engine, everything must be assembled with care in a spotlessly clean environment, using the correct lubricant where directed.

Disassembly

4 Before disassembling the engine, thoroughly clean and degrease its external surfaces. This will prevent contamination of the engine internals, and will also make the job a lot easier and cleaner. A high flash-point solvent, such as paraffin (kerosene) can be used, or better still, a proprietary engine degreaser such as Gunk. Use old paintbrushes and toothbrushes to work the solvent into the various recesses of the casings. Take care to exclude solvent or water from the electrical components and intake and exhaust ports.

⚠️ *Warning: The use of petrol (gasoline) as a cleaning agent should be avoided because of the risk of fire.*

5 When clean and dry, position the engine on the workbench, leaving suitable clear area for working. Gather a selection of small containers, plastic bags and some labels so that parts can be grouped together in an easily identifiable manner. Also get some paper and a pen so that notes can be taken. You will also need a supply of clean rag, which should be as absorbent as possible.

6 Before commencing work, read through the appropriate section so that some idea of the necessary procedure can be gained. When removing components note that great force is seldom required, unless specified (checking the specified torque setting of the particular bolt being removed will indicate how tight it is, and therefore how much force should be needed). In many cases, a component's

4.23a Unscrew the nuts (arrowed) and remove the washers

4.23b Withdraw the bolts and remove the engine

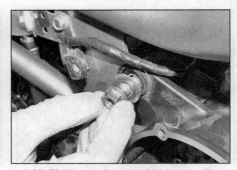

4.25 Fit the washers and nuts onto the rear mounting bolts

6.3a Unscrew the bolts (arrowed)...

6.3b ...and remove the valve cover

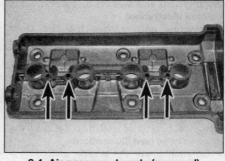

6.4 Air passage dowels (arrowed)

reluctance to be removed is indicative of an incorrect approach or removal method; if in any doubt, re-check with the text.

7 When disassembling the engine, keep 'mated' parts together (including gears, pistons, connecting rods, valves, etc, that have been in contact with each other during engine operation). These 'mated' parts must be reused or replaced as an assembly.

8 A complete engine disassembly should be done in the following general order with reference to the appropriate Sections (or Chapters, where indicated).

Remove the valve cover
Remove the cam chain tensioner
Remove the camshafts
Remove the cylinder head
Remove the clutch
Remove the alternator rotor and starter clutch
Remove the starter motor (see Chapter 8)
Remove the gearchange mechanism
Remove the water pump (see Chapter 3)
Remove the oil cooler
Remove the oil sump
Remove the oil pump
Separate the crankcase halves
Remove the crankshaft
Remove the connecting rods and pistons
Remove the transmission output shaft
Remove the selector drum and forks
Remove the transmission input shaft

Reassembly

9 Reassembly is accomplished by reversing the general disassembly sequence.

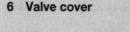

6 Valve cover

Removal

1 Remove the fuel tank and the air filter housing (see Chapter 4). Displace the throttle bodies and support them clear of the valve cover (see Chapter 4) – you need to disconnect the throttle cables, and after displacing the throttle bodies disconnect the ECT sensor wiring connector, but you can leave the coolant hoses and all other wiring connected. Remove the AIS air cut-off valve and hoses, then remove the reed valves (see Chapter 4).

2 Release the cable-ties and remove the rubber heat shield, noting how it fits **(see illustrations 4.11a, b and c)**. Clean the area around each spark plug cap to prevent any dirt falling into the spark plug wells. Check that the cylinder location is marked on each HT lead (numbered 1 to 4 from the left-hand side), then pull the cap off each spark plug **(see illustration 4.11d)**. Poke the caps through the holes in the frame so they are out of the way.

3 Unscrew and remove the valve cover bolts **(see illustration)**. Lift the cover off the cylinder head and remove it **(see illustration)**. If it is stuck, break the gasket seal by tapping gently around the edge with a soft-faced hammer or block of wood. Do not lever the

cover off as this will damage the sealing surface.

4 Remove the gasket. Note the four AIS system air passage dowels and remove them if they are loose **(see illustration)**.

Installation

5 Examine the valve cover gasket rim and circular spark plug seals for signs of damage or deterioration and fit a new gasket if necessary **(see illustration)**. Similarly check the cover bolt sealing washers for cracks, hardening and deterioration and use new ones if necessary **(see illustration)**.

6 Clean the mating surfaces of the cylinder head and the valve cover with a suitable solvent.

7 Fit the gasket onto the valve cover, making sure It locates correctly **(see illustration 6.5a)**. If the new gasket has a bridge piece between the cam chain end and the adjacent spark plug seal cut it away using a sharp knife. Apply a smear of a suitable sealant to the raised sections of the gasket that fit into the cut-outs in the cylinder head **(see illustration)**. Make sure the AIS system dowels are pushed fully into place **(see illustration 6.4)**.

8 Position the valve cover on the cylinder head, making sure the gasket stays in place **(see illustration 6.3b)**. Fit the sealing washers if removed **(see illustration 6.5b)**. Fit the bolts and tighten them to the torque setting specified at the beginning of this Chapter **(see illustration 6.3a)**.

9 Install the remaining components in the reverse order of removal.

6.5a Check the gasket...

6.5b ...and the sealing washers

6.7 Apply some silicone sealant to the raised sections

7.5 Cam chain tensioner mounting bolts (arrowed)

7.6a Pinch the spring ends together...

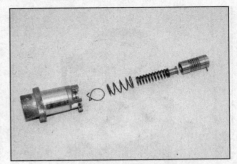

7.6b ...and remove the plunger, spring seat and springs

7 Cam chain tensioner

1 The cam chain tensioner is located on the rear of the cylinder head on the right-hand side (see illustration 7.3).

Removal

2 To access the cam chain tensioner, on XJ6-N models remove the right-hand side cover, on XJ6-S models remove the right-hand fairing side panels, and on XJ6-F and FZ6R models remove the right-hand lower fairing panel (see Chapter 7).
3 Remove the valve cover (see Section 6). Remove the spark plugs (see Chapter 1). Place a drain tray under the timing rotor cover

and unscrew the cover bolts (see illustration 8.3). Note the guide for the coolant hose. Ease the cover off. Remove the gasket – a new one must be used.
4 Refer to Section 8, Step 4 and position cylinder No. 1 at TDC compression.
5 Unscrew the two mounting bolts, evenly and a little at a time, and withdraw the tensioner, noting that the plunger will be pushed out under spring pressure (see illustration). Remove the gasket – a new one must be used (see illustration 7.9a).
6 Hold the ends of the resister spring together and withdraw the plunger, spring seat, coil springs and resistor spring (see illustrations). Drain the oil out of the body.

Inspection

7 Clean all components. Examine them for

signs of wear or damage. If the tensioner is worn or damaged, or if the plunger does not run smoothly in the body, the tensioner must be replaced with a new one – individual components are not available.

Installation

8 Clean and dry the tensioner and cylinder head mating surfaces. Fit the outer spring into the tensioner body (see illustration). Fit the resister spring, locating it in its groove (see illustration). Fit the inner spring, then fit the spring seat into it (see illustrations). Fit the plunger, aligning the pin on its top with the latch on the tensioner body, then hold the ends of the resister ring together to expand it and push the plunger through it and all the way in, keep it held there and fit the latch over the pin to lock it, then slowly release the plunger

7.8a Fit the outer spring...

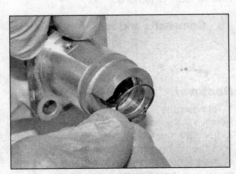

7.8b ...the resister spring...

7.8c ...the inner spring...

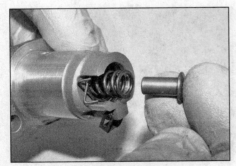

7.8d ...and the spring seat

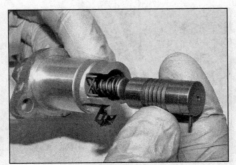

7.8e Fit the plunger over the seat and springs, aligning the pin with the latch...

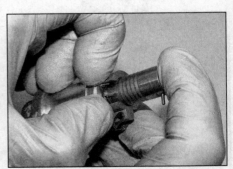

7.8f ...then pinch the spring ends to allow the plunger through it...

7.8g ...and hook the latch over the pin

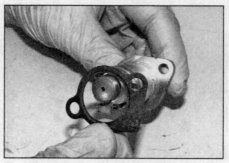

7.9a Fit a new gasket...

7.9b ...so it is positioned as shown

7.9c Fit the tensioner...

7.9d ...and keep it pushed in while fitting and tightening the bolts

8.2 CKP sensor wiring connector (arrowed)

so the latch holds it in the retracted position **(see illustration)**. Now push on the plunger to check that the latch drops off under its own weight, then reset it in the locked position.

9 Hold the tensioner so the triangular mark points up, and fit a new gasket with the tab marked L on the lower left side (when viewed from the outer side) relative to the triangular mark **(see illustrations)**. Fit the tensioner with the triangular mark at the top, push it all the way in and keep it held against the engine while tightening the bolts to the torque setting specified at the beginning of the Chapter **(see illustrations)**.

10 Turn the engine clockwise through two full turns using the timing rotor bolt – make sure the tensioner releases and all slack in the chain is taken up, then check again that all the timing marks still align (see Section 8, Steps 4

and 5). Refer to Section 8, Steps 46 and 47, and install the timing rotor cover.

11 Install the remaining components in the reverse order of removal.

8 Camshafts and followers

Removal

1 Remove the valve cover (see Section 6). Remove the spark plugs (see Chapter 1).

2 Trace the crankshaft position sensor wiring from the timing rotor cover and disconnect it at the connector **(see illustration)**. Feed the wiring back to the cover, noting its routing.

3 Place a drain tray under the timing rotor

cover and unscrew the cover bolts **(see illustration)**. Note the guide for the coolant hose. Ease the cover off. Remove the gasket – a new one must be used.

4 The engine must now be turned to position the No. 1 (left hand) cylinder at TDC (top dead centre) on the compression stroke. Using a spanner on the timing rotor bolt, turn the engine clockwise until the 'T' mark on the ignition rotor faces to the rear and aligns with the crankcase mating surfaces **(see illustrations)**. The camshaft lobes on each camshaft for the No. 1 cylinder should face away from each other; if the cam lobes are facing towards each other, rotate the engine clockwise 360° (one full turn) so that the 'T' mark again faces to the rear and aligns with the crankcase mating surfaces. The camshaft lobes should now be facing away from each other and the No. 1 cylinder will be

8.3 Unscrew the bolts (arrowed) and remove the cover

8.4a Turn the engine clockwise...

8.4b ...until the T mark aligns with the crankcase joint...

8.4c ...and the No. 1 cam lobes (arrowed) point away from each other

8.5 Check the camshaft sprocket marks (arrowed) are as shown

at TDC (top dead centre) on the compression stroke (see illustration).

5 Before disturbing the camshafts, check that the 'I' (intake camshaft) and 'E' (exhaust camshaft) timing marks on the camshaft sprockets face away from each other and align with the cylinder head mating surface (see illustration). If you are in any doubt as to the alignment of the markings, or if they are not visible, make your own alignment marks between all components, and also between a tooth on each sprocket (including the timing sprocket) and its corresponding link on the chain, before disturbing them. These markings ensure that the valve timing can be correctly set up on assembly. As it is easy to be a tooth out on installation, marking between a tooth on each sprocket and its link in the chain is especially useful.

6 Remove the cam chain tensioner (see Section 7).

7 There are three camshaft holders for each camshaft (see illustration). Each has an identity mark (I1 or I2 on the intake side and E1 or E2 on the exhaust side, with the holders marked 1 on the right-hand (cam chain) side of the engine), and an arrow which points to the right-hand side of the engine (see illustration). Note the position of each holder for correct installation later. If the marks are unclear make your own.

8 Note the camshaft identification markings – the intake camshaft is marked green and the exhaust camshaft is coloured red, and the I or E on the sprocket is marked with white paint according to the camshaft it fits on (see illustrations).

9 Working on one camshaft at a time and starting with the intake shaft if removing both, unscrew the camshaft holder bolts evenly and a little at a time in a criss-cross pattern, starting from the outside and working towards the centre (see illustration 8.7a). Slacken the bolts above any cam lobes that are pressing onto a valve last in the sequence so that the pressure from the open valves cannot cause the camshaft to bend.

Caution: If the bolts are loosened carelessly and the holders do not come away from the head squarely, a holder is likely to break. If this happens the complete cylinder head assembly must be replaced with a new one as the holders are matched to the head and cannot be obtained separately. Also, the camshaft could be damaged if the holder bolts are not slackened evenly and the pressure from a depressed valve causes a shaft to bend.

10 Remove the bolts, then lift off the camshaft holders. Retrieve the dowels from either the holder or the cylinder head if they are loose.

11 Disengage the chain from the camshaft sprocket and lift the camshaft out of the head (see illustration 8.38a or 8.35a). With both

camshafts removed secure the cam chain with a length of wire to prevent it dropping into the crankcase, and avoid rotating the crankshaft in case the chain jams between the timing sprocket and the case.

12 If required remove the cam chain front guide blade, the tensioner blade and the cam chain (see Section 9).

13 If the followers and shims are being removed from the cylinder head, obtain a container which is divided into sixteen compartments, and label each compartment with the location of its corresponding valve in the cylinder head. If a container is not available, use labelled plastic bags (egg cartons also work very well). Remove the cam

8.7a Camshaft holders (arrowed)...

8.7b ...are marked for identification and orientation

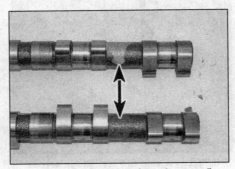

8.8a Note the colour marking (arrowed) on each camshaft...

8.8b ...and the painted letter on the camshaft sprocket

follower of the valve in question, then retrieve the shim from the inside of the follower **(see illustrations)**. If it is not in the follower, pick it out of the top of the valve using either a magnet, a small screwdriver with a dab of grease on it (the shim will stick to the grease), or a screwdriver and a pair of pliers. Do not allow the shim to fall into the engine.

Inspection

14 Inspect the bearing surfaces of the cylinder head and camshaft holder and the corresponding journals on the camshaft. Look for score marks, deep scratches and evidence of spalling (a pitted appearance) **(see illustration 8.15a)**. If damage is noted or wear is excessive, the relevant parts must be replaced with new ones. The cylinder head and holder must be replaced as a new matched set – individual parts are not available.

15 Check the camshaft lobes for heat discoloration (blue appearance), score marks, chipped areas, flat spots and spalling **(see illustration)**. Measure the height of each lobe with a micrometer **(see illustration)** and compare the results to the minimum lobe height listed in this Chapter's Specifications. If damage is noted or wear is excessive, the camshaft must be replaced with a new one. Also check the condition of the cam followers.

16 Check the amount of camshaft runout by supporting each end of the camshaft on V-blocks, and measuring any runout at the journals using a dial gauge. If the runout

exceeds the specified limit the camshaft must be replaced with a new one.

17 The camshaft journal oil clearance should now be checked. There are two possible ways of doing this, either by direct measurement (see Steps 18 to 21) or by the use of a product known as Plastigauge (see Steps 22 to 27).

18 If the direct measurement method is to be used, make sure the camshaft holder dowels are in place then fit the holders in their correct location (see Step 7). Lubricate the threads of the holder bolts with clean engine oil, then tighten the bolts evenly and a little at a time in a criss-cross pattern to the torque setting specified at the beginning of this Chapter. Using telescoping gauges and a micrometer (see *Tools and Workshop Tips*), measure the inside diameter of the holder journals.

19 Now measure the diameter of the corresponding camshaft journals with a micrometer. To determine the journal oil clearance, subtract the journal diameter from the holder diameter and compare the result to the clearance specified. If any clearance is greater than specified, it is an indication of wear on the camshaft, the holder, or both.

20 First check to see if the camshaft journals are worn below the service limit. If they are, a new camshaft must be fitted. However, since it is likely that the holder is also worn, ensure that the specified journal diameter for a new camshaft will restore the oil clearance to within specification before buying a new camshaft.

21 If the camshaft journals are good, or if fitting a new camshaft will not restore the oil

clearance to within specification, the holders and cylinder head will have to be replaced as a new matched set.

22 If the Plastigauge method is to be used, work on one camshaft at a time and clean the camshaft being checked, the corresponding bearing surfaces in the cylinder head and the camshaft holders with a suitable solvent and a clean, lint-free cloth, then lay the camshaft in place in the cylinder head, making sure the timing marks are correctly aligned (see Step 4 and 5).

23 Cut some strips of Plastigauge and lay one piece on each journal, parallel with the camshaft centreline **(see illustration)**. Make sure the camshaft holder dowels are in place then fit the holders in their correct location (see Step 7). Lubricate the threads of the holder bolts with clean engine oil, then tighten the bolts evenly and a little at a time in a criss-cross pattern to the torque setting specified at the beginning of this Chapter – work from the centre of the camshafts outwards, starting with the bolts that are above valves that will be opened when the camshafts are tightened down. Whilst tightening the bolts, make sure each holder is being pulled down squarely and is not binding on the dowels. Whilst doing this, don't let the camshaft rotate.

24 Now unscrew the bolts evenly and a little at a time in a criss-cross pattern, starting from the outside and working towards the centre, and carefully lift off the camshaft holders.

25 To determine the oil clearance, compare the crushed Plastigauge (at its widest point) on each journal to the scale printed on the Plastigauge container **(see illustration)**.

8.13a Lift out the follower using a magnet if available...

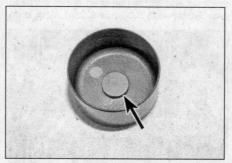

8.13b ...and retrieve the shim (arrowed) from inside it

8.15a Check the camshaft lobes as described – damage as shown requires immediate attention

8.15b Measure the height of the camshaft lobes with a micrometer

8.23 Lay a strip of Plastigauge across each bearing journal parallel with the centreline

8.25 Compare the width of the crushed Plastigauge with the scale printed on the container

8.29 Camshaft sprocket bolts

8.31a Fit each shim into its recess...

8.31b ...then fit the follower

Compare the results to this Chapter's Specifications. Carefully clean away all traces of Plastigauge using a fingernail or other object which will not score the bearing surfaces. If any clearance is greater than specified, it is an indication of wear on the camshaft, the holder, or both.

26 First check to see if the camshaft journals are worn below the service limit by measuring them with a micrometer. If they are, a new camshaft must be fitted. However, since it is likely that the holder is also worn, ensure that the specified journal diameter for a new camshaft will restore the oil clearance to within specification before buying a new camshaft.

27 If the camshaft journals are good, or if fitting a new camshaft will not restore the oil clearance to within specification, the holders and cylinder head will have to be replaced as a matched set.

28 Inspect the cam chain guide blade, tensioner blade and cam chain (see Section 9).

29 Inspect the camshaft sprockets; if they show signs of wear, cracks or other damage, replace them and the cam chain with a new set. The camshaft sprockets are retained by two bolts (see illustration) – unscrew the bolts and remove the sprockets. Fit the new sprockets on their respective camshafts with the marks facing out, and tighten the bolts to the specified torque setting.

30 Inspect the outer surfaces of the cam followers for evidence of wear, scoring or other damage. If the side of a follower is in poor condition, it is probable that the bore in which it works is also damaged. Check for clearance between the followers and their bores. Whilst no specifications are given, if slack is excessive, replace the followers with new ones. If the bores are seriously out-of-round or tapered, then replace the cylinder head and followers with new ones.

Installation

31 If removed, lubricate each valve shim and follower with molybdenum disulphide oil (a 50/50 mixture of molybdenum disulphide grease and engine oil) and fit each shim into its recess on the top of the valve, with the size marking on the shim facing up (see illustration). Make sure the shim is correctly seated, then fit the follower, making sure it sits squarely in its bore (see illustration). Note: It is important that the shims and followers are returned to their original valves, otherwise the valve clearances will be inaccurate.

32 Make sure the camshaft journals and the bearing surfaces in the cylinder head are clean, then apply molybdenum disulphide oil to them and to the camshaft lobes.

33 If removed, install the cam chain, the tensioner blade and the front guide blade (see Section 9).

34 Make sure that the 'T' mark on the timing rotor still aligns with the crankcase mating surfaces (see Step 4) (see illustration 8.4b).

35 Fit the exhaust camshaft (see Step 8), making sure the 'E' mark on the sprocket faces forward and aligns with the cylinder head mating surface (see illustration). Fit the cam chain around the sprocket as you position the camshaft, pulling up on the chain to remove all slack in the front run between the crankshaft and the camshaft. If alignment marks were made prior to disassembly (see Step 5), check that the marks on the cam chain and sprocket align. With the alignment correct fit a cable-tie through the hole in the sprocket and around the chain to prevent it jumping (see illustration).

36 Fit the exhaust camshaft holder dowels into the holders or cylinder head if removed. Make sure the bearing surfaces in the holders are clean, then lubricate them with molybdenum disulphide oil.

37 Fit the holders in their correct location (see Step 7). Make sure that the holder dowels, and the rib on the camshaft above the middle holder, locate correctly (see illustration). Lubricate the threads of the holder bolts with clean engine oil and fit them into the holders. Tighten the bolts evenly and a little at a time in a criss-cross pattern to the torque setting specified at the beginning of this Chapter – work from the centre of the camshaft outwards, starting with the bolts that are above valves that will be opened when the camshafts are tightened down. Whilst tightening the bolts, make sure each holder is being pulled down squarely and is not binding on the dowels.

38 Now fit the intake camshaft, making sure the 'I' mark on the sprocket faces to the rear and aligns with the cylinder head mating

8.35a Fit the exhaust camshaft as described...

8.35b ...make sure the E mark is aligned with the head, then cable-tie the chain to the sprocket

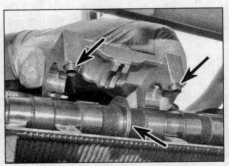

8.37 Fit the holders making sure the dowels and ring (arrowed) locate correctly

8.38a Fit the intake camshaft as described...

8.38b ...make sure the I mark is aligned with the head, then cable-tie the chain to the sprocket

8.40 Fit the holders making sure the dowels and ring (arrowed) locate correctly

surface (see illustration). Fit the cam chain around the sprocket, aligning the marks (if made) between sprocket and chain. When fitting the chain, pull it tight to make sure there is no slack between the two camshaft sprockets; any slack in the chain must lie in the rear run, so that it is taken up by the tensioner. With the alignment correct fit a cable-tie through the hole in the sprocket and around the chain to prevent it jumping (see illustration).

39 Fit the intake camshaft holder dowels into the holders or cylinder head if removed. Make sure the bearing surfaces in the holders are clean, then lubricate them with molybdenum disulphide oil.

40 Fit the holders in their correct location (see Step 7). Make sure that the holder dowels, and the rib on the camshaft above the middle holder, locate correctly (see illustration). Lubricate the threads of the holder bolts with clean engine oil and fit them into the holders. Tighten the bolts evenly and a little at a time in a criss-cross pattern to the torque setting specified at the beginning of this Chapter – work from the centre of the camshaft outwards, starting with the bolts that are above valves that will be opened when the camshafts are tightened down. Whilst tightening the bolts, make sure each holder is being pulled down squarely and is not binding on the dowels.

Caution: The camshaft holder is likely to break if it is not tightened down evenly and squarely and the camshaft is likely to

bend if it is tightened down onto the closed valves before the open ones.

41 Using a piece of wooden dowel, press on the back of the cam chain tensioner blade via the tensioner bore in the crankcase to take up any slack in the cam chain. Check that all the timing marks are still in **exact** alignment as described in Steps 4 and 5. If it is necessary to turn the engine slightly to align the marks with the engine mating surfaces, keep the wooden dowel pressed onto the tensioner blade. Note that it is easy to be slightly out (by one tooth on a sprocket) without the marks appearing drastically out of alignment.

42 If the camshaft marks are out, release the tension on the chain, cut the cable-ties around the sprockets and chain, and remove the tensioner and guide blade pivot pins (Section 9), then manually feed the chain around the sprockets as required, then turn the crankshaft as required so that all timing marks align as specified, then refit the blade pivot pins and recheck the timing marks.

Caution: If the marks are not aligned exactly as described, the valve timing will be incorrect and the valves may strike the pistons, causing extensive damage to the engine.

43 With everything correctly aligned, install the cam chain tensioner (see Section 7). Turn the engine clockwise through two full turns – make sure the tensioner releases and all slack in the chain is taken up, then check again that all the timing marks still align (see Steps 4

and 5). On the engine photographed the tensioner did not fully release, leaving enough slack for the chain to jump a tooth on each sprocket, so the timing was out. To realign the marks if necessary remove the tensioner (Section 7) and the tensioner and guide blade pivot pins (Section 9), then manually feed the chain around the sprockets as required, then turn the crankshaft as required so that all timing marks align as specified, then refit the blade pivot pins and the tensioner, and turn the engine again as described at the beginning of the Step.

44 Check the valve clearances and adjust them if necessary (see Chapter 1).

45 Install the valve cover (see Section 6).

46 Clean all old gasket off the timing rotor cover and crankcase mating surfaces. Clean the threads of the cover bolts, then apply some fresh threadlock. Fit the new gasket onto the cover, then insert two of the bolts to keep it in place as you fit the cover (see illustration).

47 Fit the cover and secure it with the bolts finger-tight, making sure the guide is correctly positioned with the hose behind it (see illustration). Tighten the cover bolts evenly to the torque setting specified at the beginning of this Chapter.

48 Connect the crankshaft position sensor wiring (see illustration 8.2).

49 Install all remaining components in the reverse order of removal. On completion, check the engine oil level (see *Pre-ride* checks). Check and adjust the idle speed (see Chapter 1).

8.46 Fit the cover using a new gasket

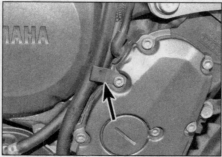

8.47 Position of guide (arrowed) on bolt and the hose and wiring behind it

9 Cam chain, tensioner blade and guides

Tensioner blade and guides

Removal

1 Remove the camshafts (see Section 8). The cam chain top guide is fixed in the valve cover and should not be removed.

2 To remove the cam chain tensioner blade, withdraw the pivot pin, then draw the blade

9.2a Withdraw the pivot pin...

9.2b ...and draw the tensioner blade out of the engine

9.3a Withdraw the pivot pin...

9.3b ...and draw the guide blade out of the engine

9.8a Using the alternator rotor bolt to prevent the crankshaft turning while unscrewing the timing rotor bolt

9.8b Remove the bolt and the washer...

out of the top of the engine, noting which way round it fits **(see illustrations)**.

3 To remove the cam chain front guide blade, withdraw the pivot pin, then draw the blade out of the top of the engine, noting which way round it fits **(see illustrations)**.

Inspection

4 Check the sliding surfaces for excessive wear, deep grooves, cracking and other obvious damage, and replace them with new ones if necessary.

Installation

5 Apply some clean engine oil to the blade

pivot pin, then fit the blade and insert the pin **(see illustrations 9.3b and a, and 9.2b and a)**.

6 Install the camshafts (see Section 8).

Cam chain

Removal

7 Remove the camshafts (see Section 8).

8 To prevent the crankshaft turning while unscrewing the timing rotor bolt, either select a gear and apply the rear brake (if the engine is in the frame), or remove the alternator cover (see Chapter 8) and counter-hold the alternator rotor bolt **(see illustration)**. Remove the bolt,

washer and the rotor, noting how it locates **(see illustrations)**.

9 Lift the cam chain off the crankshaft sprocket and out of the engine **(see illustration)**. The sprocket is an integral part of the crankshaft.

Inspection

10 Except in cases of oil starvation, the cam chain wears very little. If the chain is stiff or the links are binding, or if the links are loose, replace the chain with a new one.

Installation

11 Installation of the chain is the reverse of removal. Make sure the marked side of the

9.8c ...then remove the rotor, noting how it locates

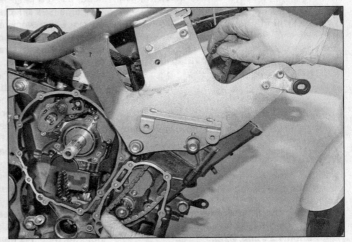

9.9 Removing the cam chain

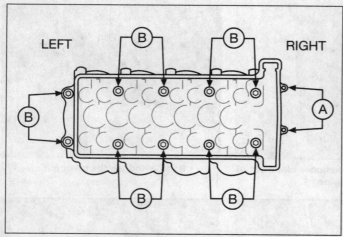

10.3a Cylinder head 6 mm bolts (A) and 10 mm bolts (B)

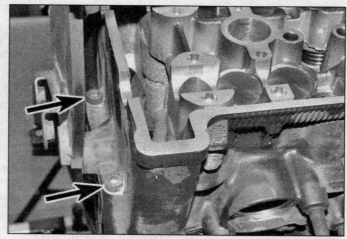

10.3b First unscrew the 6 mm bolts (arrowed)…

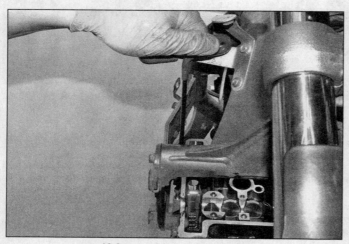

10.3c …using a long hex key

10.3d Cylinder head 10mm bolts (arrowed)

ignition rotor faces out and that the indented section on the rotor locates in the cut-out on the crankshaft (see illustration 9.8c). Tighten the rotor bolt to the torque setting specified at the beginning of the Chapter, counter-holding the crankshaft as on removal.

10 Cylinder head removal and installation

Note: *On installation new head bolts (10 mm) must be used, so it is wise to obtain them before commencing work.*

Removal

1 Remove the valve cover (see Section 6), the camshafts (see Section 8) and cam chain (see Section 9).
2 Unscrew the front engine mounting bolts on the each side, noting the washers (see illustration 4.21 and 4.22).
3 The cylinder head is secured by twelve bolts

(see illustration). First unscrew and remove the 6 mm bolts on the right-hand end of the head, using a long hex key if the engine is in the frame (see illustrations). Now unscrew the 10 mm bolts evenly and no more than a half turn at a time in the *reverse* of the tightening sequence (see illustration and 10.11b). When all the bolts are loose, remove them.
4 Pull the cylinder head up off the cylinder block (see illustration). If it is stuck, tap around the joint faces of the head with a soft-faced hammer or block of wood to free it. Do not attempt to free the head by inserting a lever between it and the cylinder block or you might damage the sealing surfaces.
5 Remove the dowels if loose (see illustration 10.9).
6 Check the cylinder head gasket and the mating surfaces on the cylinder head and block for signs of leaks from the cylinders, or the oil or coolant passages, which could indicate that the head is warped. Refer to Section 11, Step 14, for a warpage check.

7 Remove the cylinder head gasket – a new one must be used. Lay a clean cloth over the pistons while the head is off to prevent any dirt getting in.

Installation

8 Clean all traces of old gasket material from the cylinder head and block. If you need to use

10.4 Lift the head up off the block and remove it

a scraper, take care not to scratch or gouge the soft aluminium. Be careful not to let any of the gasket material fall into the crankcase, the cylinder bores or the oil or coolant passages.

9 Fit the dowels if removed, then lay the new head gasket over the dowels (see illustration).

10 Carefully fit the cylinder head, making sure it locates correctly onto the dowels (see illustration 10.4).

11 Lubricate the threads, washers and under the heads of the new 10 mm cylinder head bolts with clean engine oil. Fit the bolts and tighten them finger-tight (see illustration 10.3d). Now tighten the bolts in the sequence shown to the first stage torque setting, then tighten them in the same sequence to the second stage torque setting (see illustration). Now slacken them in reverse sequence so they are loose, then tighten them in sequence to the third stage torque setting. Finally, using a degree disc, tighten each bolt in sequence through 120° (see illustration).

12 Fit the 6 mm bolts and tighten them to the specified torque setting (see illustration 10.3b).

13 Fit the front engine mounting bolts with their washers and tighten them to the specified torque setting, tightening the bolts on the left-hand side first.

14 Install the remaining components in the reverse order of removal.

11 Cylinder head and valve overhaul

1 Because of the complex nature of this job and the special tools and equipment required, most owners leave servicing of the valves, valve seats and valve guides to a professional. However, you can make an initial assessment of whether the valves are seating correctly, and therefore sealing, by pouring a small amount of solvent into each of the valve ports. If the solvent leaks past any valve into the combustion chamber area the valve is not seating correctly and sealing.

2 With the correct tools (a valve spring compressor is essential – make sure it is suitable for motorcycle work), you can also remove the valves and associated components from the cylinder head, clean them and check them for wear to assess the extent of the work needed, and, unless seat cutting or guide replacement is required, lap the valves and reassemble them in the head.

3 A dealer service department or engine specialist can replace the guides and re-cut the valve seats.

4 After the valve service has been performed, be sure to clean it very thoroughly before installation on the engine to remove any metal particles or abrasive grit that may still be present from the valve service operations. Use compressed air, if available, to blow out all the holes and passages.

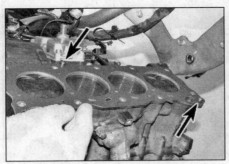
10.9 Fit the dowels (arrowed) then lay the new gasket on the block

10.11a Use new bolts and lubricate as described

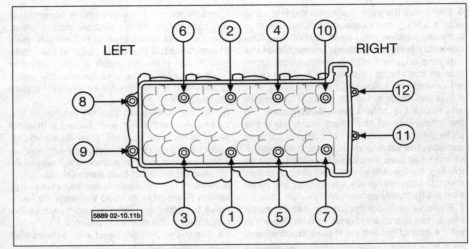
10.11b Cylinder head bolt tightening sequence

10.11c Use a degree disc for the final tightening

Disassembly

5 Before proceeding, arrange to label and store the valves along with their related components in such a way that they can be returned to their original locations without getting mixed up (see illustration). Either use the same container as the valve shims and followers are stored in (see Section 8), or obtain a separate container which is divided into sixteen compartments, and label each compartment with the identity of the valve which will be stored in it. Alternatively, labelled plastic bags will do just as well.

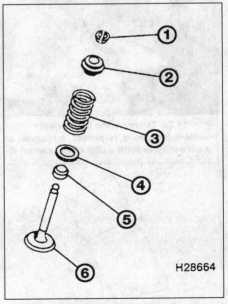
11.5 Valve components

1 Collets
2 Spring retainer
3 Valve spring
4 Spring seat
5 Valve stem oil seal
6 Valve

11.6a Compressing the valve springs using a valve spring compressor

11.6b Make sure the compressor is a good fit both on the top...

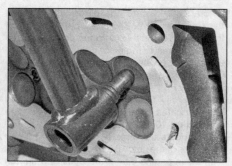

11.6c ...and the bottom of the valve assembly

6 Compress the valve spring on the first valve with a spring compressor, making sure it is correctly located onto each end of the valve assembly **(see illustration)**. On the top of the valve the adaptor needs to be about the same size as the spring retainer – if it is too big it will contact the follower bore and mark it, and if it is too small it will be difficult to remove and install the collets **(see illustration)**. On the underside of the head make sure the plate (where present) on the compressor only contacts the valve and not the soft aluminium of the head **(see illustration)** – if the plate is too big for the valve, use a spacer between them. Do not compress the springs any more than is absolutely necessary.

7 Remove the collets using needle-nose pliers, tweezers, a magnet or a screwdriver with a dab of grease on it **(see illustration)**.

Carefully release the valve spring compressor and remove the spring retainer, noting which way up it fits, the spring and the valve **(see illustrations)**. If the valve binds in the guide (won't pull through), push it back into the head and deburr the area around the collet groove with a very fine file or whetstone **(see illustration)**.

8 Pull the valve stem seal off the top of the valve guide with pliers and discard it (the old seals cannot be reused) **(see illustration)**. Remove the spring seat, noting which way up it fits – using a magnet is the easiest way to lift the seat off the head **(see illustration)**.

9 Repeat the procedure for the remaining valves. Remember to keep the parts for each valve together and labelled so they can be reinstalled in the correct location.

10 Clean the cylinder head with solvent and

dry it thoroughly. Compressed air will speed the drying process and ensure that all holes and recessed areas are clean. **Note:** *Do not use a wire brush mounted in a drill motor to clean the combustion chambers as the head material is soft and may be scratched or eroded away by the wire brush.*

11 Clean the valve components with solvent and dry them thoroughly – clean the parts from one valve at a time so parts cannot get mixed up.

12 Scrape off any deposits that may have formed on the valves, using a motorised wire brush if available and necessary. Again, make sure the valves do not get mixed up.

Inspection

13 Inspect the head very carefully for cracks and other damage. If cracks are found, a new

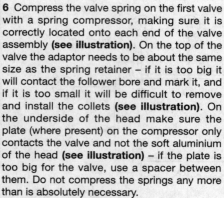

11.7a Remove the collets with needle-nose pliers, tweezers, a magnet or a screwdriver with a dab of grease on it

11.7b Remove the spring retainer and the spring...

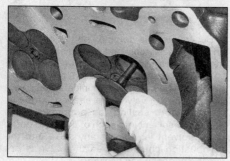

11.7c ...then push the valve down and draw it out

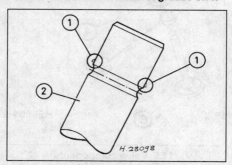

11.7d If the valve stem (2) won't pull through the guide, deburr the area above the collet groove (1)

11.8a Pull the seal off the top of the guide...

11.8b ...then remove the spring seat

11.15 Measure the valve seat width with a ruler (or for greater precision use a Vernier caliper)

11.16 Check the valve face (arrowed) for wear and damage

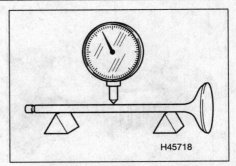

11.17 Measure valve stem runout with V-blocks and a dial gauge

head is required. Check the camshaft bearing surfaces for wear and evidence of seizure. Check the camshafts and holders for wear as well (see Section 8).

14 Using a precision straight-edge and a feeler gauge, check the head gasket mating surface for warpage. Refer to *Tools and Workshop Tips* (Section 3) in the *Reference* section for details of how to use the straight-edge. If the head is warped beyond the limit specified at the beginning of this Chapter, consult your Yamaha dealer or take it to an engineer for rectification.

15 Examine the valve seats in the combustion chamber. If they are pitted, cracked or burned, the head will require work beyond the scope of the home mechanic. Measure the valve seat width and compare it to this Chapter's Specifications **(see illustration)**. If it exceeds the service limit, or if it varies around its circumference, consult your Yamaha dealer or take the head to an engineer for rectification.

16 Examine each valve face for cracks, pits and burned spots **(see illustration)**. **Note:** *Slight imperfections between the valve face and seat may be overcome by lapping the valve (see Steps 24 to 28).*

17 Rotate the valve and check for any obvious indication that it is bent. Using V-blocks and a dial gauge if available, measure the valve stem runout and compare the results to the specifications at the beginning of this Chapter **(see illustration)**. If the measurement exceeds

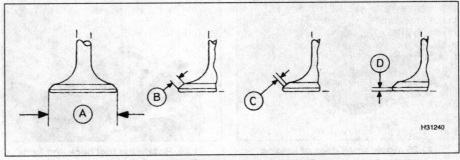

11.18 Valve head measurement points

A Head diameter   B Face width   C Seat width   D Margin thickness

the service limit specified, the valve must be replaced with a new one. Note that a slightly bent valve stem will prevent the valve from seating properly in the head.

18 Measure the various aspects of the valve head and compare them with the listed specifications **(see illustration)**. If the valve is worn it should be replaced with a new one.

19 Measure the valve stem diameter **(see illustration)**. Clean the valve guides to remove any carbon build-up, then measure the inside diameters of the guides (at both ends and the centre of the guide) with a small hole gauge and micrometer (see *Tools and Workshop Tips* (Section 3) in the *Reference* section) **(see illustration)**. The guides are measured at the ends and at the centre to determine if they

are worn in a bell-mouth pattern (more wear at the ends). Subtract the stem diameter from the valve guide diameter to obtain the valve stem-to-guide clearance. If the stem-to-guide clearance is greater than listed in this Chapter's Specifications, replace whichever components are worn beyond their specified limits with new ones. If the valve guide is within specifications, but is worn unevenly, it should be renewed.

20 Inspect the valve stem and collet groove area for scuffing and cracks **(see illustration)**. Check the end of the stem for pitting and wear. The presence of any of the above conditions indicates the need for fitting new valves.

21 Check the ends of each valve spring for wear. Measure the free length of each spring and compare it to that listed in the specifications

11.19a Measure the valve stem diameter with a micrometer…

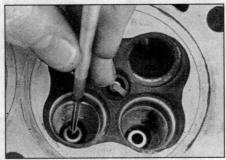

11.19b …and the guide bore width with a bore gauge

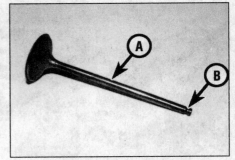

11.20 Check the stem (A) and collet groove (B)

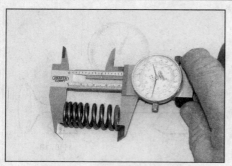

11.21a Measure spring free length with a Vernier caliper...

11.21b ...and check the spring is not bent

11.25 Apply small dabs of lapping compound to the valve face only

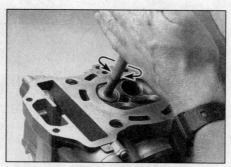

11.26 Rotate the tool back and forth between the palms of your hands

compound to the valve face **(see illustration)**. Smear some molybdenum disulphide oil (a 50/50 mixture of molybdenum disulphide grease and engine oil) to the valve stem, then slip the valve into the guide **(see illustration 11.7c)**. **Note:** *Make sure each valve is installed in its correct guide and be careful not to get any lapping compound on the valve stem.*

26 Attach the grinding tool to the valve and rotate the tool between the palms of your hands. Use a back-and-forth motion (as though rubbing your hands together) rather than a circular motion (i.e. so that the valve rotates alternately clockwise and anti-clockwise rather than in one direction only) **(see illustration)**. If a motorised tool is being used, take note of the correct drive speed for it – if your drill runs too fast and is not variable, use a hand tool instead. Lift the valve off the seat and turn it at regular intervals to distribute the lapping compound properly. Continue the procedure until the valve face and seat contact area is of uniform width, and unbroken around the entire circumference.

27 Carefully remove the valve from the guide and wipe off all traces of lapping compound. Use solvent to clean the valve and wipe the seat area thoroughly with a solvent soaked cloth.

28 Repeat the procedure for the remaining valves.

29 Working on one valve at a time, lay the spring seat in place in the cylinder head so that its shouldered side faces upwards **(see illustration 11.8b)**. Fit a new valve stem seal onto the guide and use your fingers or an appropriate size deep socket to press the seal over the end of the valve guide until it is felt to clip into place **(see illustrations)**. Don't twist or cock the seal, or it will not seal properly against the valve stem. Also, don't remove it again or it will be damaged.

30 Coat the valve stem with molybdenum disulphide oil, then slide it into its guide, rotating it slowly to avoid damaging the seal **(see illustration 11.7c)**. Check that the valve moves up and down freely in the guide. Next, fit the spring, with the closer-wound coils facing down into the cylinder head **(see**

(see illustration). If any spring is shorter than specified it has sagged and must be replaced with a new one, though it would be advisable to replace all springs as a set. Also place the spring upright on a flat surface and check it for bend by placing a ruler or engineer's square against it **(see illustration)**. If the bend in any spring exceeds the specified limit, it must be replaced with a new one.

22 Check the spring retainers and collets for obvious wear and cracks. Any questionable parts should not be reused, as extensive damage will occur in the event of failure during engine operation.

23 If the inspection indicates that no overhaul work is required, the valve components can be reinstalled in the head.

Reassembly

24 Unless a valve service has been performed, before installing the valves in the head they should be lapped to ensure a positive seal between the valves and seats. **Note:** *Do not lap the valves after the seats have been re-cut. The valve seat must be soft and unpolished for final seating to occur when the engine is first run.* This procedure requires fine lapping compound and a valve grinding tool (either hand-held or drill driven). If a grinding tool is not available, a piece of rubber or plastic hose can be slipped over the valve stem (after the valve has been installed in the guide) and used to turn the valve.

25 Apply a small amount of lapping

11.29a Fit the valve stem seal, using a rod as a guide...

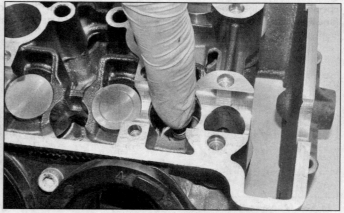

11.29b ...and carefully push it on until it clicks into place

11.30a Fit the valve spring with the closer-wound coils facing down...

11.30b ...then fit the spring retainer

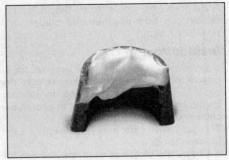

11.31 A small dab of grease will help to keep the collets in place on the valve while the spring is released

11.33 Tap the valve stem gently to seat the collets in the groove

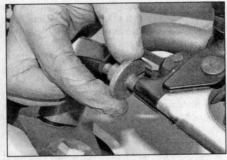

12.2 Turn the adjuster fully in then align the slots

12.3a Bend back the tab in the cable retainer...

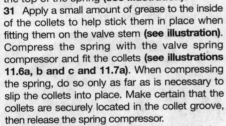
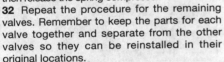

12.3b ...and release the cable end

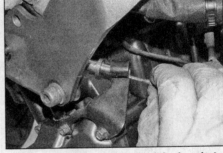

12.3c Draw the cable out of the bracket

illustration). Fit the spring retainer, with its shouldered side facing down so that it fits into the top of the spring **(see illustration)**.

31 Apply a small amount of grease to the inside of the collets to help stick them in place when fitting them on the valve stem **(see illustration)**. Compress the spring with the valve spring compressor and fit the collets **(see illustrations 11.6a, b and c and 11.7a)**. When compressing the spring, do so only as far as is necessary to slip the collets into place. Make certain that the collets are securely located in the collet groove, then release the spring compressor.

32 Repeat the procedure for the remaining valves. Remember to keep the parts for each valve together and separate from the other valves so they can be reinstalled in their original locations.

33 Support the cylinder head on blocks so the valves can't contact the workbench top, then very gently tap the top of each valve stem to seat the collets in the groove **(see illustration)**.

34 After the camshafts have been installed, check the valve clearances (see Chapter 1).

12 Clutch cable

Removal

1 On XJ6-N models remove the left-hand side cover, on XJ6-S models remove the left-hand fairing side panel, and on XJ6-F and FZ6R models remove the left-hand lower fairing panel (see Chapter 7).

2 Turn the adjuster at the handlebar end of the cable fully into the lever bracket, then turn it out to align the slot in the adjuster with that in the lever bracket **(see illustration)**.

3 Bend back the tab in the cable retainer on the end of the clutch release mechanism arm,

then release the cable end from the retainer, noting how it fits **(see illustrations)**. Slip the cable out of the bracket **(see illustration)**.

4 Pull the outer cable from the socket in the adjuster and release the inner cable end from the lever **(see illustrations)**.

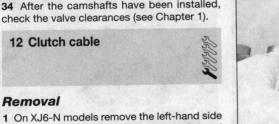

12.4a Release the cable from the adjuster...

12.4b ...and the lever

5 Remove the cable from the machine, releasing it from any ties and guides, and noting its routing.

Installation

6 Installation is the reverse of removal. Apply grease to the cable ends and make sure the cable is correctly routed. Bend the retainer on the release mechanism arm to secure the cable end **(see illustration 12.3a)**.

7 Adjust the clutch lever freeplay (see Chapter 1).

8 Check the clutch release mechanism for smooth operation and any signs of wear or damage. Remove the release arm/shaft for cleaning and re-greasing if required (see Section 13).

9 Install the bodywork (see Chapter 7).

13 Clutch

Special tool: *A clutch centre holding tool is useful, although not essential – see Step 11.*

Removal

1 On XJ6-N models remove the right-hand side cover, on XJ6-S models remove the right-hand fairing side panels, and on XJ6-F and FZ6R models remove the right-hand lower fairing panel (see Chapter 7).

2 Make sure that the engine casing below the clutch cover and around the oil dipstick is clean. Place a drain tray under the clutch cover.

13.3a Unscrew the dipstick...

3 For clearance to remove the clutch cover, unscrew the oil dipstick and the bolt on the timing rotor cover that holds the coolant hose guide **(see illustrations)**. Plug the dipstick hole with some rag.

4 Working evenly in a criss-cross pattern, unscrew the clutch cover bolts **(see illustration)**.

5 Remove the cover, being prepared to catch any residual oil **(see illustration)**. If the cover will not lift away easily, break the gasket seal by tapping gently around the edge with a soft-faced hammer or block of wood.

6 Remove the cover gasket – a new one must be fitted. Note the position of the two dowels and remove them if they are loose – they could be in either the cover or the crankcase **(see illustration 13.43)**.

7 Working in a criss-cross pattern, gradually slacken the clutch spring bolts until spring pressure is released, counter-holding the

13.3b ...and the bolt (arrowed)

clutch using a rag **(see illustration)**. Remove the bolts and springs.

8 Remove the pressure plate, noting the alignment marks on it and the clutch centre **(see illustration)**. Remove the short push-rod from the pressure plate bearing, or draw it out of the input shaft, as required **(see illustration 13.39b)**. Use a magnet inserted in the end of the shaft to draw out the ball bearing **(see illustration)**.

9 Remove the clutch plates **(see illustrations 13.38c, b and a)** – unless the plates are being replaced with new ones, keep them in their original order. Note that the outermost friction plate is darker than the rest and has wider friction segments, and the perimeter tabs locate in the shallow slots in the clutch housing.

10 Use a small pointed tool to unstake the rim of the clutch nut from the indent in the end of the shaft **(see illustration)**.

13.4 Unscrew the bolts (arrowed)...

13.5 ...and remove the cover

13.7 Remove the clutch bolts and springs...

13.8a ...and the pressure plate

13.8b Use a magnet to draw the ball bearing out

13.10 Unstake the rim of the nut...

13.11 ...then unscrew it as described

13.14 Ease the bearing centre and bearing out...

11 To unscrew the clutch nut, the transmission input shaft must be locked. This can be done in several ways. If the engine is in the frame, engage top gear and have an assistant hold the brakes on hard with the rear tyre in firm contact with the ground. Alternatively, the Yamaha service tool Pt. No. 90890-04086 (European models) or YM-91042 (US models) or a similar commercially available tool, can be used to hold the clutch centre while the nut is loosened. Protect the footrest bracket with a piece of wood and lay the clutch holding tool against it – this saves having to counter-hold it while unscrewing the nut (see illustration). With the clutch held, unscrew the nut and remove the washers (see illustration 13.37b). A new nut should be used on reassembly.

12 Slide the clutch centre and the thrust washer off the input shaft (see illustrations 13.37a and 13.35).

13 Note how the primary driven gear on the clutch housing engages with the primary drive gear on the crankshaft. Note also the run of the oil pump drive chain in the guide behind the clutch housing – the chain loops round a sprocket on the back of the clutch housing.

14 Ease out the bearing centre and needle bearing from between the clutch housing and the input shaft – this can be done using a magnet and/or by sliding the housing on the shaft to help push them along (see illustration).

15 There is now enough clearance to draw the clutch housing out along the input shaft and expose the oil pump drive chain behind it (see illustration). Disengage the chain from the drive sprocket and remove the clutch housing. Note: *Depending on the position of the crankshaft it may be necessary to rotate it to obtain clearance between the primary driven gear and the connecting rod of No. 4 cylinder or the right-hand web on the crankshaft. To rotate the crankshaft, unscrew the inspection plug in the timing rotor cover and turn the rotor bolt on the end of the crankshaft in a clockwise direction only.*

16 Slip the chain off the shaft and remove the thrust washer and spacer (see illustrations 13.33b and a).

17 If required, unscrew the oil pump drive chain guide bolts and remove the guide (see illustration).

Inspection

18 After an extended period of service the clutch friction plates will wear and promote clutch slip. Measure the thickness of each friction plate using a Vernier caliper (see illustration). If any plate has worn to or beyond the service limit given in the Specifications at the beginning of this Chapter, the friction plates must be replaced with a new set. Also, if any of the plates smell burnt or are glazed, they must be replaced as a set. If this is the case, and also if there has been any juddering from the clutch,

release and remove the anti-judder spring retaining ring, noting how its ends locate and how it seats in the groove, then remove the inner plain plate and friction plate and the anti-judder spring and spring seat (see illustrations 13.36g, f, e, d, c, and a). Note that the friction plate has a wider internal diameter than all the other plates to allow it to sit around the anti-judder components. Check the wire retainer ring for deformation – note that Yamaha specify to fit a new one whenever it is removed.

19 The plain plates should not show any signs of excess heating (bluing). Check for warpage using a flat surface and feeler gauges (see illustration). If any plate exceeds the maximum permissible amount of warpage, or

13.15 ...then displace the clutch centre and disengage the oil pump chain

13.17 Oil pump drive chain guide bolts (arrowed)

13.18 Measuring clutch friction plate thickness

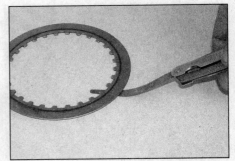

13.19 Checking the plain plates for warpage

13.20 Measure the free length of the clutch springs

13.21a Check for wear of the friction plate tabs and the clutch housing slots...

13.21b ...and of the plain plate tongues and clutch centre slots

shows signs of bluing, all the plain plates must be renewed as a set.

20 Measure the free length of each clutch spring **(see illustration)**. If any spring is below the service limit specified, replace all the springs with a new set.

21 Inspect the friction plate tabs and the clutch housing slots for burrs and indentations **(see illustration)**. Similarly check for wear between the inner teeth of the plain plates and the slots in the clutch centre **(see illustration)**. Wear of this nature will cause clutch drag and slow disengagement during gear changes as the plates will snag when the pressure plate is lifted. With care a small amount of wear can be corrected by dressing with a fine file, but if this is excessive the worn components should be replaced with new ones.

22 Inspect the needle roller bearing, the internal bearing surface of the clutch housing

and the external surface of the bearing centre **(see illustration)**. If there are any signs of wear, pitting or other damage the affected parts must be replaced with new ones.

23 Check the teeth of the primary driven gear on the clutch housing and the corresponding teeth of the primary drive gear on the end of the crankshaft. Replace the clutch housing with a new one if any teeth are worn or chipped. The primary drive gear is an integral part of the crankshaft (see Section 24 for removal of the crankshaft).

24 Check the teeth of the oil pump drive sprocket on the back of the clutch housing. If any are worn or chipped, replace the housing with a new one and remove the oil pump and chain for inspection (see Section 18).

25 The clutch housing incorporates a cush-drive mechanism; check that the springs

on the back are not loose and that there is no backlash between the centre of the housing and the primary driven gear.

26 Check the pressure plate and its bearing for signs of wear or damage and roughness **(see illustration)**. Check the push-rod for signs of wear or damage **(see illustration)**. Replace any parts, as necessary, with new ones. To replace the bearing drive it out from the outside using a socket. Drive the new bearing in from the inside using a socket that bears on the outer race until it seats.

27 Check the clutch release mechanism shaft (on the left-hand side of the engine) turns smoothly in its housing. If it is rough, remove the front sprocket cover **(see illustration)**. Release the wiring guide from the clutch release shaft housing **(see illustration)**. Unscrew the two bolts and remove the housing **(see illustration)**. Remove the drive

13.22 Inspect the needle bearing, the bearing centre and the bearing surface in the housing

13.26a Check the pressure plate and bearing...

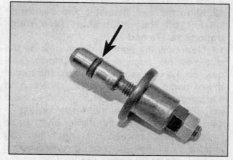

13.26b ...and the short pushrod and its O-ring (arrowed) for wear

13.27a Unscrew the bolts (arrowed) and remove the cover

13.27b Displace the wiring guide (arrowed)

13.27c Clutch release mechanism housing bolts (arrowed)

13.27d Remove the chain guide...

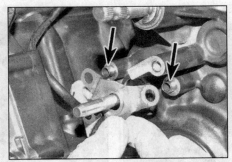

13.27e ...and the plate, and the dowels (arrowed) if required

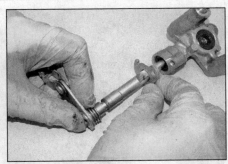

13.28a Remove the shaft and retainer plate

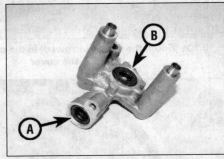

13.28b Shaft oil seal and bearing (A), long pushrod oil seal (B)

chain guide **(see illustration)**. Remove the oil seal plate, and if required the two dowels **(see illustration)**.

28 Unscrew the shaft retainer bolt and withdraw the shaft, noting how the spring ends locate **(see illustration)**. Clean all components. Check the condition of the shaft and its oil seal and bearing, and fit new parts if necessary **(see illustration)**. First lever the oil seal out using a seal hook or screwdriver **(see illustration 13.29c)**, then draw the bearing out (see *Tools and Workshop Tips* (Sections 5 and 6) in the *Reference* section). The oil seal and bearing must be replaced with new ones if removed. Lubricate the new bearing with grease and press it into the housing until it seats. Push the new seal in, marked side facing out, using your fingers or a socket until it is flush **(see illustration 13.29d)**. Lubricate the seal lips with grease.

29 The long pushrod runs through two seals, one in the crankcase and one in the housing. If new seals are needed, withdraw the long pushrod **(see illustration)**. Lever the old seals out using a seal hook or screwdriver, then push the new ones in, marked side facing out, using your fingers or a socket until they are flush **(see illustrations)**. Make sure the pushrod is straight. Smear grease over it before sliding it back into the crankcase.

30 Fit the spring and retainer onto the shaft **(see illustration 13.28a)**. Slide the shaft into the housing, align the retainer and seat the spring ends, then fit the retainer bolt **(see illustration)**. Fit the dowels if removed, then fit the seal plate **(see illustration 13.27e)**. Fit the chain guide **(see illustration 13.27d)**. Clean the threads of the housing bolts and apply some fresh threadlock, then fit the housing

and tighten the bolts to the torque setting specified at the beginning of the Chapter **(see illustration)**. Fit the wiring guide **(see**

13.29a Withdraw the pushrod

13.29b Lever the crankcase seal...

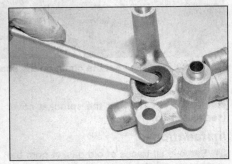

13.29c ...and the housing seal out using a screwdriver or hook

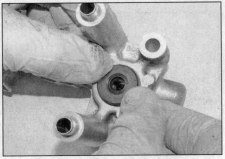

13.29d Push the new seals in

13.30a Make sure the spring ends are located as shown

13.30b Keep the housing square to prevent distorting the oil seal as it fits over the pushrod

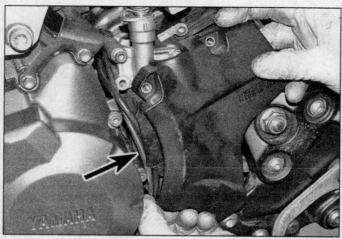

13.30c Route the wiring (arrowed) in the channel in the front of the cover

13.33a Fit the spacer and thrust washer...

13.33b ...then seat the chain on the shaft and in its guide

13.35 Fit the thrust washer

illustration 13.27b). Fit the sprocket cover (see illustration).

Installation

31 Remove all traces of old gasket from the crankcase and clutch cover surfaces.
32 If removed, clean the threads of the oil pump chain guide bolts and apply some fresh threadlock, then fit the guide and tighten the bolts to the torque setting specified at the beginning of the Chapter (see illustration 13.17).
33 Slide the spacer and the thrust washer onto the transmission input shaft and seat them against the bearing (see illustration). Loop the chain over the shaft and seat each run in the guide (see illustration). Slide the clutch housing onto the shaft and engage the oil pump chain onto the drive sprocket on the back of the housing (see illustration 13.15). Make sure that the chain is correctly routed in the guide.
34 Lubricate the needle roller bearing with clean engine oil. Support the clutch housing

and engage the primary driven and drive gears, then slide the bearing and the bearing centre onto the shaft and into the housing (see illustrations 13.14).
35 Lubricate the thrust washer with clean engine oil and slide it onto the shaft (see illustration).

36 If removed from the clutch centre, fit the anti-judder spring seat, then fit the spring so that its outer rim is raised off (see illustrations). Fit the inner friction plate (with the wider internal diameter) over the spring and spring seat, then fit the plain plate (see illustrations). Secure the assembly with a new

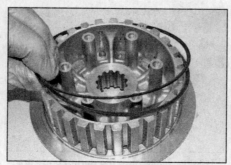

13.36a Fit the spring seat and spring...

13.36b ...so the outer rim of the spring is raised off the seat

13.36c Fit the friction plate...

13.36d ...and the plain plate

13.36e Fit one end of the new ring into the hole...

retainer ring, making sure it locates properly in its groove and the ends are secure in the back of the hole (see illustrations).

37 Slide the clutch centre onto the shaft splines (see illustration). Fit the thrust washer and the spring washer, with the OUT mark facing out (see illustration). Fit the clutch centre nut with the thin rim facing out, then lock the input shaft as before (see Step 11) and tighten the nut to the torque setting specified at the beginning of this Chapter (see illustrations). Note: Check that the clutch centre rotates freely after tightening the nut. Stake the rim of the nut into the indent in the end of the shaft (see illustration).

13.36f ...then feed the ring round in the groove and fit the other end in the hole...

13.36g ...making sure the ends are secure

13.37a Fit the clutch centre...

13.37b ...the washers...

13.37c ...and a new clutch nut

13.37d Tighten the nut to the specified torque...

13.37e ...then stake the rim into the indent

13.38a Fit a friction plate...

13.38b ...then a plain plate, and so on

13.38c Fit the outer friction plate tabs into the offset shallow slots

38 Coat each clutch plate with clean engine oil prior to installation. Build up the plates, starting with a friction plate, then a plain plate and so on, fitting the tabs of the outermost friction plate (that is darker and has wider friction segments) into the shallow slots in the housing so they are offset from the rest **(see illustrations)**.

39 Lubricate the ball bearing and push it into the shaft **(see illustration)**. Lubricate the short pushrod and fit it into shaft **(see illustration)**.
40 Lubricate the bearing in the pressure plate with clean engine oil. Align the reference marks on the clutch pressure plate and the clutch centre and fit the pressure plate, locating the castellations in its rim locate into the slots in the clutch centre **(see illustration)**.
41 Fit the clutch springs and bolts, then hold the clutch housing and tighten the bolts evenly and a little at a time in a criss-cross sequence to the specified torque setting **(see illustration)**.
42 Now check the adjustment of the release mechanism: on the left-hand side of the engine push the release arm forwards as far as it will go – the pointer on the arm should align with the raised rib on the housing **(see illustration)**. If not, slacken the locknut on the short pushrod, then hold the nut behind it and turn the adjuster screw using a Phillips screwdriver as required until the marks do align, then tighten the locknut **(see illustration)**.
43 If removed, fit the dowels into the crankcase. Fit the new gasket onto the dowels **(see illustration)**.
44 Clean the threads of the clutch cover bolts and apply some fresh threadlock, then fit the cover, locating it on the dowels and making sure it is seated all round, then tighten the bolts evenly in a criss-cross sequence to the torque setting specified at the beginning of the Chapter **(see illustrations 13.5 and 13.4)**.

13.39a Fit the ball bearing...

13.39b ...and short pushrod into the shaft

13.40 Align the marks when fitting the pressure plate

13.41 Fit the springs and bolts and tighten as described

13.42a Push the arm forwards and check the pointer aligns with the rib

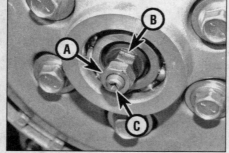

13.42b Slacken the locknut (A), hold the nut (B) and turn the pushrod (C) to align the marks

13.43 Fit a new gasket onto the dowels (arrowed)

14.2a Alternator wiring connector (arrowed)

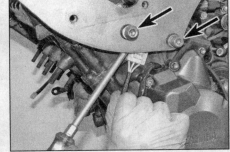

14.2b Slacken the bolts (arrowed) then lever the frame away slightly to provide clearance for the connector

14.3 Alternator cover bolts (arrowed)

45 Check the engine oil level (see *Pre-ride checks*) and fit the dipstick.
46 Adjust the clutch cable (see Chapter 1).
47 Fit the timing rotor cover bolt with the hose guide **(see illustration 13.3b)**.
48 Install the body panels (see Chapter 7).

14 Starter clutch and gears

1 On XJ6-N models remove the left-hand side cover, on XJ6-S models remove the left-hand fairing side panels, and on XJ6-F and FZ6R models remove the left-hand lower fairing panel (see Chapter 7).
2 Raise the fuel tank (see Chapter 4). Trace the alternator wiring to its connector (with three white wires) inside the boot behind the engine and disconnect it **(see illustration)**. Feed the wiring to the alternator cover, noting its routing – the connector is just too large to fit between the engine and frame, so you need to slacken the left-hand front engine mounting bolts, then use a screwdriver or pry bar to lever the frame plate slightly away from the engine until there is enough clearance **(see illustration)**.
3 Place a drain tray under the alternator cover. Unscrew and remove the cover bolts, noting the wiring clip and clutch cable bracket **(see illustration)**. Remove the cover, being

prepared to catch any residual oil, and noting that you need to pull against the attraction of the magnets in the alternator rotor. If necessary break the gasket seal by tapping gently around the edge with a soft-faced hammer or block of wood – do not try to lever between the cover/crankcases mating surfaces as they could be damaged. Remove the gasket – a new one must be used. Remove the dowels from either the cover or the crankcase if they are loose.

Check
4 The operation of the starter clutch can be checked while it is in place. Check that the idle/reduction gear is able to rotate freely anti-clockwise as you look at it from the left-hand side of the bike, but locks when rotated clockwise **(see illustration 14.5)**. If not, the starter clutch is faulty and should be removed for inspection.

Removal
5 Withdraw the idle/reduction gear shaft from the crankcase and remove the gear **(see illustration)**.
6 Remove the alternator rotor (see Chapter 8) – the starter clutch is mounted on the back of it.

Inspection
7 Inspect the teeth on the idle/reduction gear and replace it with a new one if any are chipped or worn. Similarly check the teeth on the starter driven gear and on the starter motor shaft. Check the gear shaft bearing surfaces

for signs of wear or damage, and replace with a new one if necessary.
8 With the alternator rotor face down, check that the starter driven gear rotates freely in an anti-clockwise direction and locks against the rotor in a clockwise direction **(see illustration)**.
9 Remove the driven gear from the clutch **(see illustration 14.13)**. Inspect the condition of the sprags in the clutch and the outer surface of the driven gear hub **(see illustration)**. If they are damaged or worn at any point, the worn components(s) should be replaced with a new one.
10 To remove the starter clutch hold the rotor using a rotor strap and unscrew the clutch bolts **(see illustration)**.
11 Inspect the bush in the driven gear and its

14.5 Withdraw the shaft and remove the gear

14.8 Check the gear rotates anti-clockwise, and locks clockwise

14.9 Check the sprags in the clutch and the driven gear hub

14.10 Starter clutch bolts (arrowed)

14.11 Check the bush (arrowed) for wear

14.13 Rotate the gear as you fit the hub into the clutch

bearing surface on the crankshaft for signs of wear and scoring **(see illustration)**. If the bush is worn, evident by the lack of oil retention groove, replace the gear with a new one.

Installation

12 Clean the starter clutch bolt threads and apply a drop of locking compound. Fit the clutch onto the back of the alternator rotor, then tighten the bolts to the torque setting specified at the beginning of the Chapter, holding the rotor as before **(see illustration 14.10)**.

13 Lubricate the starter driven gear hub with clean engine oil, then fit it into the starter clutch, rotating it anti-clockwise to spread the sprags and allow the hub to enter **(see illustration)**. Check the operation of the starter clutch as described in Step 8.

14 Install the alternator (see Chapter 8).

15 Lubricate the idle/reduction gear shaft with clean engine oil. Position the gear, making sure the smaller pinion faces inwards and engages the driven gear teeth, and the teeth of the larger pinion mesh with the teeth of the starter motor shaft, then insert the gear shaft **(see illustration 14.5)**.

16 If removed, fit the dowels in the crankcase, then fit a new gasket onto the dowels **(see illustration)**. Fit the alternator cover onto the dowels and the idle gear shaft, noting that it will be forcibly drawn on by the magnets, and make sure it is seated all around **(see illustration)**. Clean the threads of the cover bolts and apply some fresh threadlock. Fit the bolts, not forgetting the wiring clip and the cable bracket, and tighten them evenly in a criss-cross sequence to the specified torque setting **(see illustrations)**.

17 Feed the wiring back to the connector, levering the frame plate away from the engine as on removal, and reconnect it, then fit the boot over the connectors **(see illustrations 14.2b and a)**. Tighten the engine mounting bolts to the specified torque setting.

18 Install the fuel tank (see Chapter 4) and the body panels (see Chapter 7). Check the oil level (see *Pre-ride checks*).

15 Gearchange mechanism

Removal

1 Make sure the transmission is in neutral.

2 Note the alignment of the line on the gearchange shaft with the punch mark on the gearchange linkage arm (see illustration 4.16a). Unscrew the pinch bolt and slide the arm off the shaft (see illustration 4.16b). **Note:** *If necessary make your own alignment mark before removing the arm so that it can be correctly aligned with the shaft on installation.*

3 Release the E-clip and remove the washer from the left-hand end of the shaft **(see illustration)**.

4 Remove the clutch (see Section 13).

14.16a Fit a new gasket onto the dowels (arrowed)...

14.16b ...and make sure the cover locates correctly on the shaft

14.16c Fit the wiring clip...

14.16d ...and cable bracket with the relevant bolts

15.3 Release the clip and remove the washer

15.6a Unhook the spring...

15.6b ...and withdraw the shaft

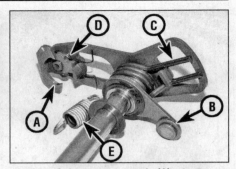

15.8a Selector arm pawls (A), stopper arm roller (B), centralising spring (C), pawl spring (D), stopper arm return spring (E)

5 Note how the gearchange shaft centralising spring ends fit on each side of the locating pin in the crankcase, how the pawls on the selector arm locate onto the pins on the end of the selector drum, how the stopper arm spring locates, and how the roller on the stopper arm locates in the neutral detent on the selector drum (see illustration 15.15).

6 Unhook the stopper arm spring from its anchor pin, then withdraw the gearchange shaft assembly (see illustrations). Check whether the washer is on the inner end of the shaft as you remove the assembly – it may stick to the crankcase wall, in which case remove it and slide it onto the shaft.

Inspection

7 Inspect the splines on the end of the gearchange shaft; if they are worn or damaged, or if the shaft is bent, replace the shaft with a new one.

8 Check the shaft selector arm for cracks, distortion and wear of its pawls, and check for any corresponding wear on the selector pins on the selector drum (see illustrations). Check the stopper arm roller and the detents in the selector drum for any wear or damage, and make sure the roller turns freely. Replace any components that are worn or damaged with new ones.

9 Inspect the centralising spring, the pawl spring and the stopper arm return spring for fatigue, wear or damage (see illustration 15.8a). Make sure the selector arm turn freely and returns to the centre (see illustration). If any faults are found, replace the components with new ones. Note how the ends of the centralising spring locate each side of the tab on the selector arm.

10 To disassemble the shaft, slide the washer off, then remove the circlip, the second washer and the stopper arm (see illustration). Slide the collar off, then the centralising spring. Reassemble in reverse order, making sure the centralising spring ends seat on each side of the tab, and fit the long end of the collar between the spring and the shaft. Make sure the stopper arm is the correct way round. It is

advisable to use a new circlip, and make sure it is seated in the groove.

11 Check that the centralising spring locating pin in the crankcase is tight. If it is loose, remove it, clean the threads and apply a non-permanent thread locking compound, then tighten it to the torque setting specified at the beginning of this Chapter.

12 Check the condition of the gearchange shaft oil seal and bearing in the crankcase – it is wise to fit a new seal if the shaft is removed. Lever out the old seal with a flat-bladed screwdriver or seal hook (see illustration). If the bearing is damaged or does not run smoothly and freely, it must be replaced with a new one (see Section 5 of *Tools and Workshop Tips* in the *Reference* section) (see illustration). Push the new seal squarely into place, with its marked side facing out, using your fingers or a suitable socket (see illustration). Grease the lips of the seal.

15.8b Selector drum pins (A) and detents (B)

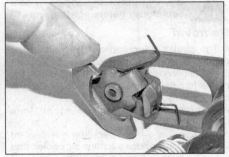

15.9 Check the action of the selector arm

15.10 Release the circlip (arrowed) to disassemble the shaft

15.12a Lever the seal out...

15.12b ...and check the bearing (arrowed)

15.12c Press the new seal in

15.14 Raise the stopper arm onto the top of the drum

15.15 Check that everything is correctly in place

Installation

13 Lubricate the gearchange shaft with clean engine oil. If removed, slide the washer onto the shaft, and fit the stopper arm spring onto the stopper arm **(see illustration 15.8a)**.

14 Slide the gearchange shaft assembly into the crankcase, lifting the stopper arm onto the neutral detent on the top of the selector drum, making sure that the centralising spring ends fit on each side of the locating pin and that the selector arm pawls engage the pins on the selector drum **(see illustration)**.

15 Hook the spring over its anchor pin **(see illustration 15.6a)**. Check that everything is correctly positioned **(see illustration)**.

15.16 Slide the washer on then fit the clip into the groove

16 Fit the washer onto the left-hand end of the shaft, then slide the E-clip into its groove **(see illustration)**.

17 Fit the gearchange linkage arm, aligning the slit in the clamp with the mark on the shaft, and tighten the pinch bolt **(see illustrations 4.16b and a)**.

18 Check the gearchange mechanism by raising the rear wheel off the ground, and spinning it forwards by hand while selecting each gear in turn, then back to neutral.

19 Install the clutch (see Section 13).

16 Oil cooler

⚠ **Warning: Allow the engine to cool completely before starting work.**

Removal

1 The cooler is located on the front of the engine. Drain the engine oil and the coolant (see Chapter 1). Leave a drain tray under the cooler to catch residual oil and coolant as the cooler is removed.

2 Remove the exhaust system (see Chapter 4).

3 Release the clamps securing the coolant inlet and outlet hoses to the oil cooler and

slide them along the hoses **(see illustration)**. Detach the outlet hose from the top.

4 Unscrew the bolt and remove the cooler, detaching it from the inlet hose **(see illustration 16.3)**.

5 Remove the washer from the bolt and the O-ring from the cooler body – new ones must be used **(see illustrations)**.

6 Check the cooler body for cracks and dents and any evidence of coolant leaking and replace it with a new one if necessary. Also check the hoses for splits, cracks, hardening and deterioration and fit new ones if required.

Installation

7 Installation is the reverse of removal, noting the following:

● Clean the mating surfaces of the crankcase and the cooler with a rag and solvent.
● Before reassembly, lubricate the new O-ring with grease and seat it in the groove in the cooler body **(see illustration 16.5b)**.
● Slide the inlet hose onto its union as you locate the cooler – the outlet hose union should be pointing up **(see illustration 16.3)**.
● Fit a new washer onto the cooler bolt **(see illustration 16.5a)**. Lubricate the threads of the bolt and tighten it to the torque setting specified at the beginning of this Chapter.
● Make sure the coolant hoses are pressed

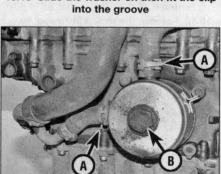

16.3 Squeeze the clamp ends (A) together and slide the clamps along the hoses. Oil cooler bolt (B)

16.5a Remove the washer...

16.5b ...and the O-ring

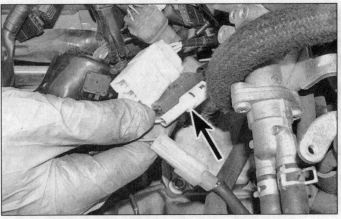

17.2 Oil level sensor wiring connector (arrowed)

17.3 Unscrew the bolts (arrowed) and remove the sump

fully onto their unions and secured by the clamps (see illustration 16.3).

● Refill the engine with oil and refill the cooling system, both to the correct levels (see Chapter 1 and *Pre-ride checks*).

● Start the engine and check that there are no leaks before taking the machine on the road.

17 Oil sump, oil strainer and pressure relief valve

Removal

1 Drain the engine oil (see Chapter 1). Remove the fuel tank and the exhaust system (see Chapter 4).

2 Trace the wire from the oil level sensor underneath the sump and disconnect it at the connector inside the boot (see illustration). Feed the wire through to the underside of the engine, noting its routing. If required remove the belly-pan/lower fairing brackets (see illustration 4.3).

3 Unscrew the sump bolts, slackening them evenly in a criss-cross sequence and noting the position of the oil level sensor wiring clamp, and remove the sump (see illustration). If necessary, break the gasket seal by tapping gently around the edge of the sump with a soft-faced hammer or block of wood; do not

lever the sump off as this will damage the sealing surface. Remove the gasket – a new one must be used.

4 Pull the oil strainer out of its socket in the oil pump, noting how the tab locates between the lugs (see illustration). Remove the seal – a new one must be used.

5 Pull the pressure relief valve out of the crankcase (see illustration). Discard the O-ring – a new one must be used.

Inspection

6 If required remove the oil level sensor (see Chapter 8). Remove all traces of gasket from the sump and crankcase mating surfaces, and clean the inside of the sump with a suitable solvent.

7 Clean the strainer in solvent, flushing it

through from the inside, and remove any debris caught in the mesh (see illustration). Check the mesh for any signs of wear or damage and replace the strainer with a new one if necessary.

8 Push the relief valve plunger into the valve body and check that it moves smoothly and freely against spring pressure (see illustration). If not, remove the circlip, noting that it is under spring pressure, and remove the spring seat, spring and plunger (see illustration). Clean all the components in solvent and check them for scoring, wear or damage. If any is found, replace the relief valve with a new one – individual components are not available. Otherwise, coat the inside of the valve body and the plunger with clean engine oil, then

17.4 Remove the strainer and its seal

17.5 Remove the pressure relief valve and its O-ring (arrowed)

17.7 Clean and check the strainer mesh (arrowed)

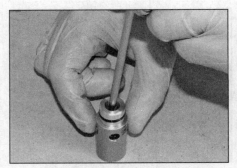

17.8a Check the plunger can be pushed down and returns under spring pressure

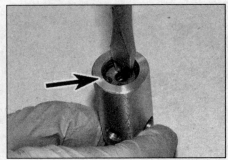

17.8b Press down on the spring seat to remove the circlip (arrowed)

17.10a Lubricate the new seal and fit it into the pump

17.10b Make sure the tab (arrowed) seats between the lugs

17.11 Use a new gasket, aligning it with the sump bolt holes

insert the plunger, spring and spring seat and secure them with the circlip. Check the action of the valve plunger again – if it is still suspect, replace the valve with a new one.

Installation

9 Fit a new O-ring onto the relief valve and smear it with grease **(see illustration 17.5)**. Push the valve into its socket in the crankcase.
10 Lubricate the new seal for the oil strainer with grease and fit it into the pump **(see illustration)**. Fit the strainer into the seal with the arrow pointing to the front of the engine **(see illustration 17.4)** and locating the tab between the lugs **(see illustration)**.
11 Lay a new gasket onto the sump (if the engine is in the frame) or onto the crankcase (if the engine has been removed and is upside down on the work surface) **(see illustration)**. Make sure the holes in the gasket align correctly with the bolt holes – if the engine is

in the frame insert two bolts into the sump and through the gasket to keep it aligned.
12 Position the sump on the crankcase and finger-tighten all bolts, not forgetting the oil level sensor wiring clamp **(see illustration)**. Tighten the bolts evenly and a little at a time in a criss-cross pattern to the torque setting specified at the beginning of the Chapter **(see illustration 17.3)**.
13 If removed fit the belly-pan/lower fairing brackets **(see illustration 4.3)**. Connect the oil level sensor wire at the connector **(see illustration 17.2)**.
14 Install the exhaust system and the fuel tank (see Chapter 4).
15 Fill the engine with the correct type and quantity of oil (see Chapter 1 and *Pre-ride checks*).
16 Start the engine and check that there are no leaks around the sump before taking the bike on the road.

18 Oil pump

Removal

1 Remove the water pump (see Chapter 3). Remove the clutch (see Section 13). Remove the sump and the oil strainer (see Section 17).
2 Remove the pump drive chain **(see illustration)**.
3 Unscrew the U-shaped oil pipe bolts and pull the pipe out of its sockets in the crankcase **(see illustration)**. Remove the O-rings – new ones must be used.
4 Unscrew the pump mounting bolts and remove the oil return pipe **(see illustrations)**.
5 Remove the pump **(see illustration)**. Remove the pump dowels if they are loose.

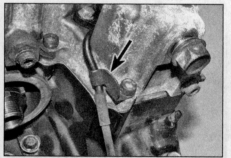

17.12 Correct fitting of the wiring clamp (arrowed)

18.2 Remove the drive chain

18.3 Unscrew the bolts (arrowed) and remove the pipe

18.4a Unscrew the bolts (arrowed)...

18.4b ...and remove the pipe...

18.5 ...and the pump, and the dowels (arrowed) if required

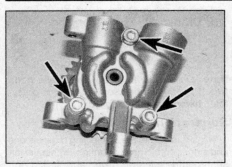

18.6a Unscrew the bolts (arrowed)...

18.6b ...and remove the cover. Note the locating pins (arrowed)

18.7a Remove the outer rotor...

Inspection

6 Unscrew the oil pump assembly bolts, then remove the cover from the pump housing **(see illustrations)**. Remove the locating pins if loose.

7 Remove the outer and inner rotors, noting how they fit **(see illustrations)**. The outer rotor is not marked but it should be installed in the pump the same way round on reassembly.

8 Withdraw the drive pin from the shaft, then slide the washer off and pull the shaft out of the pump body **(see illustrations)**.

9 Clean all components in solvent. Check that the oilways in the body are clear by blowing them through with compressed air.

10 Inspect the components for scoring and wear. If any damage, scoring or uneven or excessive wear is evident, replace the pump with a new one – individual components are not available.

11 Reassemble the shaft, washer drive pin and rotors in the housing, then measure the clearance between the outer rotor and housing with a feeler gauge and compare it to the maximum clearance listed in the specifications at the beginning of this Chapter **(see illustration)**. If the clearance measured is greater than the maximum, replace the pump with a new one.

12 Position the inner rotor as shown and measure the clearance between the inner rotor tip and the outer rotor with a feeler gauge and compare it to the maximum clearance specified **(see illustration)**. If the clearance measured is greater than the maximum, replace the pump with a new one.

13 Check the pump driven sprocket and the chain for wear or damage, and replace them with new ones if necessary. **Note:** *When replacing the chain and driven sprocket, also check the condition of the drive sprocket*

on the back of the clutch housing (see Section 13).

14 If the pump is good, make sure all the components are clean, then lubricate them with clean engine oil. Slide the pump shaft into the housing and fit the washer and drive pin **(see illustrations 18.8c, b and a)**. Slide the inner rotor onto the shaft so that the slots locate over the drive pin, then fit the outer rotor onto the inner rotor, remembering to fit it the same way round as noted on removal **(see illustrations 18.7b and a)**.

15 Fit the locating pins if removed **(see illustration 18.6b)**. Fit the cover and tighten the bolts to the torque setting specified at the beginning of the Chapter **(see illustration 18.6a)**.

16 Rotate the pump shaft by hand and check that the rotors turn freely. If not, strip and reassemble the pump.

18.7b ...and the inner rotor

18.8a Withdraw the pin...

18.8b ...remove the washer...

18.8c ...and draw the shaft out

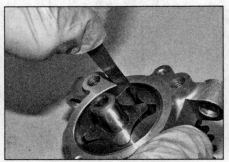

18.11 Measure the outer rotor to body clearance as shown

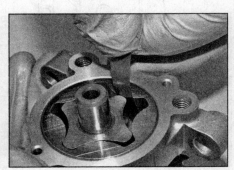

18.12 Measure the inner rotor tip to outer rotor clearance as shown

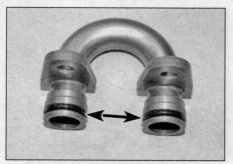

18.19a Fit new O-rings (arrowed)...

18.19b ...then fit the pipe

Installation

17 Before fitting the pump, prime it with clean engine oil. Check the dowels are in place, then fit the pump onto them **(see illustration 18.5)**.

18 Fit the oil return pipe and pump mounting bolts and tighten them to the torque setting specified at the beginning of this Chapter **(see illustrations 18.4b and a)**.

19 Smear the new O-rings for the U-shaped oil pipe with grease and fit them onto the pipe **(see illustration)**. Clean the threads of the pipe bolts and apply a suitable non-permanent thread locking compound. Fit the pipe and tighten the bolts to the specified torque **(see illustration)**.

20 Loop the drive chain over the sprocket and transmission shaft **(see illustration 18.2)**.

21 Fit the oil strainer and the sump (see Section 17), the clutch (see Section 13), and the water pump (see Chapter 3).

22 Fill the engine with the specified quantity and type of new engine oil and coolant (see Chapter 1 and *Pre-ride checks*).

19.4 Remove the oil filter boss (arrowed) to allow removal of crankcase bolt No. 12

19.5a Unscrew bolt No. 21 (arrowed) first, then turn the engine over

19 Crankcase separation and reassembly

Note: *On reassembly new crankcase bolts Nos. 1 to 10 must be used. It is wise to obtain them before commencing work.*

Separation

1 To gain access to the connecting rods, pistons and rings, crankshaft, bearings, transmission shafts and selector drum and forks, the crankcase must be split into two parts.

2 Remove the engine from the frame (see Section 4). **Note:** *To reduce the weight of the engine, where possible remove as many of the components listed below before removing the engine from the frame; do not, however, remove the oil sump at this stage.*

3 Before the separating the crankcases for a full engine strip remove the following components:

    Camshafts and cam chain tensioner
      (Sections 7 and 8).
    Cylinder head (Section 10).
    Alternator rotor (Chapter 8).
    Starter motor (Chapter 8).
    Cam chain (Section 9).
    Clutch (Section 13).
    Gearchange mechanism (Section 15).
    Oil cooler (Section 16).
    Water pump (Chapter 3)
    Oil sump, strainer and pressure relief valve
      (Section 17).
    Oil pump and drive chain (Section 18).

4 Remove the oil filter (see Chapter 1). To allow crankcase bolt No. 12 to be removed unscrew the filter mounting boss from the crankcase **(see illustration)** – the bolt can be unscrewed and tightened with the boss in place, but cannot be removed, so if you are happy for it to stay loose in its hole there is no need to remove the boss.

5 The crankcases are joined by twelve 8 mm bolts (Nos. 1 to 12) and fifteen 6 mm bolts (Nos. 13 to 27). Bolt No. 21 on the back right-hand corner is fitted from the top (all the rest fit from the underside), so unscrew this bolt first **(see illustration)**. Turn the engine upside down. Unscrew the remaining bolts a quarter turn at a time in a **reverse** of the

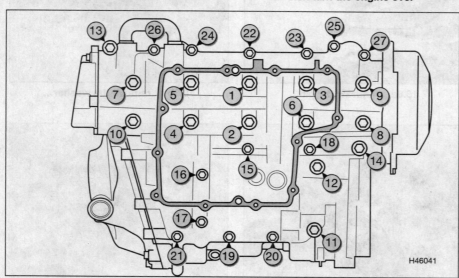

19.5b Crankcase bolt location and TIGHTENING sequence. Loosen bolts in REVERSE order

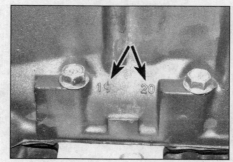

19.5c Bolt numbers (arrowed) are cast into the crankcase

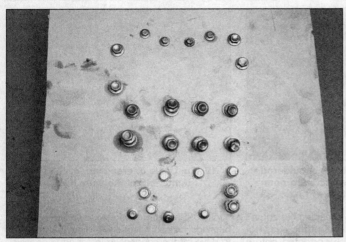

15.5d Example of a cardboard template for storing the crankcase bolts

19.6 Lift the lower half of the crankcase off the upper half

numerical sequence shown and as marked on the crankcase, until they are finger-tight, then remove them – as there are many different types and length of bolt it is best to store them in a cardboard template of the crankcase to ensure correct installation (see illustrations). Note the washers fitted to bolts Nos. 1 to 10 – these bolts must be replaced with new ones.

6 Carefully lift the lower crankcase half off the upper half, using a soft-faced hammer or block of wood to tap around the joint to initially separate the halves, if necessary (see illustration). Note: *If the halves do not separate easily, make sure all fasteners have been removed. Do not try and separate the halves by levering between the sealing surfaces as they are easily damaged and will leak oil on reassembly.*

7 Remove the three locating dowels from the crankcase (they could be in either half) (see illustration 19.13).

8 Refer to Sections 20 to 28 for the removal and installation of the components housed within the crankcases.

Reassembly

9 Remove all traces of sealant from the crankcase mating surfaces.

10 Check that all components and their bearings are in place in the upper and lower crankcase halves. If the transmission shafts have not been removed, remove the oil seal from the left-hand end of the output shaft and replace it with a new one – apply some grease to its lip (see illustration 25.10b). Check that the selector drum is in the neutral position.

11 Generously lubricate the crankshaft, transmission shafts and selector drum and forks, particularly around the bearings, with clean engine oil, then use a rag soaked in high flash-point solvent to wipe over the mating surfaces of both crankcase halves to remove all traces of oil.

12 Apply a small amount of suitable sealant (such as Yamaha Bond 1215) to the mating surface of one crankcase half as shown (see illustration).

Caution: Do not apply an excessive amount

of sealant as it will ooze out when the case halves are assembled and may obstruct oil passages. Do not apply the sealant on or too close (within 2 to 3 mm) to any of the bearing shells or surfaces.

13 If removed, fit the three locating dowels into the crankcase (see illustration).

14 Check again that all components are in position, particularly that the bearing shells are located in their seats in the lower crankcase half. Fit the lower crankcase half onto the upper crankcase half, making sure the dowels locate correctly (see illustration 19.6).

15 Check that the lower crankcase half is seated all the way round. Note: *The crankcase halves should fit together without being forced. If the casings are not correctly seated, remove the lower crankcase half and investigate the problem. Do not attempt to pull them together using the crankcase bolts as the casing could crack and be ruined.*

16 Clean the threads of the crankcase bolts, then lubricate the threads of all except bolt No. 18, and under the heads of all bolts, and

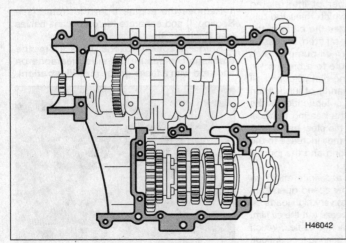

19.12 Apply sealant to the shaded area

19.13 Fit the dowels (arrowed) if removed

19.17a New 8mm bolts with washers must be used

19.17b The bolts with the shouldered shanks fit with the two forwardmost dowels (Nos. 13 and 14)

19.17c Use a degree disc for the final tightening of the 8mm bolts

the washers of the new bolts Nos. 1 to 10, with clean engine oil (see illustration 19.5b). Apply a suitable thread locking compound to the threads of bolt No. 18.

17 Fit the bolts in their correct locations and secure them finger-tight (see illustrations) – make sure the two longer new 8 mm bolts are fitted in positions 8 and 9. First tighten bolts Nos. 1 to 10 in the sequence shown to the first stage torque setting (see illustration 19.5b). Now slacken them in reverse sequence so they are loose, then tighten them in sequence to the second stage torque setting. Finally, using a degree disc, tighten each bolt in sequence through the third stage angle specified for each bolt at the beginning of the Chapter (the angle for bolts 8 and 9 is different to that for 1 to 7 and 10) (see illustration). Now tighten bolts 11 to 27, evenly and a little at a time, in the correct numerical sequence as shown and as marked on the crankcase (see illustrations 19.5b and c), to the torque settings specified at the beginning of this Chapter – make sure the correct torque is applied to each bolt according to number.

18 With all crankcase bolts tightened, check that the crankshaft and transmission shafts rotate smoothly and easily. Check that all gears can be selected and that the shafts rotate freely in every gear. If there are any signs of undue stiffness, rough spots, or of any other problem, the fault must be rectified before proceeding further.

19 If the filter boss was removed tighten it to the specified torque setting.

20 Install all the removed assemblies in the reverse order of removal, according to your procedure (see Steps 2 and 3).

20 Main and big-end bearing information

1 Even though main and connecting rod bearings are generally replaced with new ones during an engine overhaul, the old bearings should be carefully examined as they can reveal valuable information about the condition of the engine.

2 Bearing failure occurs mainly because of lack of lubrication, the presence of dirt or

other foreign particles, overloading the engine and/or corrosion. Regardless of the cause of bearing failure, it must be corrected before the engine is reassembled to prevent it from happening again.

3 When examining the bearings, match them with their corresponding journal on the crankshaft to help identify the cause of any problem.

4 Dirt and other foreign particles get into the engine in a variety of ways. They may be left in the engine during assembly or they may pass through filters or breathers, then get into the oil and from there into the bearings. Metal chips from machining operations and normal engine wear are often present. Abrasives are sometimes left in engine components after reconditioning operations, especially when parts are not thoroughly cleaned using the proper cleaning methods. Whatever the source, foreign objects often end up imbedded in the soft bearing material and are easily recognised. Large particles will not imbed in the bearing and will score or gouge the bearing and journal. The best prevention for this type of bearing failure is to clean all parts thoroughly and keep everything spotlessly clean during engine reassembly. Regular oil and filter changes are also essential.

5 Lack of lubrication or lubrication breakdown have a number of interrelated causes. Excessive heat (which thins the oil), overloading (which squeezes the oil from the bearing face) and oil throw-off (from excessive bearing clearances, a worn oil pump or high engine speeds) all contribute to a breakdown of the protective lubricating film. Blocked oil passages will starve a bearing of lubrication and destroy it. When lack of lubrication is the cause of bearing failure, the bearing material is wiped or extruded from the steel backing of the bearing. Temperatures may increase to the point where the steel backing and the journal turn blue from overheating.

6 Riding habits can have a definite effect on bearing life. Full throttle, low speed operation, or labouring the engine, puts very high loads on bearings, which tend to squeeze out the oil film. These loads cause the bearings to flex, which produces fine cracks in the bearing face (fatigue failure). Eventually the bearing material will loosen in pieces and tear away from the steel

backing. Short trip riding leads to corrosion of bearings, as insufficient engine heat is produced to drive off the condensed water and corrosive gases produced. These products collect in the engine oil, forming acid and sludge. As the oil is carried to the engine bearings, the acid attacks and corrodes the bearing material.

7 Incorrect bearing installation during engine assembly will lead to bearing failure as well. Tight fitting bearings which leave insufficient bearing oil clearances result in oil starvation. Dirt or foreign particles trapped behind a bearing shell result in high spots on the bearing which lead to failure.

8 To avoid bearing problems, clean all parts thoroughly before reassembly, double check all bearing clearance measurements and lubricate the new bearings with clean engine oil during installation.

21 Connecting rods and bearings

Note: On installation new connecting rod bolts must be used, so it is wise to obtain them before commencing work.

Removal

1 Remove the engine from the frame (see Section 4) and separate the crankcase halves (see Section 19).

2 Before separating the rods from the crankshaft, measure the side clearance on each rod with a feeler gauge (see illustration).

21.2 Measuring the connecting rod side clearance with a feeler gauge

21.4 Unscrew the bolts (arrowed) and pull the cap off the connecting rod

21.5 Push each rod down off its crankpin

21.6 Remove each piston and connecting rod from the top of its bore

If the clearance on any rod is greater than that listed in this Chapter's Specifications, replace that rod with a new one.

3 Using paint or a marker pen, mark the cylinder identity on the top of each piston and across the front of each connecting rod and cap. Cylinders are numbered 1 to 4 from the left-hand side of the motorcycle (as seated). Note that the number and letter already written across the back of the rod and cap are the rod size code and weight grade respectively, not the cylinder number.

4 Unscrew the connecting rod cap bolts and separate the caps, complete with the lower bearing shells from the crankpins **(see illustration)**. If a cap appears stuck, tap it on one end with a hammer while pulling it. If it still won't release thread the bolts part-way in, then tap them lightly and evenly to push the rod down.

5 Detach the connecting rods from the crankpins and push them down the bore until they are clear **(see illustration)**. Lift the crankshaft out, taking care not to dislodge the main bearing shells **(see illustration 24.2)**.

6 Raise the front of the crankcase and rest it on some wood, or turn it onto its side. Push each piston/connecting rod assembly to the top end of the cylinder bore and remove it, making sure the connecting rod does not mark the bore walls **(see illustration)**. Note the 'Y' mark on each connecting rod that must face to the left-hand side of the engine, and the arrow on the top of each piston which points to the front of the engine. If this is not visible, mark the piston accordingly so that it can be installed the correct way round.

Caution: Do not try to remove the piston/ connecting rod from the bottom of the cylinder bore. The piston will not pass the crankcase main bearing webs. If the piston is pulled right to the bottom of the bore the oil control ring will expand and lock the piston in position. If this happens it is likely the ring will be broken.

7 Fit the related bearing shells (if removed), bearing cap, and bolts on each piston/ connecting rod assembly so that they are all kept together as a matched set. **Note:** *New bolts must be used on final assembly, but use the old bolts for the oil clearance check and for seating the bearing shells.*

8 If required remove the pistons from the connecting rods (see Section 22).

Inspection

9 Check the connecting rods for cracks and other obvious damage.

10 Apply clean engine oil to the No. 1 piston pin, insert it into its connecting rod small-end and check for any freeplay between the two **(see illustration)**. If freeplay is excessive, measure the external diameter at the centre of the pin. Compare the result to the specifications at the beginning of this Chapter. Replace the pin with a new one if it is worn beyond its specified limits. If the pin diameter is within specifications, replace the connecting rod with a new one. Repeat the measurements for all the pins and rods.

11 Refer to Section 20 and examine the connecting rod bearing shells. If they are scored, badly scuffed or appear to have seized, new

shells must be installed. Always renew the shells in the connecting rods as a set. If they are badly damaged, check the corresponding crankpin. Evidence of extreme heat, such as bluing, indicates that lubrication failure has occurred. Be sure to thoroughly check the oil pump and pressure relief valve as well as all oil holes and passages before reassembling the engine.

12 Have the rods checked by a Yamaha dealer if you are in doubt about their straightness.

Oil clearance check

Note: *It is essential that, throughout this procedure, the connecting rod does not rotate on the crankshaft. If the procedure is being carried out on a bench find some way of clamping the crankshaft so it cannot move, and also the connecting rod once it has been fitted onto its journal. The alternative is to fit the rod and piston back into its bore and lay the crankshaft in the crankcase to keep them held steady.*

13 Whether new bearing shells are being fitted or the original ones are being re-used, the connecting rod big-end bearing oil clearance should be checked prior to reassembly. Bearing oil clearance is measured with a product known as Plastigauge.

14 Remove the bearing shells from the rods and caps, keeping them in order **(see illustration)**. Clean the backs of the shells, the bearing housings in both the connecting rod and cap, and the crankpin journal with a suitable solvent.

15 Press the bearing shells into their locations, locating the tab on each shell in the notch in the connecting rod or cap **(see illustration)**. Make sure the shells are fitted

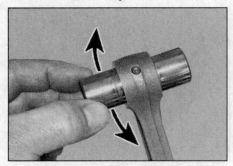

21.10 Check for freeplay between the pin and the small-end

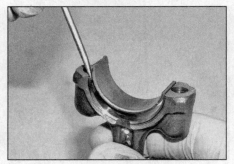

21.14 Remove the shells from the rods and caps

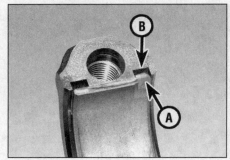

21.15 Locate the tab (A) in the notch (B)

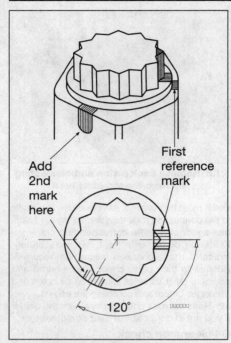

21.18 After initial tightening mark the bolt and cap as shown to ensure correct angle tightening

in the correct locations and take care not to touch any shell's bearing surface with your fingers.

16 Work on one rod at a time. Cut an appropriate size length of Plastigauge (it should be slightly shorter than the width of the crankpin) and place it on the crankpin journal to be checked **(see illustration 8.23)**. Do not place Plastigauge over the oil holes in the journal.

17 Apply molybdenum disulphide grease to the threads and under the heads of the bolts. Fit the connecting rod and cap onto the crankpin. Make sure the cap is fitted the correct way around so the previously made markings align (see Step 3), and that the 'Y' mark on the rod is facing to the left-hand end of the crankshaft (see Step 6). Fit the bolts and tighten them finger-tight. **Note:** *It is essential that, throughout this procedure, the connecting rod does not rotate on the crankshaft.*

18 Tighten the bolts to the initial torque setting specified at the beginning of this Chapter with a torque wrench. Now tighten each bolt in turn and in one continuous movement through the specified angle using a degree disc (torque angle gauge) **(see illustration 21.34)**. **Note:** *If a torque angle gauge is not available, tighten the cap bolts as follows. Paint a small reference mark on one point of the bolt bi-hex after tightening the bolt to the initial torque setting, then go clockwise around the bolt a distance of four points and paint another mark corresponding to this on the connecting rod cap* **(see illustration)** *– the angle between two points is 30°, so going around four points equals 120°. Now, using a ring spanner so that you can see the two marks, tighten the bolt clockwise in one continuous movement until the marks align.*

19 Slacken the bolts and remove the cap and rod from the crankshaft.

20 Compare the width of the crushed Plastigauge on the crankpin to the scale printed on the Plastigauge envelope to obtain the connecting rod bearing oil clearance **(see illustration 8.25)**. Compare the reading to the specifications at the beginning of this Chapter. If the clearance is within the range specified and the bearings are in perfect condition, they can be reused.

21 Carefully clean away all traces of the Plastigauge from the crankpin journal and bearing shells using a fingernail or other object which will not score the bearing surfaces.

22 If the clearance is beyond the service limit, replace the bearing shells with new ones (see Steps 25 and 26) and check the oil clearance once again. Always renew all of the shells at the same time.

23 If the clearance is still greater than the service limit listed in this Chapter's Specifications, the big-end bearing journal is worn and the crankshaft should be replaced with a new one.

24 Repeat the procedure for the remaining connecting rods, then discard the old big-end bolts.

Bearing shell selection

25 Replacement bearing shells for the big-end bearings are supplied on a selected fit basis. Code numbers for the crankshaft journals are stamped on the outside of the crankshaft web on the left-hand end of the crankshaft **(see illustration)**. The right-hand block of four numbers are the size codes for the big-end bearing journals (the left-hand block of five numbers are the size codes for the main bearing journals). The first number of the block is for the left-hand (No. 1 cylinder) journal, and so on. Each connecting rod size code number is marked in ink on the flat face of the connecting rod and cap **(see illustration)**.

26 A range of bearing shells are available. To select the correct shells for a particular journal, subtract the big-end bearing journal number on the crankshaft from the number on the connecting rod and compare the result with the table below to find the colour coding of the replacement shells, e.g. connecting rod number 5 minus crankshaft journal number 1 = 4; No. 4 bearing shells are colour-coded yellow-green. The colour codes are marked on the side of each bearing shell **(see illustration)**.

Number	Colour
1	yellow-blue
2	yellow-black
3	yellow-brown
4	yellow-green

Installation

Note: *New big-end bolts must be used on final assembly.*

27 If removed, fit the pistons onto the connecting rods (see Section 22) – make sure the piston ring end gaps are correctly spaced (see Section 23).

28 Make sure that the backs of the bearing shells, the bearing seats in the caps and rods and the crankpin journals are clean. If new shells are being fitted, remove any protective grease using paraffin (kerosene). Dry the shells, caps, rods and journals with a clean, lint-free cloth. Fit the shells, locating the tab on each shell in the notch in the cap or rod, and making sure the end of each shell is flush with the cap or rod **(see illustration 21.15)**. If the original bearing shells are to be fitted, make sure that they are in their correct locations.

21.25a Big-end bearing size codes (arrowed)

21.25b Connecting rod size code number

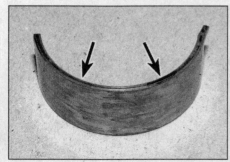

21.26 Big-end bearing shell colour codes (arrowed)

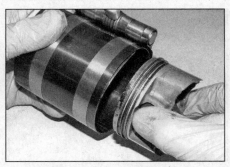

21.30a Fit the ring compressor over the piston...

21.30b ...and tighten it to compress the rings

21.30c Insert the rod assembly into the top of the bore...

21.30d ...and carefully press the piston into the bore

21.32 Align the markings and fit the cap onto the rod

21.34 Use a degree disc for the final tightening of the bolts

Take care not to touch any bearing surfaces with your fingers.

29 Lubricate the pistons, rings and cylinder bores with clean engine oil. When fitting the piston/rod assembly into its bore make sure the arrow on the top of the piston points to the front and the 'Y' mark on the rod faces the left-hand side of the engine (see Step 6).

30 If available, use a piston ring compressor as shown to fit the piston assembly into the bore **(see illustrations)**. If a compressor is not available, insert the piston/connecting rod assembly into its bore, **(see illustration 21.6)**, then carefully compress and feed each piston ring into the bore until the piston crown is flush with the top of the bore. In either case take care not to allow the connecting rod to mark the bore.

31 Turn the crankcase over. Make sure all the main bearing shells are in place, then lower the crankshaft into position **(see illustration 24.2)**.

32 Working on one connecting rod at a time, lubricate the crankpin and the shells in the connecting rod and cap with clean engine oil. Pull the rod onto the crankpin **(see illustration 21.5)**. Fit the cap onto the rod **(see illustration)**. Make sure the cap is fitted the correct way around so the previously made markings align (see Step 3).

33 Apply molybdenum disulphide grease to the threads and under the heads of the new

big-end bolts. Fit the bolts and tighten them finger-tight. Check that all components have been returned to their original locations using the marks made on disassembly.

34 Tighten the bolts to the initial torque setting specified at the beginning of this Chapter with a torque wrench. Now tighten each bolt in turn and in one continuous movement through the specified angle using a degree disc (torque angle gauge) **(see illustration)**. If a disc is not available, follow the procedure in Step 18 and mark the bolts with a dab of paint in order to tighten them to the specified angle. Fit the remaining rods onto the crankshaft in the same way.

35 Check that the crankshaft rotates smoothly and freely. If there are any signs of roughness or tightness, detach the rods and recheck the assembly. Sometimes tapping the bottom of the connecting rod cap will relieve tightness.

36 Reassemble the crankcase halves (see Section 19).

22 Pistons

Removal

1 Remove the engine from the frame (see Section 4), separate the crankcase halves (see

Section 19). Remove the piston/connecting rod assemblies (see Section 21).

2 Before removing the piston from the connecting rod, make sure both are marked with their cylinder identity. If the piston is going to be cleaned, scratch the identity lightly on the inside of the piston skirt. Each piston must be installed in its original cylinder on reassembly. Note the arrow on the top of each piston that points to the front of the engine **(see illustration)**. If this is not visible, mark the piston accordingly so that it can be installed the correct way round.

3 Carefully prise out the circlips on each side of the piston pin using needle-nose pliers or a small flat-bladed screwdriver inserted into

22.2 Note the arrow that points to the front of the engine

22.3a Prise out the circlip...

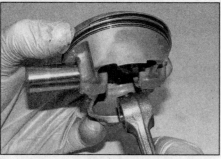

22.3b ...then push out the pin and remove the piston

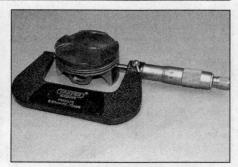

22.10 Measuring the piston diameter with a micrometer

the notch (see illustration). Check for burring around the circlip grooves and remove any with a very fine file or knife blade, then push the piston pin out to free the piston from the connecting rod (see illustration). Discard the circlips as new ones must be used on reassembly. When the piston has been removed from the rod, keep the piston and its pin together so that related parts do not get mixed up.

4 Using your thumbs or a piston ring removal and installation tool, carefully remove the rings from the pistons, working on one piston at a time (see Section 23). Do not nick or gouge the pistons in the process. Note which way up each ring fits and in which groove, as they must be installed in their original positions if being re-used. The upper surface of the two top rings (compression rings) should have a manufacturer's mark or letter at one end (though on the engine photographed only the second ring had a mark) – note which mark is

for the top ring and which is for the second (see illustration 23.2).

5 Scrape all traces of carbon from the tops of the pistons. A hand-held wire brush or a piece of fine emery cloth can be used once most of the deposits have been scraped away. Do not, under any circumstances, use a wire brush mounted in a drill motor; the piston material is soft and is easily damaged.

6 Use a piston ring groove cleaning tool to remove any carbon deposits from the ring grooves. If a tool is not available, a piece broken off an old ring will do the job. Be very careful to remove only the carbon deposits. Do not remove any metal and do not nick or gouge the sides of the ring grooves.

7 Once the carbon has been removed, clean the pistons with a suitable solvent and dry them thoroughly. Make sure the oil return holes at the back of the oil ring groove are clear. If the identification mark previously applied to the piston is cleaned off, be sure to re-mark it correctly.

Inspection

8 Inspect each piston for cracks around the skirt, at the pin bosses and at the ring lands. Normal piston wear appears as even, vertical wear on the thrust surfaces of the piston and slight looseness of the top ring in its groove. If the skirt is scored or scuffed, the engine may have been suffering from overheating and/or abnormal combustion, resulting in excessively high operating temperatures.

9 A hole in the top of the piston (only likely in extreme circumstances), or burned areas around the edge of the piston crown, indicate that pre-ignition or knocking under load have occurred. If you find evidence of any problems the cause must be corrected or the damage will occur again (see Fault Finding in the Reference section).

10 Check the piston-to-bore clearance by measuring the bore (see Section 28) and the piston diameter. Make sure each piston is matched to its correct cylinder. Measure the piston 5 mm up from the bottom of the skirt and at 90° to the piston pin axis (see illustration). Subtract the piston diameter from the bore diameter to obtain the clearance. If it is greater than the figure specified at the beginning of this Chapter, check whether it is the bore or piston that is worn beyond its service limit. If the bores are good, fit new pistons and rings. If the bores are worn, replace the crankcases, pistons and rings.

11 Measure the piston ring-to-groove clearance by laying each compression ring in its groove and slipping a feeler gauge in beside it (see illustration). Make sure you have the correct ring for the groove (see Step 4). Check the clearance at three or four locations around the groove. If the clearance is greater than specified, renew both the piston and rings as a set. If new rings are being used, measure the clearance using the new rings. If the clearance is greater than that specified, the piston is worn and must be replaced with a new one.

12 Apply clean engine oil to the piston pin, insert it part way into the piston and check for any freeplay between the two (see illustration). Measure the pin external diameter at each end, and the pin bores in the piston (see illustrations). Subtract the pin diameter from the bore diameter to obtain the clearance. If it is greater than the specified

22.11 Measuring the piston ring-to-groove clearance with a feeler gauge

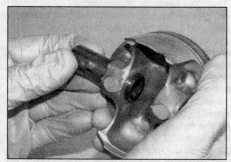

22.12a Insert the pin into the piston and check for freeplay

22.12b Measure the pin external diameter...

22.12c ...and the pin bore in the piston

figure, check whether it is the bore or pin that is worn beyond its service limit and replace them with new ones as required. Check for excessive play between the pin and the connecting rod small-end (see Section 21).

Installation

13 Inspect and install the piston rings (see Section 23).
14 Fit a **new** circlip into one side of the piston (never re-use old circlips). Lubricate the piston pin, the piston pin bore and the connecting rod small-end bore with clean engine oil.
15 Line up the piston on its connecting rod so that the arrow on the top of the piston will point to the front and the 'Y' mark on the rod will face the left-hand side of the engine when they are installed. Insert the piston pin from the side without the circlip **(see illustration 22.3b)**. Secure the pin with the other **new** circlip. When fitting the circlips, compress them only just enough to fit them in the piston, and make sure they are properly seated in their grooves with the open end away from the removal notch **(see illustration)**.
16 Install the connecting rods (see Section 21).

23 Piston rings

1 It is good practice to fit new piston rings when an engine is being overhauled. Before fitting the rings on the pistons, the ring end gaps must be checked with the rings in the cylinder.

Inspection

2 Lay out each piston with its new ring set so the rings will be matched with the same piston and cylinder during the measurement procedure and engine reassembly. The upper surface of the two top rings (compression rings) should have a manufacturer's mark or letter at one end, though on the engine photographed only the second (middle) ring was marked **(see illustration)** – if the mark on each ring is different, note which mark is for the top ring and which is for the second.
3 To measure the ring end gap, fit the ring into the top of the cylinder and square it up

22.15 Fit the circlip with the open end away from the removal notch

with the cylinder walls by pushing it in with the top of the piston. The ring should be about 5 mm below the top edge of the cylinder. Slip a feeler gauge between the ends of the ring and compare the measurement to the specifications at the beginning of this Chapter **(see illustrations)**.
4 If the gap is larger or smaller than specified, double check to make sure that you have the correct rings before proceeding.
5 Excess end gap is not critical unless it exceeds the service limit. Check that the bore is not worn (see Section 28).
6 Repeat the procedure for each ring and each cylinder in turn. Note that the end gaps differ between the top, second and oil ring. When checking the oil ring, only the side-rails can be checked as the ends of the expander ring should contact each other. Remember to keep the rings together with their matched pistons and cylinders.

23.3a Set the ring square using the piston

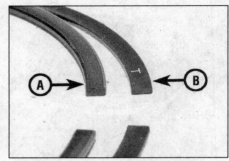

23.2 Top ring (A), middle ring (B)

Installation

7 Once the ring end gaps have been checked and corrected as necessary, the rings can be installed on the pistons.
8 Fit the oil control ring (lowest on the piston). It is composed of three separate components, namely the expander and the upper and lower side rails. First slip the expander into the ring groove, making sure the ends do not overlap **(see illustration)**. Next fit the lower side rail – do not use a piston ring installation tool on the oil ring side rails as they may be damaged **(see illustration)**. Instead, place one end of the side rail into the groove between the expander and the ring land. Hold it firmly in place and slide a finger around the piston while pushing the rail into the groove. Next, fit the upper side rail in the same manner **(see illustration)**. Make sure the ends of the expander touch but do not overlap.

23.3b Measuring piston ring end gap

23.8a Fit the oil ring expander in its groove...

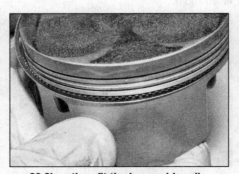

23.8b ... then fit the lower side rail...

23.8c ... and the upper side rail as described

23.10 Carefully feed the second ring into its groove

23.11 Finally, fit the top ring

24 Crankshaft and main bearings

Removal

1 Remove the engine from the frame (see Section 4), separate the crankcase halves (see Section 19) and disconnect the piston/connecting rod assemblies from the crankshaft (see Section 21). There is no need to remove the piston/connecting rod assemblies from the cylinders, but push them up the bores so that the connecting rod ends are clear of the crankshaft and wrap clean rag around the rod ends to prevent damage to the bores **(see illustration 21.5)**. **Note:** *New big-end bolts must be used on reassembly.*
2 Lift the crankshaft out of the upper crankcase half, taking care not to dislodge the main bearing shells **(see illustration)**.
3 If required, remove the main bearing shells from the crankcase halves **(see illustration)**. Keep the shells in order so that they can be fitted in their original locations for the oil clearance check.

Inspection

4 Clean the crankshaft with a suitable solvent, paying particular attention to flush out the oil passages. If available, blow the crank dry with compressed air, and also blow through the oil passages. Check the primary drive gear for wear or damage. If any of the teeth are excessively worn, chipped or broken, the crankshaft must be replaced with a new one. Check the primary driven gear on the clutch housing for corresponding wear or damage. Also check the cam chain sprocket, the sprockets on the camshafts and the cam chain itself and replace them with new ones, if necessary.
5 Refer to Section 20 and examine the main bearing shells. If they are scored, badly scuffed or appear to have seized, new bearings must be installed. Always renew the main bearings as a set. If they are badly damaged, check the corresponding crankshaft journals. Evidence of extreme heat, such as bluing, indicates that lubrication failure has occurred. Be sure to thoroughly check the oil pump and pressure relief valve as well as all oil holes and passages before reassembling the engine.
6 Give the crankshaft journals a close visual examination, paying particular attention where damaged bearings have been discovered. If the journals are scored or pitted in any way, a new crankshaft will be required. Note that undersized bearing shells are not available, precluding the option of re-grinding the crankshaft.
7 Place the crankshaft on V-blocks and check the runout at the main bearing journals using a dial gauge (see *Tools and Workshop Tips* in the *Reference* section). Compare the reading to the maximum specified at the beginning of this Chapter. If the runout exceeds the limit,

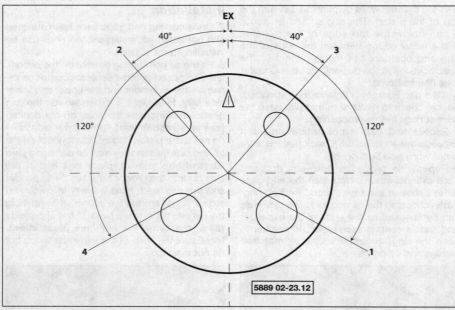

23.12 Piston ring installation details - stagger the ring end gaps as shown

1 Top ring and oil ring expander   2 Lower side rail   3 Upper side rail   4 Second ring

9 After the three oil ring components have been fitted, check to make sure that both the upper and lower side rails can be turned smoothly in the ring groove.
10 Fit the second ring into the middle groove in the piston (T mark uppermost) – use a feeler gauge blade to help slip the ring into place **(see illustration)**. Do not expand the ring any

more than is necessary – they are brittle and break easily.
11 Finally, fit the top ring in the same manner into the top groove in the piston **(see illustration)**.
12 Once the rings are correctly installed, check they move freely without snagging and stagger their end gaps as shown **(see illustration)**.

24.2 Lift the crankshaft out of the crankcase carefully

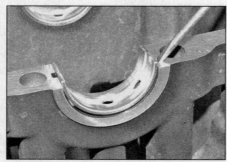

24.3 Remove the main bearing shells from their housings

the crankshaft must be replaced with a new one.

Oil clearance check

8 Whether new bearing shells are being fitted or the original ones are being re-used, the main bearing oil clearance should be checked before the engine is reassembled. Main bearing oil clearance is measured with a product known as Plastigauge.

9 If not already done, remove the bearing shells from the crankcase halves (see Step 3). Clean the backs of the shells and the bearing seats in both crankcase halves, and the main bearing journals on the crankshaft.

10 Press the bearing shells into their seats, locating the tab on each shell in the notch in the crankcase **(see illustration)**. Make sure the bearings are fitted in the correct locations and take care not to touch the bearing surfaces with your fingers.

11 Make sure the shells and crankshaft are clean and dry. Lay the crankshaft in position in the upper crankcase.

12 Cut five appropriate size lengths of Plastigauge (they should be slightly shorter than the width of the crankshaft journals). Place a strand of Plastigauge on each journal **(see illustration 8.23)**. Do not place Plastigauge over the oil holes in the crankshaft. Make sure the crankshaft is not rotated.

13 If removed, fit the dowels into the crankcase **(see illustration 19.13)**. Carefully fit the lower crankcase half onto the upper half, making sure the dowels locate correctly and the Plastigauge is not disturbed **(see illustration 19.6)**. Check that the lower crankcase half is correctly seated all round. **Note:** *Do not tighten the crankcase bolts if the casing is not correctly seated.*

14 Clean and lubricate the threads, the underside of the heads and the washers of the crankcase bolts Nos. 1 to 10 **(see illustration 19.5b)** with clean engine oil. Fit the bolts in their correct locations and secure them finger-tight – make sure the two longer 8 mm bolts are fitted in positions 8 and 9. First tighten the bolts in the sequence shown to the first stage torque setting **(see illustration 19.5b)**. Now slacken them in reverse sequence so they are loose, then tighten them in sequence to the second stage torque setting. Finally, using

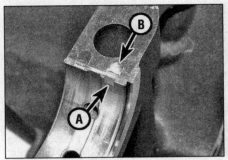

24.10 Locate the tab (A) in the notch (B)

a degree disc, tighten each bolt in sequence through the angle specified for each bolt at the beginning of the Chapter (the angle for bolts 8 and 9 is different to that for 1 to 7 and 10) **(see illustration 19.17c)**.

15 Unscrew the bolts a quarter turn at a time in a **reverse** of the numerical sequence shown in illustration **19.5b**, until they are loose, then remove them. Carefully lift off the lower crankcase half, making sure the Plastigauge is not disturbed.

16 Compare the width of the crushed Plastigauge on each crankshaft journal to the scale printed on the Plastigauge envelope to obtain the main bearing oil clearance **(see illustration 8.25)**. Compare the reading to the specifications at the beginning of this Chapter. If the clearance is within the range specified and the bearings are in perfect condition, they can be reused.

17 Carefully clean away all traces of the Plastigauge from the journals and bearing shells using a fingernail or other object which will not score the bearing surfaces.

18 If the clearance is beyond the service limit, replace the bearing shells with new ones (see Steps 20 to 22) and check the oil clearance once again. Always renew all of the shells at the same time.

19 If the clearance is still greater than the service limit listed in this Chapter's Specifications, the crankshaft journal is worn and the crankshaft should be renewed.

Bearing shell selection

20 Replacement bearing shells for the main

24.20 Crankshaft journal size codes (arrowed)

bearings are supplied on a selected fit basis. Code numbers for the crankshaft journals are stamped on the outside of the crankshaft web on the left-hand end of the crankshaft **(see illustration)**. The left-hand block of five numbers are the size codes for the main bearing journals (the right-hand block of four numbers are the size codes for the big-end bearing journals). The first number of the block is for the left-hand (No. 1) journal, and so on.

21 The main bearing size code(s) is/are stamped into the back of the lower crankcase half **(see illustration)**. If there are five numbers the first is for the left-hand (No. 1) bearing, and so on. If there is only one number stamped into the crankcase, it means that all the bearings are the same size code.

22 A range of bearing shells are available. To select the correct shells for a particular journal, subtract the crankshaft journal number on the crankshaft from the number on the crankcase, and then subtract 1. Compare the result with the table below to find the colour code of the replacement shells, e.g. crankcase number 6 minus crankshaft journal number 2 minus 1 = 3; No. 3 bearing shells are colour coded brown. The colour code is marked on the side of each bearing shell **(see illustration)**.

Number	Colour
0	white
1	blue
2	black
3	brown
4	green

Installation

23 Make sure the backs of the bearing shells, the bearing seats in both crankcase halves, and the main bearing journals on the crankshaft are clean. If new shells are being fitted clean any protective grease off using paraffin (kerosene). Wipe the shells and crankcase halves dry with a lint-free cloth. Make sure all the oil passages and holes are clear, and blow them through with compressed air if it is available.

24 Press the bearing shells into their seats, locating the tab on each shell in the notch in the crankcase **(see illustration 24.10)**. Make sure the bearings are fitted in the correct locations and take care not to touch any

24.21 Main bearing size code(s) (arrowed)

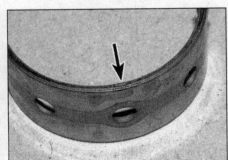

24.22 Main bearing shell colour code (arrowed)

bearing surfaces with your fingers. Lubricate the shells with clean engine oil.

25 Lower the crankshaft into position in the upper crankcase, making sure all bearing shells remain in place **(see illustration 24.2)**.

26 Refer to Section 21, Steps 32 to 35, and fit the connecting rods onto the crankshaft using new bolts.

27 Reassemble the crankcase halves (see Section 19).

---

25 Transmission shaft removal and installation

Special tool: Although not strictly a tool, this procedure requires the use of two M6 x 1.0 bolts of 30 mm thread length and three M6 x 1.0 bolts of 25 mm thread length with plain washers – see Steps 5 and 7.

Removal

1 Remove the engine from the frame (see Section 4). Remove the gearchange mechanism (see Section 15), then separate the crankcase halves (see Section 19) – there is no need to remove the camshafts or cylinder head, but you have to remove the alternator cover and timing rotor cover, and the sump.

2 Note how the pin on the output shaft bearing locates in the cut-out in the upper crankcase half, and how the output shaft selector forks locate in the grooves on the 5th and 6th gear pinions, and how the guide pins on the forks locate in the grooves in the selector drum. Lift the output shaft out of the crankcase **(see illustration)**; if it is stuck, use a soft-faced hammer and gently tap on the ends of the shaft to free it.

3 Remove the bearing half-ring retainer from the crankcase or bearing, noting how it fits

(see illustration 25.10a). Remove the oil seal from the left-hand end of the shaft – a new one must be used **(see illustration 25.10b)**.

4 Remove the selector drum and forks (see Section 27).

5 Undo the Torx screws securing the input shaft bearing housing **(see illustration)** – note that new screws must be used on reassembly. Obtain two 6 mm bolts, 30 mm long excluding the bolt head, and with a 1 mm thread pitch, and screw them into the two threaded holes in the bearing housing as shown **(see illustration)**. Turn the bolts until they contact the surface of the crankcase, then continue turning them evenly and a little at a time until the bearing housing is displaced **(see illustration)**. Withdraw the input shaft from the crankcase **(see illustration 25.7)**.

6 To remove the left-hand input shaft bearing, see *Tools and Workshop Tips* in the *Reference* section **(see illustration)**.

Installation

7 Slide the input shaft into the crankcase far enough for the left-hand end of the shaft to locate in its bearing **(see illustration)**. Obtain three 6 mm bolts, 25 mm long excluding the bolt head, and three flat washers. Fit the washers onto the bolts, insert the bolts through the bearing housing screw holes and thread them into the crankcase **(see illustration)**. Tighten the bolts evenly and a little at a time to draw the bearing housing into its location in the crankcase **(see illustration)**. When the housing is fully seated, unscrew the bolts.

25.2 Lift the output shaft out of the crankcase

25.5a Undo the screws (arrowed)

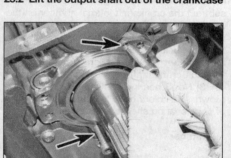
25.5b Screw the bolts into the threaded holes...

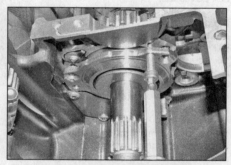
25.5c ...and against the crankcase surface, and keep turning them to push the bearing housing out

25.6 Input shaft left-hand bearing (arrowed)

25.7a Locate the end of the input shaft in the bearing (arrowed)

25.7b Fit and evenly tighten the bolts...

25.7c ...to draw the bearing housing into the crankcase

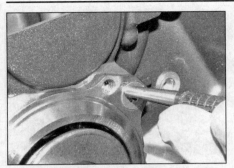

25.8 Tighten the new Torx screws as specified and then stake them in place

25.10a Fit the retainer into its slot...

25.10b ...and fit a new oil seal

8 Apply a suitable thread locking compound to the new Torx screws and tighten them to the torque setting specified at the beginning of this Chapter. Stake the edge of each screw into the indent in the housing using a suitable punch **(see illustration)**.

9 Install the selector drum and forks (see Section 27).

10 Fit the output shaft bearing half-ring retainer into its slot in the upper crankcase **(see illustration)**. Smear the lip of the new output shaft seal with grease. Slide the seal onto the left-hand end of the shaft **(see illustration)**.

11 Lower the output shaft into position in the upper crankcase **(see illustration 25.2)** – make sure the selector forks locate in their pinion grooves and selector drum tracks correctly, and the groove in the bearing engages correctly with the half-ring retainer and the pin on the bearing locates correctly in the crankcase **(see illustration)**.

Caution: If the half-ring retainer is not correctly engaged, the crankcase halves will not seat correctly.

12 Make sure output shaft is correctly seated and that the selector forks are located in the grooves in the appropriate gear pinions (see Section 27).

13 Position the gears in the neutral position and check the shafts are free to rotate easily and independently (i.e. the input shaft can turn whilst the output shaft is held stationary) before proceeding further.

14 Reassemble the crankcase halves (see Section 19).

26 Transmission shaft overhaul

1 Remove the transmission shafts from the crankcase (see Section 25). Always disassemble the transmission shafts separately to avoid mixing up the components.

Input shaft disassembly

2 Slide the 2nd gear pinion off the left-hand end of the shaft, noting which way around it is fitted – mark its outer face with a marker pen as an aid to reassembly **(see illustration 26.26)**.

3 Note how the tabs on the lock washer fit into the slotted splined washer and remove the lockwasher **(see illustration 26.25)**.

4 Turn the slotted splined washer to offset the splines and slide it off the shaft **(see illustration 26.24a)**.

5 Slide the 6th gear pinion and its splined bush off the shaft, followed by the splined washer **(see illustrations 26.23c, b and a)**.

6 Remove the circlip securing the combined 3rd/4th gear pinion, then slide the pinion off the shaft noting which way round it fits **(see illustrations 26.22b and a)**. Discard the circlip as a new one must be fitted on reassembly.

7 Remove the circlip securing the 5th gear pinion, then slide the splined washer, the pinion and its bush off the shaft **(see illustrations 26.21b and a and 26.20b and a)**. Discard the circlip as a new one must be fitted on reassembly.

8 The 1st gear pinion is integral with the shaft **(see illustration)**.

9 If required, remove the bearing and its housing from the right-hand end of the shaft, referring to *Tools and Workshop Tips* (Section 5) in the *Reference* section **(see illustration 26.8)**.

Shaft inspection

10 Wash all the components in solvent and dry them off.

11 Check the gear teeth for cracking, chipping, pitting and other obvious wear or damage. Any pinion that is damaged must be replaced with a new one.

12 Inspect the dogs and the dog holes in the gears for cracks, chips, and excessive wear especially in the form of rounded edges. Make sure mating gears engage properly. Replace mating gears as a set if necessary.

13 Check for signs of scoring or bluing on the pinions, bushes and shaft. This could be caused by overheating due to inadequate lubrication. Check that all the oil holes and passages are clear. Replace any worn or damaged parts with new ones.

14 Check that each pinion moves freely on the shaft or bush but without undue freeplay. Check that each bush moves freely on the shaft but without undue freeplay.

15 The shaft is unlikely to sustain damage unless the engine has seized, placing an unusually high loading on the transmission, or the machine has covered a very high mileage. Check the surface of the shaft, especially where a pinion turns on it, and replace the shaft with a new one if it has scored or picked up, or if there are any cracks. Check the shaft runout using V-blocks and a dial gauge and replace the shaft with a new one if the runout exceeds the limit specified at the beginning of this Chapter.

16 Check the washers and replace any that are bent or worn with new ones.

17 Check the bearings referring to *Tools and Workshop Tips* (Section 5) in the *Reference* section. Do not forget the input shaft left-hand bearing, which is housed in the crankcase.

Input shaft reassembly

18 During reassembly, apply clean engine oil or molybdenum disulphide oil (a 50/50

25.11 Make sure the ring (A) locates in the groove and the pin (B) seats in the cut-out

26.8 The 1st gear pinion (arrowed) is integral with the shaft

26.20a Slide the 5th gear pinion bush...

26.20b ...the 5th gear pinion...

26.21a ...and the splined washer onto the shaft...

26.21b ...and secure them with the circlip...

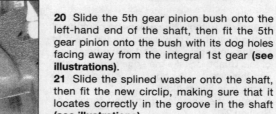

26.21c ...making sure it locates correctly

20 Slide the 5th gear pinion bush onto the left-hand end of the shaft, then fit the 5th gear pinion onto the bush with its dog holes facing away from the integral 1st gear **(see illustrations)**.

21 Slide the splined washer onto the shaft, then fit the new circlip, making sure that it locates correctly in the groove in the shaft **(see illustrations)**.

22 Slide the combined 3rd/4th gear pinion onto the shaft with the smaller 3rd gear pinion facing the 5th gear pinion, aligning the oil holes **(see illustration)**. Fit the new circlip, making sure it locates correctly in its groove in the shaft **(see illustrations)**.

23 Slide the splined washer onto the shaft, followed by the splined 6th gear pinion bush, aligning the oil hole in the bush with the hole in the shaft **(see illustrations)**. Fit the 6th gear pinion, making sure its dog holes face the 3rd/4th gear pinion **(see illustrations)**.

mixture of molybdenum disulphide grease and engine oil) to the mating surfaces of the shaft, pinions and bushes. Use new circlips and do not expand their ends any further than is necessary to slide them along the shaft. Install them so that their chamfered side faces the pinion they secure (see *Correct fitting of* a stamped circlip illustration in *Tools and Workshop Tips* (Section 2) in the *Reference* section).

19 If removed, fit the bearing and its housing onto the right-hand end of the shaft, referring to *Tools and Workshop Tips* (Section 5) in the *Reference* section **(see illustration 26.8)**.

26.22a Slide the 3rd/4th gear pinion onto the shaft...

26.22b ...and secure it with the circlip...

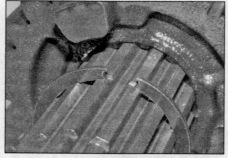

26.22c ...making sure it locates correctly

26.23a Fit the splined washer...

26.23b ...align the oil holes and fit the 6th gear pinion bush...

26.23c ...and slide on the 6th gear pinion

24 Slide the slotted splined washer onto the shaft and locate it in its groove, then turn it in the groove, so that the splines on the washer locate against the splines on the shaft and secure the washer in the groove **(see illustrations)**.

25 Slide the lockwasher onto the shaft, so that the tabs on the lockwasher locate in the slots on the outside edge of the splined washer **(see illustration)**.

26 Slide the 2nd gear pinion onto the shaft, the correct way around as noted on removal **(see illustration)**.

27 Check that all components have been correctly installed. The assembled shaft should look as shown **(see illustration)**.

Output shaft disassembly

28 Slide the bearing off the right-hand end of the shaft **(see illustration 26.49)**.

29 Slide the thrust washer off the shaft, followed by the 1st gear pinion and its bush **(see illustrations 26.48c, b and a)**.

30 Slide the 5th gear pinion off the shaft **(see illustration 26.47)**.

31 Remove the circlip securing the 3rd gear pinion, then slide the splined washer, the pinion and its splined bush off the shaft **(see illustrations 26.46d, c, b and a)**. Discard the circlip as a new one must be fitted on reassembly.

32 Note how the tabs on the lock washer fit into the slotted splined washer and remove the lockwasher **(see illustration 26.45)**.

33 Turn the slotted splined washer to align it with the splines on the shaft and slide it off the shaft **(see illustrations 26.44)**.

34 Slide the 4th gear pinion and its splined bush, followed by the splined washer, off the shaft **(see illustrations 26.43c, b and a)**.

35 Remove the circlip securing the 6th gear pinion, then slide the pinion off the shaft **(see illustrations 26.42b and a)**. Discard the circlip as a new one must be fitted on reassembly.

36 Remove the circlip securing the 2nd gear pinion, then slide the splined washer,

26.24a Fit the slotted splined washer...

26.24b ...then turn it to align the splines so it is locked

26.25 ...then slide on the tabbed lockwasher...

26.26 ...and the 2nd gear pinion

the pinion and its bush off the shaft **(see illustrations 26.41d, c, b and a)**.

37 If required, remove the collar and bearing from the left-hand end of the shaft, referring to *Tools and Workshop Tips* (Section 5) in the *Reference* section **(see illustration)**.

Shaft inspection

38 Refer to Steps 10 to 17 above.

Output shaft reassembly

39 During reassembly, apply engine oil or molybdenum disulphide oil (a 50/50 mixture of molybdenum disulphide grease and engine

oil) to the mating surfaces of the shaft, pinions and bushes. When installing the new circlips, do not expand their ends any further than is necessary to slide them along the shaft. Install them so that their chamfered side faces the pinion they secure (see *Correct fitting of a stamped circlip* illustration in *Tools and Workshop Tips* (Section 2) in the *Reference* section).

40 If removed, fit the bearing and collar onto the left-hand end of the shaft, referring to *Tools and Workshop Tips* (Section 5) in the *Reference* section **(see illustration 26.37)**.

41 Slide the 2nd gear pinion bush onto the

26.27 The assembled gearbox input shaft

26.37 Remove the collar and bearing if required

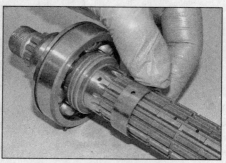

26.41a Slide the 2nd gear pinion bush...

26.41b ...the 2nd gear pinion...

26.41c ...and the splined washer onto the shaft...

26.41d ...and secure them with the circlip...

26.41e ...making sure it locates correctly

26.42a Align the oil holes and slide the 6th gear pinion onto the shaft...

26.42b ...and secure it with the circlip...

26.42c ...making sure it locates correctly

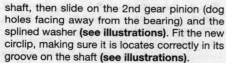

shaft, then slide on the 2nd gear pinion (dog holes facing away from the bearing) and the splined washer (see illustrations). Fit the new circlip, making sure it is locates correctly in its groove on the shaft (see illustrations).

42 Align the oil holes in the shaft and the 6th gear pinion, and slide the pinion onto the shaft with its selector fork groove facing away from the 2nd gear pinion, then fit the new circlip, making sure it locates correctly in its groove on the shaft (see illustrations).

43 Slide the splined washer and the splined 4th gear pinion bush onto the shaft, making sure the oil hole in the bush aligns with the hole in the shaft, then fit the 4th gear pinion so that its dished side and dog holes face the 6th gear pinion (see illustrations).

26.43a Fit the splined washer...

26.43b ...then align the oil holes and fit the 4th gear pinion bush...

26.43c ...and slide on the 4th gear pinion

26.44a Fit the slotted splined washer...

26.44b ...then turn it to align the splines so it is locked...

26.45 ...then slide on the tabbed lockwasher

26.46a Align the oil holes and fit the 3rd gear pinion bush...

26.46b ...then slide on the 3rd gear pinion...

26.46c ...and the splined washer...

44 Slide the slotted splined washer onto the shaft and locate it in its groove, then turn it in the groove so that the splines on the washer align against the splines on the shaft and secure the washer in the groove **(see illustrations)**.

45 Slide the lockwasher onto the shaft, so that the tabs on the lockwasher locate into the slots in the outer rim of the splined washer **(see illustration)**.

46 Slide the splined 3rd gear pinion bush onto the shaft, making sure the oil hole in the

bush aligns with the hole in the shaft, then fit the 3rd gear pinion (dished side and dog holes facing away from the 4th gear pinion) and the splined washer **(see illustrations)**. Fit the new circlip, making sure it locates correctly in its groove in the shaft **(see illustrations)**.

47 Align the oil holes in the shaft and the 5th gear pinion, and slide the pinion onto the shaft with its selector fork groove facing the 3rd gear pinion **(see illustration)**.

48 Slide the 1st gear pinion bush onto the shaft, followed by the 1st gear pinion (dished

26.46d ...and secure them with the circlip...

26.46e ...making sure it locates correctly

26.47 Align the oil holes and slide the 5th gear pinion onto the shaft

side facing the 5th gear pinion) and the thrust washer **(see illustrations)**.

49 Fit the bearing onto the end of the shaft with its open side facing the 1st gear pinion **(see illustration)**.

50 Check that all components have been correctly installed. The assembled shaft should look as shown **(see illustration)**.

27 Selector drum and forks

Removal

1 Remove the engine from the frame (see Section 4). Remove the gearchange mechanism (see Section 15), then separate the crankcase halves (see Section 19) – there is no need to remove the camshafts or cylinder head, but you have to remove the alternator and timing rotor covers, and the sump.

2 Note how the output shaft selector forks locate in the grooves on the 5th and 6th gear pinions and how the guide pins on the forks locate in the grooves in the selector drum, then remove the output shaft (see Section 25).

3 Note that each selector fork is lettered for identification. The right-hand fork has an 'R', the centre fork a 'C', and the left-hand fork an 'L'. These letters face the right-hand side (clutch side) of the engine. If no letters are visible, mark the forks yourself using a felt pen.

4 Note how the input shaft selector fork locates in the groove on the 3rd/4th gear pinion and how the guide pin on the fork locates in the groove in the selector drum.

5 Unscrew the bolt securing each retainer plate and remove the plates, noting how they fit **(see illustration)**.

6 Hold the output shaft selector forks (L and R), withdraw the shaft and remove the forks **(see illustrations 27.18b and a)**. Slide the forks back onto the shaft in the correct order and the right way round.

7 Support the input shaft selector fork (C) and withdraw the fork shaft from the crankcase **(see illustration 27.17b)**. Move the fork guide pin out of its track in the selector drum, then withdraw the selector drum from the left-hand side of the casing **(see illustration 27.15b)**.

8 Move the selector fork around in its groove

in the 3rd/4th gear pinion and remove it **(see illustration 27.14)**. Slide the fork back onto the shaft.

Inspection

9 Inspect the selector forks for any signs of wear or damage, especially around the fork ends where they engage with the grooves in the pinions; the thickness of the fork ends can be measured and compared with the limit in the Specifications to check whether they're worn. Check that each fork fits correctly in its

26.48a Fit the 1st gear pinion bush...

26.48b ...then slide the 1st gear pinion...

26.48c ...and the thrust washer onto the shaft...

26.49 ...and fit the bearing

26.50 The assembled gearbox output shaft

27.5 Unscrew the bolts (arrowed) and remove the retainer plates

27.9 Check the fit of each fork in its pinion groove

27.10 Check the fit of each fork on its shaft

27.12 Check the tracks and guide pins for wear and damage

pinion groove **(see illustration)**. Check closely to see if the forks are bent. If the forks are in any way damaged they must be replaced with new ones.

10 Check that the forks fit correctly on their shaft **(see illustration)**. They should move freely with a light fit but no appreciable freeplay. Check that the fork shaft holes in the casing are not worn or damaged.

11 Check the selector fork shaft runout using V-blocks and a dial gauge and replace the shaft with a new one if the runout exceeds the limit specified at the beginning of this Chapter. A bent shaft will cause difficulty in selecting gears and make the gearchange action heavy.

12 Inspect the selector drum tracks and selector fork guide pins for signs of wear or damage **(see illustration)**. If either show signs of wear or damage they must be replaced with new ones.

13 Check the selector drum bearing referring to *Tools and Workshop Tips* (Section 5) in the *Reference* section **(see illustration)**. If the bearing is worn a new selector drum will have to be fitted as the bearing is not available separately. Also check that the neutral switch contact on the right-hand end of the drum is not damaged or worn away. If required, remove the contact and replace it with a new one.

Installation

14 Locate the input shaft selector fork (C) in its groove in the 3rd/4th gear pinion, making sure the letter faces the right-hand (clutch) side of the engine, then slide the fork around and below the input shaft so that it does not get in the way when installing the selector drum **(see illustration)**.

15 Lubricate the end of the selector drum with clean engine oil, then align the drum so that the neutral detent points to the upper rear engine mounting and slide it into the crankcase **(see illustrations)**. Make sure the drum end locates in its bore in the crankcase, and that the neutral contact on the drum locates against the neutral switch contact on the inside back of the crankcase.

16 Lubricate the fork shafts with clean engine oil.

17 Move the input shaft selector fork around in its groove and locate the fork guide pin into its track in the selector drum, then slide the fork shaft into the crankcase and through the fork **(see illustrations)**.

18 Position the output shaft fork R in the crankcase, making sure the letter faces the right-hand (clutch) side of the engine and the fork guide pin locates in its tracks in the drum, and slide the shaft into the crankcase

27.13 Selector drum bearing (arrowed)

27.14 Fit the C fork as described

27.15a Align the neutral contact (arrowed) as described...

27.15b ...and slide the drum into the crankcase

27.17a Locate the guide pin in its track (arrowed)...

27.17b ...then slide the shaft in

27.18a Fit the R fork and slide the shaft through it...

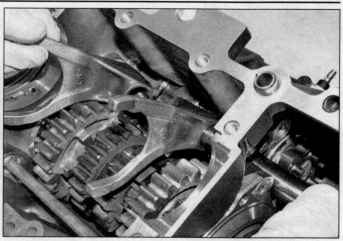

27.18b ...then fit the L fork and slide the shaft all the way in

and through the fork, then repeat for the L fork **(see illustrations)**.

19 Clean the threads of the retainer plate bolts and apply a suitable non-permanent thread locking compound. Fit the plates with the OUT marks facing out and tighten the bolts to the torque setting specified at the beginning of this Chapter **(see illustration 27.5)**.

20 Install the transmission output shaft (see Section 25).

21 Check that the output shaft is correctly seated and that the transmission shafts rotate easily and independently (see Section 25).

28 Crankcases and cylinder bores

Crankcase halves

1 After the crankcases have been separated, remove the crankshaft, connecting rods and pistons, bearings, transmission shafts, selector drum and forks, and any other components or assemblies, referring to the relevant Sections of this and other Chapters (see Step 3 of Section 19).

2 Withdraw the oil feed pipe from the upper crankcase – it is a push-fit **(see illustration)**. Check the condition of the pipe O-rings and replace them with new ones if they are in any way damaged, deformed or deteriorated **(see illustration)**.

4 If required unscrew the main oil gallery plug from each side of the lower crankcase – new O-rings must be fitted on reassembly.

5 If required unscrew the breather plate bolts in the clutch housing and remove the plate. If required unscrew the crankcase breather cover bolts, remove the cover and discard its gasket.

6 Clean the crankcases thoroughly with solvent and dry them with compressed air. Blow out all oil passages and pipes with compressed air.

7 Remove all traces of old gasket sealant from the mating surfaces. Minor damage to the surfaces can be cleaned up with careful use of a fine sharpening stone.

Caution: Be very careful not to nick or gouge the crankcase mating surfaces, or oil leaks will result. Check both crankcase halves very carefully for cracks and other damage.

8 Before proceeding further, check the cylinder bores (see Steps 18 to 21).

9 Inspect the bearing seats for signs of damage, especially if an engine or transmission bearing has overheated or seized (see Section 20). If bearing shells or a ball bearing cage are not a precise fit in their seats, ask your Yamaha dealer for a suitable bearing locking compound which will overcome small amounts of wear. Otherwise the crankcase halves will have to be replaced with a new set.

10 Small cracks or holes in aluminium castings can be repaired with an epoxy resin adhesive as a temporary measure. Permanent

28.2a Withdraw the oil feed pipe (arrowed) from the crankcase...

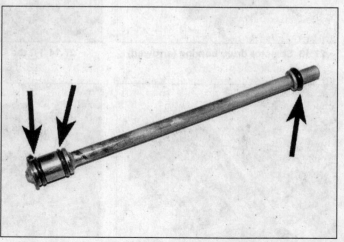

28.2b ...and check the condition of the O-rings (arrowed)

28.16 Seat the tab (arrowed) in the cut-out

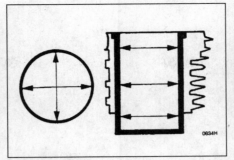

28.19a Measure the cylinder bore in the directions shown…

28.19b …with a telescoping gauge

repairs can only be effected by argon-arc welding, and only a specialist in this process is in a position to advise on the economy or practical aspect of such a repair. Note that low temperature aluminium welding kits are available for minor repairs. If any damage is found that can't be repaired, renew the crankcase halves as a set.

11 Damaged threads can be economically reclaimed by using a diamond section wire insert which is easily fitted after drilling and re-tapping the affected thread.

12 Sheared studs or screws can usually be removed with stud or screw extractors; if you are in any doubt consult your Yamaha dealer or specialist motorcycle engineer.

13 Install the breather plate, then apply a suitable non-permanent thread locking compound to the threads of the bolts and tighten them to the torque setting specified at the beginning of this Chapter. Fit the crankcase breather cover using a new cover and tighten its bolts to the specified torque.

14 Lightly grease the new O-rings for the oil gallery plugs and fit the plugs, tightening them securely.

16 Lightly grease the O-rings on the oil feed pipe **(see illustration 28.2b)**. Fit the pipe, locating the tab on the outer end in the cut-out in the crankcase **(see illustration)**.

17 Install the remaining components in the reverse order of removal.

Cylinder bores

18 Check the cylinder walls carefully for scratches and score marks.

19 Using telescoping gauges and a micrometer (see *Tools and Workshop Tips*), check the dimensions of each cylinder to assess the amount of wear, taper and ovality. Measure near the top (but below the level of the top piston ring at TDC), the centre and bottom (but above the level of the oil ring at

BDC) of the bore. Measure both parallel to and across the crankshaft axis in each case and calculate the average cylinder dimension at each point **(see illustrations)**. Compare the results to the specifications at the beginning of this Chapter.

20 If the precision measuring tools are not available, take the crankcase to a Yamaha dealer or specialist motorcycle engineer for assessment and advice.

21 If the cylinders are worn beyond the service limit, or badly scratched, scuffed or scored, replace the crankcases with a new set. The cylinders cannot be rebored. If new crankcases are fitted, new pistons and rings must be used.

29 Running-in procedure

1 Make sure the engine oil and coolant levels are correct (see *Pre-ride checks*).

2 Make sure there is fuel in the tank.

3 Turn the ignition 'ON' and check that the oil level warning light and the engine management warning light come on for a few seconds and then go off. Ensure that the transmission is in neutral and that the neutral light is illuminated.

4 Start the engine, then allow it to run at a moderately fast idle until it reaches normal operating temperature.

5 As no oil pressure warning light is fitted, an oil pressure check is advised (see Section 3).

6 If a lubrication failure is suspected, stop the engine immediately and try to find the cause. If an engine is run without oil, even for a short period of time, severe damage will occur. After running the rebuilt engine for 600 miles (1000 km), change the engine oil and filter (see Chapter 1).

7 Check carefully that there are no oil or

coolant leaks and make sure the transmission and controls, especially the brakes and clutch, work properly before road testing the machine.

8 Treat the machine gently for the first few miles to allow the oil to circulate throughout the engine and any new parts installed to seat.

9 Great care is necessary if the engine has been extensively overhauled – the bike will have to be run in as when new. This means more use of the transmission and a restraining hand on the throttle until at least 600 miles (1000 km) have been covered. There is no point in keeping to any set road speed, the main idea is to keep from labouring the engine and to gradually increase performance up to the 1000 mile (1600 km) mark. These recommendations apply less when only a partial overhaul has been done, though it does depend to an extent on the nature of the work carried out and which components have been renewed. Experience is the best guide, since it is easy to tell when an engine is running freely. If in any doubt, consult a Yamaha dealer. The following maximum engine speed limitations, which Yamaha provide for new motorcycles, can be used as a guide.

Up to 600 miles (1000 km)
Do not exceed 5800 rpm
600 to 1000 miles (1000 to 1600 km)
Vary throttle position/speed. Do not exceed 7000 rpm for long periods
Over 1000 miles (1600 km)
Normal riding. Do not exceed tachometer red line

10 Upon completion of the road test, and after the engine has cooled down completely, recheck the valve clearances (see Chapter 1) and check the engine oil and coolant levels (see *Pre-ride checks*).

Chapter 3
Cooling system

Contents

Degrees of difficulty

Easy, suitable for novice with little experience ✎	**Fairly easy,** suitable for beginner with some experience ✎	**Fairly difficult,** suitable for competent DIY mechanic ✎	**Difficult,** suitable for experienced DIY mechanic ✎	**Very difficult,** suitable for expert DIY or professional ✎

Specifications

Coolant

Coolant type	Pre-mixed coolant for motorcycle engines, or a mixture of 50% distilled water and 50% ethylene glycol anti-freeze with corrosion inhibitors for aluminium engines. *Note that Yamaha specify that soft tap water can be used, but NOT hard water. If in doubt, boil the water first or use only distilled water.*

Coolant capacity
Radiator and all passages	2.0 litres
Reservoir	0.25 litre

Radiator

Cap valve opening pressure	13.2 to 17.8 psi (0.9 to 1.2 Bar)

Coolant temperature sensor

Resistance @ 0°C	5.21 to 6.37 K-ohms
Resistance @ 10°C	approx. 4 K-ohms
Resistance @ 20°C	approx 2.5 K-ohms
Resistance @ 80°C	290 to 354 ohms

Thermostat

Opening temperature	71 to 85°C
Valve lift	8 mm @ 85°C

Water pump

Impeller shaft tilt (max.)	0.15 mm

Torque wrench settings

Coolant inlet union bolts	10 Nm
Coolant temperature sensor	18 Nm
Radiator mounting bolts	7 Nm
Thermostat cover bolts	12 Nm
Water pump cover/drain bolts	10 Nm
Water pump mounting bolts	10 Nm

1 General information

The cooling system uses a water/antifreeze mixture to carry excess heat away from the engine. The cylinders are surrounded by a water jacket, through which the coolant is circulated by a water pump. The water pump is driven by the oil pump, which is driven by chain and sprockets off the back of the clutch.

Heated coolant rises through the system to a thermostat on the back of the cylinder head, and then to the radiator. It flows across the radiator, where it is cooled by the airflow, then down to the water pump and back into the engine, where the cycle is repeated. The thermostat is fitted in the system to prevent the coolant flowing through the radiator when the engine is cold, therefore accelerating the speed at which the engine reaches normal operating temperature.

A coolant temperature sensor is fitted into the back of the cylinder head, and provides signals for the coolant temperature display on the instrument panel and for the ECU as part of the engine management system.

A relay-controlled cooling fan is fitted behind the radiator, to aid cooling in extreme conditions. The relay is controlled by a signal from the ECU.

Some coolant is routed from the engine through the fast idle unit on the throttle bodies then back to the radiator – when the coolant is cold the unit increases engine idle speed for fast warm-up.

The complete cooling system is partially sealed and pressurised, the pressure being controlled by a spring-loaded valve contained in the radiator cap. By pressurising the coolant the boiling point is raised, preventing premature boiling in adverse conditions. The overflow hose from the system is connected to a reservoir mounted on the front of the engine, into which excess coolant is expelled under pressure. The discharged coolant automatically returns to the radiator when the engine cools.

⚠️ *Warning: Do not remove the pressure cap from the radiator when the engine is hot. Scalding hot coolant and steam may be blown out under pressure and could cause serious injury. When the engine has cooled, place a thick rag such as a towel over the pressure cap; slowly rotate the cap anti-clockwise to the first stop. This procedure allows any residual pressure to escape. When the pressure has stopped escaping, press down on the cap while turning it anti-clockwise, and remove it.*
Do not allow antifreeze to come into contact with your skin, or painted surfaces of the motorcycle. Rinse off any spills immediately with plenty of water. Antifreeze is highly toxic if ingested. Never leave antifreeze lying around in an open container or in puddles on the floor; children and pets are attracted by its sweet smell and may

drink it. Check with the local authorities about disposing of used antifreeze. Many communities will have collection centres which will see that antifreeze is disposed of safely.
Caution: At all times use the specified type of antifreeze, and always mix it with distilled water in the correct proportion. The antifreeze contains corrosion inhibitors which are essential to avoid damage to the cooling system. A lack of these inhibitors could lead to a build-up of corrosion which will block the coolant passages inside the engine, resulting in overheating and severe engine damage. Distilled water should be used as opposed to tap water to avoid a build-up of scale which would also block the passages. Alternatively purchase pre-mixed motorcycle coolant.

Read the *Safety first!* section of this manual carefully before starting work.

2 Radiator

Removal

⚠️ *Warning: The engine must be completely cool before carrying out this procedure.*

1 On XJ6-N models remove the side covers, on XJ6-S models remove the fairing side panels, and on XJ6-F and FZ6R models remove the lower fairing panels (see Chapter 7).
2 Drain the cooling system (see Chapter 1).
3 Remove the fuel tank and the air filter housing (see Chapter 4).
4 Trace the wiring from the cooling fan motor on the back of the radiator and disconnect it at the black connector **(see illustration)**. Release the wiring from the tie and feed it to the radiator **(see illustration)**.
5 Release the clamps securing the hoses on each side of the radiator, then detach the hoses, noting which fits where **(see illustrations)**.
6 On machines fitted with ABS, undo the bolt securing the brake pipes to the support bracket on the left-hand end of the radiator **(see illustration)**.

2.4a Cooling fan wiring connector (arrowed)

2.4b Release the cable-tie (arrowed) and draw the wiring out

2.6 Unscrew the bolt (arrowed)

2.5a Release the clamps (arrowed)...

2.5b ...on each side, and detach the hoses

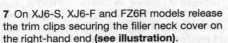

2.7 Release the trim clips (arrowed)

2.8 Unscrew the bolts (arrowed)...

2.9 ...then displace the radiator from the lug (arrowed)

7 On XJ6-S, XJ6-F and FZ6R models release the trim clips securing the filler neck cover on the right-hand end **(see illustration)**.

8 Unscrew the radiator mounting bolts, and on ABS models remove the brake pipe support bracket **(see illustration)**.

9 Carefully move the radiator to the right to free its grommet from the frame lug, and remove it **(see illustration)**.

10 If necessary, remove the cooling fan (see Section 4).

11 Check the radiator for signs of damage and clear any dirt or debris that might obstruct airflow and inhibit cooling. Radiator fins can be straightened carefully with a flat-bladed screwdriver, but if the fins are badly damaged or broken the radiator must be replaced with a new one. Remove the two collars for the mounting bolts and check the three mounting grommets, and replace them with new ones if necessary **(see illustration)**.

Installation

12 Installation is the reverse of removal, noting the following.

- Make sure the two collars for the mounting bolts are fitted in the grommets **(see illustration 2.11)**. Tighten the bolts to the torque setting specified at the beginning of this Chapter.
- Where fitted make sure the ABS pipe support bracket and filler neck cover are correctly fitted **(see illustrations 2.6 and 2.7)**.
- Make sure the coolant hoses are in good condition (see Chapter 1), and are securely

retained by their clamps – use new clamps if necessary (see Step 5).

- Make sure that the wiring is correctly routed and the connector is secure **(see illustrations 2.4b and a)**.
- Refill the cooling system as described in Chapter 1.

Radiator pressure cap

13 If problems such as overheating or loss of coolant occur, check the entire system as described in Chapter 1. The radiator cap opening pressure should be checked by a Yamaha dealer with the special tester required for the job. If the cap is defective, replace it with a new one.

3 Coolant reservoir

Removal

1 Remove the exhaust system (see Chapter 4).

2 Release the reservoir cap and draw out the end of the radiator overflow hose **(see illustration)**.

3 Unscrew the reservoir mounting bolts and remove the reservoir and its cover **(see illustration 3.2)**. Tip the coolant out of the reservoir into a suitable container.

4 If required, release the clip securing the radiator overflow hose from the union on the filler neck **(see illustration 2.5a)**. Release the

hose from the guide on the timing rotor cover and remove the hose, noting its routing **(see illustration)**.

Installation

5 Installation is the reverse of removal, noting the following:

- Make sure the breather hose and the overflow hose are correctly routed and secured.
- Fill the reservoir with the specified coolant up to the correct level (see *Pre-ride checks*).

4 Cooling fan and cooling fan relay

Note: *For circuit testing, refer to Section 2 in Chapter 8, and to the wiring diagram for your model at the end of Chapter 8.*

Cooling fan

Check

1 If the engine is overheating and the coolant temperature display flashes and the coolant temperature warning light is on, yet the cooling fan isn't cutting in, first check the fan fuse in the fusebox (see Chapter 8). If the fuse is good, make sure there is battery voltage at the red wire to the fuse with the ignition OFF. If there is no voltage check the red wire for continuity from the fan fuse to the main fuse.

2 If the fan fuse is good, remove the right-hand rear cowl (see Chapter 7). Check that voltage

2.11 Make sure the grommets (arrowed) are in good condition

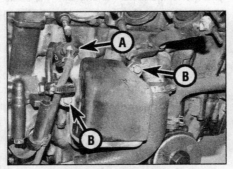

3.2 Reservoir cap (A) and mounting bolts (B)

3.4 Release the hose (arrowed) from behind the guide

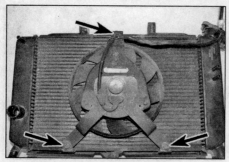

4.6 Cooling fan screws (arrowed)

4.8 Cooling fan relay (arrowed)

is present at the brown/black wire to the fan relay with the ignition OFF, and at the red/white wire to the relay when the ignition is ON **(see illustration 4.14)**. If there is voltage, the fault lies in either the wiring and connectors between the relay and the fan, the cooling fan motor or the fan relay (see below). If not check the circuit between the cooling fan relay and the ignition switch, referring to the wiring diagram for your model (see Chapter 8).

3 To test the cooling fan motor, remove the fuel tank and the air filter housing (see Chapter 4).

4 Trace the wiring from the fan motor and disconnect it at the connector **(see illustration 2.4a)**. Using a 12 volt battery and two jumper wires, connect the positive (+) battery lead to the blue wire terminal on the fan side of the wiring connector and the negative (–) lead to the black wire terminal. Once connected, the fan should operate. If it does not, and the wiring between the connector and the fan is good, then the fan motor is faulty. Replace the fan assembly with a new one – individual components are not available.

Removal and installation

 Warning: The engine must be completely cool before carrying out this procedure.

5 Remove the radiator (see Section 2).

6 Undo the fan screws and remove the fan **(see illustration)**.

7 Installation is the reverse of removal.

Cooling fan relay

8 Remove the right-hand rear cowl (see Chapter 7). If not already done, refer to Step 2 and check the power to the relay **(see illustration)**.

9 If the voltage is good, disconnect the fan relay wiring connector. Set a multimeter to the ohms x 1 scale and connect the positive (+) probe to the brown/black wire terminal on the relay, and the negative (-) probe to the blue wire terminal. There should be no continuity (infinite resistance).

10 Using a fully-charged 12 volt battery and two insulated jumper wires, connect the positive (+) battery terminal to the red/white wire terminal on the relay, and the negative (–) battery terminal to the green/yellow wire terminal. At this point the relay should be

heard to click and the multimeter should read 0 ohms (continuity).

11 If this is the case, the relay is proved good. If there is continuity through the relay at all times, or if the relay does not click when battery voltage is applied and indicates no continuity (infinite resistance) across its terminals, it is faulty and must be replaced with a new one.

12 If the relay is good, test the fan motor (if not already done), and the coolant temperature sensor (see Section 5), then if necessary check the wiring and connectors between the relay, the fan motor and the ECU.

5 Coolant temperature display and sensor

Temperature display

Check

1 The circuit consists of the sensor mounted in the back of the cylinder head and the coolant temperature display and warning light on the instrument cluster.

2 The temperature display and warning light should function as follows: when the ignition switch is turned ON, all the segments of the temperature display should appear and the warning light should come for a few seconds as a test of the circuit. When the engine is cold (below 40°C), 'LO' will be shown. Between 40°C and 116°C the actual temperature will be displayed. Between 117°C and 134°C the actual temperature will be displayed flashing, and the temperature warning light will come

5.8 Coolant temperature sensor wiring connector (arrowed)

on. Above 134°C 'HI' will be displayed flashing, and the temperature warning light be on.

3 If the temperature display begins flashing and the temperature warning light comes on, the coolant is over-heating – turn the engine OFF immediately. When the engine has cooled, check the coolant level (see *Pre-ride checks*). If the level is low, check the cooling system for leaks (see Chapter 1, Section 9). If insufficient coolant is not the cause of the over-heating, check the thermostat (see Section 6).

4 If the temperature display malfunctions, first check the ignition fuse and the back-up fuse in the fusebox (see Chapter 8). If the fuses are good, check the wiring and connections between the sensor and the ECU, then between the ECU and the instrument cluster, and between the fuses and the instrument cluster. If required, the operation of the temperature sensor can be checked as described below.

5 If no problems are found, take the instrument cluster to a Yamaha dealer for further assessment – Yamaha provide no specific test data for the instruments themselves. If there are any faults, a new cluster will have to be fitted, as no individual components are available.

Removal and installation

6 Refer to Chapter 8, Section 16, for removal and installation details.

Coolant temperature sensor

Check

7 The sensor is mounted in the back of the cylinder head, below the throttle bodies **(see illustration 5.8)**. The resistance of the sensor changes with changes in temperature – see the Specifications at the beginning of the chapter. While in theory it is possible to bench-test the sensor at those temperatures, in practice the test is difficult to set up and perform. However you can test the resistance of the sensor in the bike with the engine cold, warm and hot.

8 Remove the fuel tank, and if required for best access the throttle bodies (see Chapter 4). If you don't remove the throttle bodies, disconnect the sensor wiring connector **(see illustration)**. Check that the sensor is tight in the cylinder head

9 Connect the probes of a multimeter set to read resistance to the terminals on the sensor and take several readings as the engine warms up **(see illustration)**. Resistance

5.9 Connect the meter probes to the sensor terminals (arrowed)

6.3 Unscrew the bolts (arrowed), detach the cover...

6.4 ...and remove the thermostat (arrowed)

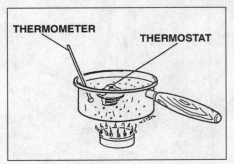

6.7 Thermostat testing set-up

should decrease as temperature increases – if the sensor fails it is most likely to give a zero, constant, or infinite resistance reading at all temperatures.

10 If the meter readings obtained are widely different the sensor is faulty and must be replaced with a new one.

Removal and installation

 Warning: The engine must be completely cool before carrying out this procedure.

11 Drain the cooling system (see Chapter 1). Remove the throttle bodies (see Chapter 4).

12 Disconnect the sensor wiring connector, then unscrew the sensor from the head **(see illustration 5.8)**. Remove the sealing washer – a new one must be used.

13 Fit the sensor using a new sealing washer and tighten it to the torque setting specified at the beginning of this Chapter.

14 Install the throttle bodies (see Chapter 4) and fill the cooling system (see Chapter 1).

6 Thermostat

 Warning: The engine must be completely cool before carrying out this procedure.

1 The thermostat is automatic in operation and should give many years' service without requiring attention. In the event of a failure, the valve will probably jam open, in which case the engine will take much longer than normal

to warm up. Conversely, if the valve jams shut, the coolant will be unable to circulate and the engine will quickly overheat. Neither condition is acceptable, and the fault must be investigated promptly.

Removal

2 Drain the cooling system (see Chapter 1). Remove the throttle bodies (see Chapter 4).

3 Unscrew the thermostat cover bolts and remove the cover, being prepared to catch any residual coolant **(see illustration)**.

4 Lift the thermostat out of the cylinder head, noting how it fits **(see illustration)**.

5 Inspect the cover for cracks and corrosion, especially around the hose union. If required slacken the hose clamp and pull the cover out of the hose, and clean off any corrosion with a wire brush or steel wool.

Check

6 Examine the thermostat visually before carrying out the test. If it remains in the open position at room temperature, it should be replaced with a new one. Check the condition of the seal around the rim. If it is damaged or has deteriorated, or there has been leakage from the thermostat cover, fit a new thermostat – the seal is not available separately.

7 To check the operation of the thermostat, suspend it in a container of cold water. Place a thermometer capable of reading temperatures up to 100°C in the water so that the bulb is close to the thermostat **(see illustration)**.

8 Heat the water whilst stirring it gently, noting the temperature when the thermostat

opens, and compare the result with the specifications given at the beginning of this Chapter. Also check the amount the valve opens after it has been heated at 85°C for a few minutes and compare the measurement to the specifications. If the readings obtained differ from those given, the thermostat is faulty and must be replaced with a new one.

9 In the event of the thermostat jamming closed, *as an emergency measure only*, it can be removed and the machine used without it. **Note:** *Take care when starting the engine from cold, as it will take much longer than usual to warm up. Ensure that a new unit is installed as soon as possible.*

Installation

10 Fit the thermostat into the cylinder head, making sure that it seats correctly and that the breather hole is at the top **(see illustration 6.4)**.

11 Clean the threads of the cover bolts and apply some fresh threadlock, then fit the cover and tighten the bolts to the torque setting specified at the beginning of the Chapter. If detached make sure the hose is pushed fully onto its union as far as the spigot, and tighten the clamp securely **(see illustration 6.3)**.

12 Install the throttle bodies (see Chapter 4) and fill the cooling system (see Chapter 1).

7 Water pump

Check

1 See Section 9 in Chapter 1.

Removal

2 Drain the coolant (see Chapter 1).

3 Release the clamps securing the hoses to the pump and detach the hoses, noting which fits where **(see illustration)**.

4 Unscrew the pump mounting bolts and draw the pump out of the crankcase **(see illustration)**.

5 Remove the O-ring on the back of the pump body – a new one must be used **(see illustration 7.22a)**.

6 If required unscrew the pump cover bolts and remove the cover **(see illustration 7.4)**.

7.3 Release the clamps (arrowed) and detach the hoses

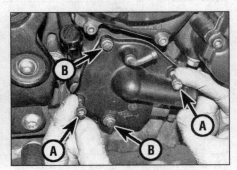

7.4 Pump mounting bolts (A), pump cover bolts (B)

7.8a Release the circlip...

7.8b ...and withdraw the impeller

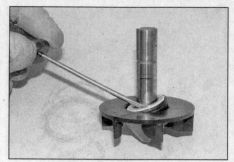

7.9a Remove the damper using a screwdriver...

7.9b ...and push the new one in with your fingers

7.13 Drive the mechanical seal out using a punch

Remove the seal – a new one must be used (see illustration 7.21a).

Inspection

7 To check the pump impeller bearing, wiggle the impeller back-and-forth and turn it by hand. If there is excessive movement, or the bearing is noisy or rough when turned, the bearing must be replaced with a new one.

8 Release the circlip on the inner end of the shaft and withdraw the impeller from the pump body (see illustrations). If there are signs of wear or other damage to the shaft or impeller, replace it with a new one. Check that the shaft is straight – if it tilts by more than the specified limit, replace it with a new one.

9 Check the condition of the rubber damper on the rear (inside) face of the impeller. If it is damaged or deteriorated, replace it with a new one (see illustrations) – it is not available on its own, but comes as a kit along with a mechanical seal.

10 Inspect the pump body for corrosion or a build-up of scale and clean with steel wool as necessary, then rinse the pump body in running clean water.

11 Lubricate the impeller shaft and damper with coolant and slide it into the pump body (see illustration 7.8b). Invert the pump so the impeller is on the work surface and push the pump down so the impeller compresses the mechanical seal and the circlip groove is

exposed, and fit a new circlip into the groove (see illustration 7.8a).

Seal and bearing renewal

Note: *Once removed, neither of the seals or the bearing can be re-used – they must be replaced with new ones.*

12 Remove the pump from the engine and the cover and impeller from the pump (Steps 2 to 6 and 8).

13 To remove the mechanical seal, drive it out using a suitable punch inserted through the bearing and oil seal and located against the inner rim of the seal (see illustration).

14 To remove the oil seal, first remove the mechanical seal (see Step 13). Lever the oil seal out using a flat-bladed screwdriver, noting which way round it fits (see illustration).

15 To remove the bearing, first remove the mechanical seal and the oil seal (see Steps 13 and 14). Drive the bearing out using a socket seated against the inner race (see illustration).

16 Clean any traces of sealant from around the mechanical seal seat with a suitable solvent.

17 Drive the new bearing into the pump body using a socket that bears on the outer race only until it is seated (see illustration).

18 Apply a smear of coolant to the outside of

7.14 Lever the oil seal out using a screwdriver

7.15 Drive the bearing out using a 13mm socket, supporting the pump on a 28mm socket as shown

7.17 Drive the new bearing in using a 20mm socket until seated

7.18a Push the new seal in...

7.18b ...so the drain is fully exposed

7.19a Position the new seal in the pump...

7.19b ...then seat a 25mm bi-hex ring spanner or socket over it as an interface and drive or press it in

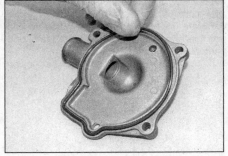

7.21a Fit a new O-ring into the groove...

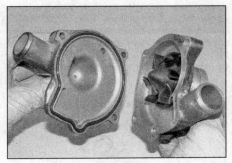

7.21b ...then fit the cover

the new oil seal. Press or drive the seal into the body until the drain hole is fully exposed **(see illustrations)**.

19 Smear Yamaha Bond 1215 or a suitable equivalent onto the mechanical seal seat. Press or carefully drive the new mechanical seal into the pump body using a suitable a 25mm bi-hex ring spanner or socket that bears only on the outer rim of the seal as an interface between the press or hammer head **(see illustrations)**. Alternatively Yamaha produce a special tool, Part No. 90890-04078

(European models) or YM-33221-A (US models), for installing the seal if required.
20 Refer to Step 9 and fit the new damper into the back of the impeller, then refer to Step 11 to fit the impeller.

Installation

21 Fit the new cover O-ring into its groove **(see illustration)**. Fit the cover and the cover bolts, fitting a new sealing washer to the bottom (drain) bolt **(see illustrations)**. Tighten the bolts to the torque setting specified at the beginning of this Chapter.

22 Fit a new pump body O-ring and smear it lightly with grease **(see illustration)**. Turn the impeller shaft as required to align the slot in its end with the drive tab on the end of the oil pump shaft **(see illustration)**. Fit the pump into the crankcase, locating the slot over the tab, and tighten the mounting bolts to the specified torque.

23 Connect the hoses and secure them with the clamps, using new ones if necessary **(see illustration 7.3)**. Refill the cooling system (see Chapter 1).

7.22a Fit a new O-ring (arrowed) into the groove...

7.22b ...and align the slot with the drive tab (arrowed)

8 Coolant hoses, pipes and unions

Removal

 Warning: Allow the engine to cool completely before disconnecting a coolant hose.

1 Before removing a hose, pipe or union, drain the coolant (see Chapter 1). **Note:** *When removing components of the cooling system, be prepared to catch any residual fluids.*

2 Use a screwdriver to slacken the larger-bore hose clamps **(see illustration 7.3)**. Slide the clamp back along the hose and clear of the union spigot, then pull the hose off the union. The smaller-bore hoses are secured by spring clips, which can be expanded by squeezing their ears together with pliers.
Caution: The radiator unions are fragile. Do not use excessive force when attempting to remove the hoses.

3 If a hose proves stubborn, release it by rotating it on its union before working it off. If all else fails, cut the hose with a sharp knife then slit it at each union so that it can be peeled off in two pieces. Whilst this means renewing the hose, it is preferable to buying a new radiator.

4 Remove the union on the front of the engine by detaching the hose, then unscrewing the union bolts **(see illustration)**. Remove the O-ring – a new one must be used.

Installation

5 Slide the clip onto the hose and then work the hose onto its union, up against the spigot where present.

6 Rotate the hose on its union to settle it in position before sliding the clip into place and tightening it securely.

7 If the union on the engine has been

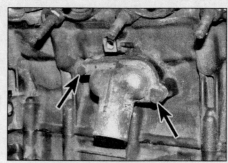

8.4 Coolant inlet union bolts (arrowed)

removed, fit a new O-ring into the groove and smear it with grease. Clean the threads of the bolts and apply some fresh threadlock, then fit the union and tighten the bolts to the torque setting specified at the beginning of the Chapter.

Chapter 4
Engine management system

Contents

Degrees of difficulty

Easy, suitable for novice with little experience	**Fairly easy,** suitable for beginner with some experience	**Fairly difficult,** suitable for competent DIY mechanic	**Difficult,** suitable for experienced DIY mechanic	**Very difficult,** suitable for expert DIY or professional

Specifications

General information

Cylinder numbering	1 to 4 from left to right
Ignition timing	6.5° BTDC @ 1300 rpm
Spark plugs	see Chapter 1

Component test data

AIS solenoid valve resistance	20.0 to 24.0 ohms @ 20°C
AIS reed valve bending limit	0.4 mm (max)
Crankshaft position sensor resistance	248 to 372 ohms @ 20°C
Coolant temperature sensor	
Resistance @ 0°C	5.21 to 6.37 K-ohms
Resistance @ 10°C	approx. 4 K-ohms
Resistance @ 20°C	approx. 2.5 K-ohms
Resistance @ 80°C	290 to 354 ohms
Fuel level sensor resistance	
Fuel tank full	19 to 21 ohms
Fuel tank empty	139 to 141 ohms
Fuel pump pressure	36.3 psi (2.5 Bar)
Intake air pressure sensor output voltage	3.594 to 3.684 V
Intake air temperature sensor resistance	
Resistance @ 0°C	5.4 to 6.6 K-ohms
Resistance @ 80°C	290 to 390 ohms
Speed sensor output voltage	
On	5V
Off	0V
Throttle position sensor	
Resistance (max)	1.75 to 3.25 K-ohms @ 20°C
Output voltage (at idle)	0.63 to 0.73V
Lean angle sensor output voltage	
Sensor upright	0.4 to 1.4 V
Sensor tilted at 65°	3.7 to 4.4 V

Fuel

Grade	Unleaded, minimum 95 RON (Research Octane Number)
Fuel tank capacity (including reserve)	17.3 litres
Reserve	3.2 litres

Throttle bodies

Type	1 x Mikuni 32EIDW
Throttle valve size.	# 50
Intake vacuum	see Chapter 1

Fuel injector

Manufacturer	DENSO
Type/quantity	0290/4

Ignition coils

Primary resistance	1.53 to 2.07 ohms @ 20°C
Secondary resistance.	12.0 to 18.0 K-ohms @ 20°C
Minimum spark gap	6 mm
Spark plug cap resistance	10.0 K-ohms @ 20°C

Torque wrench settings

Crankshaft position sensor bolts	10 Nm
Exhaust header pipe nuts.	20 Nm
Exhaust mounting bolts	20 Nm
Fuel pump bolts	4 Nm
Intake duct bolts.	10 Nm
Oxygen sensor	15 Nm
Timing rotor cover bolts	10 Nm

1 General information and precautions

General information

All models are fitted with a fully electronic engine management system that controls both the fuelling and ignition from one engine control unit, or ECU.

Fuel system

The fuel system consists of the fuel tank, inside of which is located the fuel pump with integral filter and fuel level sensor, the fuel supply hose, the fuel injectors and throttle body assembly, and the throttle cables. Air is drawn into the throttle bodies via an air filter, which is housed under the fuel tank.

The fuel pump is activated initially by the ignition switch, and fuel pressure is controlled by a regulator in the pump.

To aid cold starting and engine warm-up, a fast idle unit that responds to the temperature of the engine coolant is fitted to the throttle body assembly.

In the event of the machine falling over, a lean angle sensor cuts power to the fuel and ignition systems.

The fuel injection system is controlled by the engine control unit (ECU), which monitors data sent from the various system sensors and adjusts fuel delivery to the engine and ignition timing accordingly. The ECU has its own fault diagnosis function and displays fault codes and diagnostic codes on the LCD display in the instrument cluster.

The exhaust is an underslung four-into-one design and incorporates a catalytic converter and an oxygen sensor. An air induction system (AIS) introduces filtered air into the exhaust ports to promote the burning of excess fuel in the exhaust gases to reduce harmful emissions.

Ignition system

The ignition system consists of the timing rotor, crankshaft position sensor (CKP sensor), the engine control unit (ECU) and ignition coils.

The timing rotor on the right-hand end of the crankshaft generates a signal in the CKP sensor as the crankshaft rotates. The CKP sensor sends that signal to the ECU, which, in conjunction with data sent from the various other system sensors, calculates the best ignition timing and supplies the ignition coils with the power necessary to produce a spark at the plugs. There is no provision for adjusting the ignition timing.

The system incorporates a starter safety circuit that will cut the ignition if the sidestand is extended whilst the engine is running and in gear, or if a gear is selected whilst the engine is running and the sidestand is extended. It also prevents the engine from being started if the engine is in gear unless the clutch lever is pulled in and the stand is up.

Models sold in certain markets are fitted with an immobiliser system, which will not allow the engine to be started unless the correct key is used. The immobiliser system has its own fault diagnosis function. An alarm system is available as an optional extra.

Note: *Individual engine management system components can be checked but not repaired if faulty. If system troubles occur,* *and the faulty component can be isolated, the only cure for the problem in most cases is to replace the part with a new one. Keep in mind that most electronic parts, once purchased, cannot be returned. To avoid unnecessary expense, make very sure the faulty component has been positively identified before buying a new part.*

Precautions

⚠ *Warning: Petrol (gasoline) is extremely flammable, so take extra precautions when you work on any part of the fuel system. Don't smoke or allow open flames or bare light bulbs near the work area, and don't work in a garage where a natural gas-type appliance is present. If you spill any fuel on your skin, rinse it off immediately with soap and water. When you perform any kind of work on the fuel system, wear safety glasses and have a fire extinguisher suitable for a class B type fire (flammable liquids) on hand.*

● Always perform service procedures in a well-ventilated area to prevent a build-up of fumes.
● Never work in a building containing a gas appliance with a pilot light, or any other form of naked flame. Ensure that there are no naked light bulbs or any sources of flame or sparks nearby.
● Do not smoke (or allow anyone else to smoke) while in the vicinity of petrol (gasoline), or of components containing petrol. Remember the possible presence of vapour from these sources and move well clear before smoking.
● Check all electrical equipment belonging to the house, garage or workshop where

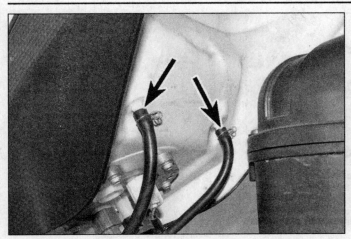

2.4a Partially raise the tank and disconnect the hoses (arrowed)...

2.4b ...then raise it fully and support it as shown

work is being undertaken (see the Safety First! section of this manual). Remember that certain electrical appliances such as drills, cutters, etc, create sparks in the normal course of operation and must not be used near petrol (gasoline) or any component containing it. Again, remember the possible presence of fumes before using electrical equipment.

● Always mop up any spilt fuel and safely dispose of the rag used.

● Any stored fuel that is drained off during servicing work must be kept in sealed containers that are suitable for holding petrol (gasoline), and clearly marked as such; the containers themselves should be kept in a safe place. Note that this last point applies equally to the fuel tank if it is removed from the machine; also remember to keep its filler cap closed at all times.

● Read the Safety first! section of this manual carefully before starting work.

2 Fuel tank

Warning: Refer to the precautions given in Section 1 before starting work.

Removal

Note: To reduce the weight of the tank remove it when it is nearly empty, or if the tank is full siphon the fuel into a suitable container using a hand pump (available from tool suppliers).

1 Make sure the fuel filler cap is secure. Remove the seat(s) (see Chapter 7). On XJ6-N models remove the side covers, on XJ6-S, XJ6-F and FZ6R models remove the cockpit side panels (see Chapter 7).

2 Loosen but do not remove the bolt securing the rear of the tank.

3 Unscrew the bolts securing the front of the tank.

4 Raise the tank at the front and disconnect the breather and overflow hoses **(see illustration)**. Raise the tank some more and support it using a piece of wood as shown **(see illustration)**.

5 Disconnect the fuel pump (green) and fuel level sensor (white) wiring connectors **(see illustration)**.

6 Remove the cover from the fuel hose connector, then slide the security clip down, press in the two tabs on the connector and pull it off the union **(see illustrations)**. Have a rag ready to catch any residual fuel from the hose.

7 Remove the support and lower the tank. Remove the bolt securing the rear of the tank, then carefully lift the tank off the frame **(see illustration)**. Support the tank on a block of

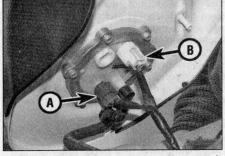

2.5 Fuel pump wiring connector (A – green), fuel level sensor connector (B – white)

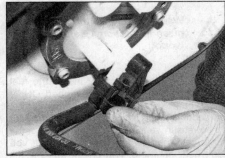

2.6a Remove the cover...

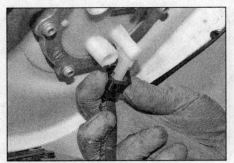

2.6b ...press the tabs in...

2.6c ...and pull the hose connector off

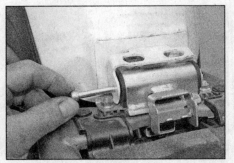

2.7 Withdraw the rear bolt and remove the tank

wood so it does not rest on the underside of the fuel pump.

8 Inspect the tank support and mounting bolt rubbers for signs of damage or deterioration and replace them with new ones if necessary.

Installation

9 Installation is the reverse of removal, noting the following:
● Make sure the mounting rubbers are in place.
● Make sure the hoses are properly attached and secured by their clamps. Make sure the wiring connectors are secure.
● Start the engine and check that there are no fuel leaks. If the tank has been emptied, make sure it is refilled before turning the ignition switch ON.

Repair

10 All repairs to the fuel tank should be carried out by a professional who has experience in this critical and potentially dangerous work. Even after cleaning and flushing of the fuel system, explosive fumes can remain and ignite during repair of the tank.

11 If the fuel tank is removed from the bike, it should not be placed in an area where sparks or open flames could ignite the fumes coming out of the tank. Be especially careful inside garages where a natural gas-type appliance is located, because the pilot light could cause an explosion.

3 Fuel pump and pressure regulator

⚠ **Warning: Refer to the precautions given in Section 1 before starting work.**

Check

1 The fuel pump is located inside the fuel tank. When the ignition is switched ON, it should be possible to hear the pump run for a few seconds until the system is up to pressure – the pressure regulator, an integral part of the pump, will then switch the pump off. If you can't hear anything, first check that the kill switch is set to run and the battery is not flat,

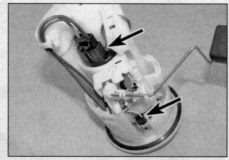

3.3 Check the internal wiring and connectors (arrowed)

then check the main, ignition and fuel injection system fuses.

2 Next, check the fuel injection system relay (see Section 8). If they are good, check the wiring and terminals in the circuit for physical damage or loose or corroded connections and rectify as necessary (see the *Wiring Diagrams* at the end of Chapter 8).

3 If the pump still will not run, make sure the ignition switch is OFF, then raise the fuel tank and disconnect the pump (green) wiring connector (see Section 2). Connect the positive (+) lead from a fully charged battery to the red/blue wire terminal in the connector and the negative (-) lead to the black wire terminal – the pump should run. If it does there is a fault in the wiring circuit to the pump. If it doesn't, remove the pump and check the internal wiring **(see illustration)**. If the wiring is good replace the pump with a new one.

Fuel pressure check

Special tools: *A fuel pressure gauge with an appropriate adapter is required for this procedure.*

4 Fuel pressure is governed by a regulator that is an integral part of the fuel pump.

5 Raise the fuel tank, then disconnect the fuel supply hose from the fuel tank (see Section 2). Connect the adapter and fuel pressure gauge between the fuel tank and the fuel hose. Yamaha can provide a gauge (Pt. No. 90890-03153 in Europe, YU-03153 in the US)

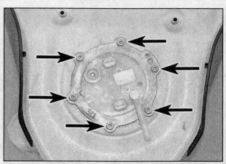

3.10 Fuel pump retaining ring bolts (arrowed)

and gauge adapter (Pt. No. 90890-03176 or YM 03176) for this purpose.

6 Start the engine and note the pressure recorded on the gauge – it should be similar to that given in the specifications at the beginning of this Chapter. Stop the engine.

7 If the pressure is not as specified, make sure the fuel hose has not become kinked. If the hose is in good condition, a new pump will have to be fitted – individual components are not available. Note that the fuel filter is an integral part of the fuel pump.

Removal and installation

8 Siphon the fuel from the tank into a suitable container using a hand-pump, available from good tool and DIY stores.

9 Remove the fuel tank (see Section 2), and lay it upside down on plenty of clean rag.

10 Unscrew the pump retaining ring bolts and remove the ring, noting how it fits **(see illustration)**.

11 Carefully lift the pump and manoeuvre it out of the tank. On the model photographed it was found that there was not quite enough clearance for the level sensor float arm rest to clear the rim; it was necessary to carefully bend it using a screwdriver in order to get the pump out **(see illustration)**.

12 Remove the sealing ring **(see illustration)** - a new one must be fitted.

13 Fit a new sealing ring flat side down onto the pump base **(see illustration)**.

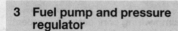

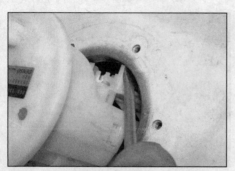

3.11 Carefully remove the pump, using gentle leverage if required

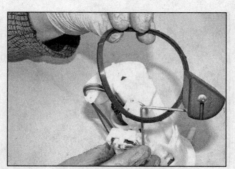

3.12 Remove the sealing ring

3.13 Fit the new sealing ring with the shaped side facing up

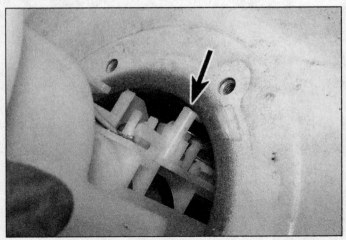

3.14 Carefully fit the pump, taking care with the float arm rest (arrowed)

3.15 Align the pump and ring as shown and fit the cut-out in the ring over the stud (arrowed)

14 Manoeuvre the pump into the aperture in the tank **(see illustration)**.

15 Align the pump so the fuel supply hose union points to the back, and align the cut-out in the retaining ring with the stud on the underside of the pump **(see illustration)**. Tighten the bolts evenly and in a criss-cross sequence to the torque setting specified at the beginning of this Chapter.

4 Fuel level display and sensor

Fuel level display
Check

1 The circuit consists of the sensor mounted inside the fuel tank and the fuel level display that is part of the multi-function display in the instrument cluster.

2 The fuel level display should function as follows. When the ignition switch is turned ON, all the segments of the display should appear in sequence as a test of the circuit. Then, depending upon how much fuel is in the tank, the requisite number of segments between 'F' (full) and 'E' (empty) will be shown.

3 When the fuel content in the tank falls to approx. 3.2 litres, the E segment on the display begins flashing and the odometer display automatically changes to fuel reserve trip meter mode.

4 If required, the trip meter can be reset using the SELECT button on the instrument cluster (see Chapter 8). Once the tank has been topped-up, the fuel reserve trip meter should reset automatically after the machine has travelled approx. 3 miles.

5 The fuel level display has its own self-diagnosis function. If it malfunctions, the display and the fuel symbol will flash eight times, then go out for three seconds, on a repeating cycle. First check the fuel level sensor wiring connector (white) on the underside of the tank (see Section 2), then check the wiring from the sensor to the instrument cluster, referring to Section 2 in Chapter 8 and to the wiring diagram for your model at the end of Chapter 8. If all is good, check the sensor as described below.

6 If no problems are found, take the instrument cluster to a Yamaha dealer for further assessment – Yamaha provide no specific test data for the instruments themselves. If there are any faults, a new cluster will have to be fitted, as no individual components are available.

Removal and installation

7 Refer to Chapter 8, Section 16.

Fuel level sensor

8 Remove the fuel pump from the tank (see Section 3).

9 Using an ohmmeter or multimeter set to the ohms x 10 scale, measure the resistance between the sensor terminals on the pump as shown, first with the sensor float in the empty position, and then held up in the full position **(see illustrations)**.

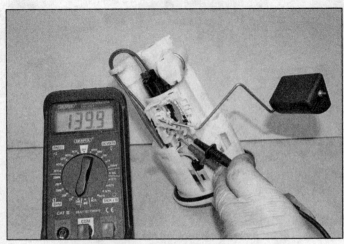

4.9a Measure the resistance in the empty position...

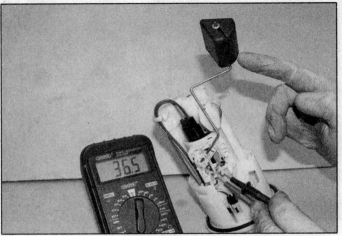

4.9b ...and the full position

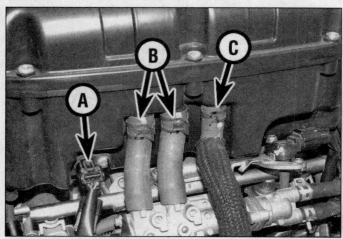

5.2a Disconnect the wiring connector (A), release the clamps (B)
and detach the breather hose (C)

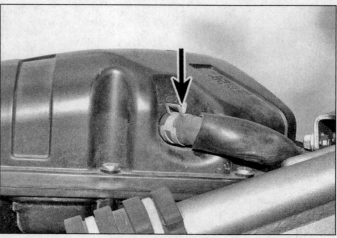

5.2b Detach the AIS hose (arrowed)

10 If the results are widely different from that specified at the beginning of this Chapter, the sensor is faulty and a new pump will have to be fitted – individual components are not available (see Section 3).

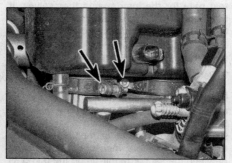

5.3 Slacken the clamp screws (arrowed)
on each side

5 Air filter housing

Removal

1 Remove the fuel tank (see Section 2).
2 Disconnect the air temperature sensor wiring connector (**see illustration**). Release the synchronising unit hose clamps and slide them down the hoses – the hoses will detach when you remove the housing. Release the crankcase breather hose clamp and detach the hose from the housing. Release the AIS hose clamp and detach the hose from the housing (**see illustration**).
3 Slacken the clamps on the underside

securing the housing to the throttle body intakes (**see illustration**).
4 Unscrew the bolt at the front, then lift the housing up off the throttle bodies (**see illustrations**).

Installation

5 Installation is the reverse of removal, noting the following:
● Check the condition of the various hoses and the clamps and replace them with new ones if necessary.
● Make sure that the clamps are correctly positioned over the tabs (**see illustration 5.3**).
● Lubricate the inside of the housing outlets with a squirt of WD40 or a smear of grease to aid installation on the throttle bodies.

5.4a Unscrew the bolt...

5.4b ...and remove the housing

6 Fuel injection system description

1 The fuel injection system consists of two main component groups, the fuel circuit and the electronic control circuit.
2 The fuel circuit consists of the tank, the integrated pump, filter and pressure regulator, the throttle bodies and the injectors. Fuel is pumped under pressure from the tank to the fuel rail, from which the individual injectors are fed. Operating pressure is maintained by the pressure regulator in the pump. The injectors spray pressurised fuel into the throttle bodies where it mixes with air and vaporises, before entering the cylinder where it is compressed and ignited.
3 The electronic control circuit consists of the ECU, which operates and co-ordinates both the fuel injection and ignition systems, and the various sensors which provide the ECU with information on engine operating conditions.
4 The ECU monitors signals from the following sensors:
  Intake air temperature sensor
  Intake air pressure sensor
  Throttle position sensor
  Crankshaft position sensor
  Coolant temperature sensor
  Oxygen sensor
  Speed sensor
  Lean angle sensor
5 Based on the information it receives, the ECU calculates the appropriate ignition and fuel requirements of the engine. By varying the length of the electronic pulse it sends to each injector, the ECU controls the length of time the injectors are held open and thereby the amount of fuel that is supplied to the engine. Fuel supply varies according to the engine's needs for starting, warming-up, idling, cruising and acceleration.
6 In the event of an abnormality in any of the sensor signals, the ECU will determine whether the engine can still be run safely. If it can, a back-up mode substitutes the sensor signal with a fixed signal, restricting performance but allowing the bike to be ridden home or to a dealer. When this occurs, the engine trouble warning light in the instrument cluster will come on and stay on. If the fault is serious, the fuel injection system will be shut down and the engine will not run. When this occurs, the engine trouble warning light will flash when the ignition switch is ON and the start button is being pressed. **Note:** *The warning light should come on for 1.4 seconds after the ignition switch has been turned ON and while the starter button is being pressed. If the warning light does not come on, check its LED circuit in the instrument cluster (see Chapter 8).*
7 After the engine has been stopped, the appropriate self-diagnostic fault code will appear instead of the clock on the instrument display. If more than one fault has occurred, the lowest code numerically will be displayed. See Section 7 for fault diagnosis.

7 Fuel injection system fault diagnosis

1 The system incorporates a self-diagnostic function whereby most faults, when they occur, are identified by a fault code, which is displayed on the clock LCD after the engine has been stopped. The codes are stored in the ECU memory until a deletion operation is performed. In the case of a minor fault in the injection system, the engine trouble warning light in the instrument cluster will come on and stay on and the engine will continue to run, enabling the machine to be ridden, although performance will be reduced. In the case of a major fault the warning light will flash when the ignition switch is turned ON and the start button is pressed, and it will not be possible to run the engine. Certain faults will not activate the warning light and are not subject to a fault code, but will be recorded as a diagnostic code. If the engine does not run correctly but no warning light and fault code are shown, enter diagnostic mode (see Step 3 onwards), check the code given and refer to the table.
2 Compare the fault code displayed with those in Table 1 to identify the faulty component and the appropriate diagnostic code (where given). Next, follow the appropriate steps and set the instrument cluster to diagnostic mode to confirm the appropriate test information. If a diagnostic code is not given for a particular fault code (i.e. 12 or 24), refer to Section 8 and check the component as described.

Table 1 Fuel system fault codes

Fault code	Faulty component – symptoms	Possible causes	Diagnostic code
12	Crankshaft position sensor – engine will stop and will not restart	Faulty wiring or wiring connector Damaged or improperly installed sensor or timing rotor Faulty ECU	-
13	Intake air pressure sensor – engine will run	Faulty wiring or wiring connector Damaged or faulty sensor Faulty ECU	03
14	Intake air pressure sensor hose system – engine will run	Kinked, clogged or detached hose Faulty ECU	03
15	Throttle position sensor – engine will run	Faulty wiring or wiring connector Damaged or improperly installed sensor Faulty ECU	01
16	Throttle position sensor – engine will run	Throttle position sensor stuck Faulty ECU	01
19	Sidestand switch – engine will not run	Faulty wiring or wiring connector Faulty ECU	20
21	Coolant temperature sensor – engine will run	Faulty wiring or wiring connector Damaged or improperly installed sensor Faulty ECU	06
22	Intake air temperature sensor – engine will run	Faulty wiring or wiring connector Damaged or improperly installed sensor Faulty ECU	05
24	Oxygen sensor – engine will run	Faulty wiring or wiring connector Damaged or improperly installed sensor Faulty ECU	-

Table 1 Fuel system fault codes (continued)

Fault code	Faulty component – symptoms	Possible causes	Diagnostic code
30	Lean angle sensor – engine will not run, fuel system turned OFF	Machine overturned Damaged or improperly installed sensor Faulty ECU	08
33	Ignition coil, Nos. 1 and 4 cylinders – engine will run dependent on how many cylinders are affected	Faulty primary wiring or wiring connector Damaged ignition coil Faulty component in ignition cut-off safety circuit Faulty ECU	30
34	Ignition coil, Nos. 2 and 3 cylinders – engine will run dependent on how many cylinders are affected	Faulty primary wiring or wiring connector Damaged ignition coil Faulty component in ignition cut-off safety circuit Faulty ECU	31
-	Fuel injector, Nos. 1 and 4 cylinders	Faulty wiring or wiring connector	36
-	Fuel injector, Nos. 2 and 3 cylinders	Faulty wiring or wiring connector	37
-	Air induction system cut-off valve	Faulty wiring or wiring connector	48
-	Starter safety cut-off relay	Faulty wiring or wiring connector Damaged relay	50
-	Radiator cooling fan relay	Faulty wiring or wiring connector Damaged relay	51
-	Headlight relay	Faulty wiring or wiring connector Damaged relay	52
41	Lean angle sensor – engine will not run	Faulty wiring or wiring connector Damaged sensor Faulty ECU	08
42	Speed sensor/neutral switch – engine will run	Damaged speed sensor/neutral switch Faulty wiring or wiring connector Faulty ECU	07/21
43	Power supply to the fuel pump or injectors – engine will run	Faulty wiring or wiring connector Faulty ECU	50
44	Carbon monoxide (CO) density reading/writing error – engine will run	Error writing CO adjustment value to EEPROM Faulty ECU	60
46	Power supply to fuel injection system – engine will run	Faulty charging system	-
50	ECU malfunction, fault code may not be displayed – engine will not run	ECU internal memory malfunction	-
Start unable warning	Engine warning light flashes when the ignition switch is ON and the start button is pushed	Error detected – refer to fault codes 12, 19, 30, 41 or 50	-
Er-1 Er-2 Er-3 Er-4	No communication or unreadable communication between ECU and instrument cluster – engine will not run	Faulty wiring or wiring connector Damaged instrument cluster Damaged ECU	-

Diagnostic mode set-up

3 To set-up the diagnostic mode, first ensure that the ignition switch is OFF and that the engine stop switch is OFF, then disconnect the fuel pump wiring connector (see Section 2).
4 Press the SELECT and RESET buttons on the instrument cluster simultaneously, then turn the ignition switch ON, keeping the SELECT and RESET buttons pressed for at least 8 seconds – all displays on the meter should disappear except for the clock, which will show 'di', and the tripmeter.

5 Confirm the selection of 'di' by pressing the SELECT and RESET buttons simultaneously for 2 seconds.
6 Turn the engine stop switch OFF.
7 Referring to Table 1 above, verify the diagnostic code that corresponds with the fault code originally displayed. Now press the SELECT or RESET button until the appropriate diagnostic code is displayed on the clock LCD. The SELECT button scrolls through the code numbers in ascending order, the RESET button scrolls through the numbers in descending order. The corresponding

operating data, as found, is displayed on the trip LCD.
8 Select the diagnostic code on Table 2, and the corresponding operating data, to identify the test action required. Note that in some instances it will be necessary to turn the engine stop switch ON to verify the operating data.
9 After each check the ignition switch must be turned OFF and the set-up procedure repeated for subsequent checks.
10 To cancel the diagnostic mode, turn the ignition switch OFF.

Table 2 Fuel system diagnostic codes and data

Diagnostic code	Action required	Data displayed
01	Check angle data displayed with throttle fully closed Check angle data displayed with throttle fully open	Fully closed – 15 to 17 Fully open – 97 to 100
03	Turn the engine stop switch ON and crank the engine using the starter motor to generate a pressure difference	10 to 200 mmHg
05	Check the temperature* in the air filter housing and compare with data displayed	-
06	Check the temperature** of the coolant and compare with data displayed – see Chapter 3 to check the operation of the sensor	-
07	Turn the rear wheel in the normal direction of rotation and check pulses generated are displayed. On machines fitted with ABS, check the rear wheel ABS wiring connector and sensor-to-rotor clearance (see Chapter 6)	0 to 999 -
08	Check the operation of the lean angle sensor	Sensor upright – 0.4 to 1.4V Tilted more than 65° – 3.7 to 4.4V
09	Turn the engine stop switch ON and check for battery voltage Check the operation of the fuel injection system relay	Approx.12V
20	Check the operation of the sidestand switch. Select a gear position other than neutral – see Chapter 8 for access and further checks	Stand retracted – ON Stand down – OFF
21	Check the operation of the neutral switch – see Chapter 8 for access and further checks	Gearbox in neutral – ON In gear – OFF
30 and 31	Check the operation of the appropriate ignition coil (see Section 17) – turning the engine stop switch ON will generate five sparks in the appropriate plug and the engine warning light will come on.	-
36 and 37	Check the operation of the appropriate fuel injector (see Section 10) – turning the engine stop switch ON will generate five pulses in the appropriate injector and the engine warning light will come on. Check for the pulses using a sounding rod.	-
48	Check the operation of the air induction system solenoid – turning the engine stop switch ON will actuate the solenoid five times and the engine warning light will come on. You should be able to hear the solenoid click – (see Section 14)	-
50	Check the operation of the fuel injection system (starter safety cut-off relay) – turning the engine stop switch ON will actuate the relay five times and the engine warning light will flash. You should be able to hear the relay click – see Chapter 8 for access and further checks	-
51	Check the operation of the radiator cooling fan relay – turning the engine stop switch ON will actuate the relay five times and the engine warning light will come on. You should be able to hear the relay click – see Chapter 3 for access and further checks	-
52	Check the operation of the headlight relay – turning the engine stop switch ON will actuate the relay five times and the engine warning light will come on. When the relay is ON the headlight should be ON. You should be able to hear the relay click – see Chapter 8 for access and further checks	-
60	Check the carbon monoxide density in the exhaust gas	01 – faulty cylinders 1 and 4 02 – faulty cylinders 2 and 3
61	Fault history code display – once corrected, delete the fault codes No history History	 00 12 to 50 as appropriate
62	Fault history No history History To erase History	 00 00 to 17 Turn the engine stop switch ON
63	Fault history – reinstate codes	Turn the engine stop switch ON

* If possible, check the temperature next to the sensor, otherwise use the ambient temperature as the standard
** Check the temperature of the coolant as close as possible to the sensor

11 Once the fault has been corrected, confirm that the fault code is no longer displayed by turning the ignition switch OFF and then ON again. If the code is no longer displayed on the clock LCD the repair is complete.
12 To delete a fault code from the ECU memory,

follow the appropriate procedure above to set-up the diagnostic mode, then enter code 62 on the clock LCD. The total number of stored codes will be displayed on the trip LCD (00 to 17). Turn the engine stop switch ON to delete the stored codes – the LCD should display 00 codes.

8.5 CKP sensor wiring connector (arrowed)

8.8 Timing rotor cover bolts (arrowed)

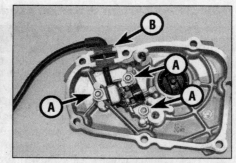

8.9 CKP sensor and wiring guide bolts (A), wiring grommet (B)

8 Fuel injection system components

1 If a fault is indicated in any of the system components, first check the wiring and connectors between the appropriate component and the ECU (refer to Section 2 in Chapter 8 and to the wiring diagram for your model at the end of Chapter 8). A continuity test of all wires will locate a break or short in any circuit. Inspect the terminals inside the wiring connectors and ensure they are not loose, bent or corroded. Spray the inside of the connectors with a proprietary electrical terminal cleaner before reconnection.

2 It is possible to undertake most checks on system components using a multimeter and comparing the results with the specifications at the beginning of the Chapter. **Note:** *Different meters may give slightly different results to those specified even though the component being tested is not faulty – do not consign a component to the bin before having it double-checked.* However, some faults will only become evident when a component is tested with specialised equipment, in which case the checks should be undertaken by a Yamaha dealer.

3 If after a thorough check the source of a fault has not been identified, it is possible that the ECU itself is faulty. Yamaha provides no test specifications for the ECU. In order to determine conclusively that the unit is defective, it should be substituted with a

known good one. If the problem is rectified, the original unit is confirmed faulty.

Crankshaft position sensor

Check

4 Make sure the ignition is OFF. Remove the fuel tank (see Section 2).

5 The crankshaft position sensor is located inside the timing rotor cover on the right-hand side of the engine. Trace the wiring from the cover and disconnect it at the connector inside the boot **(see illustration)**.

6 Using an ohmmeter or multimeter set to the ohms x 100 scale, measure the resistance between the terminals on the sensor side of the connector. Connect the positive (+) meter probe to the grey wire terminal in the connector and the negative (-) probe to the black wire terminal. Compare the result with the specification at the beginning of this Chapter. If the result is not as specified, replace the sensor with a new one.

Removal and installation

7 Follow Steps 4 and 5, then feed the wiring down to the rotor cover, noting its routing.

8 Place a drain tray under the rotor cover and unscrew the cover bolts **(see illustration)**. Note the guide for the coolant hose. Ease the cover off. Remove the gasket - a new one must be used.

9 Undo the bolts securing the sensor and the wiring guide to the inside of the cover, then free the wiring grommet from the cut-out and remove the sensor **(see illustration)**.

10 Clean the threads of the sensor and wiring

guide bolts. Apply a suitable sealant to the wiring grommet and some threadlock to the bolts. Fit the sensor, wiring guide and wiring grommet and tighten the bolts to the torque setting specified at the beginning of this Chapter **(see illustration 8.9)**.

11 Clean all old gasket off the timing rotor cover and crankcase mating surfaces. Clean the threads of the cover bolts, then apply some fresh threadlock. Fit the new gasket onto the cover, then insert two of the bolts to keep it in place as you fit the cover **(see illustration)**. Fit the cover and secure it with the bolts finger-tight, making sure the guide is correctly positioned with the hose behind it **(see illustration)**. Tighten the cover bolts evenly to the torque setting specified at the beginning of this Chapter.

12 Feed the wiring up to the connector and reconnect it **(see illustration 8.5)**.

13 Install the remaining components in the reverse order of removal.

Intake air pressure sensor

Check

14 Make sure the ignition is OFF. Remove the air filter housing (see Section 5).

15 The intake air pressure sensor is located on the right-hand end of the fuel rail **(see illustration)**. Check the condition of the vacuum hoses between the underside of the sensor and the throttle bodies. If any hose is cracked or perished remove the throttle bodies (se Section 9) and replace them all with a new set. Make sure the hoses are a tight fit on the

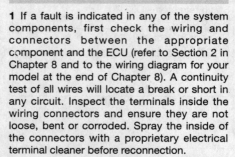

8.11a Fit a new gasket

8.11b Fit the hose guide (arrowed) as shown

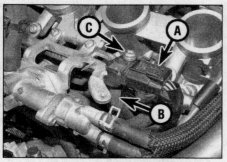

8.15 IAP sensor wiring connector (A), vacuum hose (B) and mounting screw (C)

8.21 TP sensor wiring connector (arrowed)

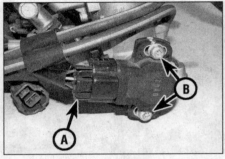

8.25 TP sensor wiring connector (A) and screws (B)

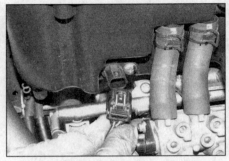

8.30 Disconnect the wiring connector

sensor, the hose connectors and the throttle bodies.

16 Using a voltmeter or multimeter set to the volts (DC) scale, measure the sensor output voltage as follows – do not disconnect the wiring connector for this test. Insert the positive (+) probe of the meter into the pink/white wire terminal in the back of the sensor wiring connector, and the negative (-) probe into the black/blue wire terminal. Turn the ignition switch ON and note the output voltage. Turn the ignition OFF.

17 If the voltage is not as specified, replace the sensor with a new one. Note that the wiring for the air pressure sensor is connected to the main wiring loom via a sub loom (see Section 9) – ensure that the sub loom connector is clean and secure.

Removal and installation

18 Follow Step 14, then disconnect the sensor wiring connector and undo the sensor screw **(see illustration 8.15)**. Lift the sensor and disconnect the vacuum hose.

19 Prior to installation, check the condition of the vacuum hoses (Step 15). Make sure that the hose is a tight fit on the sensor union and that the wiring connector terminals are clean.

Throttle position sensor
Check

20 Make sure the ignition is OFF. On XJ6-N models remove the right-hand side cover, on XJ6-S models remove the right-hand fairing side panel, and on XJ6-F and FZ6R models remove the right-hand lower fairing panel (see Chapter 7).

21 The throttle position sensor is on the right-hand end of the throttle body assembly. Disconnect the wiring connector **(see illustration)**.

22 Using an ohmmeter or multimeter set to the K-ohms scale, connect the meter positive (+) probe to the blue wire terminal and the negative (-) probe to the black/blue wire terminal on the sensor and measure the sensor maximum resistance.

23 If the resistance is not as specified at the beginning of the Chapter, replace the sensor with a new one.

Removal and installation

24 Remove the throttle body assembly (see Section 9).

25 Disconnect the wiring connector from the sensor **(see illustration)**. The sensor is secured by two Torx security screws, for which a special Torx bit (that has a hole in its middle) is required. Undo the screws and draw the sensor off, noting how the slot fits over the throttle shaft.

26 To fit the sensor, align the slot with the throttle shaft and tighten the screws finger-tight. Connect the wiring connector.

27 To adjust the position of the sensor, first place the throttle bodies on the bike so the sensor is accessible and temporarily connect the throttle body sub-loom wiring connectors. Using a voltmeter or multimeter set to the volts (DC) scale, insert the positive (+) probe of the meter into the yellow wire terminal in the back of the sensor connector and the negative (-) probe into the black/blue wire terminal. Turn

the ignition switch ON and carefully adjust the position of the sensor until the output voltage is within the range specified at the beginning of the Chapter, then tighten the sensor screws. Turn the ignition OFF. Install the throttle body assembly (see Section 9).

Intake air temperature sensor

28 Make sure the ignition switch is OFF.

29 Raise the fuel tank (see Section 2).

30 The sensor is mounted in the back of the air filter housing. Disconnect the wiring connector **(see illustration)**.

31 Using an ohmmeter or multimeter set to the ohms x 100 scale, connect the meter positive (+) probe to the brown/white wire terminal on the sensor and the negative (-) probe to the black/blue wire terminal and measure the resistance.

32 If the result is not as specified at the beginning of the Chapter, replace the sensor with a new one – it is secured to the housing by a screw **(see illustration)**.

33 Make sure that the wiring connector terminals are clean.

Oxygen sensor

34 Make sure the ignition is OFF. The sensor is located in the right-hand side of the exhaust system **(see illustration)**. Inspect the sensor for damage.

35 Remove the fuel tank (See Section 2). Trace the wiring to the connector and check that the wiring is not damaged or trapped, and that the connector is secure **(see illustration)**.

8.32 Undo the screw (arrowed) and remove the IAT sensor

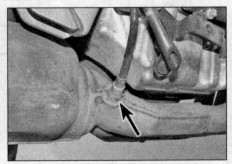

8.34 Oxygen sensor (arrowed) – belly-pan shown removed for clarity

8.35 Oxygen sensor wiring connector (arrowed)

8.39 Lean angle sensor (arrowed)

8.45 Speed sensor (arrowed)

8.46 Speed sensor wiring connector (arrowed)

36 If the correct socket is available (that has a slot in the side to accommodate the wiring), check that the sensor is tightened to the torque setting specified at the beginning of this Chapter.

37 No test specifications for the sensor are available – if no physical damage can be found, it must be assumed that the sensor is defective. Replace it with a new one – on N and S models remove the belly-pan for access (see Chapter 7). Tighten the new sensor to the torque setting specified at the beginning of the Chapter.

Lean angle sensor

Check

38 Make sure the ignition is OFF. Remove the seat (see Chapter 7).

39 The lean angle sensor is located next to the fusebox **(see illustration)** – undo the screws and lift the sensor off. Do not disconnect the wiring connector.

40 Using a voltmeter or multimeter set to the volts (DC) scale, insert the positive meter (+) probe into the yellow/green wire terminal in back of the connector and the negative (-) probe into the black/blue wire terminal.

41 Hold the sensor in its normal position with the UP mark facing up, then turn the ignition switch ON and note the output voltage. Now tilt the sensor 65° to one side and then 65° to

the other, noting the output voltage. Turn the ignition OFF.

42 If the output voltage is not as specified when the sensor is upright and tilted over, replace it with a new one.

Removal and installation

43 Follow the procedure in Steps 38 and 39 to remove the sensor, then disconnect the wiring connector. Note the top surface of the sensor is marked UP – make sure this is uppermost when the sensor is installed.

Speed sensor (non-ABS models)

Check

44 Support the machine on the centrestand or an auxiliary stand so the rear wheel is off the ground. Make sure the ignition is OFF.

45 Remove the fuel tank (see Section 2). The speed sensor is located on the top of the crankcase to the rear of the starter motor **(see illustration)**.

46 Trace the wiring from the sensor to the white three-pin connector inside the wiring boot at the back of the engine **(see illustration)**. Do not disconnect the wiring connector.

47 Using a voltmeter or multimeter set to the volts (DC) scale, insert the positive meter (+) probe into the white/yellow wire terminal in the connector, and the negative (-) probe into the black/blue terminal. Turn the ignition switch ON. Turn the rear wheel in its normal direction

of rotation and check the reading on the meter – it should be seen to fluctuate between 0 and 5 volts as the wheel is turned. Turn the ignition switch OFF.

48 If the voltage is not as specified, replace the sensor with a new one.

Removal and installation

49 Remove the throttle bodies (see Section 9). Disconnect the wiring connector **(see illustration 8.46)**. Unscrew the bolt and remove the sensor **(see illustration 8.45)**. Remove the O-ring - a new one must be fitted.

50 Use a new O-ring on installation, and make sure the wiring connector terminals are clean and that the pins are not damaged.

Fuel injection system relay

51 Make sure the ignition is OFF. Remove the seat(s) (see Chapter 7). The relay unit is mounted on the right-hand side of the rear sub-frame and contains the fuel injection system relay and starter circuit safety cut-off relay **(see illustration)**.

52 Lift the relay assembly off its bracket and disconnect the wiring connector.

53 Using an ohmmeter or continuity tester, connect the positive (+) probe to the red wire terminal on the relay and the negative (-) probe to the red/blue wire terminal **(see illustration)**. There should be no continuity.

54 Using a fully-charged 12V battery and

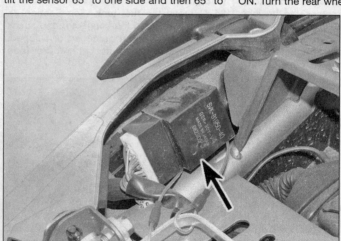

8.51 FI system relay is within the relay unit (arrowed)

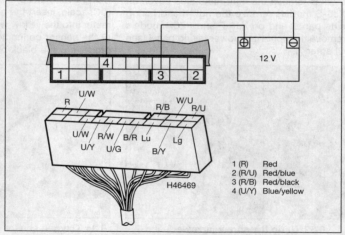

8.53 Test connections for the fuel injection system relay

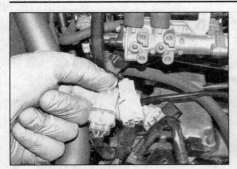

9.4 Disconnect the sub-loom connectors

9.5 Release the clamps (arrowed) and detach the hoses

9.6a Access the left-hand clamps screws (arrowed)...

some insulated jumper leads, connect the positive (+) battery terminal to the red/black wire terminal on the relay, and the negative (–) battery terminal to the blue/yellow wire terminal **(see illustration 8.53)**. There should now be continuity between the red and red/blue wire terminals.

55 If the relay does not operate as described, replace it with a new one.

Exhaust gas oxygen content

56 Follow the procedure in Section 14 to check the AIS.

57 Have the exhaust gases analysed by a Yamaha dealer.

9.6b ...from the right...

9.6c ...and the right-hand clamp screws (arrowed) from the left

9 Throttle bodies

Warning: Refer to the precautions given in Section 1 before starting work.

Special tool: *Access to the clamp screws requires the use of a long reach 3 mm Allen key.*

Removal

1 Remove the air filter housing (see Section 5). On California models, detach the EVAP hose from the throttle body assembly.

2 Partially drain the cooling system to avoid coolant leaking when the hoses are disconnected from the fast idle unit (see Chapter 3).

3 Disconnect the throttle cables (see Section 12, Steps 2 to 5).

4 Disconnect the throttle body sub loom wiring connectors **(see illustration)**.

5 Place some rag under the fast idle unit to catch any residual coolant. Release the clips and disconnect the coolant hoses from the unit, noting which fits where **(see illustration)**. If required, plug the hoses to prevent further loss of coolant.

6 Slacken the clamps on the cylinder head intake manifolds – you will need a long 3 mm Allen bit with a socket extension if necessary to access them, accessing the right-hand clamps from under the left-hand side of the frame and the left-hand clamps from the right-hand side **(see illustrations)**.

7 Ease the throttle body assembly off the intake manifolds then disconnect the coolant temperature sensor wiring connector **(see illustration)**.

8 Note how the clamps locate on the intake ducts **(see illustration)**. If required unscrew the bolts and remove the ducts – they are

9.7 Displace the throttle bodies and disconnect the ECT sensor connector (arrowed)

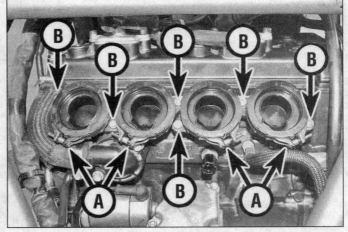

9.8 Note the orientation of the clamps (A) and how they locate. Intake duct bolts (B)

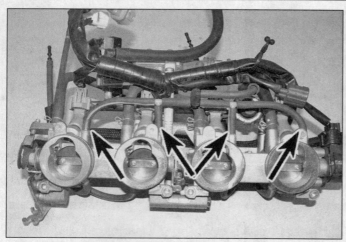

9.11a Throttle body vacuum hose arrangement – IAP sensor hoses (arrowed)...

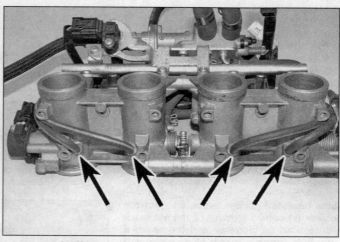

9.11b ...and synchronising hoses (arrowed)

numbered 1 to 4 from left-to right (according to cylinder numbering) to ensure correct installation.

Caution: Stuff clean rag into each intake manifold to prevent anything from falling inside.

Disassembly

9 Refer to Section 11 and remove the throttle synchronising/fast idle unit.
10 Refer to Section 10 and remove the fuel rail and injectors.
11 Note the arrangement of the IAP sensor vacuum hoses and where they connect on the throttle body assembly, then pull them off their unions and remove the sensor and hose assembly **(see illustration)**. Also disconnect and remove the vacuum take-off hoses (for synchronising the throttle bodies) **(see illustration)**.
12 If required, remove the throttle position sensor (see Section 8).

Cleaning

Caution: Use only a petroleum-based solvent for cleaning. Do not use caustic cleaners.

13 Ensure that only metal components come into contact with the cleaning solvent and always follow manufacturer's recommendations as to cleaning time. If a spray cleaner is used, direct the spray into all passages.
14 After the cleaner has loosened and dissolved most of the varnish and other deposits, use a nylon-bristle brush to remove the stubborn deposits. Rinse the throttle bodies, then dry them with compressed air.
15 Use compressed air to blow out all of the fuel and air passages.

Inspection

16 Check the throttle bodies for cracks, distorted sealing surfaces and other damage. If any defects are found, fit a new throttle body assembly.
17 Operate the throttle pulley and ensure that the throttle butterfly valves open and

close smoothly. If they don't, clean the throttle linkage, and check the throttle bodies for wear where butterfly valves close against them.
18 Check all the vacuum hoses for cracks, splits and kinks and replace them with new ones if necessary.

Reassembly

19 Reassemble the throttle bodies in the reverse order of disassembly. Ensure that all the hoses are securely clipped in place.

Installation

20 Installation is the reverse of removal, noting the following.
● Check for cracks or splits in the intake manifolds and make sure the sealing rings fitted in the grooves on the underside are in good condition. Replace the ducts with new ones if necessary – the sealing rings are not available separately. Fit the ducts in their correct location (see Step 8) and tighten the bolts to the torque setting specified at the beginning of the Chapter.
● Make sure the clamps are correctly aligned with the tabs on the manifolds **(see illustration 9.8)**.
● Lubricate the inside lip of each manifold with a squirt of WD40 or a smear of grease to aid installation of the throttle body assembly.

10.6 Undo the screw (arrowed) and displace the sensor

● Once the assembly is correctly aligned, press it firmly into place and tighten the clamps.
● Refer to Section 12 for installation of the throttle cables.
● Make sure the terminals in the wiring connectors are clean and that the connectors are secure.
● Top-up the cooling system (see Chapter 1 and *Pre-ride checks*).
● Check idle speed and throttle body synchronisation and adjust as necessary (see Chapter 1).

10 Fuel rail and injectors

⚠️ *Warning: Refer to the precautions given in Section 1 before proceeding.*

Check

1 Remove the fuel tank (see Section 2).
2 Follow the procedure in Section 7 to set-up the diagnostic mode on your machine. Confirm that the diagnostic codes for checking the fuel injectors are 36 (injectors No. 1 and 4) and 37 (injectors No. 2 and 3).
3 Check the operation of each injector in turn, using a stethoscope or sounding rod held against the injector being checked. Turn the engine stop switch ON – if the injector is good it will click five times. If any injector is silent, either the injector or its wiring harness is faulty.
4 Disconnect the wiring connector from the injector **(see illustration 10.7)**. Using the wiring diagrams at the end of Chapter 8, check for continuity in the wiring and connectors between the injectors, the sub loom and the ECU, and between the injectors and earth (ground).

Removal

5 Remove the throttle bodies (see Section 9).
6 Displace the intake air pressure sensor **(see illustration)**. Undo the screws securing

the throttle synchronising/fast idle unit and displace the unit **(see illustrations 11.6a, b and c)**.

7 Disconnect the wiring connectors from the fuel injectors **(see illustration)**.

8 Undo the screws securing the fuel rail **(see illustration)**. Carefully lift the fuel rail off the throttle body assembly **(see illustration 10.12)** – the injectors will come away with the rail. Remove the seal from each injector port or on the lower end of each injector **(see illustration)**.

9 Pull the injector(s) out of the fuel rail as required, noting which way round it fits **(see illustration)**. Remove the O-ring from the upper end of each injector **(see illustration)**. New seals and O-rings must be fitted on reassembly.

10 Modern fuels contain detergents which should keep the injectors clean and free of gum or varnish from residue fuel. If an injector is suspected of being blocked, clean it through with injector cleaner.

Installation

Note: Apply a smear of clean engine oil to all new seals and O-rings before reassembly.

11 Fit a new seal into each injector port **(see illustration)**. Fit a new O-ring into the groove in the top of each injector **(see illustration 10.9b)**. Align each injector so the wiring connector will face back, then carefully press the injectors into the rail **(see illustration 10.9a)**. **Note:** *Avoid twisting*

10.7 Disconnect the wiring from each injector

the injectors as this may damage the seals.

12 Align the injectors with their ports and fit the fuel rail into place evenly **(see illustration)**. Make sure that all four injectors are seated correctly and the rail brackets are flush with the screw holes before fitting the screws – do not use the screws to correctly seat and align the fuel rail.

13 Fit the fuel rail screws **(see illustration 10.8a)**.

14 Connect the injector wiring connectors **(see illustration 10.7)**.

15 Fit the throttle synchronising/fast idle unit and intake air pressure sensor **(see illustrations 11.6c, b and a, and 10.6)**.

16 Install the throttle bodies (see Section 9). Run the engine and make sure there are no fuel leaks before riding the bike.

11 Fast idle unit

⚠ **Warning: Refer to the precautions given in Section 1 before proceeding.**

Operation

1 The fast idle unit is located on the right-hand side of the assembly that incorporates the throttle body synchronising screws and the idle speed adjuster. The throttle synchronising/fast idle unit is part of the complete throttle body assembly and is not available separately.

2 The unit allows extra air to pass from the air filter housing into the throttle body assembly, which in turn draws more fuel through the injectors, raising the idle speed even though the throttle twistgrip is closed.

3 Operation of the unit is dependant upon the temperature of coolant that circulates through it between the cylinder head and the radiator. As the coolant temperature rises, a wax element inside the unit expands, gradually closing the intake airways to the throttle body assembly.

4 The intake airways should be fully open when the engine is cold, and fully closed when the engine reaches normal operating temperature, which is usually reached after 10 to 15 minutes of stop-and-go riding. If a smooth, steady idle cannot be achieved, and all other components have been checked, the

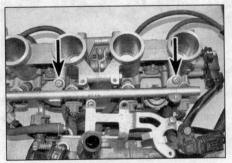

10.8a Undo the screws (arrowed) and remove the rail

10.8b Remove the seal from each port

10.9a Carefully pull the injector out of the rail

10.9b Injector O-ring (arrowed)

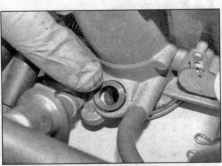

10.11 Fit a new seal into each port

10.12 Align and insert the injectors

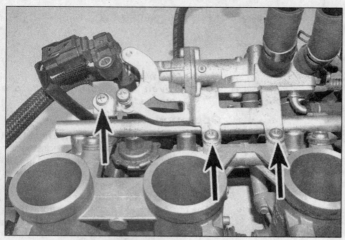

11.6a Undo the screws (arrowed)...

11.6b ...and the screw (arrowed)...

11.6c ...noting the spacer fitted with it

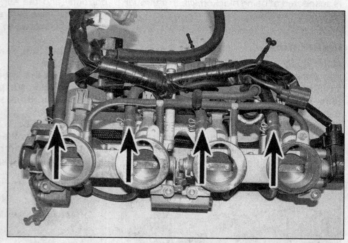

11.6d Detach the hoses (arrowed) and remove the unit

fast idle unit may be faulty. Have the operation of the unit checked by a Yamaha dealer. **Note:** *Where fitted, the oxygen sensor may try to compensate for an incorrect fuel/air mixture caused by a faulty fast idle unit. A fuel injection system fault code based upon incorrect carbon monoxide density in the exhaust gas will result.*

Removal and installation

5 Remove the throttle bodies (see Section 9).
6 Displace the intake air pressure sensor **(see illustration 10.6)**. Undo the screws securing the throttle synchronising/fast idle unit and displace the unit **(see illustrations)**. Release the clips securing the synchronising unit hoses to the unions on the throttle bodies and detach the hoses, then lift the unit off **(see illustration)**.
7 Installation is the reverse of removal. Make sure all hoses are in good condition, correctly routed and secured and not trapped or kinked.

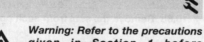

12 Throttle cables

Warning: Refer to the precautions given in Section 1 before proceeding.

Removal

1 On XJ6-N models remove the left-hand side cover, on XJ6-S models remove the left-hand fairing side panel, and on XJ6-F and FZ6R models remove the left-hand lower fairing panel (see Chapter 7).
2 Remove the bracket from the left-hand side of the frame **(see illustration)**.
3 Note the differences between the lower (throttle opening) cable and the upper (throttle closing) cable on the left-hand end of the throttle body assembly and how they seat in the bracket. Note the differences between the front (throttle opening) cable and the rear (throttle

closing) cable on the underside of the housing on the handlebar. If required, mark each cable according to its location at both ends. If new cables are being fitted, match them to the old cables to ensure they are correctly installed.
4 Loosen the locknut on the lower cable and thread it up until the adjuster nut clears the

12.2 Unscrew the bolts (arrowed) and remove the bracket

12.4a Fully slacken the locknut (arrowed)...

12.4b ...and free the cable from the bracket

12.4c Slacken the hex and free the upper cable

bracket, then slip the cable out of the bracket **(see illustrations)**. Unscrew the hex on the upper cable until the nut clears the bracket, then slide the cable out of the bracket **(see illustration)**.
5 Detach the inner cable ends from the throttle pulley **(see illustrations)**.

6 Undo the switch housing and cable cover screws on the underside of the housing and remove the cover, noting the locating tab **(see illustrations)**. Note the arrangement of the throttle opening and closing cable elbows in the lower half of the twistgrip housing.

7 Separate the housing halves from the handlebar **(see illustration 12.12)**.
8 Detach the inner cable ends from the pulley then draw the cable elbows from the housing, noting how they fit **(see illustrations)**.
9 Withdraw the cables from the machine, noting their routing.

12.5a Detach the opening cable end...

12.5b ...and the closing cable end

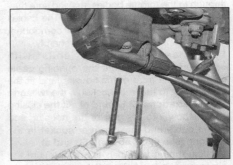

12.6a Undo the housing screws...

12.6b ...and the cover screw...

12.6c ...and remove the cover

12.8a Detach the closing cable end...

12.8b ...and draw the cable out of the housing

12.8c Detach the opening cable end...

12.8d ...and draw the cable out of the housing

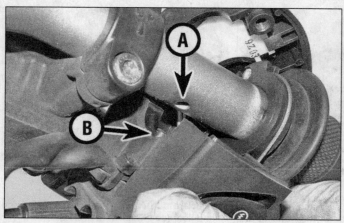

12.12 Locate the pin (B) in the hole (A)

13.3 Unscrew the eight nuts (four arrowed)...

Installation

10 Feed the cables from the handlebar through to the throttle bodies, making sure they are correctly routed and arranged. The cables must not interfere with any other component and should not be kinked or bent sharply.

11 Lubricate the cable ends with multi-purpose grease. Fit the opening cable elbow into the front of the housing and fit the cable end into the front socket in the twistgrip (see illustrations 12.8d and c). Fit the closing cable elbow into the rear of the housing and fit the cable end into the rear socket in the twistgrip (see illustration 12.8b and a).

12 Join the housing halves, making sure the pin locates in the hole in the handlebar (see illustration). Fit the cover onto the bottom, making sure the elbows remain correctly seated, and locating the tab in the cut-out, and secure it with the short screw (see illustrations 12.6c and b).

13 Fit the housing screws – the shorter of the two screws goes in the front (see illustration 12.6a).

14 Fit the closing cable end into the upper socket in the throttle pulley, then fit the opening cable end into the lower socket (see illustrations 12.5b and a).

15 Seat the closing cable in the upper holder on the bracket, the pull it forwards to lock the nut and tighten the hex against the bracket (see illustration 12.4c). Seat the opening cable in the lower holder on the bracket, adjusting the position of the locknut as required so there is minimal freeplay in the cable, then finger-tighten the locknut against the bracket (see illustrations 12.4b and a).

16 Follow the procedure in Chapter 1 to adjust the cable freeplay. Start the engine and check that the idle speed does not rise as the handlebars are turned. If it does, the throttle cables are routed incorrectly. Correct the problem before riding the motorcycle.

17 Fit the bracket (see illustration 12.2). Install the body panels.

13 Exhaust system

⚠️ **Warning: If the engine has been running the exhaust system will be very hot. Allow the system to cool before carrying out any work.**
Caution: The header pipe flange nuts on the model photographed were extremely corroded, to the point that no amount of wire brushing and penetrating fluid would release them, and we had to resort to applying extreme heat using an oxy-acetylene torch before the nuts came undone. As this sort of equipment is not usually available to the home mechanic, if necessary try using a blow-torch instead, but if this does not work take the bike to a workshop equipped with oxy-acetylene, rather than trying to apply too much force which could end with sheared studs in the cylinder head. Also, when applying heat in this way take care not to overheat surrounding components and the alloy cylinder head itself.

Removal

1 Remove the fuel tank (see Section 2). On XJ6-N and XJ6-S models remove the belly pan (see Chapter 7).

2 Trace the wiring from the oxygen sensor on the right-hand side of the exhaust and disconnect it at the connector (see illustration 8.35). Feed the wiring down to the sensor, noting its routing.

3 Unscrew the eight header pipe flange nuts and draw the flanges off the studs (see illustration).

4 Support the silencer and undo the mounting bolt on each side (see illustrations).

5 Draw the header pipes off the cylinder head and manoeuvre the exhaust out from underneath the engine. **Note:** The exhaust contains a catalytic converter – handle it carefully to avoid damage to the cat.

6 Remove the gasket from each exhaust port in the cylinder head and discard them, as new ones must be fitted (see illustration).

13.4a ...then unscrew the left-hand bolt (arrowed)...

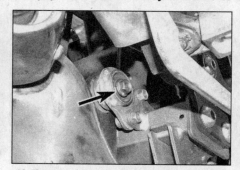

13.4b ...and the right-hand bolt (arrowed) and remove the exhaust assembly

13.6 Remove the old gaskets

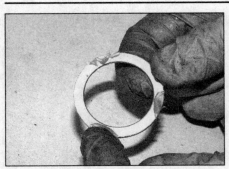

13.10a Dab grease onto the new gaskets…

13.10b …to keep them in place

13.11 Locate the head of each pipe in its port

7 Check the condition of the rubber bush in each mounting bolt bracket and replace the brackets with new ones if necessary – each is secured to the frame by two bolts **(see illustrations 13.4a and b)**. If the flange nuts are corroded replace them with new ones.

Installation

8 Fit the mounting brackets if removed **(see illustrations 13.4a and b)**.
9 Clean the threads of the studs in the cylinder head and the mounting bolts and smear copper grease over them.
10 Apply dabs of multi-purpose grease to the new gaskets to keep them in place, then fit a gasket into each exhaust port **(see illustrations)**.
11 Manoeuvre the exhaust into position, locating each header pipe in its port **(see illustration)**. Fit the mounting bolts finger-tight **(see illustrations 13.4a and b)**.
12 Locate the header pipe flanges onto the studs, then fit the nuts and tighten them to the torque setting specified at the beginning of the Chapter **(see illustration 13.3)**.
13 Tighten the mounting bolts to the specified torque.
14 Reconnect the oxygen sensor wiring connector **(see illustration 8.35)**.
15 Run the engine and check that there are no exhaust gas leaks.

16 Install the remaining components in the reverse order of removal.

14 Air induction system (AIS)

Function

1 The air induction system uses negative (low pressure) exhaust gas pulses to suck fresh air from the air filter housing via a solenoid valve and reed valves into the exhaust ports, where it mixes with hot combustion gases. The extra oxygen causes continued combustion, allowing un-burnt hydrocarbons to burn off, thereby reducing emissions.
2 The solenoid valve, controlled electronically by signals from the ECU, allows air to flow when the engine is cold and when it is at idle. The valve shuts off the flow of air when the engine reaches normal operating temperature and is being ridden. If, however, the coolant temperature drops, the valve opens and air is added to aid combustion and raise the gas temperature inside the exhaust system.
3 The reed valves located in the engine valve cover ensure a one-way flow of air into the ports, only opening when there is negative pressure in the ports, and preventing exhaust

gases flowing back into the cut-off valve and air filter housing.
4 A general inspection of the AIS should be carried out at the specified service interval (see Chapter 1, Section 5).

Testing

Solenoid valve

5 Remove the valve (see below).
6 Clean the end of the air supply hose. Manually check the operation of the system by blowing through the hose – air should flow through the solenoid valve and out of the reed valve hoses **(see illustration)**. Using a pair of auxiliary wires now apply battery voltage (12 volts) across the terminals, positive (+) probe to the red/white wire terminal and the negative (-) probe to the brown/red wire terminal, in the solenoid valve connector and repeat the check **(see illustration)** – no air should flow through the solenoid valve. Disconnect the battery. If the valve does not function as described replace it with a new one.
7 Check the resistance of the valve - using an ohmmeter or multimeter set to the ohms x 1 scale, connect the meter positive (+) probe to the red/white wire terminal and the negative (-) probe to the brown/red wire terminal and measure the resistance **(see illustration 14.6b)**. If the result is not as specified

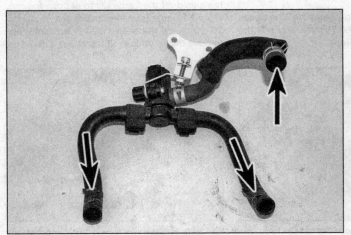

14.6a Air should flow as shown

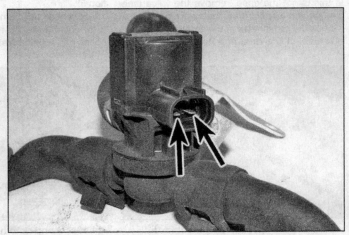

14.6b With power to the terminals (arrowed) no air should flow

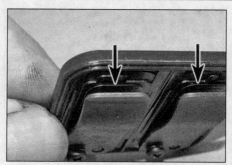

14.11a Check each reed (arrowed) seals correctly on its seat

14.11b Gently push the reeds to check they are not stuck

14.13 Detach the hoses (arrowed)

14.14a Unscrew the bolts (arrowed)...

14.14b ...and disconnect the wiring

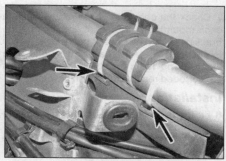

14.19a Release the two cable-ties (arrowed) on the left-hand side...

at the beginning of the Chapter, replace the valve with a new one.

Reed valves

8 Remove the air filter housing (see Section 5).

9 Release the clamps securing the hoses to the unions on the reed valves and pull the hoses off (see illustration 14.13). Attach a length of clean auxiliary hose to one of the unions.

10 Check the valve by blowing and sucking on the auxiliary hose end. Air should flow through the hose only when blown down it (valve open) and not when sucked back up (valve closed). If this is not the case, remove the valve (see below) and inspect it as described in Step 11. Check the other valve in the same way.

11 Inspect the reed and its seat for carbon

deposits or gum that might impair its operation. The reed should sit flat against its seat to act as a seal against back pressure in the exhaust port (see illustration). If necessary, clean the surface or the reed carefully with a rag and a suitable solvent – do not bend the reed. Also check the valve is not stuck to its seat by carefully pushing with a finger to lift it off (see illustration) – do not push it too far, just check that it is not stuck

Removal and installation

Solenoid valve

12 Remove the air filter housing (see Section 5).

13 Release the clamps securing the hoses to the unions on the reed valves and pull hoses off (see illustration).

14 Unscrew the valve bracket bolts, displace the valve and disconnect the wiring connector (see illustrations).

15 Detach the valve from the bracket and the hoses from the valve as required, noting which fits where.

16 Installation is the reverse of removal.

Reed valves

17 Remove the air filter housing (see Section 5).

18 Release the clamps securing the hoses to the unions on the reed valves and pull the hoses off (see illustration 14.13).

19 Release the heat shield cable-ties and lift the shield off the frame rail to expose the reed valve housings (see illustrations).

20 Unscrew the reed valve cover bolts and remove the cover (see illustration). Lift out the

14.19b ...and the single cable-tie (arrowed) on the right...

14.19c ...and note how the shield locates before removing it

14.20a Reed valve cover bolts (arrowed)

14.20b Remove the valve...

14.20c ...and the baseplates

reed valve and the baseplates, noting which way around they are fitted (see illustrations).
21 Installation is the reverse of removal.

15 Catalytic converter

General information

1 A catalytic converter is incorporated in the exhaust system to minimise the level of exhaust pollutants released into the atmosphere.
2 The catalytic converter consists of a canister containing a fine ceramic honeycomb impregnated with a catalyst material, over which the hot exhaust gases pass. The catalyst speeds up the oxidation of harmful carbon monoxide, unburned hydrocarbons and soot, effectively reducing the quantity of harmful products released into the atmosphere via the exhaust gases.
3 The catalytic converter is a closed-loop design – an oxygen sensor in the exhaust system enables the ECU to vary the intake fuel/air mixture dependant upon engine operating conditions (see Section 8).

Precautions

4 The catalytic converter is a reliable and simple device which needs no maintenance in itself, but there are some facts of which an owner should be aware if the converter is to function properly for its full service life.

● DO NOT use leaded or lead replacement petrol (gasoline) – the additives will coat the precious metals, reducing their converting efficiency and will eventually destroy the catalytic converter.
● Always keep the ignition and fuel systems well-maintained in accordance with the manufacturer's schedule – if the fuel/air mixture is suspected of being incorrect have the exhaust gas CO content checked by a Yamaha dealer.
● If the engine develops a misfire, do not ride the bike at all (or at least as little as possible) until the fault is cured.
● DO NOT use fuel or engine oil additives – these may contain substances harmful to the catalytic converter.

● DO NOT continue to use the bike if the engine burns oil to the extent of leaving a visible trail of blue smoke.
● Remember that the catalytic converter is FRAGILE – handle the exhaust mid-section carefully if removing it from the machine.

16 Ignition system check

Warning: The energy levels in electronic systems can be very high. On no account should the ignition be switched on whilst the plugs or plug caps are being held. Shocks from the HT circuit can be most unpleasant. Secondly, it is vital that the engine is not turned over or run with any of the plug caps removed and isolated, and that the plugs are soundly earthed (grounded) when the system is checked for sparking. The ignition system components can be seriously damaged if the HT circuit becomes isolated.

1 As no means of adjustment is available, any failure of the system can be traced to failure of a system component or a simple wiring fault. Of the two possibilities, the latter is by far the most likely. In the event of failure, check the system in a logical fashion, as described below.
2 Make sure the ignition is OFF. Work on one cylinder at a time.
3 Refer to Chapter 1, Section 2 for access to the spark plugs. Pull the cap off the plug being

16.3 Pull the cap off the plug

tested (see illustration). Connect the cap to a spare spark plug (preferably use a new plug).
4 Use a length of fairly thick insulated wire with crocodile clips at each end to link the plug threads to the cylinder head, or some other known good earth point. Hold the plug cap and shade the plug electrodes so the spark will be easy to see.

Warning: Do not remove any of the spark plugs from the engine to perform this check – atomised fuel being pumped out of the open spark plug hole could ignite, causing severe injury! Make sure the plugs are earthed – if they are not the ECU could be damaged when the engine is turned over.

5 Check that the kill switch is in the RUN position and the transmission is in neutral, then turn the ignition switch ON and turn the engine over on the starter motor. If the system is in good condition a regular, fat blue spark should be evident at the plug electrode. If the spark appears thin or yellowish, or is non-existent, further investigation is necessary. Turn the ignition OFF and repeat the check for each plug cap.
6 The ignition system must be able to produce a spark that is capable of jumping at least a 6 mm gap. Simple ignition spark gap testing tools are commercially available (see illustration) – follow the manufacturer's instructions, and set the gap at 6 mm.
7 If the test results are good the entire ignition system can be considered good. If the spark appears thin or yellowish, or is non-existent, further investigation is necessary.
8 Ignition faults can be divided into two categories, namely those where the ignition system has failed completely, and those that are due to a partial failure. The likely faults are listed below, starting with the most probable source of failure. Work through the list systematically, referring to the subsequent sections for full details of the necessary checks and tests. Note: Before checking the following items ensure that the battery is fully charged and that all fuses are in good condition.
● Loose spark plug cap or lead connection, faulty spark plug cap or HT lead, faulty spark plug, dirty, worn or corroded plug electrodes.

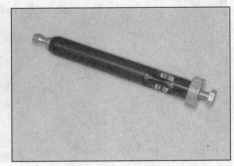

16.6 A typical ignition spark testing tool

● Loose, corroded or damaged wiring connections, broken or shorted wiring between any of the component parts of the ignition system.
● Faulty neutral, clutch or sidestand switch (see Chapter 8).
● Faulty ignition coil(s) (Section 17).
● Faulty ignition switch or engine kill switch (see Chapter 8).
● Faulty crankshaft position (CKP) sensor (Section 8) or damaged triggers on timing rotor (Chapter 2).
● Faulty lean angle sensor or starting circuit cut-off relay (see Section 8 and Chapter 8).
● Faulty ECU (Section 18).

9 If the above checks don't reveal the cause of the problem, have the ignition system tested by a Yamaha dealer.

17 Ignition coils

Check

1 Refer to Steps 7 to 9 for access to the coils. The HT leads on the left-hand coil are connected to cylinders 1 and 4, and the leads on the right-hand coil are connected to cylinders 2 and 3. Note which primary wiring connector connects to which terminal (see illustration 17.4a).

2 Inspect the coils for cracks and other damage. Check that each HT lead is securely connected to the coil body and spark plug cap, and that the primary wiring connectors and terminals are clean and secure (see illustration 17.4a).

3 Pull the cap off each spark plug (see illustration 16.3). Unscrew the plug caps from the HT leads (see illustration). Set the meter to the K-ohm scale and measure the resistance between the terminals in either end of the cap (see illustration). If the reading obtained differs from the one shown in the Specifications, fit a new cap.

4 Disconnect the primary wiring connectors from the coil being tested, noting which fits where (see illustration). Measure the ignition coil primary circuit resistance as follows: set the meter to the ohms x 1 scale, then connect the positive (+) meter probe to the red/black wire terminal on the coil and the negative (-) probe to the orange/black (cyls 1 and 4) or grey/black (cyls 2 and 3) wire terminal (see illustration). If the reading obtained is not within the range shown in the Specifications, it is likely that the coil is defective.

5 Finally, measure the secondary circuit resistance as follows. Set the meter to the K-ohm scale. Connect one meter probe to the exposed end of one HT lead and the other meter probe to the other HT lead, ensuring that the probes make good contact with the core wire inside the leads. If the reading obtained is not within the range shown in the Specifications, it is likely that the coil is defective.

6 If a coil is confirmed to be faulty, it must be replaced with a new one – the coils are sealed units and cannot therefore be repaired.

Removal and installation

7 Remove the AIS control valve and hoses (see Section 14).

8 Release the heat shield cable-ties and remove the shield, noting how it fits (see illustrations 14.19a, b and c).

9 Note the routing of the HT leads. Pull the caps off the relevant spark plugs (see illustration 16.3). Disconnect the primary wiring connectors from the coil, noting which fits where (see illustration 17.4a).

10 Undo the screw and remove the coil, noting how it locates at the front (see illustration).

17.3a Unscrew the caps from the leads...

17.3b ...and check the resistance of each cap

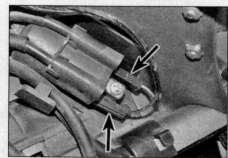

17.4a Primary circuit wiring connectors (arrowed)

17.4b To test the coil primary resistance, connect the meter as shown

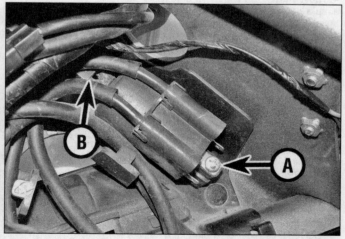

17.10 Undo the screw (A). Note how the front of the coil locates in the holder (B)

11 Installation is the reverse of removal. Make sure that the coils are fitted in their correct locations according to the cylinder numbers marked on the HT leads (see Step 1), and that the wiring connectors are secure.

12 Make sure the HT leads are connected to the spark plugs in the correct order.

18 Engine Control Unit (ECU)

18.4 Lift the ECU out and disconnect the wiring

Check

1 If the tests shown in the preceding Sections have failed to isolate the cause of an ignition fault, it is possible that the ECU itself is faulty. No details are available for testing the ECU – it must taken to a Yamaha dealer for assessment.

2 On machines not fitted with an immobiliser system, it is possible to substitute a known good ECU in place of the suspect one for testing purposes. If an immobiliser system is fitted, the only solution in the event of an ECU failure is to fit a new unit. If a new ECU is fitted, the (red) immobiliser code re-registering key must be registered to the unit (see Section 19).

Removal and installation

3 Remove the battery (see Chapter 8).

4 Lift the ECU out and disconnect the wiring connector **(see illustration)**.

5 Installation is the reverse of removal. Make sure the wiring terminals are clean and none of the pins are bent, and make sure that the connector is pushed fully onto the ECU.

19 Immobiliser system

General information

1 The immobiliser system will only allow the machine to be started if a registered key is used to turn the ignition switch ON. The system consists of a transponder in the ignition key, the immobiliser unit (transceiver) fitted on the front of the ignition switch, and the engine control unit (ECU).

2 When the ignition is switched ON, the ECU sends power through the immobiliser transceiver to the transponder. The transponder sends a coded signal back through the transceiver to the ECU. If the code sent by the transponder matches the code stored in the ECU memory, the immobiliser indicator light in the instrument cluster comes on for about a second, then goes out, and the ECU allows the engine to be started.

3 If the key code is not recognised, or if there is a fault in the system, the indicator

light flashes. If the light flashes, or does not come on at all, refer to the *Fault diagnosis* and *Troubleshooting* Sections below.

4 The ECU can store the codes for up to three registered keys, two of which are standard-use keys with black casings, the other being the code re-registering key with a red casing. The three keys should be kept separately i.e. not on the same key-ring. The proximity of another key to the one being used in the switch can lead to the signal from the switch key transponder being jammed, and the bike will not start.

5 The transponder in the ignition key can be damaged if the key is dropped or knocked, gets too hot, is too close to a magnetic object, or is submerged in water. If this happens, a new key can be obtained from a Yamaha dealer and registered using the (red) code re-registering key. It is important, therefore, to keep the (red) code re-registering key in a safe place and never to use it on a daily basis.

6 Always make sure you have a spare standard-use key. If an existing key is damaged or lost, obtain a new key and register it with the immobiliser system as soon as possible.

7 If all the keys are lost, or if the ignition switch is faulty, all the components in the immobiliser system must be renewed.

Standard-use key registration procedure

Note: *This must be done when a standard-use key is lost and a new one is obtained. The procedure automatically renders the lost key useless – even if you don't replace the lost key with a new one and just have one standard-use key, following this procedure will re-register your remaining standard-use key and so doing will de-register the lost key.*

8 Obtain a new key from a Yamaha dealer, and have it cut to match the original key.

9 Have all three keys ready to hand – when a new standard-use key is registered, the code in the remaining standard-use key is cancelled, so this will also have to be registered.

10 Using the (red) code re-registering key, turn the ignition switch ON, then turn it OFF and remove the key. Within 5 seconds, turn the ignition ON with the new key. **Note:** *The immobiliser indicator light should flash on and off every half second. This indicates that the system is in registration mode. If at any time during the procedure the light stops flashing, more than 5 seconds have elapsed and the system is no longer in registration mode, in which case start again to register both keys.*

11 While the light is still flashing, turn the ignition OFF, remove the new key (placing it well away from the transceiver) and within 5 seconds turn the ignition ON with the remaining standard-use key. When the light stops flashing the registration is complete. Turn the ignition OFF and remove the key.

12 Check that both standard-use keys can start the motorcycle.

Code re-registering key registration procedure

Note: *This must be done when a new ECU has been fitted, or when a new immobiliser system has been installed.*

13 Turn the ignition switch ON using the (red) code re-registering key. The immobiliser light will come on for about one second, then go out, indicating that the key has been registered.

14 Check that the key can start the motorcycle.

15 Now register the standard-use keys as described in Steps 8 to 12.

Installing a new ECU

16 Install the ECU (see Section 18).

17 Turn the ignition switch ON using the code re-registering key. This registers the key to the new ECU.

18 Check that the key can start the motorcycle.

19 Now register the standard-use keys as described in Steps 8 to 12.

Installing a new immobiliser transceiver

20 Remove the ignition switch, then remove the old immobiliser transceiver from it and fit the new one (see Chapter 8).

21 Turn the ignition switch ON using the code re-registering key. This registers the key to the transceiver.

22 Check that the key can start the motorcycle.

23 Now register the standard-use keys as described in Steps 8 to 12

Fault diagnosis

24 If there is a fault in the system, the immobiliser indicator light in the instrument cluster flashes and a fault code is shown in the LCD display.

Fault code	Symptoms	Possible causes
51	Signal from key not being received by immobiliser transceiver	Interference from other keys or magnet Faulty key transponder Faulty immobiliser transceiver
52	Code from key not recognised by immobiliser transceiver	Interference from other key Unregistered key being used
53	Signal from immobiliser transceiver not being received by ECU	Faulty wiring or wiring connector Faulty immobiliser transceiver Faulty ECU
54	Codes do not match between immobiliser and ECU	Code re-registering key not registered Faulty wiring or wiring connector Faulty immobiliser transceiver Faulty ECU
55	Key registration error	Same key being registered twice
56	Code not recognised by ECU	Interference Faulty wiring or wiring connector Faulty immobiliser transceiver Faulty ECU

Troubleshooting procedure

25 If fault code 51 or 52 is shown, first check that none of the other registered keys are close to the receiver. If they are, remove them and try the ignition again. The key transponder

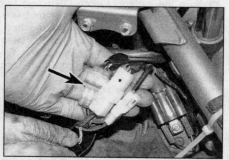

19.27 Immobiliser transceiver wiring connector (arrowed)

may be faulty – try starting the bike with another key.

26 If any fault code is shown, first check the fuses, wiring and connectors between the immobiliser receiver, ignition switch and the ECU (see below and Chapter 8, Sections 2 and 18, and to the *Wiring diagrams* at the end of Chapter 8). A continuity test of all wires will locate a break or short in any circuit. Inspect the terminals inside the wiring connectors and ensure they are not loose, bent or corroded. Spray the inside of the connectors with a proprietary electrical terminal cleaner before reconnection. Also make sure the battery is in good condition and that the ignition switch is not faulty (see Chapter 8).

27 Remove the air filter housing (see Section 5). Trace the wiring from the immobiliser transceiver to the wiring connector and disconnect the connector (**see illustration**). Using a voltmeter, connect the positive (+)

probe to the red/white wire terminal on the loom side of the connector and the negative (–) probe to the black/white wire terminal. Turn the ignition ON – there should be battery voltage. Now repeat the test with the positive (+) probe connected to the red/green wire terminal. If no voltage was recorded in either test refer to the wiring diagrams and check the red/white and red/green circuits to their power sources, and check the black wire for continuity to earth. If there is voltage, the immobiliser transceiver is probably faulty and must be replaced with a new one.

28 If the immobiliser LED or the LCD display in the instrument cluster do not come on, refer to Chapter 8 and check the instrument cluster.

29 If all indications are that either the immobiliser transceiver or the ECU are faulty, it is worth having them checked by a Yamaha dealer before buying new parts.

Chapter 5
Frame and suspension

Contents

Degrees of difficulty

Easy, suitable for novice with little experience	**Fairly easy**, suitable for beginner with some experience	**Fairly difficult**, suitable for competent DIY mechanic	**Difficult**, suitable for experienced DIY mechanic	**Very difficult**, suitable for expert DIY or professional

Specifications

Front forks
Fork oil type	Yamaha suspension fluid '01' or equivalent
Fork oil capacity (per leg)	473 cc
Fork oil level*	115 mm
Fork spring free length	
Standard	365 mm
Service limit	358 mm

*Oil level is measured from the top of the inner tube with the fork spring removed and the leg fully compressed.

Torque wrench settings
Centrestand pivot bolts	73 Nm
Clutch lever bracket clamp bolt	11 Nm
Clutch release mechanism shaft housing bolts	10 Nm
Footrest bracket bolts	30 Nm
Fork clamp bolts	
Bottom yoke	30 Nm
Top yoke	20 Nm
Fork damper bolt	23 Nm
Fork top bolt	24 Nm
Front brake master cylinder clamp bolts	10 Nm
Handlebar clamp bolts	24 Nm
Handlebar end-weights	26 Nm
Rear brake master cylinder mounting bolts	23 Nm
Rear shock absorber nuts	
Upper mounting	51 Nm
Lower mounting	55 Nm
Sidestand bracket bolts	63 Nm
Sidestand pivot bolt nut	54 Nm
Steering stem nut	110 Nm
Swingarm pivot bolt nut	110 Nm

1 General information

All models use a steel frame, incorporating the engine as a stressed member.

Front suspension is by a pair of conventional telescopic forks with internal coil springs. The forks are not adjustable.

At the rear, an aluminium alloy swingarm acts directly onto a single shock absorber. The shock absorber is adjustable for spring pre-load only.

2 Frame

1 The frame should not require attention unless accident damage has occurred. In most cases, fitting a new frame is the only satisfactory remedy for such damage. A few frame specialists have the jigs and other equipment necessary for straightening the frame to the required standard of accuracy, but even then there is no simple way of assessing to what extent the frame may have been over-stressed.

2 After the machine has covered a high mileage, the frame should be examined closely for signs of cracking or splitting at the welded joints. Loose engine mount bolts can cause ovaling or fracturing of the mounts themselves. Minor damage can often be repaired by welding, depending on the extent and nature of the damage, but this is a task for an expert.

3 Remember that a frame that is out of alignment will cause handling problems. If misalignment is suspected as the result of an accident, first check the wheel alignment (see Chapter 6). To have the frame checked thoroughly it will be necessary to strip the machine completely.

3 Footrests, gearchange lever and rear brake pedal

Footrests

1 To remove the rider's footrests, remove the split pin from the pivot pin, then pull the pivot pin out (see illustration). Note the location of the footrest return spring ends.

2 If required, the footrest rubbers can be removed by undoing the screws on the underside of the footrest.

3 Follow the same procedure to remove the passenger's footrests – note that a spring-loaded ball and detent plate are located between the footrest and its bracket to secure the footrest in the UP position when not in use (see illustration). Take care not to loose the ball and spring when the footrest is removed.

4 Installation is the reverse of removal. Use new split pins.

Gearchange lever

5 Measure and note the amount of exposed thread on each end of the gearchange lever linkage rod (this determines the position of the lever), then slacken the linkage rod locknuts (see illustrations). Unscrew the rod from the lever and the arm and remove the rod – the rod is reverse-threaded on one end, so will unscrew from both lever and arm simultaneously when turned in the one direction.

6 Unscrew the gearchange lever pivot bolt and remove the bolt, washers (noting their order) and lever (see illustration).

7 Installation is the reverse of removal. Clean and grease the gearchange lever pivot bolt and make sure the washers are correctly fitted – the wave washer goes between the plain washer and the pivot bolt. Clean the threads of the pedal pivot bolt and apply some fresh threadlock.

8 Set the linkage rod in the arm as lever as noted on removal or so the lever is at the desired height, then tighten the locknuts (see illustrations 3.5a and b).

Rear brake pedal

9 Unscrew the pedal pivot bolt (see illustration).

10 Unscrew the bolts securing the rear brake master cylinder to the footrest bracket and the footrest bracket to the frame and remove the bracket, drawing the brake pedal off as you

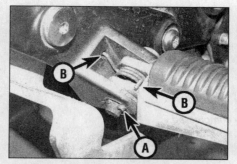

3.1 Remove the split pin (A) and withdraw the pivot pin – note how the return spring ends (B) locate

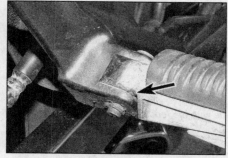

3.3 Note the fitting of the ball, spring and plate (arrowed)

3.5a Slacken the locknuts (arrowed)...

3.5b ...on each end of the rod

3.6 Gearchange lever pivot bolt (arrowed)

3.9 Brake pedal pivot bolt (arrowed)

do, and noting that there is a wave washer fitted on the pivot against the pedal (see illustrations).

11 Remove the split pin and washer from the clevis pin connecting the brake pedal to the master cylinder pushrod, then push the clevis pin out (see illustration). A new split pin must be used on reassembly.

12 Unhook the rear brake light switch spring and the pedal return spring (see illustration).

13 Installation is the reverse of removal, noting the following:

● Check for wear and damage to the pivot bush in the footrest bracket and replace it with a new one if necessary – if the pedal is a sloppy fit the bush is worn. Clean and grease the pedal pivot shaft and make sure the wave washer is on the pivot against the lever (see illustration 3.10b).

● Make sure the springs are hooked up correctly (see illustration 3.12).

● Fit the clevis pin from the inside (see illustration 3.11). Fit the washer and secure the clevis pin with a new split pin – bend both ends of the split pin around the clevis pin for security.

● Clean the threads of the footrest bracket bolts and apply some fresh threadlock, and tighten the bolts to the torque setting specified at the beginning of the Chapter. Tighten the rear brake master cylinder mounting bolts to the specified torque setting. Clean the threads of the pedal pivot bolt and apply some fresh threadlock.

14 If required, follow the procedure in Chapter 1, Section 11, to adjust the rear brake light switch and pedal position.

4 Stands

Sidestand

1 To remove the sidestand, support the motorcycle securely in an upright position using the centrestand if fitted, or an auxiliary stand. Tie the front brake on.

2 To remove the stand, unhook the spring with the stand in the raised position (see illustration). Counterhold the bolt head, unscrew the nut and remove the washer (see illustration). Support the stand leg and withdraw the bolt.

 HAYNES HINT *Fit a washer in between each coil of the stand spring – this expands it, making it a lot easier to unhook and hook back up.*

3 To remove the bracket, undo the sidestand switch nuts and bolts and displace the switch (see illustration). Undo the stand bracket bolts and lift the assembly off (see illustration).

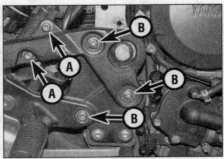
3.10a Unscrew the master cylinder bolts (A) and bracket bolts (B)...

3.11 Remove the split pin (arrowed) and detach the pushrod from the pedal

3.10b ...displace the bracket from the pedal pivot, noting the washer (arrowed)

3.12 Unhook the springs (arrowed) and remove the pedal

4 Installation is the reverse of removal, noting the following points:

● Apply lithium-based grease to the pivot contact areas.

● Clean the bracket and stand bolt threads and apply a suitable thread locking compound.

● Tighten the bracket bolts and pivot bolt

nut to the torque settings specified at the beginning of the Chapter.

● Check the spring tension – it must hold the stand up when it is not in use. If the spring has sagged, replace it with a new one.

● Check the operation of the sidestand switch and starter safety circuit (see Chapter 1, Section 15).

4.2a Unhook the springs (arrowed)

4.3a Displace the sidestand switch

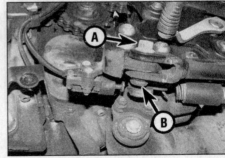
4.2b Sidestand pivot bolt (A) and nut (B)

4.3b Sidestand bracket bolts (arrowed)

4.6 Unhook the springs (arrowed)

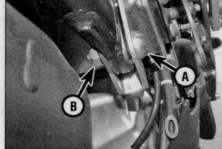

4.7 Centrestand pivot bolt (A) and nut (B) (one on each side)

Centrestand (where fitted)

5 Support the motorcycle on its sidestand.
6 Unhook the springs with the stand in the raised position (see illustration).
7 Counterhold the stand pivot bolts and unscrew the nuts (see illustration). Support the stand and withdraw the bolts.
8 Installation is the reverse of removal, noting the following points:
- Apply lithium-based grease to the pivot contact areas.
- Clean the stand bolt threads and apply a suitable thread locking compound.
- Tighten the nuts/bolts to the torque setting specified at the beginning of this Chapter.
- Check the spring tension – they must hold

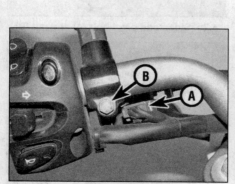

5.2 Brake light switch connectors (arrowed)

the stand up when it is not in use. If the springs have sagged, replace them with new ones.

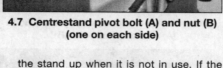

5 Handlebars and levers

Handlebars

Removal

Note: *The handlebars can be displaced from the top yoke without having to remove the throttle twistgrip, switch assemblies or levers (see Step 10). In all cases, take care to avoid straining the handlebar wiring. Support or tie the handlebar assembly using rags to cushion*

5.3 Handlebar end-weight (arrowed)

it and anything it sits against. Also cover the front brake master cylinder with rag in case of leakage.

1 On XJ6-N models remove the mirrors (see Chapter 7).
2 Disconnect the brake light switch wiring connectors (see illustration). Follow the procedure in Chapter 4 to disconnect the throttle cables and displace the throttle twistgrip housing/right-hand switch assembly. Free the wiring from any ties on the handlebar.
3 Unscrew the end-weight from the right-hand end of the handlebar with a suitable Allen key, then slide the twistgrip off the handlebar (see illustration).
4 Follow the procedure in Chapter 6 and displace the front brake master cylinder. There is no need to disconnect the brake hose. Keep the reservoir upright to prevent fluid spillage and make sure no strain in placed on the hose.
5 Disconnect the clutch switch wiring connector (see illustration). Follow the procedure in Chapter 8 to displace the left-hand switch assembly. Free the wiring from any ties on the handlebar.
Caution: Wear eye protection when using a spray lube for this purpose – it can spray back into your face.
6 Unscrew the end-weight from the left-hand end of the handlebar (see illustration 5.3). Pull the grip off the handlebar – push a plastic tool or screwdriver covered with tape between the grip and the bar and use spray lubricant and/or compressed air to loosen the grip. If the grip has been bonded in place you may need to cut it free.
7 Follow the procedure in Chapter 2, Section 12, to disconnect the clutch cable from the clutch lever.
8 Loosen the clutch lever bracket pinch bolt and slide the lever off the handlebar (see illustration 5.5).
9 Carefully prise the plugs off the handlebar clamp bolts (see illustration).
10 Support the handlebars, unscrew the handlebar clamps bolts and remove the clamps, then lift the handlebars off (see illustration).

5.9 Remove the plugs...

5.10 ...then unscrew the bolts (arrowed)

5.5 Clutch switch connector (A); clutch lever bracket pinch bolt (B)

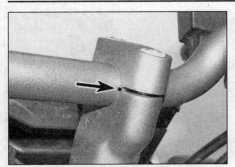
5.11 Align the clamp mating surfaces with the punch mark (arrowed)

5.12 Fit the clamps with the arrow to the front

5.13a Align the slit with the punch mark (arrowed)

5.13b Align the clamp mating surfaces with the punch mark (arrowed)

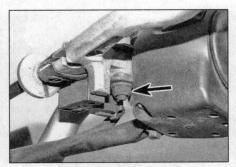
5.15 Clutch lever pivot bolt locknut (arrowed)

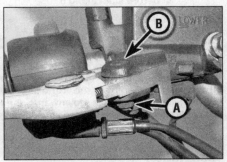
5.17 Brake lever pivot bolt locknut (A), pivot bolt (B)

Installation

11 Position the handlebars centrally, aligning the punch mark on the bar with the top edge of the right-hand bracket (see illustration).

12 Fit the handlebar clamps with the arrow mark pointing to the front (see illustration). Tighten the front clamp bolts first, then the rear clamp bolts, to the torque setting specified at the beginning of this Chapter. Fit the plugs into the bolts (see illustration 5.9).

13 Install the remaining components in the reverse order of removal, noting the following.

● Align the slit in the clutch lever bracket with the punch mark on the underside of the handlebar (see illustration). Tighten the clamp bolt to the specified torque.

● Align the front brake master cylinder clamp mating surfaces with the punch mark on the top of the handlebar, and fit the clamp with the UP mark facing up (see illustration). Tighten the clamp bolts to the specified torque, tightening the top bolt first.

● Make sure that the peg on the lower half of each switch housing locates in the hole in the underside of the handlebar.

● Lubricate the right-hand bar end before sliding on the throttle twistgrip.

● Tighten the handlebar end-weights to the specified torque.

● Check and adjust throttle and clutch cable freeplay (see Chapter 1).

● Do not forget to reconnect the front brake light switch and clutch switch wiring connectors (see illustrations 5.2 and 5.5).

● Check the operation of all switches, the front brake and clutch before taking the machine on the road.

Clutch lever

14 Follow the procedure in Chapter 2, Section 12, to disconnect the clutch cable from the clutch lever.

15 Unscrew the lever pivot bolt locknut, then push the pivot bolt out of the bracket and remove the lever (see illustration). Note there is a sleeve in the lever pivot – make sure it does not drop out.

16 Installation is the reverse of removal. Apply grease to the pivot bolt shaft and sleeve and to the contact areas between the lever and its bracket, and to the inner clutch cable end. Adjust the clutch cable freeplay (see Chapter 1).

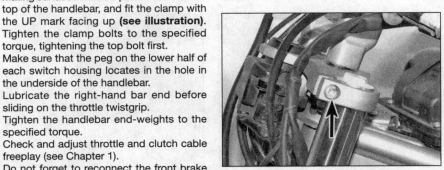
6.5a Slacken the clamp bolt (arrowed) in the top yoke

Front brake lever

17 Undo the lever pivot bolt locknut, then unscrew the pivot bolt and remove the lever from the master cylinder, noting how it locates against the pushrod (see illustration).

18 Installation is the reverse of removal. Apply silicone grease to the pivot bolt shaft and to the contact areas between the lever and its bracket and where the pushrod locates in the cup in the lever.

6 Fork removal and installation

Removal

1 Support the motorcycle upright on level ground so that the front wheel is off the ground. On XJ6-S and F and FZ6R models remove the fairing (see Chapter 7).

2 Remove the front wheel (see Chapter 6).

3 Remove the front mudguard (see Chapter 7).

4 Work on each fork leg individually. Note the routing of the cables, wiring and hoses around the forks.

5 Note the alignment between the top of the fork inner tube and the top yoke, then slacken the fork clamp bolt in the top yoke (see illustration). If the fork leg is to be disassembled, or if the fork oil is being

6.5b Stick a single layer of masking tape around the fork top bolt to protect its finish before slackening it

6.6a Slacken the clamp bolt (arrowed) in the bottom yoke...

6.6b ...then draw the fork down and out of the yokes

changed, loosen the fork top bolt, but don't remove it **(see illustration)**.

6 Support the fork leg, then loosen the fork clamp bolt in the bottom yoke **(see illustration)**. Remove the fork leg by twisting it and pulling it downwards **(see illustration)**. Note which fork leg fits on which side.

Installation

7 Remove all traces of corrosion from the fork tubes and the yokes.

8 Slide the fork leg up through the bottom yoke and into the top yoke, making sure the wiring, cables and hoses are the correct side of the leg as noted on removal **(see illustration 6.6b)**. Align the top of the fork tube with the top yoke, so the top bolt itself is raised above it **(see illustration 6.5b)**.

9 Tighten the fork clamp bolt in the bottom yoke to the torque setting specified at the beginning of this Chapter **(see illustration 6.6a)**. If the fork leg has been dismantled or if the oil has been changed, tighten the top bolt to the specified torque setting. Tighten the fork clamp bolt in the top yoke to the specified torque setting **(see illustration 6.5a)**.

10 Install the remaining components in the reverse order of removal.

11 Check the operation of the front forks and brakes before taking the machine on the road.

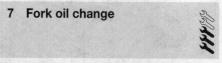

7 Fork oil change

Note: *After a high mileage the fork oil will deteriorate and its damping and lubrication qualities will be impaired. Always change the oil in both fork legs.*

1 Remove the fork leg, making sure that the top bolt is loosened while the leg is still clamped in the bottom yoke (see Section 6).

2 Unscrew the top bolt from the top of the inner tube carefully as it is under spring pressure **(see illustration)**. Check the

condition of the O-ring on the top bolt and replace it with a new one if necessary.

3 Withdraw the spacer, then slide the inner tube down and remove the washer, then pull out the fork spring, noting which way round it fits **(see illustrations)**. Wipe any excess oil off the spring and spacer.

4 Invert the fork leg over a suitable container and pump the inner tube to expel as much oil as possible **(see illustration)**.

5 Support the fork upside down and allow it to drain for a few minutes, then pump the fork again. If required, the fork spring free length can be checked (see Section 8). **Note:** *If the fork oil contains metal particles, follow the procedure in Section 8 and inspect the*

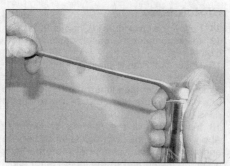

7.2 Unscrew the top bolt

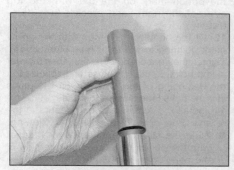

7.3a Remove the spacer...

7.3b ...the spring seat...

7.3c ...and the spring

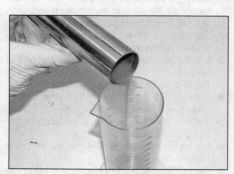

7.4 Drain and pump the oil from the fork

fork bushes and the surface of the tube for wear.

6 Fully compress the inner tube in the outer tube. Hold the leg upright and slowly pour in the correct quantity of the specified grade of fork oil **(see illustration)**. Pump the inner tube to distribute the oil, then stand the leg upright for ten minutes to allow any air bubbles to disperse.

7 Make sure the inner tube is fully compressed into the outer tube, then measure the fork oil level from the top of the inner tube **(see illustration)**. Add or subtract fork oil until it is at the level specified at the beginning of this Chapter.

8 Fit the spring with its closer-wound coils at the top **(see illustration)**. Pull the inner tube out until the spring is just recessed, then fit the washer onto it, then fully extend the inner tube and fit the spacer **(see illustrations 7.3b and a)**.

9 Lubricate the top bolt O-ring, using a new one if necessary, with fork oil. Carefully thread the top bolt into the tube and tighten it finger-tight **(see illustration)**. **Note:** *The top bolt can be tightened to the specified torque setting when the fork leg has been installed and is securely held in the bottom yoke.*

10 Install the fork leg (see Section 6).

8 Fork overhaul

Special Tools: *Yamaha service tools are available for holding the damper and installing the fork top bush and oil seal, although alternatives are given in the procedure.*

Disassembly

Note: *Always dismantle the fork legs separately to avoid interchanging parts and thus causing an accelerated rate of wear. Store all components in separate, clearly marked containers.*

1 Remove the fork leg, making sure that the top bolt is loosened while the leg is still clamped in the bottom yoke (see Section 6).

2 If the right-hand fork leg is being

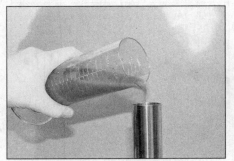

7.6 Pour in the correct type and quantity of oil and pump the inner tube to circulate it

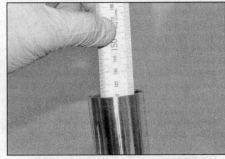

7.7 Measure the oil level and adjust if necessary

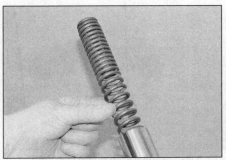

7.8 Make sure the spring is the correct way round

7.9 Check and lubricate the O-ring (arrowed), then thread the top bolt into the tube

disassembled, unscrew the axle pinch bolt. If required remove the stone guard by carefully easing it off its seat on the top of the outer tube.

3 Slacken the damper bolt in the base of the outer tube **(see illustration)**. If the damper turns inside the fork, turn the leg upside down and compress the fork so the pressure of the spring holds the damper while the bolt is loosened. If the bolt cannot be loosened at this stage, Yamaha produce a service tool (Part No. 90890-01460) and T-bar (Part No. 90890-01326) which can be inserted down inside the inner tube once the spring has been removed (see Step 7) – the tool has a tapered head that engages in the top end of the

damper to hold it while the bolt is loosened. As an alternative we used a broom handle tapered at the end, and it did the job **(see illustration 8.7b)**.

4 Follow the procedure in Section 7 to remove the top bolt, spacer, washer and spring, and drain the oil form the fork.

5 Carefully prise off the dust seal **(see illustration)**. A new seal must be used.

6 Compress the fork leg to avoid damaging its working surface, then using a small screwdriver, carefully remove the oil seal retaining clip, taking care not to scratch the surface of the inner tube **(see illustration)**.

7 Unscrew the previously slackened damper bolt from the bottom of the outer tube **(see**

8.3 Slacken the damper rod bolt

8.5 Prise out the dust seal using a flat-bladed screwdriver...

8.6 ...then remove the retaining clip

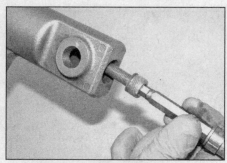

8.7a Remove the damper rod bolt

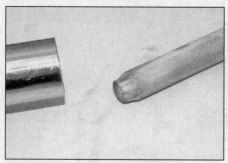

8.7b A tapered broom handle end can be used to hold the damper rod to prevent it turning

8.8 Remove the damper rod

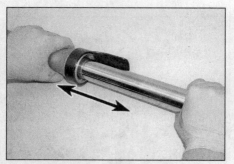

8.9a Repeatedly draw the tubes apart...

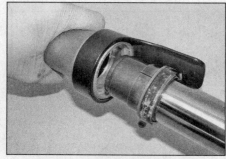

8.9b ...until the seal and bush are displaced

8.11 Remove the damper seat

illustration). If necessary, use the Yamaha service tool or the broom handle described in Step 4 to hold the damper **(see illustration)**. A new sealing washer must be used on the bolt on reassembly.

8 Tip the damper rod and rebound spring from inside the inner tube **(see illustration)**.

9 To separate the inner tube from the outer tube it is necessary to displace the oil seal and top bush from the top of the outer tube. The bottom bush on the inner tube will not pass through the top bush in the outer tube, and this can be used to good effect. Gently compress the fork until the inner tube stops against the damper. Now pull the inner tube sharply outwards until the bottom bush strikes the top bush **(see illustration)**. Repeat this operation until the seal and top bush are tapped out of the outer tube and the inner tube can be fully withdrawn **(see illustration)**.

10 Slide the oil seal, washer and the top bush off the inner tube, noting which way up they fit. A new oil seal must be fitted on reassembly.

11 Tip the damper seat out of the outer tube, noting which way up it fits **(see illustration)**.

Inspection

12 Clean all parts in solvent and blow them dry with compressed air, if available. Check the inner tube for score marks, scratches, flaking or pitted chrome finish and excessive or abnormal wear. Look for dents in the inner tube and replace the tubes in both forks with new ones if any are found. Check the fork seal seat for nicks, gouges and scratches. If damage is evident, leaks will occur. Also check the oil seal washer for damage or distortion; replace damaged or worn parts with new ones as necessary.

13 Check the fork inner tube for runout

(bending) using V-blocks and a dial gauge, or have it done by a Yamaha dealer or suspension specialist **(see illustration)**. Yamaha specify a runout limit of 0.2 mm, so if the inner tube is bent beyond the limit fit new inner tubes.

⚠️ *Warning: If either inner tube is bent, it should not be straightened (particularly after an accident) – replace both inner tubes with a new pair.*

14 Check the spring for cracks and other damage. Measure the spring free length and compare the measurement to the specifications at the beginning of this Chapter **(see illustration)**. If a spring is defective or has sagged below the service limit, replace the springs in both fork legs with new ones. Never replace only one spring.

15 Examine the working surfaces of the two bushes **(see illustration)**. If there is any

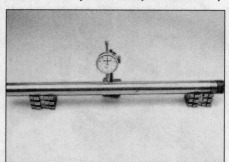

8.13 Check the inner tube for runout

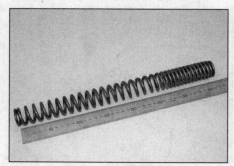

8.14 Measure spring free length

8.15a Check the working surface (arrowed) of each bush

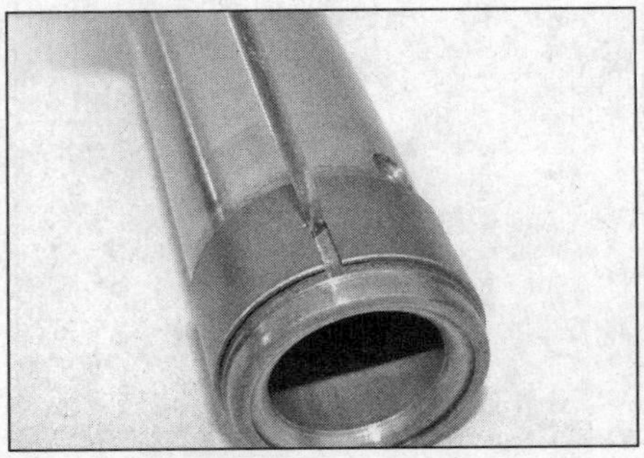

8.15b Lever the ends apart just enough to slide the bush off

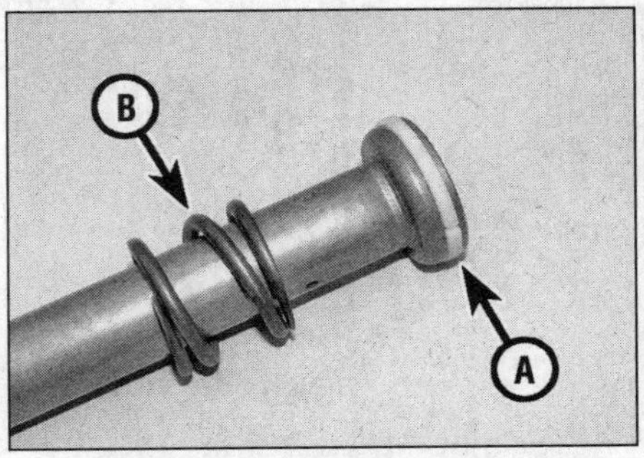

8.16 Damper rod piston ring (A) and rebound spring (B)

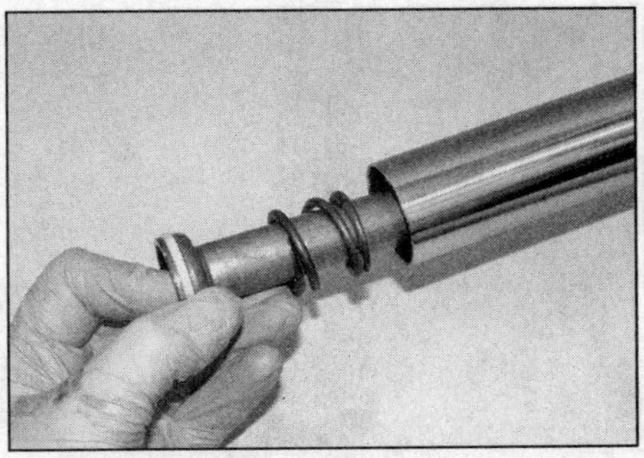

8.19a Slide the damper into the top of the tube and down to the bottom so its end protrudes...

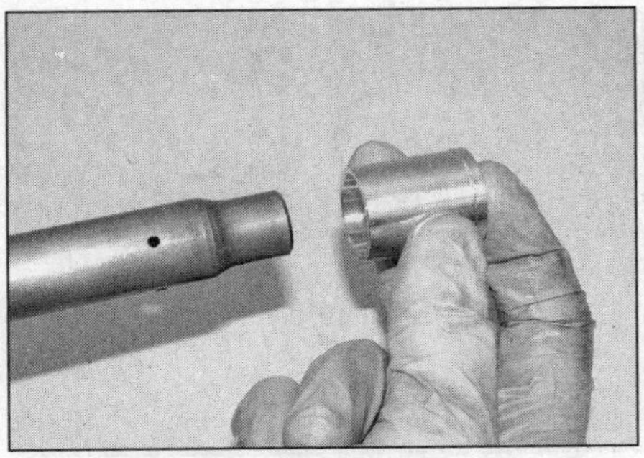

8.19b ...then fit the seat onto it...

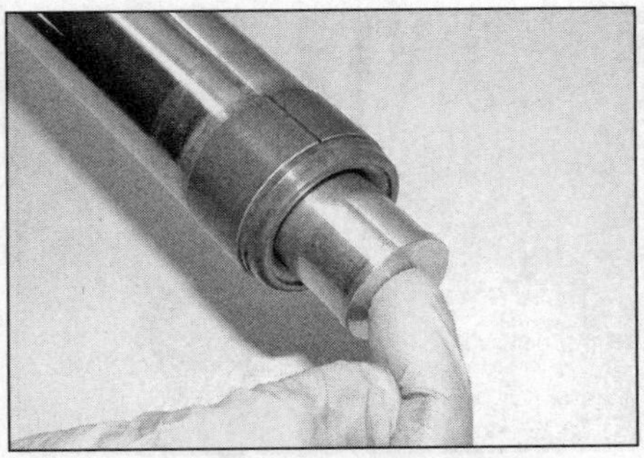

8.19c ...and push it up into the tube

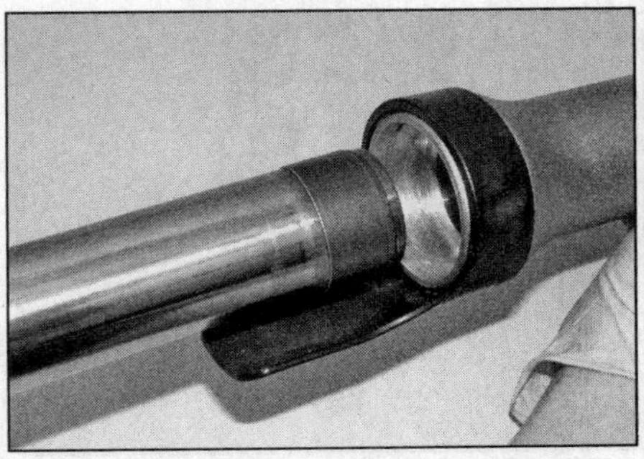

8.20 Slide the inner tube into the outer tube

evidence of wear or scuff marks they should be replaced with new ones. **Note:** *Yamaha advises that new top and bottom bushes should be fitted whenever the forks are disassembled.* The bottom bush (on the inner tube) can be removed by carefully opening out its slot with a large flat-bladed screwdriver so that it will slide off the end of the tube **(see illustration)**; use the same method to install the new bush.

16 Check the damper rod, the piston ring in its head, and the rebound spring for damage and wear, and replace any components as necessary with new ones **(see illustration)**.

17 Examine the damper seat and replace it with a new one if it is worn or distorted **(see illustration 8.11)**.

Reassembly

18 If removed, fit the bottom bush on the fork tube (see Step 15).

19 Fit the rebound spring onto the damper rod, then slide the rod into the inner tube, and let the bottom end slide out of the hole in the bottom of the tube **(see illustration)**. Fit the seat onto the bottom of the rod, then push the seat up inside the tube **(see illustrations)**.

20 Lubricate the inner tube and bottom bush with fork oil, then insert the inner tube as far as it will go into the outer tube, so that the damper seat locates in the bottom of the outer tube **(see illustration)**.

21 Clean the threads of the damper bolt. Fit a new sealing washer onto the bolt and apply a few drops of a suitable non-permanent thread-locking compound to the threads, then screw the bolt into the bottom of the damper rod **(see illustration)**.

22 Hold the damper head with the tapered broom handle or the Yamaha service tools to prevent it turning (see Step 3), and tighten the damper bolt to the torque setting specified at the beginning of the Chapter.

23 Push the inner tube fully into the outer tube. Lubricate the top bush, then slide it down over the inner tube and press it squarely into its recess in the outer tube **(see illustration)**. Fit the washer on top of the bush **(see illustration)**.

24 If available, slide a suitable piece of tubing down over the inner tube to tap the bush into its recess. Yamaha produce service tools to do this (Part Nos. 90890-01367 and 90890-01381), or there are aftermarket fork bush/seal fitting tools available from good

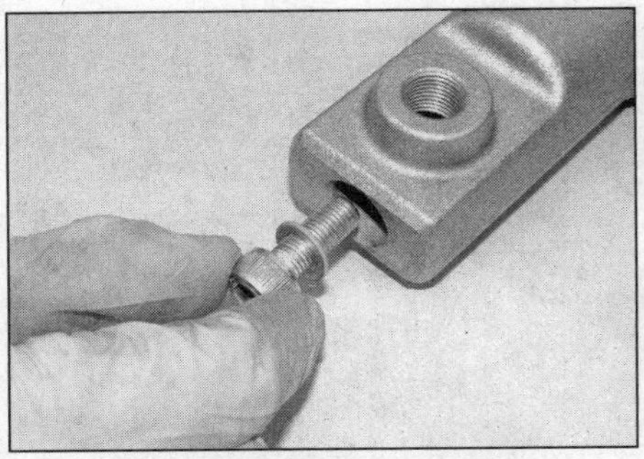

8.21 Use a new sealing washer and threadlock on the bolt

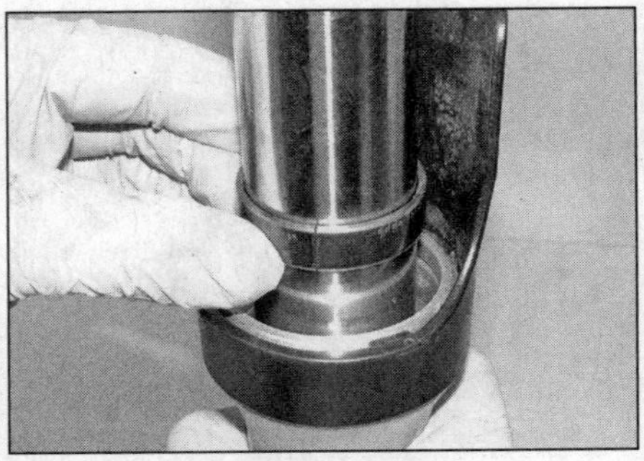

8.23a Fit the top bush...

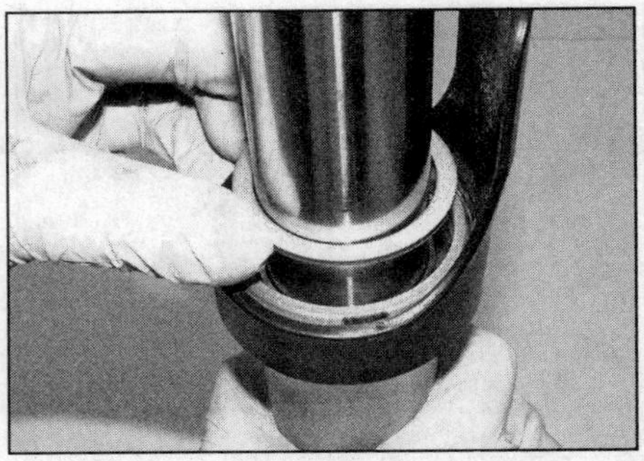

8.23b ...then seat the washer on it

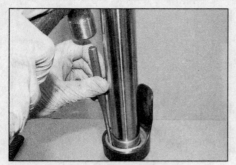

8.24 Using a punch to drive the bush in

8.25a Slide the seal down into the top of the outer tube

8.25b Using a dedicated tool to drive the seal in

8.25c Fit the old seal on top of the new one…

8.25d …to prevent damage if using a punch…

8.25e …then lever the old seal out and discard it

suppliers **(see illustration 8.25b)**. If necessary, the bush can be tapped into place using a pin punch and hammer – take great care to drive the bush in evenly **(see illustration)**. **Note:** *Excessive force should be unnecessary and will damage the bush. Take care not to scratch the inner tube during reassembly; if the inner tube is pushed fully into the outer tube any accidental scratching is confined to the area above the oil seal.*

25 Lubricate the **new** oil seal with lithium-based grease and slide it down over the inner tube with its markings facing upwards **(see illustration)**. Press the seal squarely into the outer tube. Tap it lightly into place, preferably using a dedicated tool as described in Step 24, until the retaining clip groove is

visible above the seal **(see illustration)**. If you are using a punch to drive the seal in it is advisable to fit the old seal on top of the new one to act as an interface to avoid any damage to the new seal **(see illustrations)**. Once the new seal is fitted the old seal can be pushed out easily using a small screwdriver **(see illustration)**.

26 Fit the retaining clip, making sure it is correctly located in its groove **(see illustration)**.

27 Lubricate the inside of the new dust seal then slide it down the inner tube and press it into position **(see illustration)**.

28 If removed fit the stone guard, locating the tab in the notch in the top of the outer tube.

29 Follow the procedure in Section 7 to fill the fork leg with the correct amount of specified

fork oil, and install the spring, washer, spacer and top bolt.

30 Install the fork leg (see Section 6).

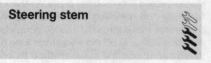

9 Steering stem

Removal

1 Support the motorcycle upright on level ground so that the front wheel is off the ground. Remove the fuel tank (see Chapter 4).

2 On XJ6-N models remove the headlight (see Chapter 8). Release the hose clip from the right-hand side of the instrument cluster bracket **(see illustration)**. Disconnect the

8.26 Fit the retaining ring into the groove…

8.27 …then press the dust seal in

9.2a Release the clip

9.2b Disconnect the instrument wiring...

9.2c ...then unscrew the bolts (arrowed)...

9.2d ...and remove the instrument assembly

instrument wiring connector **(see illustration)**. Unscrew the instrument bracket bolts on the underside of the top yoke and remove the instrument assembly **(see illustrations)**.

3 On XJ6-S and F and FZ6R models remove the fairing (see Chapter 7).

4 Remove the front forks (see Section 6).

5 Unscrew the bolts securing the horn/front brake hose support bracket to the bottom yoke and displace the bracket **(see illustration)**.

6 Unscrew the steering stem nut and remove the washer **(see illustrations)**. Lift the top yoke/handlebar assembly up off the steering stem and rest it across the air filter housing as shown, using rag as cushioning and protection as required **(see illustrations)**.

7 Remove the tabbed lockwasher, noting how it fits, then unscrew and remove the locknut, using a C-spanner if necessary (it shouldn't

be tight and will probably undo by hand) **(see illustrations)**. Remove the rubber washer **(see illustration)**.

8 Supporting the bottom yoke, slacken

the adjuster nut using a C-spanner **(see illustration)**. Remove the adjuster nut and the bearing cover from the steering stem **(see illustrations 9.14b and a)**.

9.5 Unscrew the bolts (arrowed)

9.6a Unscrew the nut and remove the washer

9.6b Displace the yoke/handlebar assembly...

9.6c ...and rest it on the air filter housing

9.7a Remove the lockwasher...

9.7b ...then unscrew the locknut...

9.7c ...and remove the rubber washer

9.8 Slacken the adjuster nut using a C-spanner

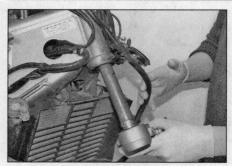

9.9 Remove the steering stem...

9.10 ...then remove the inner race and upper bearing from the head

9.11a Remove the rubber washer...

9.11b ...and the lower bearing and seal (arrowed) from the stem

9.14a Fit the bearing cover...

9.14b ...then thread the adjuster nut on

9 Carefully lower the bottom yoke and steering stem out of the frame (see illustration).

10 Remove the inner race and bearing from the top of the steering head (see illustration).

11 Remove the rubber washer from the steering stem (see illustration). Remove the bearing and dust seal from the base of the steering stem (see illustration). It is advisable to fit a new dust seal. Use a suitable solvent to remove all traces of old grease from the bearings and races and check them for wear or damage as described in Section 10. Note: Do not remove the races from the steering head or the steering stem unless they are to be replaced with new ones – do not re-use the races if they have been removed.

Installation

12 Smear a liberal quantity of lithium-based grease onto the bearing races and work some grease well into both the upper and lower bearings. Fit the new dust seal over the lower bearing inner race on the steering stem, then fit the bearing (see illustration 9.11b). Fit the rubber washer (see illustration 9.11a).

13 Fit the upper bearing and the inner race into the top of the steering head (see illustration 9.10).

14 Carefully lift the bottom yoke and steering stem up through the steering head and upper bearing, taking care not to dislodge it (see illustration 9.9). Fit the bearing cover then thread the adjuster nut onto the steering stem and tighten it enough to hold the stem in the head without any play (see illustrations).

15 Install the forks, mudguard and wheel,

as their leverage and inertia need to be taken into account to properly set the bearings, then refer to the procedure in Chapter 1, Section 14, and adjust the bearings as described. Note that if new bearings have been fitted, you may need to carry out the procedure several times to allow them to settle.

16 Fit the rubber washer and the locknut, making sure the flat side of the nut faces down onto the washer (the upper side has a slight ridged section) (see illustrations 9.7c and b). Tighten the locknut finger-tight, then tighten it further until its notches align with those in the adjuster nut. Fit the tabbed lockwasher so that the tabs locate in the notches in both the locknut and adjuster nut (see illustration 9.7a).

17 Fit the top yoke assembly onto the steering stem, then fit the washer and steering stem nut and tighten it to the torque setting specified at the beginning of this Chapter (see illustrations 9.6b and a).

18 Install the remaining components in the reverse order of removal. Carry out a check of the steering head bearing freeplay as described in Chapter 1, and if necessary re-adjust.

10 Steering head bearings

Inspection

1 Remove the steering stem (see Section 9). Using a suitable solvent, remove all traces of old grease from the bearings and races.

2 Check for wear or damage – the races should be polished and free from indentations (see illustration). Inspect the bearing balls for signs of wear, damage or discoloration, and examine the retainer cages for distortion, cracks or splits. Spin the bearing balls by hand. They should spin freely and smoothly. If there are signs of wear on any of the above components, both upper and lower bearing assemblies must be replaced with a new set. Note: Do not remove the races from the steering head or the steering stem unless they are to be replaced with new ones – do not re-use the races if they have been removed.

Renewal

3 The outer races are an interference fit in the steering head and can be tapped out with a suitable drift located in the cut-outs in the

10.2 Check the inner and outer races for wear and damage

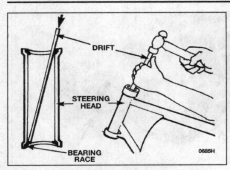

10.3a Drive the outer races from the steering head using a drift...

10.3b ...located in the cut-outs provided (arrowed)

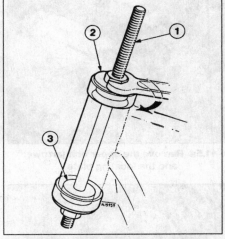

10.5 Drawbolt arrangement for fitting steering stem bearing races

1 *Long bolt or threaded bar*
2 *Thick washer*
3 *Guide for lower race*

head **(see illustrations)**. Alternate between the cut-outs so that the race is driven out squarely. It may prove advantageous to curve the end of the drift slightly to improve access.
4 Alternatively, the races can be removed using a slide-hammer type bearing extractor – these can often be hired from tool shops.
5 The new outer races can be fitted using a drawbolt arrangement **(see illustration)**, or by using a suitable tubular drift or socket that bears only on the outer flat rim of the race, and does not touch the sloping bearing surface of the race itself. Freezing the races first to shrink them will make them easier to fit.
6 To remove the lower bearing race from the steering stem, first thread the steering stem nut onto the top of the stem to protect the threads, they lay the stem over on its side and drive a chisel between the base of the race and the bottom yoke, taking great care not to

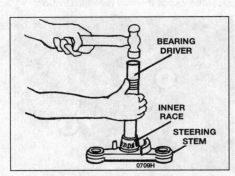

10.6 Lower bearing inner race (arrowed)

damage the yoke – heating the race first with a hot-air gun should expand it a little to ease removal **(see illustration)**. Work the chisel around the race to ensure it lifts squarely. Once there is clearance beneath the race, use two levers placed on opposite sides of the race to work it free, using blocks of wood to improve leverage and protect the yoke. If the race is firmly in place, carefully cut it off using a Dremel or angle grinder – you will probably not need to cut all the way through, as often the race may crack after a groove has been cut, or you can work a screwdriver or chisel in the groove to finally split it. Alternatively, take the steering stem to a Yamaha dealer.
7 Fit the new lower race onto the steering stem. A length of tubing with an internal diameter slightly larger than the steering stem that bears only on the inner flat rim of the race, and does not touch the sloping bearing surface of the race itself, will be needed to tap the new race into position **(see illustration)**. Heating the race first to expand it will make it easier to fit.
8 Install the steering stem (see Section 9).

11 Rear shock absorber

⚠️ *Warning: Do not attempt to disassemble the shock absorber. It is nitrogen-charged under high pressure. Improper disassembly*

could result in serious injury. Take the shock to a Yamaha dealer or suspension specialist for servicing or disposal.

Removal

1 Support the motorcycle upright on level ground on its centrestand if fitted, or on an auxiliary stand or stands (but not a rear paddock stand) – make sure that no weight is transmitted through any part of the rear suspension. Position a support under the rear wheel or swingarm so that it does not drop when the shock absorber is removed. Tie the front brake lever on so the bike can't roll forward.
2 Remove the seat and the side panels (see Chapter 7).
3 Unscrew the nuts on the shock absorber mounting bolts and remove the washers **(see illustrations)**.
4 Withdraw the lower mounting bolt.
5 Support the shock absorber and withdraw the upper mounting bolt along with the locating

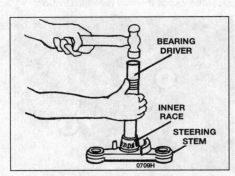

10.7 Drive the new bearing on using a suitable driver or a length of pipe

11.3a Unscrew the nut (arrowed) on the upper bolt...

11.3b ...and the lower bolt

11.5a Remove the upper bolt (arrowed) and the locating plate...

11.5b ...and manoeuvre the shock absorber out

11.8 Check the upper mounting bush (arrowed)

11.9a Withdraw the collars and check the seals

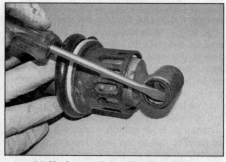

11.9b Lever the seals out with a screwdriver

11.10 Press the new seals in with your fingers

plate, then remove the shock absorber (see illustrations).

Inspection

6 Inspect the body of the shock absorber for obvious physical damage and the coil spring for looseness, cracks or signs of fatigue.

7 Inspect the shock damper rod for signs of bending, pitting and oil leakage.

8 Inspect the pivot bush in the upper mounting for wear (see illustration). If the bush is loose, worn or deteriorated, a new one must be fitted. Follow the procedure in *Tools and Workshop Tips* in the *Reference* section to press the old bush out and a new one in.

9 Withdraw the collar from each side of the lower mounting and check them for wear and damage (see illustration). Inspect the seals. If new ones are needed, lever out the old seals with a small screwdriver (see illustration). Clean any the old grease out of the lower mount and the collars with a suitable solvent.

10 Grease the lips of new bearing seals and press them into place with their marked side facing out (see illustration). Grease the collars inside and out and fit them into the mounting.

11 With the exception of the upper and lower mounting components, Yamaha do not supply replacement parts for the shock, although it is worth seeking advice from a suspension specialist on the possibility of repair.

Installation

12 Installation is the reverse of removal. Make sure the upper mounting bolt plate locates correctly and the bolt head sits inside it so it cannot turn (see illustration 11.5a). Tighten

the nuts to the torque settings specified at the beginning of this Chapter.

12 Suspension adjustment

Caution: Never attempt to turn the adjuster beyond the minimum or maximum setting.

1 The rear shock absorber is adjustable for spring pre-load.

2 Spring pre-load is adjusted using a suitable C-spanner (one is provided in the bike's toolkit, along with an extension handle) to turn the adjuster ring on the bottom of the shock absorber (see illustration).

3 There are seven positions. Position 1 is the softest setting, position 3 is the standard, and position 7 is the hardest. Align the setting required with the adjustment stopper. Turn the

12.2 Adjusting spring pre-load

spring seat clockwise to increase pre-load and anti-clockwise to decrease it.

13 Swingarm

Removal

1 Support the motorcycle upright on level ground on its centrestand if fitted, or on an auxiliary stand or stands (but not a rear paddock stand) – make sure that no weight is transmitted through any part of the rear suspension. Tie the front brake lever on so the bike can't roll forward.

2 Remove the rear wheel (see Chapter 6).

3 Release the rear brake hose from the swingarm and tie or support the rear caliper assembly out of the way (see illustration).

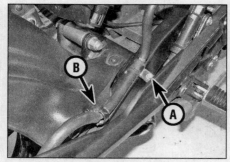

13.3 Unscrew the bolt (A) and release the clip (B)

13.4a Unscrew the bolts (arrowed) and remove the cover

13.4b Note the alignment of the arm on the shaft…

13.4c …then unscrew the bolt and slide the arm off

4 Remove the front sprocket cover **(see illustration)**. Note the alignment of the punch mark on the gearchange linkage arm with the line across the end of the shaft, then unscrew the bolt, slide the arm off, and position it clear **(see illustrations)**.

5 Release the wiring guide from the clutch release shaft housing **(see illustration)**. Unscrew the bolts and displace the housing **(see illustration)**. Remove the chain guide **(see illustration)**. Note how the oil seal plate is located over the two dowels. Disengage the chain from the sprocket and rest it over the front of the swingarm **(see illustration)**.

6 Unscrew the nut on the shock absorber lower mounting bolt and remove the washer **(see illustration 11.3b)**. Withdraw the lower mounting bolt.

7 Before removing the swingarm it is advisable to check for play in the bearings (see Chapter 1). Any problems that were not evident with the shock absorber attached may now show up.

8 Unscrew the nut on the left-hand end of the swingarm pivot bolt **(see illustration)**. Push the pivot bolt in slightly so the head is accessible on the opposite side. Note how the flat edges of the pivot bolt head locate in the recess in the pivot plate.

9 Slacken the two bolts securing the bottom of each pivot plate to the frame **(see illustrations)**.

10 Support the swingarm, then withdraw the

13.5a Release the wiring guide (arrowed)

13.5b Unscrew the bolts and displace the housing…

13.5c …and remove the chain guide

13.5d Lift the chain off the sprocket

13.8 Unscrew the nut

13.9a Slacken the two bolts (arrowed)…

13.9b …on each side

13.10 Withdraw the bolt and remove the swingarm

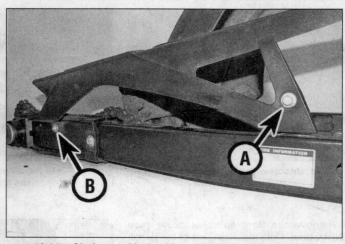

13.11a Chainguard bolt with washer (A) and screw with collar (B)...

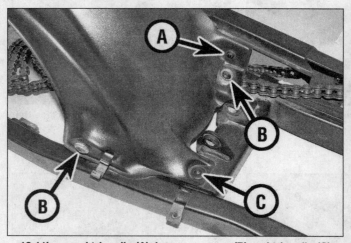

13.11b ...and trim clip (A); hugger screws (B) and trim clip (C)

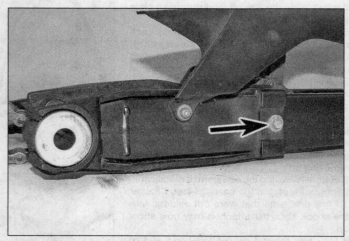

13.11c Chain slider bolt with washer and collar (arrowed)

pivot bolt and remove the swingarm together with the chain (see illustration). If required, knock the pivot bolt through using a large drift, but be careful not to damage the threaded end.

Inspection

11 If required remove the chainguard, hugger and chain slider, noting how they fit (see illustrations). If the slider is badly worn or damaged, it should be replaced with a new one.
12 Thoroughly clean the swingarm, removing all traces of dirt, corrosion and grease. Check the swingarm for cracks or distortion due to accident damage.
13 Remove the bearing cover from each side of the swingarm (see illustration). Clean the covers and check the condition of the seal inside. Also check the condition of the seal on the inner end of each pivot. Replace the seals with new ones if necessary.
14 Withdraw the sleeve from each pivot

(see illustration). Clean all old grease off the sleeves and the bearings in each pivot.
15 Inspect the bearings for signs of wear such as pitting and heavy scoring. Replace them with new ones if necessary (see below).
16 Remove any old grease and corrosion from the swingarm pivot bolt and the inner

sleeves. Check they are straight by rolling them on a flat surface such as a piece of plate glass.

Bearing renewal

17 If not already done remove the bearing covers (see illustration 13.13), then lever out

13.13 Remove the covers and check the seal (arrowed) inside

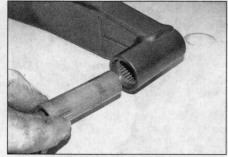

13.14 Withdraw the sleeves to check the bearings

13.17 Lever the seals out

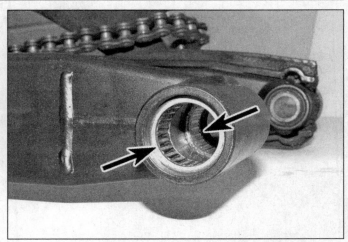
13.18 There are two bearings (arrowed) in each pivot

13.25 Make sure the bolt head flats locate correctly

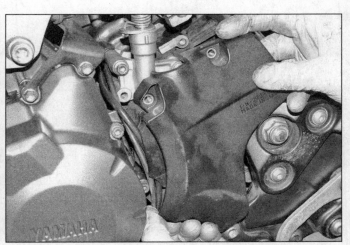
13.30 Route the wiring in the channel in the front of the cover

the grease seal on the inner end of each pivot **(see illustration)**. New seals must be used.

18 Two needle roller bearings are fitted in each pivot **(see illustration)**. Follow the procedure in *Tools and Workshop Tips* in the *Reference* section to remove the old bearings. Note that once removed, the bearings cannot be reused.

19 Inspect the bearing seats and remove any scoring or corrosion carefully with steel wool or a suitable scraper.

20 The new bearings must be pressed or drawn into their bores, rather than driven into position. In the absence of a press, a suitable drawbolt arrangement can be made up as described in *Tools and Workshop Tips* (Section 5) in the *Reference* section. Make sure the bearings are set to a depth of 4 mm on the outer end of each pivot, and to a depth of 8.5 mm on each inner end. Lubricate the bearings with lithium-based grease.

21 Press a new seal into the inner end of each pivot.

Installation

22 If removed, fit the chain slider, hugger and chainguard **(see illustrations 13.11c, b and a)**.

23 Grease the sleeves, the inside of the bearing covers and the seal lips with molybdenum disulphide grease. Slide the sleeves into the bearings, then fit the covers **(see illustrations 13.14 and 13.13)**.

24 Lubricate the swingarm pivot bolt with molybdenum disulphide grease.

25 Loop the drive chain over the left-hand pivot on the swingarm, then manoeuvre the swingarm into position. Slide the pivot bolt all the way through from the right-hand side **(see illustration 13.10)** – locate the flats on its head in the flats in the pivot bracket **(see illustration)**.

26 Tighten the pivot plate bolts on each side **(see illustrations 13.9a and b)**.

27 Fit the nut onto the pivot bolt and tighten the nut to the torque setting specified at the beginning of the Chapter **(see illus-**tration 13.8)**. Check that the swingarm moves up and down freely.

28 Align the shock absorber lower mounting and insert the bolt, then fit the washer and tighten the nut to the specified torque **(see illustration 11.3b)**.

29 Check the clutch pushrod seal plate is located on the dowels. Fit the chain guide **(see illustration 13.5c)**. Clean the threads of the housing bolts and apply some fresh threadlock, then fit the housing and tighten the bolts to the torque setting specified at the beginning of the Chapter **(see illustration 13.5b)**. Fit the wiring guide **(see illustration 13.5a)**.

30 Align the slit in the gearchange linkage arm with the mark on the shaft, then slide the arm on and tighten the bolt **(see illustrations 13.4c and b)**. Fit the sprocket cover **(see illustration)**.

31 Install the remaining components in the reverse order of removal. Check and adjust the drive chain slack (see Chapter 1), and check the operation of the rear suspension before taking the machine on the road.

Chapter 6
Brakes, wheels and final drive

Contents

Degrees of difficulty

Easy, suitable for novice with little experience	**Fairly easy,** suitable for beginner with some experience	**Fairly difficult,** suitable for competent DIY mechanic	**Difficult,** suitable for experienced DIY mechanic	**Very difficult,** suitable for expert DIY or professional

Specifications

Brakes

Brake fluid type	DOT 4
Brake pad friction material wear limit	
Rear caliper	1.5 mm (7.0 mm when new)
Front calipers	0.8 mm (6.0 mm when new)
Front caliper bore ID	
Upper bore	30.16 mm
Lower bore	25.40 mm
Front disc thickness	
Standard	4.5 mm
Service limit	4.0 mm
Front disc maximum runout	0.1 mm
Front master cylinder bore ID	16.0 mm
Rear caliper bore ID	38.1 mm
Rear disc thickness	
Standard	5.0 mm
Service limit	4.5 mm
Rear disc maximum runout	0.15 mm
Rear master cylinder bore ID	12.7 mm

Wheels

Rim size
  Front . . . . 17 x MT3.50
  Rear . . . . 17 x MT4.50
Wheel runout (max)
  Axial (side-to-side) . . . . 0.5 mm
  Radial (out-of-round) . . . . 1.0 mm

Tyres

Tyre pressures . . . . see *Pre-ride checks*
Tyre sizes*
  Front 120/70-ZR17 (58W)
  Rear 160/60-ZR17 (69W)
Refer to the owners manual or your Yamaha dealer for approved tyre brands.

Final drive

Chain type . . . . DAIDO 520VP2 (118 links)
Chain slack. . . . . 45 to 55 mm
Chain stretch service limit (see text). . . . . 239.3 mm
Sprocket sizes . . . . Front 16T, Rear 46T

Torque wrench settings

ABS rotor screws . . . . 8 Nm
ABS sensor mounting screw . . . . 7 Nm
Brake hose banjo bolts. . . . . 30 Nm
Front brake caliper bracket mounting bolts. . . . . 40 Nm
Front brake caliper slider pins . . . . 27 Nm
Front brake caliper bleed valves . . . . 6 Nm
Front brake disc bolts . . . . 18 Nm
Front brake master cylinder clamp bolts . . . . 10 Nm
Front sprocket nut . . . . 85 Nm
Front wheel axle. . . . . 65 Nm
Front wheel axle pinch bolt . . . . 19 Nm
Rear brake caliper bleed valve. . . . . 5 Nm
Rear brake caliper front slider pin . . . . 27 Nm
Rear brake caliper rear mounting bolt/slider pin . . . . 22 Nm
Rear brake pad retaining pin . . . . 17 Nm
Rear brake disc bolts . . . . 20 Nm
Rear sprocket nuts. . . . . 80 Nm
Rear wheel axle nut . . . . 90 Nm

1 General information

All models are fitted with cast alloy wheels designed for tubeless tyres only.

Both front and rear brakes are hydraulically-operated disc brakes. The front brakes are twin floating discs with two-piston sliding calipers at the front. The rear brake is a single disc with a single-piston sliding caliper. ABS is fitted on XJ6-NA, XJ6-SA and XJ6-FA models.

Drive from the gearbox to the rear wheel is by chain and sprockets.

Caution: Disc brake components rarely require disassembly. Do not disassemble components unless absolutely necessary. If an hydraulic brake line is loosened, the entire system must be disassembled, drained, cleaned and then properly filled and bled upon reassembly. Do not use solvents on internal brake components. Solvents will cause the seals to swell and distort. Use only clean DOT 4 brake fluid or denatured alcohol for cleaning. Use care when working with brake fluid as it can injure your eyes and it will damage painted surfaces and plastic parts.

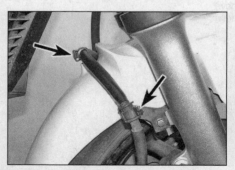

2.1a Release the clip(s) (arrowed) for greater freedom of movement as required...

2.1b ...and release the sensor wire from the clips (arrowed) on ABS models

2 Front brake pads

1 Release the clip(s) holding the brake hose(s), and on ABS models (for the right-hand caliper only) the wheel sensor wire **(see illustrations)**.

2.1c Unscrew the pins (arrowed) and displace the caliper

2.2 Remove the pads from the bracket

2.8 You should be able to push the pistons in using finger pressure

Undo the caliper slider pins and draw the caliper off the disc **(see illustration)**. The pads will remain in the caliper bracket. **Note:** *Do not operate the brake lever while the caliper is off the bracket.*

2 Lift the pads off the bracket, noting how they locate **(see illustration)**. Note any anti-chatter shims on the backs of the pads.

3 Note the location of the pad plates on the bracket and the pad spring inside the caliper **(see illustrations 2.13 and 2.15a)**.

4 Inspect the surface of each pad for contamination and check that the friction material has not worn down to the service limit (see Chapter 1, Section 11). If either pad is worn down to, or beyond the limit, is fouled with oil or grease, or is heavily scored or damaged, both pads in each caliper must be replaced with new ones. **Note:** *It is not possible to degrease the friction material – if the pads are contaminated in any way they must be replaced with new ones.*

5 Check that each pad has worn evenly at each end, and that each has the same amount of wear as the other. If uneven wear is noticed, one of the pistons is probably sticking in the caliper, in which case the caliper must be overhauled (see Section 3).

6 If the pads are in good condition clean them carefully, using a fine wire brush that is completely free of oil and grease, to remove all traces of road dirt and corrosion. Using a pointed instrument, dig out any embedded particles of foreign matter. Spray the pads with brake system cleaner.

7 Spray the inside of the caliper with brake system cleaner, paying particular attention to the exposed section of both pistons to remove any dirt or debris that could cause the seals to be damaged. If required, remove the pad spring, noting how it fits, and clean it **(see illustration 2.15a)**. Remove any traces of corrosion that might cause sticking of the caliper/pad operation.

8 If new pads are being fitted, push the pistons all the way back into the caliper to create room for them (but see Step 10 for machines fitted with ABS) **(see illustration)**. Push the pistons using finger pressure or a piece of wood as leverage, or place the old pads back in the caliper and use a large, flat-bladed screwdriver inserted between them. Alternatively obtain a piston retracting tool from a good tool supplier.

9 On standard (non-ABS) models, as the pistons are pushed into the caliper, brake fluid will be displaced back into the reservoir on the master cylinder. Depending on the initial level, it may be necessary to remove the reservoir cap, plate and diaphragm, and siphon out some fluid (see *Pre-ride checks*).

10 On ABS models it is necessary to open the caliper bleed valve to enable the pistons to be pushed back into the caliper. Remove the bleed valve cap, then attach a length of clear hose to the valve and place the open end in a suitable container **(see illustrations 11.6a and b)**. Open the valve and push the pistons in as described in Step 8. Take great care not to draw any air into the system. If in doubt, bleed

the brake afterwards (see Section 11). When the pistons are fully retracted tighten the bleed valve, remove the hose and fit the cap.

11 If either piston appears to be sticking in the caliper, the caliper must be overhauled (see Section 3).

12 Check the condition of the brake disc (see Section 4).

13 Clean and check the condition of the rubber boots, and replace them with new ones if necessary **(see illustration)**. Clean the faces of the pad plates on the bracket, and make sure they are correctly in place. Clean the caliper slider pins and remove any corrosion.

14 Smear the backs of the pads lightly with copper-based grease, making sure that none gets on the front or sides of the pads. Make sure any shims are correctly fitted on the backs of the pads. Fit the pads so that the friction material faces the disc **(see illustration 2.2)**.

15 If removed, fit the pad spring **(see illustration)**. Slide the caliper over the pads and onto the bracket, taking care not to dislodge the pads **(see illustration)**. Apply silicone grease to the slider pins and tighten them to the torque setting specified at the beginning of the Chapter. Secure the brake hose(s), and where fitted the wheel sensor wire, in the clip(s) **(see illustrations 2.1a and b)**.

16 Pump the brake lever several times to bring the pads into contact with the discs.

17 Check the fluid level in the master cylinder reservoir (see *Pre-ride checks*).

18 Check the operation of the brake before riding the motorcycle.

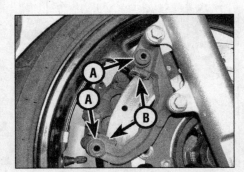

2.13 Clean and check the rubber boots (A) and the pad plates (B)

2.15a Pad spring (arrowed)

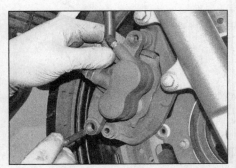

2.15b Slide the caliper over the pads and onto the bracket

3 Front brake calipers

⚠️ **Warning: If a caliper is in need of an overhaul all old brake fluid should be flushed from the system. Overhaul must be done in a spotlessly clean work area to avoid contamination and possible failure of the brake hydraulic system components. Do not, under any circumstances, use petroleum-based solvents to clean brake parts. Use clean DOT 4 brake fluid, dedicated brake cleaner or denatured alcohol only, as described. To prevent damage from spilled brake fluid, always cover paintwork when working on the braking system.**

Note: *If the caliper is being overhauled (usually due to sticking pistons or fluid leaks) read through the entire procedure first and make sure that you have obtained all the new parts required, including some new DOT 4 brake fluid.*

Removal

1 To displace the left-hand caliper (e.g. for wheel removal), first release the clip(s) holding the brake hose(s) **(see illustration 2.1a)**. Undo the caliper bracket mounting bolts and slide the caliper assembly off the disc **(see**

illustration 3.2a**)**. Secure the caliper to the motorcycle with a cable-tie to avoid straining the hose. **Note:** *Do not operate the brake lever while either caliper is off its disc.*

2 To displace the right-hand caliper (e.g. for wheel removal), first release the clip(s) holding the brake hose(s), and on ABS models release the sensor wire from the brake hoses **(see illustrations 2.1a and b)**. Undo the caliper bracket mounting bolts noting, where fitted, the ABS wiring guide, and slide the caliper assembly off the disc **(see illustrations)**. Secure the caliper to the motorcycle with a cable-tie to avoid straining the brake hose. **Note:** *Do not operate the brake lever while either caliper is off its disc.*

3 If the caliper is being completely removed or overhauled, note the alignment of the brake hose banjo fitting(s) with the caliper, then unscrew the banjo bolt and detach the hose(s), noting the positions of the sealing washers **(see illustration)**. Be prepared with a rag to catch any drops of brake fluid. Seal the banjo union(s) with a suitable nut and bolt and the two sealing washers **(see illustration)**. Note that new sealing washers must be used on reassembly.

4 Remove the brake pads (see Section 2) – this covers removing the caliper. If required undo the caliper bracket mounting bolts and remove the bracket (see Steps 1 and 2 as applicable).

Overhaul

5 Clean the exterior of the caliper with brake system cleaner.

6 To remove the pistons you need either a supply of compressed air, or a piston removal tool, or if neither are available a good pair of external circlip removal pliers.

7 If you are using compressed air make sure the bleed valve is tight. Place a piece of wood or a wad of rag between the pistons and the caliper, then apply compressed air gradually and progressively, starting with a fairly low pressure, to the fluid inlet in the caliper and allow the pistons to ease out of the bores **(see illustrations)**. If one piston is being pushed out before the other, block that one so more pressure is applied to the sticking one, but do not use your fingers.

8 If you are using a dedicated tool or the circlip pliers, grip the inner wall of the piston then twist and pull the piston out, keeping it square to the bore wall until it is free **(see illustration 7.8)**. Do not try to remove a piston by levering it out or by using pliers or other grips that may scratch the outer wall, unless you are prepared to fit new pistons.

9 If a piston sticks in its bore and cannot be displaced, the caliper will have to be replaced with a new one.

10 Remove the dust seals and the piston seals from the piston bores using a wooden

3.2a Caliper bracket bolts (arrowed)

3.2b Note the sensor guide (arrowed) on ABS models

3.3a Brake hose banjo bolt (arrowed)

3.3b Seal the banjo using a nut and bolt and the sealing washers

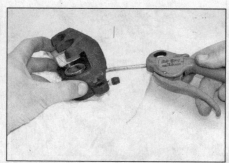

3.7a Position the wood as shown then apply compressed air...

3.7b ...until both pistons are displaced

or plastic tool to avoid scratching the bores **(see illustration)**. New seals must be fitted on reassembly. Note that the pistons and their corresponding seals are different sizes (see Specifications at the beginning of this Chapter).

11 Clean the pistons and bores with clean DOT 4 brake fluid. Blow compressed air through the fluid passages in the caliper to ensure they are clear (make sure the air is filtered and unlubricated).

Caution: Do not, under any circumstances, use a petroleum-based solvent to clean brake parts.

12 Inspect the caliper bores and pistons for signs of corrosion, nicks and burrs and loss of plating **(see illustration)**. If surface defects are present, the pistons or caliper assembly must be replaced with a new one. If the caliper is in bad shape the master cylinder should also be checked.

13 Compare the new seals and measure them if necessary to ensure that the correct seals are fitted in the correct bores **(see illustration)**.

14 Lubricate the new piston seals with clean DOT 4 brake fluid, then carefully fit them into the lower grooves in the caliper bores **(see illustrations)**.

15 Lubricate the new dust seals with silicone grease and fit them into the upper grooves in the caliper bores.

16 Lubricate the pistons with brake fluid and fit them, closed-end first, into the caliper bores

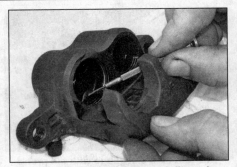

3.10 Remove the seals and discard them

3.12 Check the surfaces of the pistons and bores – the plating on this piston is lifting off

(see illustration). Using your thumbs, push the pistons all the way in, making sure they enter the bores squarely and do not displace the seals **(see illustration)**. Wipe away any excess lubricant as it will attract dirt.

Installation

17 If the caliper assembly was simply displaced, ease the brake pads apart with a large flat-bladed screwdriver to provide clearance for the disc, then slide the caliper into place **(see illustration)**. Make sure the pads sit squarely each side of the disc, then fit the bracket mounting bolts and tighten them to the torque setting specified at the beginning of this Chapter. Don't forget to

secure the ABS wiring guide, where fitted **(see illustration 3.2b)**. Secure the brake hose(s), and where fitted the sensor wire, in the clip(s) **(see illustrations 2.1a and b)**. Operate the brake lever several times to bring the pads into contact with the discs.

18 If the caliper has been overhauled, and if removed, fit the caliper bracket and tighten the mounting bolts to the torque setting specified at the beginning of this Chapter.

19 Refer to Section 2, Step 4 onwards to clean and check all components and to fit the brake pads, ignoring any Steps that do not apply following a caliper overhaul.

20 Connect the brake hose to the caliper, using **new** sealing washers on each side of

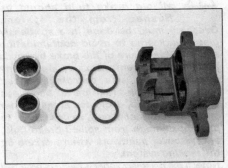

3.13 Make sure the correct seals are fitted into the correct bore, according to size

3.14a Lubricate the new piston seals with brake fluid...

3.14b ...then fit them into their grooves, followed by the new dust seals

3.16a Fit the pistons...

3.16b ...and push them all the way in

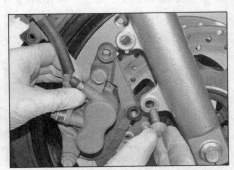

3.17 Slide the caliper onto the disc and fit the bolts

4.2 Using a micrometer to measure disc thickness

4.3 Set up a dial gauge with the probe contacting the brake disc, then rotate the wheel to check for runout

4.5 Unscrew the bolts (arrowed) and remove the disc

the banjo fitting(s). Align the fitting(s) as noted on removal **(see illustration 3.3a)**. Tighten the banjo bolt to the torque setting specified at the beginning of this Chapter.

21 Top-up the brake fluid reservoir with new DOT 4 brake fluid (see *Pre-ride checks*) and bleed the system as described in Section 11.

22 Check that there are no fluid leaks and thoroughly test the operation of the brake before riding the motorcycle.

4 Front brake discs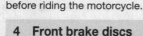

Inspection

1 Inspect the surface of each disc for score marks and other damage. Light scratches are normal after use and will not affect brake operation, but deep grooves and heavy score marks will reduce braking efficiency and accelerate pad wear. If a disc is badly grooved it must be replaced with a new one.

2 The disc must not be allowed to wear down to a thickness less than the service limit listed in this Chapter's Specifications. The thickness of the disc can be checked with a micrometer **(see illustration)**. If the thickness of the disc is less than the service limit, a new one must be fitted.

3 To check disc runout, support the bike upright so that the front wheel is raised off the ground. Mount a dial gauge to a fork leg, with the plunger on the gauge touching the surface of the disc about 10 mm (1/2 in) from the outer edge **(see illustration)**. Rotate the wheel and

watch the gauge needle, comparing the reading with the limit listed in the Specifications at the beginning of this Chapter. If the runout is greater than the service limit, check the wheel bearings for play (see Chapter 1). If the bearings are worn, fit new ones (see Section 16) and repeat this check. If disc runout is still excessive, a new pair of discs will have to be fitted.

Removal

4 Remove the front wheel (see Section 14).
Caution: Don't lay the wheel down and allow it to rest on either disc – they could become warped. Set the wheel on wood blocks so the wheel rim supports the weight of the wheel.

5 If you are not replacing the disc with a new one, mark the relationship of the disc to the wheel so that it can be installed in the same position. Unscrew the disc bolts, loosening them evenly and a little at a time in a criss-cross pattern to avoid distorting the disc, then remove the disc from the wheel **(see illustration)**.

Installation

6 Before fitting the disc, make sure there is no dirt or corrosion where it seats on the hub, particularly right in the angle of the seat. If the disc does not sit flat when it is bolted down, it will appear to be warped when checked or when the front brake is used.

7 Fit the disc onto the wheel – align the previously applied register marks if you are refitting the original disc.

8 Clean the threads of the disc bolts, then apply a suitable non-permanent thread locking compound. Install the bolts and tighten them

evenly and a little at a time in a criss-cross pattern to the torque setting specified at the beginning of this Chapter. Clean the brake disc using acetone or brake system cleaner. If a new brake disc has been installed, remove any protective coating from its working surfaces. **Note:** *If new discs have been fitted, also fit new brake pads.*

9 Install the front wheel (see Section 14).

10 Operate the brake lever several times to bring the pads into contact with the disc. Check the operation of the brake carefully before riding the motorcycle.

5 Front brake master cylinder

 Warning: If the brake master cylinder is in need of an overhaul all old brake fluid should be flushed from the system. Overhaul must be done in a spotlessly clean work area to avoid contamination and possible failure of the brake hydraulic system components. Do not, under any circumstances, use petroleum-based solvents to clean brake parts. Use clean DOT 4 brake fluid, dedicated brake cleaner or denatured alcohol only, as described. To prevent damage from spilled brake fluid, always cover paintwork when working on the braking system.

Note: *If the master cylinder is being overhauled (usually due to sticking or poor action, or fluid leaks) read through the entire procedure first and make sure that you have obtained all the new parts required, including some new DOT 4 brake fluid.*

Removal

1 On XJ6-N models remove the right-hand mirror (see Chapter 7).

2 Disconnect the brake light switch wiring connectors **(see illustration)**.

3 If the master cylinder is being completely removed or overhauled, slacken then lightly retighten the reservoir cover screws. Note the alignment of the brake hose banjo fitting, then unscrew the banjo bolt and detach the hose, noting the positions of the sealing washers **(see illustration)**. Be prepared with a rag to catch any drops of brake fluid. Seal the banjo

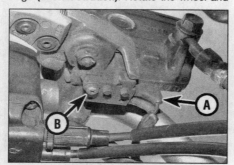

5.2 Brake light switch wiring connectors (A) and screw (B)

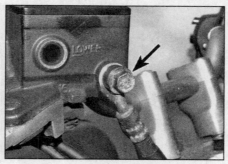

5.3 Brake hose banjo bolt (arrowed)

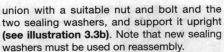

5.5 Master cylinder clamp bolts (arrowed)

5.8 Remove the pushrod and boot from the end of the master cylinder piston…

5.9a …then depress the piston, remove the circlip…

5.9b …and draw out the piston and spring

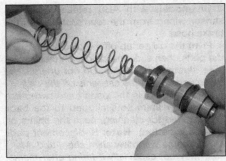

5.13 Fit the spring onto the end of the piston

union with a suitable nut and bolt and the two sealing washers, and support it upright **(see illustration 3.3b)**. Note that new sealing washers must be used on reassembly.

4 Remove the brake lever (see Chapter 5).

5 Note the alignment of the handlebar clamp with the punch mark on the handlebar, then unscrew the clamp bolts and remove the clamp **(see illustration)**. If the master cylinder is just being displaced, secure it upright with a cable-tie to avoid straining the brake hose.

6 If the master cylinder is being overhauled undo the reservoir cover screws and remove the cover, the diaphragm plate and the diaphragm. Drain the brake fluid into a suitable container. Wipe any remaining fluid out of the reservoir with a clean rag.

7 If required, undo the screw securing the brake light switch and remove the switch **(see illustration 5.2)**.

Overhaul

8 Remove the pushrod and boot **(see illustration)**.

9 The piston assembly is secured by a circlip. Remove the circlip using circlip pliers, then draw out the piston and spring assembly **(see illustrations)**.

10 Clean inside the master cylinder with fresh DOT 4 brake fluid. If compressed air is available, blow it through the fluid passages to ensure they are clear (make sure the air is filtered and unlubricated).

Caution: Do not, under any circumstances, use a petroleum-based solvent to clean brake parts.

11 Check the master cylinder bore for corrosion, scratches, nicks and score marks. If damage or wear is evident, the master cylinder must be replaced with a new one. If the master cylinder is in poor condition, then the calipers should be checked as well.

12 The pushrod and boot, circlip, piston (with seals) and spring are included in the master cylinder rebuild kit. Use all of the new parts, regardless of the apparent condition of the old ones.

13 Fit the narrow end of the spring over the inner end of the piston **(see illustration)**. Lubricate the piston and seals with clean brake fluid and fit the assembly into the master cylinder, wide end of the spring first **(see illustration 5.9b)**.

14 Push the piston in and fit the new circlip, making sure it is properly located in the groove **(see illustration)**.

15 If not already assembled, fit the boot onto the pushrod so that its outer (narrow) lip locates in the groove **(see illustration 5.8)**. Locate the pushrod against the outer end of the piston and press the inner (wide) lip of the boot into place.

16 Check the fluid reservoir top, diaphragm plate and diaphragm and replace them with new ones if they are damaged or deteriorated.

Installation

17 If removed, fit the brake light switch onto the bottom of the master cylinder, making sure the pin locates in the hole, and tighten the screw **(see illustration 5.2)**.

18 Position the master cylinder on the

5.14 Push the piston into the bore and fit the circlip

handlebar, aligning the clamp joint with the register mark on the top of the handlebar **(see illustration)**. Fit the back of the clamp with its UP mark facing up, then fit the clamp bolts and tighten them to the torque setting specified at the beginning of this Chapter, tightening the top bolt first **(see illustration 5.5)**.

19 If disconnected align the brake hose banjo fitting with the master cylinder, then fit the banjo bolt using a new sealing washer on each side and tighten it to the torque setting specified at the beginning of this Chapter **(see illustration 5.3)**.

20 Install the brake lever (see Chapter 5).

21 Connect the brake light switch wiring connectors **(see illustration 5.2)**.

22 On XJ6-N models fit the mirror (see Chapter 7).

23 If the master cylinder was overhauled, fill

5.18 Align the mating surfaces of the clamp with the punch mark (arrowed) on the handlebar

the master cylinder reservoir with new DOT 4 brake fluid (see *Pre-ride checks*). Refer to Section 11 and bleed the air from the system.
24 Check that there are no fluid leaks and thoroughly test the operation of the brake before riding the motorcycle.

6 Rear brake pads

1 Unscrew the pad retaining pin plug, then unscrew the pad pin **(see illustration)**.
2 Unscrew the rear mounting bolt/slider pin **(see illustration)**.
3 On models with ABS release the ABS sensor wiring from the rearmost clip on the brake hose.
4 Pivot the caliper up off the disc and remove the pads, then slide the caliper off the bracket **(see illustrations)**. Note: *Do not operate the brake pedal while the caliper is off the disc.*
5 On later models the pads have two-piece anti-chatter shim sets clipped to the back – if required for cleaning, ease the shims off **(see illustration)**. Note: *Replacement pads should come with new shim sets fitted. Make sure they do, especially if fitting after-market pads – if not they can be obtained separately if required, or use the ones from the old pads.*
6 Inspect the surface of each pad for contamination and check that the friction material has not worn down to the service limit (see Chapter 1, Section 11). If either pad is worn down to, or beyond the limit, is fouled with oil or grease, or is heavily scored or damaged, fit a new set of pads. Note: *It is not possible to degrease the friction material – if the pads are contaminated in any way they must be replaced with new ones.*
7 If the pads are in good condition clean them carefully, using a fine wire brush that is completely free of oil and grease, to remove all traces of road dirt and corrosion. Using a pointed instrument, dig out any embedded particles of foreign matter. Spray the pads with brake system cleaner.

8 Spray the inside of the caliper with brake system cleaner, paying particular attention to the exposed section of the piston to remove any dirt or debris that could cause the seals to be damaged. If required, remove the pad spring, noting how it fits **(see illustration 6.15)**.
9 If new pads are being fitted, push the piston all the way back into the caliper to create room for them (but see Step 11 for machines fitted with ABS). Push the piston using finger pressure or a piece of wood as leverage, or place the old pads back in the caliper and use a large, flat-bladed screwdriver inserted between them **(see illustration)**. Alternatively

obtain a piston retracting tool from a good tool supplier.
10 On standard (non-ABS) models, as the piston is pushed into the caliper, brake fluid will be displaced back through the master cylinder and into the reservoir. Depending on the initial level, it may be necessary to remove the reservoir cap, plate and diaphragm, and siphon out some fluid (see *Pre-ride checks*).
11 On ABS models it is necessary to open the caliper bleed valve to enable the piston to be pushed back into the caliper. Remove the bleed valve cap, then attach a length of clear hose to the valve and place the open end in a suitable container **(see illustrations 11.17a**

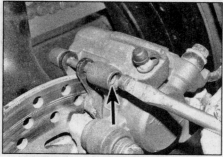

6.1 Remove the plug then unscrew the pin (arrowed)

6.2 Unscrew the rear bolt/slider pin

6.4a Pivot the caliper up and remove the pads...

6.4b ...then slide the caliper off

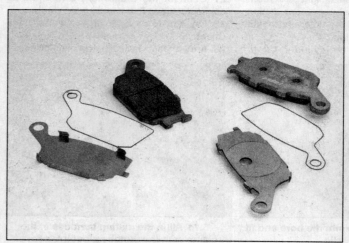

6.5 Remove the shim and its backing from each pad

6.9 You should be able to push the pistons in using finger pressure

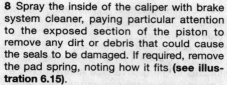

6.14a Clean and check the boot (A) and slider pin (B) on the caliper...

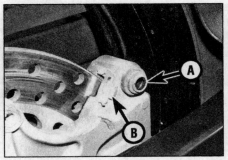

6.14b ...and the boot (A) and pad plate (B) on the bracket

6.15 Make sure the pad spring (arrowed) is correctly in place

and b). Open the valve and push the piston in as described in Step 9. Take great care not to draw any air into the system. If in doubt, bleed the brake afterwards (see Section 11). When the piston is fully retracted tighten the bleed valve, remove the hose and fit the cap.

12 If the piston appears to be sticking in the caliper, the caliper must be overhauled (see Section 7).

13 Check the condition of the brake disc (see Section 8).

14 Clean and check the condition of the rubber boots, and replace them with new ones if necessary **(see illustrations)**. Clean the face of the pad plate on the bracket, and make sure it is correctly in place. Clean the pad pin and the caliper slider pins and remove any corrosion.

15 If removed, and where fitted, clip the anti-chatter shim sets in place and make sure the outer faces are clean **(see illustration 6.5)**. If removed, fit the pad spring **(see illustration)**.

16 Apply silicone grease to the slider pins and rubber boots. Slide the caliper onto the bracket **(see illustration 6.4b)**. Position the pads in the bracket with the friction material facing the disc and so the leading edges locate against the pad plate **(see illustration 6.4a)**, then pivot the caliper down over the pads. Fit the rear mounting bolt/slider pin and tighten it to the torque setting specified at the beginning of the Chapter **(see illustration 6.2)**.

17 Apply a smear of copper-based grease to the pad pin. Push the pads up against the spring to align the holes, insert the

pad pin and tighten to the specified torque **(see illustration)**. Fit the pad pin plug **(see illustration 6.1)**.

18 On models with ABS, secure the rear ABS sensor wiring to the rear brake hose with the clip.

19 Operate the brake pedal several times to bring the pads into contact with the disc.

20 Check the fluid level in the master cylinder reservoir (see *Pre-ride checks*).

21 Check the operation of the brake carefully before riding the motorcycle.

7 Rear brake caliper

> ⚠ **Warning: If the caliper is in need of an overhaul all old brake fluid should be flushed from the system. Overhaul must be done in a spotlessly clean work area to avoid contamination and possible failure of the brake hydraulic system components. Do not, under any circumstances, use petroleum-based solvents to clean brake parts. Use clean DOT 4 brake fluid, dedicated brake cleaner or denatured alcohol only, as described. To prevent damage from spilled brake fluid, always cover paintwork when working on the braking system.**

Note: *If the caliper is being overhauled (usually due to a sticking piston or fluid leaks) read through the entire procedure first and make sure that you have obtained all the new parts required, including some new DOT 4 brake fluid.*

Removal

1 On models with ABS release the ABS sensor wiring from the rearmost clip on the brake hose.

2 If the caliper is being completely removed or overhauled, note the alignment of the brake hose banjo fitting with the caliper, then unscrew the banjo bolt and detach the hose, noting the positions of the sealing washers **(see illustration)**. Be prepared with a rag to catch any drops of brake fluid. Seal the banjo union(s) with a suitable nut and bolt and the two sealing washers **(see illustration 3.3b)**. Note that new sealing washers must be used on reassembly.

3 Remove the brake pads (see Section 6) – this covers removing the caliper.

4 If required remove the rear wheel (see Section 15), then remove the caliper bracket.

Overhaul

5 Clean the exterior of the caliper with brake system cleaner.

6 To remove the piston you need either a supply of compressed air, or a piston removal tool, or if neither are available a good pair of external circlip removal pliers.

7 If you are using compressed air make sure the bleed valve is tight. Place a piece of wood or a wad of rag between the piston and the caliper, then apply compressed air gradually and progressively, starting with a fairly low pressure, to the fluid inlet in the caliper and allow the piston to ease out of the bore **(see illustration)**.

6.17 Push the pads up to align the holes

7.2 Brake hose banjo bolt (arrowed)

7.7 Fit the wood or rag, then apply the compressed air as described until the piston is displaced

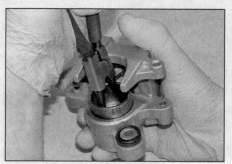

7.8 Using circlip pliers to extract a piston

7.10 Remove the seals and discard them

7.13 Dust seal (A), piston seal (B)

Warning: Never place your fingers in front of the pistons in an attempt to catch or protect them when applying compressed air, as injury could result.

8 If you are using a dedicated tool or the circlip pliers, grip the inner wall of the piston then twist and pull the piston out, keeping it square to the bore wall until it is free **(see illustration)**. Do not try to remove the piston by levering it out or by using pliers or other grips that may scratch the outer wall, unless you are prepared to fit a new piston.

9 If the piston sticks in its bore and cannot be displaced, the caliper will have to be replaced with a new one.

10 Remove the dust seal and the piston seal from the piston bore using a soft wooden or plastic tool to avoid scratching the bores **(see illustration)**. New seals must be fitted on reassembly.

11 Clean the piston and bore with clean DOT 4 brake fluid. Blow compressed air through the fluid passages in the caliper to ensure they are clear (make sure the air is filtered and unlubricated).

Caution: Do not, under any circumstances, use a petroleum-based solvent to clean brake parts.

12 Inspect the caliper bore and piston for signs of corrosion, nicks and burrs and loss of plating **(see illustration 3.12)**. If surface defects are present, the piston or caliper assembly must be replaced with a new one. If

the caliper is in bad shape the master cylinder should also be checked.

13 Compare the new seals to ensure that they are fitted correctly – the outer dust seal is thinner than the inner piston seal **(see illustration)**.

14 Lubricate the new piston seal with clean DOT 4 brake fluid, then carefully fit it into the lower groove in the caliper bore **(see illustration)**.

15 Lubricate the new dust seal with silicone grease and fit it into the upper groove in the caliper bore **(see illustration)**.

16 Lubricate the piston with brake fluid and fit it, closed-end first, into the caliper bore **(see illustration)**. Using your thumbs, push the piston all the way in, making sure it enters the bore squarely and do not displace the seals. Wipe away any excess lubricant as it will attract dirt.

Installation

17 If removed, fit the caliper bracket and install the rear wheel (see Section 15).

18 Refer to Section 6, Step 6 onwards to clean and check all components and to fit the brake pads, ignoring any Steps that do not apply following a caliper overhaul.

19 Connect the brake hose to the caliper, using **new** sealing washers on each side of the banjo fitting. Align the fitting as noted on removal **(see illustration 7.2)**. Tighten the banjo bolt to the torque setting specified at the beginning of this Chapter.

20 On models with ABS, secure the rear ABS sensor wiring to the rear brake hose with the clip.

21 Top-up the brake fluid reservoir with new DOT 4 brake fluid (see *Pre-ride checks*) and bleed the system as described in Section 11.

22 Check that there are no fluid leaks and thoroughly test the operation of the brake before riding the motorcycle.

8 Rear brake disc

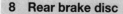

Inspection

1 Refer to Section 4 of this Chapter. To check the disc runout, support the bike upright so that the rear wheel is raised off the ground. Mount the dial gauge to the swingarm.

Removal

2 Remove the rear wheel (see Section 15).
Caution: Don't lay the wheel down and allow it to rest on the disc or the sprocket – they could become warped. Set the wheel on wood blocks so the wheel rim supports the weight of the wheel.

3 If you are not replacing the disc with a new one, mark the relationship of the disc to the wheel so that it can be installed in the same

7.14 Fit the new piston seal into its groove...

7.15 ...followed by the new dust seal

7.16 Fit the piston and push it all the way in

8.3 Rear brake disc bolts (arrowed)

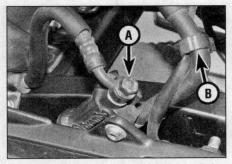

9.2 Brake hose banjo bolt (A). Brake light switch wire clip (B)

9.4 Reservoir mounting bolt (arrowed)

position. Unscrew the disc retaining bolts, loosening them evenly and a little at a time in a criss-cross pattern to avoid distorting the disc, then remove the disc from the wheel **(see illustration)**.

Installation

4 Before fitting the disc, make sure there is no dirt or corrosion where the disc seats on the hub, particularly right in the angle of the seat. If the disc does not sit flat when it is bolted down, it will appear to be warped when checked or when the rear brake is used.
5 Fit the disc onto the wheel; align the previously applied register marks if you are reinstalling the original disc.
6 Clean the threads of the disc mounting bolts, then apply a suitable non-permanent thread locking compound. Fit the bolts and tighten them evenly and a little at a time in a criss-cross pattern to the torque setting specified at the beginning of this Chapter **(see illustration 8.3)**. Clean the brake disc using acetone or brake system cleaner. If a new brake disc has been installed, remove any protective coating from its working surfaces. **Note:** *If a new disc is fitted, also fit new brake pads.*
7 Install the rear wheel (see Section 15).
8 Operate the brake pedal several times to bring the pads into contact with the disc. Check the operation of the brake carefully before riding the motorcycle.

9 Rear brake master cylinder

> **Warning: If the brake master cylinder is in need of an overhaul all old brake fluid should be flushed from the system. Overhaul must be done in a spotlessly clean work area to avoid contamination and possible failure of the brake hydraulic system components. Do not, under any circumstances, use petroleum-based solvents to clean brake parts. Use clean DOT 4 brake fluid, dedicated brake cleaner or denatured alcohol only, as described. To prevent damage from spilled brake fluid, always cover paintwork when working on the braking system.**

Note: *If the master cylinder is being overhauled (usually due to sticking or poor action, or fluid leaks) read through the entire procedure first and make sure that you have obtained all the new parts required, including some new DOT 4 brake fluid.*

Removal

1 Remove the right-hand side panel (see Chapter 7).
2 Note the alignment of the brake hose banjo fitting, then unscrew the banjo bolt and detach the hose, noting the positions of the sealing washers **(see illustration)**. Be prepared with a rag to catch any drops of brake fluid. Seal the banjo union with a suitable nut and bolt and the

two sealing washers, and support it upright **(see illustration 3.3b)**. Note that new sealing washers must be used on reassembly. Release the brake light switch wire clip from the reservoir hose.
3 Follow the procedure in Chapter 5, Section 3, and remove the footrest bracket assembly and rear brake pedal (the pedal can be left to hang on the springs if preferred).
4 Unscrew the bolt securing the fluid reservoir, then draw the reservoir out and remove the master cylinder assembly **(see illustration)**.

Overhaul

5 Remove the reservoir cap, diaphragm plate and diaphragm and drain the brake fluid into a suitable container. Wipe any remaining fluid out of the reservoir with a clean rag.
6 Release the clip securing the reservoir hose to the union on the master cylinder and detach the hose **(see illustration)**.
7 The reservoir hose union is a firm press fit in the master cylinder – unless there are signs that the seal is leaking, do not remove the union. If necessary, prise the union out, taking care not to damage the sealing surface of the master cylinder. If the union breaks in the process, both the seal and union are available as separate items.
8 Measure the position of the clevis on the pushrod, then slacken the locknut and thread the clevis and nuts off the pushrod **(see illustration)**. The clevis and nuts must be transferred to the new pushrod.
9 Pull back the boot from the end of the master cylinder to reveal the retaining circlip **(see illustration)**. Depress the pushrod and

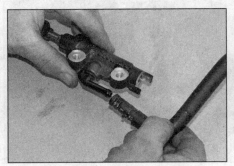

9.6 Detach the reservoir hose

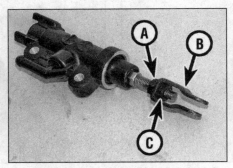

9.8 Slacken the locknut (A) and thread the clevis (B) and its nut (C) off

9.9a Pull the boot out...

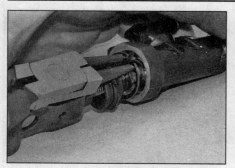

9.9b ...then release the circlip...

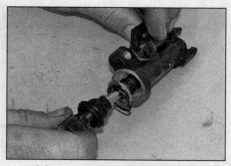

9.9c ...and remove the pushrod assembly...

9.9d ...and the piston and the spring

use circlip pliers to remove the circlip, then draw out the pushrod, the piston and spring **(see illustrations)**. Note how the spring is clipped to the inner end of the piston.

10 Clean inside the master cylinder with fresh DOT 4 brake fluid. If compressed air is available, blow it through the fluid passages to ensure they are clear (make sure the air is filtered and unlubricated).

Caution: Do not, under any circumstances, use a petroleum-based solvent to clean brake parts.

11 Check the master cylinder bore for corrosion, scratches, nicks and score marks. If damage or wear is evident, the master cylinder must be replaced with a new one. If the master cylinder is in poor condition, then the caliper should be checked as well.

12 The pushrod and boot, circlip, piston (with seals) and spring are included in the master cylinder rebuild kit. Use all of the new parts, regardless of the apparent condition of the old ones.

13 Fit one end of the spring over the inner end of the piston, clipping it into place over the metal tabs **(see illustration)**. Lubricate the piston and seals with clean brake fluid and fit the assembly into the master cylinder **(see illustration 9.9d)**.

14 Thread the locknut, clevis and nut onto the end of the pushrod. Press the pushrod into the master cylinder so that it compresses the spring, then fit the new circlip into its groove in the master cylinder **(see illustrations 9.9c and b)**.

15 Push the boot into place with its wider end located inside the groove in the master cylinder **(see illustration 9.9a)**.

16 Position the clevis as noted on removal (see Step 8), then tighten the locknut **(see illustration 9.8)**. Note that the clevis position sets brake pedal position and final adjustments can be made after installation (see Chapter 1, Section 11).

17 If removed, lubricate a new reservoir hose union seal with clean brake fluid, then press the seal into the master cylinder. Make sure the union is facing towards the top of the master cylinder, then press it firmly into place **(see illustration 9.6)**.

18 Check the reservoir, cap, diaphragm plate and diaphragm and fit new ones as required if they are damaged or deteriorated. Check the reservoir hose for cracks or splits and replace it with a new one if necessary. Check the hose clips and replace them if they are strained or corroded. Push the reservoir hose fully onto its union and secure it with the clip **(see illustration 9.6)**.

Installation

19 Secure the fluid reservoir loosely to the frame **(see illustration 9.4)**. Follow the procedure in Chapter 5, Section 3, and install the rear brake pedal and footrest bracket assembly.

20 Fit the brake hose banjo bolt using a new sealing washer on each side of the banjo union **(see illustration)**. Align the hose on the master cylinder, then tighten the bolt to the torque setting specified at the beginning of this Chapter **(see illustration 9.2)**.

21 Fill the fluid reservoir with new DOT 4 brake fluid (see *Pre-ride checks*). Refer to Section 11 and bleed the air from the system.

22 Install the right-hand side panel (see Chapter 7).

23 Check that there are no fluid leaks and thoroughly test the operation of the brake before riding the motorcycle.

10 Brake hoses and fittings

Inspection

1 Brake hose condition should be checked regularly and the hoses replaced with new ones at the specified interval (see Chapter 1).

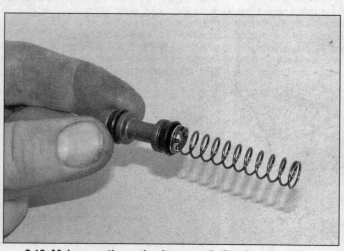

9.13 Make sure the spring is correctly fitted on the piston

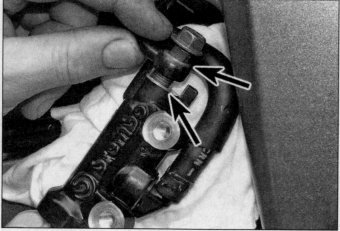

9.20 Use a new sealing washer (arrowed) on each side of the banjo union

10.4a Front brake hose/pipe joint unions – the hoses/pipe arrangements shown here come as an assembly...

10.4b ... and join secondary hoses/pipes (arrowed) on route to the control unit/modulator

2 Twist and flex the hoses while looking for cracks, bulges and seeping hydraulic fluid. Check extra carefully around the areas where the hoses connect with the banjo fittings and unions, as these are common areas for hose failure.

3 Check the banjo fittings and unions connected to the brake hoses. If the fittings are rusted, scratched or cracked, fit new hoses.

Renewal

4 On machines not fitted with ABS, the brake hoses have banjo fittings on each end **(see illustrations 3.3a, 5.3, 7.2 and 9.2)**. On machines fitted with ABS, the brake hoses connect to the calipers and master cylinders in the same way, but join to a solid brake pipe into a connecting union or to the modulator **(see illustrations)**. For full details on the ABS system see Section 17.

5 Flush the old brake fluid from the system (see Section 11).

6 Cover the surrounding area with plenty of rags to catch any drops of brake fluid. Note the alignment of the banjo fitting with the master cylinder or brake caliper. On models without ABS unscrew the banjo bolt at each end of the hose. On ABS models unscrew the banjo bolt at the caliper/master cylinder end of the hose, or on the union end of the front system secondary hoses **(see illustration 10.4b)**, and the nut at the modulator end of the pipe, then also unscrew the bolt securing the hose/pipe union block, where present – do not unscrew the nuts at the front hose unions as the hoses/pipes come as an assembly **(see illustration 10.4a)**.

7 Free the hose from any clips or guides and remove it, noting its routing. Discard the banjo sealing washers.

8 Position the new hose or hose/pipe, making sure it is correctly aligned and not twisted or otherwise strained, and ensure that it is correctly routed through any clips or guides and is clear of all moving components.

9 Check that the banjo fittings align correctly **(see illustrations 3.3a, 5.3, 7.2 and 9.2, and 10.4b)**, then fit the banjo bolts, using a new sealing washer on each side of the fitting. On the double hose fitting on the front caliper, an additional sealing washer should be fitted between the two banjo unions.

10 Tighten the banjo bolts to the torque setting specified at the beginning of this Chapter.

11 Refill the system with new brake fluid and bleed out all air (see Section 11). Check that there are no fluid leaks and thoroughly test the operation of the brake before riding the motorcycle.

11 Brake system bleeding and fluid change

Special Tool: *The brake bleeding equipment described in Step 3 will be required – ready-made bleeding kits are cheaply available from automotive stores. On models with ABS a test adaptor that plugs into the wiring loom is required to pulse test the ABS system after any work, including bleeding the system, is carried out. The test adaptor is available from Yamaha, part No. 90890-03149, or after-market versions can be sourced on-line. Refer to Step 38 for details.*

Bleeding

1 Bleeding a brake is the process of removing aerated brake fluid from the master cylinder, the hose(s)/pipe(s) and the brake caliper(s). Bleeding is necessary whenever a brake system hydraulic connection is loosened, after a component or hose is replaced with a new one, when a master cylinder or caliper is overhauled, or when there is a spongy feel to the lever and it travels all the way back to the handlebar, and where braking force is less than it should be, and it is not due

to any mechanical fault in the system (i.e. a sticking piston in the caliper, or a pad that is not moving as it should due to corrosion, for example on the pad pin). Leaks in the system may also allow air to enter, but leaking brake fluid will reveal their presence and warn you of the need for repair.

2 Brake bleeding is considered by some as a bit of a black art – seasoned professionals sometimes have trouble getting a good firm feel in the brake lever, while a first timer may have no trouble at all. One of the problems, particularly with the front brakes, is that you are working against natural principles – science dictates that air bubbles in a liquid will rise to the top, but the process entails pumping the brake fluid and any air bubbles it contains down, from the master cylinder at the top to the bleed valve in the caliper at the bottom, so while the fluid is moving down the air bubbles will want to rise. Air bubbles can also get trapped, particularly where there are high points in its path, and when there are extra components and pipes as on ABS models.

3 To bleed the brakes using the conventional method, you will need some new DOT 4 brake fluid, a length of clear flexible hose, a small container partially filled with clean brake fluid, some rags, and an 8 mm ring spanner to fit the brake caliper bleed valve. Bleeding kits that include the hose, a one-way valve and a container are available relatively cheaply from a good auto store, and simplify the task. You also need a block of wood as a support for the fluid container **(see illustrations 11.6c and 11.17c)**.

4 Cover painted components to prevent damage in the event that brake fluid is spilled. *Caution: Brake fluid attacks painted finishes and plastics – to prevent damage from spilled fluid, always cover paintwork when working on the braking system, and clean up any spills immediately using brake cleaner.*

11.5a Undo the screws...

11.5b ...and remove the cover and diaphragm

11.5c Operate the lever as described to force air from the master cylinder

Front brake system

5 Turn the handlebars so the reservoir is level. Undo the reservoir cover screws and remove the cover, diaphragm plate and diaphragm **(see illustrations)**. Slowly pump the brake lever a few times to dislodge any fine air bubbles from the small hole in the bottom of the reservoir **(see illustration)**. Now hold the lever in to force any large air bubbles out of the large hole – you can tie the lever to the handlebar and leave it pressurised for a while to prevent having to hold it, then release it and slowly pump it a few times. You can tell when all the air is gone as the large hole appears completely dark, whereas if there is any air left it will appear to have a silvery rim that is actually the edge of an air bubble.

6 Pull the dust cap off the bleed valve on the caliper **(see illustration)**. If using a ring spanner (which is preferable to an open-ended one) fit it onto the valve. Attach one end of the bleeding hose to the bleed valve and, if not using a kit, submerge the other end in the clean brake fluid in the container **(see illustrations)**.

7 Check the fluid level in the reservoir – keep it topped up and do not allow the level to drop below the bottom of the window during the procedure **(see illustration)**.

8 Slowly squeeze the brake lever and open the bleed valve a quarter turn **(see illustration)**. When the valve is opened, brake fluid will flow out of the master cylinder into the clear tubing, and the lever will move to the handlebar. If there is air in the system there will be air bubbles in the brake fluid coming out of the caliper.

9 Tighten the bleed valve, then release the

11.6a Pull the cap off the bleed valve

11.6b Fit the ring spanner over the valve then connect the hose

11.6c Bleeding kit set up for use, container supported on wood blocks

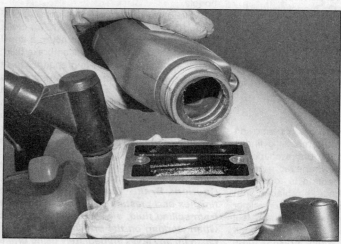

11.7 Keep the reservoir topped up

11.8 Bleed the front brake as described

11.16a Unscrew the cap...

11.16b ...and remove the diaphragm plate and diaphragm

11.17a Pull the cap off the bleed valve

brake lever. Repeat the process until no air bubbles are visible in the brake fluid leaving the caliper, and the lever is firm when applied, topping the reservoir up when necessary. On completion tighten the bleed valve and remove the equipment, then fit the dust cap.

10 Transfer the equipment to the bleed valve on the other caliper. Repeat the bleeding procedure.

11 When the system has been successfully bled there should be a good and progressively firm feel as the lever is applied, and the lever should not be able to travel all the way back to the handlebar.

12 On ABS models refer to Steps 36 to 44 and pulse test the system, then repeat the bleeding procedure.

13 On all models, when you've completed bleeding top-up the reservoir, then fit the diaphragm, diaphragm plate, and cover **(see illustrations 11.7, 11.5b and a)**. Check for spilled brake fluid and clean up as required.

14 Check that there are no fluid leaks and thoroughly test the operation of the brake before riding the motorcycle.

Rear brake system

15 Remove the right-hand side panel (see Chapter 7). Unscrew the bolt securing the

11.17b Fit the ring spanner over the valve then connect the hose

fluid reservoir, then draw the reservoir out from behind the frame tube **(see illustration 9.4)**.

16 Hold the reservoir and unscrew the cap, and remove the diaphragm plate and diaphragm **(see illustrations)**. Slowly pump the brake pedal a few times to dislodge any air bubbles from the holes in the bottom of the reservoir.

17 Pull the dust cap off the bleed valve on the caliper **(see illustration)**. If using a ring spanner (which is preferable to an open-ended one) fit it onto the valve. Attach one end of the bleeding hose to the bleed valve and, if not using a kit, submerge the other end in

11.17c Bleeding kit set up for use, container supported on wood blocks

the clean brake fluid in the container **(see illustrations)**.

18 Check the fluid level in the reservoir – keep it topped up and do not allow the level to drop below the lower level line during the procedure **(see illustration)**.

19 Slowly press the brake pedal and open the bleed valve a quarter turn **(see illustration)**. When the valve is opened, brake fluid will flow out of the master cylinder into the clear tubing, and the pedal will move down. If there is air in the system there will be air bubbles in the brake fluid coming out of the caliper.

11.18 Keep the reservoir topped up

11.19 Bleed the rear brake as described

20 Tighten the bleed valve, then release the brake pedal. Repeat the process until no air bubbles are visible in the brake fluid leaving the caliper, and the pedal is firm when applied, topping the reservoir up when necessary.

21 When the system has been successfully bled there should be a good and progressively firm feel as the pedal is applied, and the pedal should not be able to travel all the way down to its stop.

22 On ABS models refer to Steps 36 to 44 and pulse test the system, then repeat the bleeding procedure.

23 On all models, when you've completed bleeding tighten the bleed valve and remove the equipment, then fit the dust cap. Top-up the reservoir, then fit the diaphragm, diaphragm plate, and cap **(see illustrations 11.18 and 11.16b)**. Check for spilled brake fluid and clean up as required.

24 Fit the reservoir and the side panel **(see illustration 9.4)**. Check that there are no fluid leaks and thoroughly test the operation of the brake before riding the motorcycle.

Both systems

25 If it is not possible to produce a firm feel to the lever or pedal, the fluid may be full of many tiny air bubbles rather than a few big ones. To remedy this apply some pressure to the system, for the front brake by tying the front brake lever lightly back to the handlebar, and for the rear by tying a weight to the brake pedal – do not apply too much pressure or the cup and seals in the master cylinder and caliper may fail. Let the fluid stabilise for a few hours, after which the tiny bubbles should either have risen to the top in the reservoir, or have formed into one or more big bubbles that can be more easily bled out by repeating the bleeding procedure.

26 If you are still having trouble look for any high point in the system in which a pocket of air may become trapped. Displace and agitate the hose or pipe so the bubble can be dislodged (but take care not to bend a pipe) – tapping it may help. If necessary displace the master cylinder and/or the caliper(s), and free the brake hose(s) from guides and move the parts around to dislodge the air and encourage it towards a bleed valve – refer to the relevant Sections as required to displace components. On models with ABS it is not practical to disturb the modulator as the pipes have to be detached, allowing more air to enter the system – if you cannot get the system to bleed correctly take the bike to a Yamaha dealer.

27 If bleeding the system using the conventional tools and methods stated does not give satisfactory results, or if otherwise preferred, you can use a commercially available vacuum-type brake bleeding tool, such as the Mity-vac, following the manufacturer's instructions **(see illustration)**. This type of tool literally sucks the fluid out by creating a vacuum at the bleed valve. Users of such tools often get confused by the amount of air that

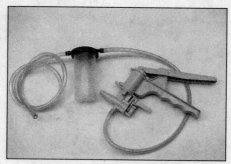

11.27 Vacuum-type brake bleeding tool

appears to be in the brake fluid – more often than not this is caused by the vacuum sucking air past the bleed valve threads (air provides less resistance to the vacuum than the brake fluid) where it mixes with the fluid being drawn out. If this is the case the vacuum applied may be too great, or the bleed valve may have been loosened too much. One way to get round this is to remove the bleed valve and thread some PTFE tape around its threads, but note that doing so will be a bit messy, so have some rag to hand.

Fluid change

28 Changing the brake fluid is a similar process to bleeding the brakes and requires the same materials plus a suitable tool (such as a syringe, or alternatively lots of absorbent rag or paper) for siphoning the fluid out of the reservoir.

29 Cover painted components and fit the equipment to the relevant caliper following the appropriate Steps in the bleeding procedure given above. Remove the reservoir cover or cap, diaphragm plate and diaphragm **(see illustrations 11.5a and b, or and 11.16a and b)**. Remove the fluid from the reservoir into a suitable container, either by sucking it up using a tool as shown, drawing it out into a syringe, or soaking it up in some paper towel. Wipe the reservoir clean. Fill the reservoir with new brake fluid **(see illustration 11.7 or 11.18)**. Squeeze or press the brake lever or pedal and open the bleed valve **(see illustrations 11.8 and 11.19)**. When the valve is opened, brake fluid will flow out of the caliper into the clear tubing, and the lever will move toward the handlebar, or the pedal will move down.

30 Tighten the bleed valve, then slowly release the brake lever or pedal. Keep the reservoir topped-up with new fluid at all times or air may enter the system and greatly increase the length of the task. Repeat the process until new fluid can be seen emerging from the caliper bleed valve.

> **HAYNES HINT** *Old brake fluid is invariably much darker in colour than new fluid, making it easy to see when all old fluid has been expelled from the system.*

31 On completion tighten the bleed valve and remove the equipment, then fit the dust cap. Top-up the reservoir, then fit the diaphragm, diaphragm plate, and cover or cap. Check for spilled brake fluid and clean up as required.

32 On ABS models, pulse test the system as described below.

33 Check that there are no fluid leaks and thoroughly test the operation of the brake before riding the motorcycle.

Draining the system for overhaul

34 Draining the brake fluid is again a similar process to bleeding the brakes. The quickest and easiest way is to use a commercially available vacuum-type brake bleeding tool (see Step 27) – follow the manufacturer's instructions. Otherwise follow the procedure described above for changing the fluid, but quite simply do not put any new fluid into the reservoir – the system fills itself with air instead.

35 When it comes to refilling the system start by adding new fluid from a sealed container to the reservoir, then perform the bleeding procedure as described above until the fluid comes out of the bleed valve, and keep at it until you are certain there is no more air left in the system.

Pulse test procedures (ABS models)

Special tool: *A method of grounding the light blue wire in the ABS test connector is required: a test adaptor (that plugs into the connector after removing the blanking cover) is available from Yamaha, part No. 90890-03149; similar after-market copies can be obtained; alternatively you can use a short length of insulated wire to bridge between the light blue and black wire terminals in the connector.*

36 On XJ6-NA models remove the left-hand side cover, and on XJ6-SA and XJ6-FA models remove the left-hand cockpit side panel (see Chapter 7).

37 Check battery voltage (see Chapter 8) – it needs to be fully charged (12.8 volts or higher).

38 Make sure the ignition is OFF. Displace the test connector and remove the blanking cover, then either plug the test adapter in or bridge between the light blue and black wire terminals in the connector using insulated wire **(see illustrations)**.

11.38a Displace the test connector (arrowed) from the bracket...

11.38b ...and remove the blanking cap

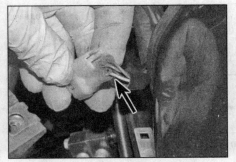

11.38c If using a jumper wire identify the light blue and black wires (arrowed)...

11.38d ...and bridge across their corresponding terminals (arrowed)

Test 1

39 Make sure the kill switch is set to OFF. Simultaneously apply the brake lever and pedal and keep them applied, then turn the ignition switch ON – a single pulse should be felt first in the lever, then in the pedal, then again in the lever (if they do not occur in that order, the brake hoses or pipes have been reconnected incorrectly). When the pulsing sequence is complete release the lever and pedal.

40 Turn the ignition OFF, remove the test adapter or jumper wire and fit the blanking cover, then turn the ignition ON and set the kill switch to RUN. Turn the ignition OFF.

Test 2

41 Put the bike on the sidestand and select a gear.

42 Make sure the kill switch is set to OFF. Turn the ignition switch ON, then push the start button for at least 4 seconds, then release it.

43 Simultaneously apply the brake lever and pedal and keep them applied – quick pulses should be felt briefly first in the lever, then in the pedal, then again in the lever (if they do not occur in that order, the brake hoses or pipes have been reconnected incorrectly). When the pulsing sequence is complete release the lever and pedal.

44 Turn the ignition OFF, remove the test adapter or jumper wire and fit the blanking cover, then turn the ignition ON and set the kill switch to RUN, select neutral and retract the sidestand. Turn the ignition OFF.

12 Wheel inspection and repair

1 In order to carry out a proper inspection of the wheels, it is necessary to support the bike securely in an upright position so that the wheel being inspected is raised off the ground. Clean the wheels thoroughly to remove mud and dirt that may interfere with the inspection procedure or mask defects. Make a general check of the wheels (see Chapter 1) and tyres (see *Pre-ride checks*).

2 Attach a dial gauge to the fork or the swingarm and position its tip against the side of the wheel rim **(see illustration)**. Spin the wheel slowly and check the axial (side-to-side) runout at the rim.

3 In order to accurately check radial (out of round) runout with the dial gauge, remove the wheel from the machine, and the tyre from the wheel. With the axle clamped in a vice and the dial gauge positioned on the top of the rim, the wheel can be rotated to check the runout.

4 An easier, though slightly less accurate, method is to attach a stiff wire pointer to the fork or the swingarm and position the end a fraction of an inch from the edge of the wheel rim where the wheel and tyre join. If the wheel is true, the distance from the pointer to the rim will be constant as the wheel is rotated.

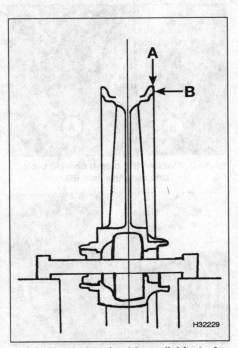

12.2 Check the wheel for radial (out-of-round) runout (A) and axial (side-to-side) runout (B)

Note: *If wheel runout is excessive, check the wheel bearings very carefully before renewing the wheel.*

5 The wheels should also be inspected for cracks, flat spots on the rim and other damage. Look very closely for dents in the area where the tyre bead contacts the rim. Dents in this area may prevent complete sealing of the tyre against the rim, which leads to deflation of the tyre over a period of time.

6 If damage is evident, or if runout in either direction is excessive, the wheel will have to be replaced with a new one. Never attempt to repair a damaged cast alloy wheel.

13 Wheel alignment check

1 Misalignment of the wheels due to a bent frame or forks can cause strange and possibly serious handling problems. If the frame or forks are at fault, repair by a frame specialist or replacement with new parts are the only options.

2 To check wheel alignment you will need an assistant, a length of string or a perfectly straight piece of wood and a ruler. A plumb bob or spirit level for checking that the wheels are vertical will also be required.

3 In order to make a proper check of the wheels it is necessary to support the bike in an upright position on its centrestand. First ensure that the chain adjuster markings coincide on each side of the swingarm (see Chapter 1, Section 1). Next, measure the width of both tyres at their widest points. Subtract the smaller measurement from the larger measurement, then divide the difference by two. The result is the amount of offset that should exist between the front and rear tyres on both sides of the machine.

4 If a string is used, have your assistant hold one end of it about halfway between the floor and the rear axle, with the string touching the back edge of the rear tyre sidewall.

5 Run the other end of the string forward and pull it tight so that it is roughly parallel to the

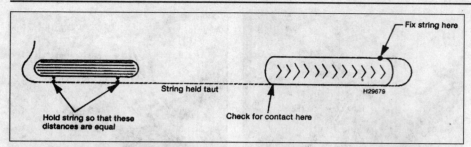

13.5 Wheel alignment check using string

floor **(see illustration)**. Slowly bring the string into contact with the front edge of the rear tyre sidewall, then turn the front wheel until it is parallel with the string. Measure the distance from the front tyre sidewall to the string.

6 Repeat the procedure on the other side of the motorcycle. The distance from the front tyre sidewall to the string should be equal on both sides.

7 As previously mentioned, a perfectly straight length of wood or metal bar may be substituted for the string **(see illustration)**.

8 If the distance between the string and tyre is greater on one side, or if the rear wheel appears to be out of alignment, have your machine checked by a Yamaha dealer.

9 If the front-to-back alignment is correct, the wheels still may be out of alignment vertically.

10 Using a plumb bob or spirit level, check the rear wheel to make sure it is vertical. To do this, hold the string of the plumb bob against the tyre upper sidewall and allow the weight to settle just off the floor. If the string touches both the upper and lower tyre sidewalls and is perfectly straight, the wheel is vertical. If it is not, adjust the stand until it is.

11 Once the rear wheel is vertical, check that the front wheel is vertical also. If both wheels are not perfectly vertical, the frame and/or major suspension components are bent.

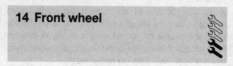

14 Front wheel

Removal

1 Support the motorcycle securely in an upright position with the front wheel off the ground.

2 Displace the front brake calipers (see Section 3).

3 Slacken the axle pinch bolt on the bottom of the right-hand fork **(see illustration)**.

4 Support the wheel, then unscrew and withdraw the axle **(see illustration)**. Remove the wheel from between the forks.

5 On models without ABS remove the shouldered spacer from each side of the wheel, noting how they fit inside the bearing seals **(see illustration)**. On models with ABS remove the shouldered spacer from the left-hand side of the wheel **(see illustration 14.5a)** and the ABS sensor mounting plate/

spacer from the right-hand side, noting how they fit inside the bearing seals **(see illustration)** – the sensor can remain in the mounting plate with its wiring attached, or the sensor can be removed.

Caution: Don't lay the wheel down and allow it to rest on either brake disc – they could become warped. Set the wheel on wood blocks so the wheel rim supports the weight of the wheel, or keep the wheel upright. Don't operate the brake lever with the wheel removed.

6 Clean the axle and remove any corrosion using steel wool. Check the axle for straightness by rolling it on a flat surface such as a piece of plate glass. If available, place the axle in V-blocks and check for runout using a dial gauge. If the axle is bent, replace it with a new one.

7 Wipe any old grease off the bearing seals and check the condition of the seals and the wheel bearings (see Section 16).

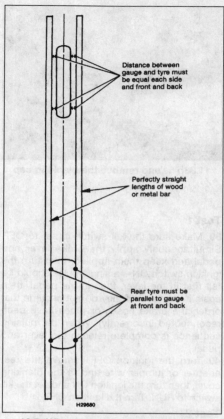

13.7 Wheel alignment check using a straight-edge

14.3 Slacken the clamp bolt (A) then unscrew the axle (B)

14.4 Withdraw the axle and remove the wheel

14.5a Remove the spacer from each side on models without ABS, and from the left on ABS models

14.5b Remove the sensor plate from the right-hand side on ABS models

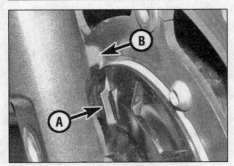

14.10a Make sure the slot (A) in the sensor plate aligns with the lug (B) on the fork...

14.10b ...and the lug locates in the slot with the wheel in position

forks by applying the brake and pressing down on the handlebars to align the wheel and the suspension.

14 Tighten the pinch bolt on the bottom of the right-hand fork to the specified torque setting (see illustration 14.3).

15 On models with ABS, install the front wheel sensor if it was removed. Note that if new front wheel bearings have been fitted or the ABS rotor renewed, the distance between the outer edge of the sensor plate and the face of the sensor rotor should be measured. Use the depth gauge on a Vernier to take this measurement, which should be between 28.7 and 29.8 mm (see illustrations 15.21a and b). In the event that the new bearing has not fully seated in the hub the air gap between the sensor head and the rotor is likely to be too great. Install the sensor once the setting has been checked.

16 Apply the front brake to bring the pads into contact with the discs. Check the operation of the front brake before riding the motorcycle.

8 Clean the axle spacers and remove any corrosion with steel wool. The spacers should be perfectly smooth where they locate in the seals.

Installation

9 Apply lithium-based grease to the insides of the bearing seals. On models without ABS fit the spacers into the seals so that the shouldered end faces out (see illustration 14.5a). On models with ABS fit the shouldered spacer into the left-hand side of the wheel (see illustration 14.5a) and the ABS sensor mounting plate/spacer into the right-hand side, making sure they fit inside the bearing seals (see illustration 14.5b).

10 Apply a thin coat of lithium-based grease to the axle, then position the wheel between the forks, making sure the directional arrow on the tyre points in the direction of normal

rotation. On ABS models make sure the sensor mounting plate is positioned with the locating slot upwards (see illustration). Lift the wheel into position between the forks, making sure the spacers remain in place, and on ABS models that the lug on the inside of the fork locates in the slot in the sensor mounting plate (see illustration).

11 Lift, align and support the wheel and slide the axle in from the right-hand side and thread it into the bottom of the left hand fork (see illustration 14.4).

12 Check that the axle is correctly located then tighten it to the torque setting specified at the beginning of the Chapter.

13 Install the brake calipers, making sure the pads sit squarely on each side of the discs (see Section 3). Apply the front brake to bring the pads back into contact with the discs. Take the bike off its stand and compress the

15 Rear wheel and sprocket coupling

Removal

1 Support the motorcycle securely in an upright position with the rear wheel off the ground.

2 Create some slack in the chain (see Chapter 1).

3 Unscrew the axle nut and remove the washer, and where fitted the adjustment marker plate (see illustration).

4 Support the wheel, then withdraw the axle with the adjustment marker plate or washer as fitted, and lower the wheel to the ground (see illustration).

5 Disengage the chain from the rear wheel sprocket and lay it over the swingarm (see illustration).

6 Withdraw the chain adjuster from each end of the swingarm (see illustration).

7 Draw the wheel back and displace the brake caliper bracket, noting how it locates on the swingarm, and support it out of the way (see illustration).

15.3 Remove the axle nut and washer, and the marker plate (arrowed) where fitted

15.4 Withdraw the axle and lower the wheel

15.5 Slip the chain off the sprocket

15.6 Remove the chain adjusters

15.7 Draw the wheel back a bit then displace the caliper bracket from its lug on the swingarm

15.8a Remove the shouldered spacer...

15.8b ...and the plain spacer

15.8c Remove the sensor plate from the right-hand side on ABS models

8 On models without ABS remove the shouldered spacer from the right-hand side of the wheel and the plain spacer from the left, noting how they fit inside the bearing seals (see illustrations). On models with ABS remove the plain spacer from the left-hand side of the wheel (see illustration 15.8b) and the ABS sensor mounting plate/spacer from the right-hand side, noting how they fit inside the bearing seals (see illustration) – the sensor can remain in the mounting plate with its wire attached or the sensor can be removed from the plate.

Caution: Don't lay the wheel down and allow it to rest on the disc or the sprocket – they could become warped. Set the wheel on wood blocks so the wheel rim supports the weight of the wheel, or keep the wheel upright. Don't operate the brake pedal with the wheel removed.

9 Check for any rotational play in the sprocket coupling – play indicates worn rubber dampers, and a new set must be fitted. If required lift the sprocket coupling out of the hub and remove the dampers (see illustrations). Check the coupling for cracks or any obvious signs of damage. Also check the sprocket studs for looseness, wear or damage.
10 Wipe any old grease off the bearing seals and check the condition of the seals and the wheel bearings in both the wheel and the sprocket coupling (see Section 16).
11 Clean the axle and remove any corrosion using steel wool. Check the axle is straight by rolling it on a flat surface such as a piece of plate glass. If available, place the axle in V-blocks and check for runout using a dial gauge. If the axle is bent, replace it with a new one.
12 Clean the spacers and remove any

corrosion with steel wool. The spacers should be perfectly smooth where they locate in the seals.

Installation

13 If removed fit the rubber dampers, using a new set if necessary (see illustration 15.9b). Make sure the spacer is in place in the sprocket coupling bearing, then press the sprocket coupling firmly into the hub, making sure it is fully and evenly seated (see illustration 15.9a).
14 Apply lithium-based grease to the insides of the bearing seals. On models without ABS fit the shouldered spacer into the right-hand side of the wheel and the plain spacer into the left, making sure they fit inside the bearing seals (see illustrations 15.8a and b). On ABS models fit the plain spacer into the left-hand side of the wheel (see illustration 15.8b).
15 Manoeuvre the wheel and the caliper bracket into place, making sure that the slot in the bracket engages with the peg on the inside of the swingarm (see illustration 15.7). On models with ABS fit the sensor mounting plate/spacer into the right-hand side of the wheel, making sure it fits inside the bearing seal, and align it so that its slot is horizontal and at the back, so it will locate over the lug on the caliper bracket (see illustration 15.8c).
16 Fit the chain adjusters into the swingarm (see illustration 15.6).
17 Fit the drive chain around the sprocket (see illustration 15.5).
18 Slide the adjustment marker plate or washer onto the axle – the tabs on the bottom of the marker must point away from the axle head.
19 Lubricate the axle with a smear of grease. Lift the wheel into position, making sure the spacers/sensor plate and caliper bracket remain in place, and that on models with ABS the slot in the wheel sensor plate is aligned with and locates over the rear of the caliper bracket (see illustration). Slide the axle through from the right-hand side (see illustration 15.4) – seat the adjustment marker tabs (where fitted) under the swingarm (see illustration).
20 Where fitted seat the left-hand adjustment marker over the end of the axle with the tabs under the swingarm, then fit the washer and the axle nut (see illustration 15.3). Follow the

15.9a Lift the sprocket coupling out...

15.9b ...and remove the dampers

15.19a Locate the rear lug on the caliper bracket in the slot in the sensor plate

15.19b Make sure the adjustment marker locates correctly

15.21a To check the wheel sensor set depth, insert the depth gauge into the sensor bore...

15.21b ...and seat the tool against the face of the plate...

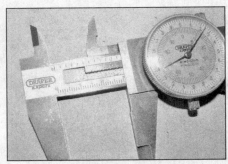

15.21c ...then note the measurement

procedure in Chapter 1 and adjust the chain tension. (see Section 17).

21 On models with ABS, install the rear wheel sensor if it was removed. Note that if new rear wheel bearings have been fitted or the ABS rotor renewed, the distance between the outer edge of the sensor plate and the face of the sensor rotor should be measured. Use the depth gauge on a Vernier to take this measurement, which should be between 29.0 and 30.1 mm **(see illustrations)**. In the event that the new bearing has not fully seated in the hub the air gap between the sensor head and the rotor is likely to be too great. Install the sensor once the setting has been checked.

22 Apply the rear brake to bring the pads into contact with the disc. Check the operation of the rear brake before riding the motorcycle.

16 Wheel and sprocket coupling bearings

Front wheel bearings

Note: *Always fit the wheel bearings in sets, never individually.*

1 Remove the wheel (see Section 14). Lay the wheel rim on wood blocks. A caged ball bearing is fitted in each side of the wheel.

2 Inspect the seals and bearings – check that each bearing inner race turns smoothly and that the outer race is a tight fit in the hub (see *Tools and Workshop Tips* (Section 5) in the Reference Section). **Note:** *Do not remove the*

bearings unless they are going to be replaced with new ones.

3 If new components are needed, it is best to remove the discs (see Section 4), and on ABS models the sensor rotor (Section 17), to prevent them being damaged or distorted during bearing removal.

4 Lever out the bearing seal from each side of the hub using a flat-bladed screwdriver or a seal hook **(see illustration)**. Take care not to damage the hub. New seals must be fitted on reassembly.

5 Move the bearing spacer aside to expose the inner race on the lower bearing **(see illustration)**.

HAYNES HINT *Position a piece of wood against the wheel to prevent the screwdriver shaft damaging it when levering the grease seal out.*

Using a metal rod (preferably a brass punch) inserted through the centre of the upper bearing drive the lower bearing from the hub, moving the spacer around and relocating the drift so it's driven out squarely **(see illustration)**. The bearing spacer will also come out. Turn the wheel over so that the remaining bearing faces down. Drive the bearing out of the wheel using a socket on the inner race and an extension bar. If you can't move the spacer, or if you can't get sufficient purchase with the drift, remove the bearings using an internal expanding puller with slide-hammer attachment, which can be obtained commercially – select the correct attachment and locate it between the inner race of the upper bearing and the spacer, then tighten the inner bolt to expand and lock the puller **(see illustration)**. Attach the slide-hammer, hold the wheel firmly down and jar the bearing out **(see illustration)**.

16.4 Lever out the grease seals

16.5a Move the spacer to the side to expose the inner race...

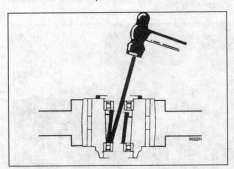

16.5b ...then locate the drift on it and drive the bearing out

16.5c Locate the knife edge of the puller in the gap between the bearing and the spacer, then expand it...

16.5d ...and use the slide-hammer to dislodge the bearing

16.7 A socket can be used to drive the new bearing in

16.9 Fit the grease seal and press or tap it into place

6 Thoroughly clean the hub area of the wheel and inspect the bearing housings for damage. If a housing is damaged, consult a Yamaha dealer or wheel specialist before reassembling the wheel.

7 Fit the new bearings with the marked side facing out. Drive the first bearing in using a bearing driver or suitable socket that bears only on the outer race, and make sure the bearing fits squarely and all the way onto its seat **(see illustration)**. Alternatively draw it in using a drawbolt arrangement (see *Tools and Workshop Tips*).

8 Turn the wheel over then fit the bearing spacer and the other new bearing.

9 Fit the new seals into the hub using finger pressure or a suitable driver that bears on the outer rim, setting them flush with the hub **(see illustration)**. Smear the seal lips with grease.

10 If removed fit the discs (see Section 4), and on ABS models the sensor rotor (Section 17). Clean the brake discs using acetone or brake system cleaner, then install the wheel (see Section 14).

11 Note that if the wheel bearings have been renewed the distance between the outer edge of the sensor plate and the face of the sensor rotor should be measured once the wheel has been reinstalled and the axle tightened.

Rear wheel bearings

12 Remove the wheel (see Section 15). Set the wheel on wood blocks. Lift the sprocket coupling out of the wheel and remove the rubber dampers **(see illustrations 15.9a and b)**. A caged ball bearing is fitted in each side of the wheel.

13 Inspect the seal and bearings – check that each bearing inner race turns smoothly and that the outer race is a tight fit in the hub (see *Tools and Workshop Tips* (Section 5) in the Reference Section). **Note:** *Do not remove the bearings unless they are going to be replaced with new ones.*

14 If new components are needed it is best to remove the disc (see Section 8), and on ABS models the sensor rotor (Section 17), to prevent them being damaged or distorted during bearing removal.

15 Lever out the bearing seal from the right-side of the hub, using a flat-bladed screwdriver or a seal hook **(see illustration 16.4)**.

Take care not to damage the hub. A new seal must be fitted on reassembly.

 HAYNES HiNT *Position a piece of wood against the wheel to prevent the screwdriver shaft damaging it when levering the grease seal out.*

16 Move the bearing spacer aside to expose the inner race on the lower bearing **(see illustration 16.5a)**. Using a metal rod (preferably a brass punch) inserted through the centre of the upper bearing drive the lower bearing from the hub, moving the spacer around and relocating the drift so it's driven out squarely **(see illustration 16.5b)**. The bearing spacer will also come out. Turn the wheel over so that the remaining bearing faces down. Drive the bearing out of the wheel using a socket on the inner race and an extension bar. If you can't move the spacer, or if you can't get sufficient purchase with the drift, remove the bearings using an internal expanding puller with slide-hammer attachment, which can be obtained commercially – select the correct attachment and locate it between the inner race of the upper bearing and the spacer, then tighten the inner bolt to expand and lock the puller **(see illustration 16.5c)**. Attach the slide-hammer, hold the wheel firmly down and jar the bearing out **(see illustration 16.5d)**.

17 Thoroughly clean the hub area of the wheel and inspect the bearing housings for damage. If a housing is damaged, consult a Yamaha dealer or wheel specialist before reassembling the wheel.

18 Fit the new bearings with the marked side facing out. Drive the first bearing in using a bearing driver or suitable socket that bears only on the outer race, and make sure the bearing fits squarely and all the way onto its seat **(see illustration 16.7)**. Alternatively draw it in using a drawbolt arrangement (see *Tools and Workshop Tips*).

19 Turn the wheel over then fit the bearing spacer and the other new bearing.

20 Fit the new seal into the right-hand side of the hub using finger pressure or a suitable driver that bears on the outer rim, setting it flush with the hub **(see illustration 16.9)**. Smear the seal lips with grease.

21 Fit the rubber dampers into the wheel. Make sure the spacer is in place in the sprocket coupling bearing, then press the coupling firmly into the hub, making sure it is fully and evenly seated **(see illustrations 15.9b and a)**.

22 If removed fit the disc (see Section 8), and on ABS models the sensor rotor (Section 17).

23 Clean the brake disc using acetone or brake system cleaner, then install the wheel (see Section 15).

24 Note that if the wheel bearings have been renewed the distance between the outer edge of the sensor plate and the face of the sensor rotor should be measured once the wheel has been reinstalled and the axle tightened.

Sprocket coupling bearing

25 Remove the rear wheel (see Section 15). Lift the sprocket coupling out of the wheel and remove the rubber dampers **(see illustrations 15.9a and b)**.

26 Inspect the seal and bearing – check that the bearing inner races turn smoothly and that the outer race is a tight fit in the coupling (see *Tools and Workshop Tips (Section 5)* in the Reference Section). **Note:** *Do not remove the bearing unless it is being replaced with a new one.*

27 If new components are needed lever out the bearing seal using a flat-bladed screwdriver or a seal hook **(see illustration)**. Take care not to damage the rim of the coupling. Discard the seal – a new one must be fitted.

28 Drive the spacer out of the centre of the bearing using a socket that bears only on the spacer and not on the bearing inner race **(see illustration)**.

16.27 Lever out the grease seal

16.28 Drive the spacer out of the centre of the bearing

29 Support the coupling on blocks of wood, sprocket side down, and drive the bearing out from the inside using a bearing driver or socket (see illustration).

30 Thoroughly clean the sprocket coupling and inspect the bearing housing for damage. If the housing is damaged, consult a Yamaha dealer or wheel specialist before reassembling the wheel.

31 Fit the new bearing with the marked side facing out. Drive the bearing in using a bearing driver or suitable socket that bears only on the outer race, and make sure the bearing fits squarely and all the way onto its seat (see illustration).

32 Support the bearing on a socket that bears on the inner race, then drive the spacer into the bearing from the inner side (see illustration).

33 Fit the new seal into the coupling using finger pressure or a suitable driver that bears on the outer rim, setting it flush with the hub (see illustration). Smear the seal lips with grease.

34 Fit the rubber dampers into the wheel. Press the sprocket coupling firmly into the hub, making sure it is fully and evenly seated.

35 Clean the brake disc using acetone or brake system cleaner then install the wheel (see Section 15).

16.29 Drive the bearing out from the inside

16.31 A socket can be used to drive in the new bearing

16.32 Support the bearing on its inner race when driving the spacer into it

16.33 Press or drive the seal into the coupling

17 Anti-lock brake system (ABS)

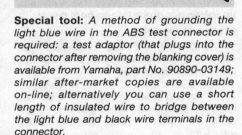

Special tool: *A method of grounding the light blue wire in the ABS test connector is required: a test adaptor (that plugs into the connector after removing the blanking cover) is available from Yamaha, part No. 90890-03149; similar after-market copies are available on-line; alternatively you can use a short length of insulated wire to bridge between the light blue and black wire terminals in the connector.*

ABS operation

1 The anti-lock brake system (ABS) prevents the wheels from locking up under hard braking or on uneven road surfaces. A sensor on each wheel transmits information about the speed of rotation to the ABS control unit; if the unit senses that a wheel is about to lock, it releases brake pressure to that wheel momentarily, preventing a skid.

2 The anti-lock system is self-checking and is activated when the ignition switch is turned on – the ABS indicator light in the instrument cluster will come on for 2 seconds, and if the ABS is normal, the light will go off. **Note:** *If the ABS indicator light does not come on initially there is a fault in the system – see below.*

3 If the indicator light remains on, flashes, or does either while the machine is being ridden, there is a fault in the system and the ABS function will be switched off – the brakes will still function but in normal mode. A fault code will be registered and stored in the ECU.

4 To retrieve any stored fault codes, a test adaptor or jumper wire is required (see **Special Tool** above). On XJ6-NA models remove the left-hand side cover, and on XJ6-SA and XJ6-FA models remove the left-hand cockpit side panel (see Chapter 7). Make sure the ignition is OFF. Displace the test connector and remove the blanking cover, and either plug the test adapter in or bridge between the light blue and black wire terminals in the connector using insulated wire (see illustrations 11.38a, b, c and d). The warning light will flash and the fault code(s) will be displayed in the instrument cluster.

5 Remove the test adaptor when the code or codes have been recorded.

6 Once the fault has been corrected, erase the fault code(s) as follows. Follow Step 4 and connect the test adapter. Turn the ignition on – the fault code(s) will be displayed. Make sure the kill switch is set to OFF. Push the starter button at least four times within ten seconds. The display should revert to normal and the ABS light flashes while the codes are being deleted. When the light stops flashing turn the ignition off then on again – no codes should be displayed. If they are there is still a fault.

7 Turn the ignition switch OFF and remove the test adapter when the code or codes have been erased. Check that the ABS is operating normally (see Step 2).

Note: *The ABS indicator may diagnose a fault if tyre sizes other than those specified by Yamaha are fitted, if the tyre pressures are incorrect, if the machine has been run continuously over bumpy roads, if the front wheel comes off the ground whilst riding (wheelie) or if the machine is on an auxiliary stand with the engine running and the rear wheel turning.*

Fault diagnosis

8 If a fault is indicated in the ABS, first check that the battery is fully charged, then check the ABS fuses (see Chapter 8).

9 If a fault appears, identify the cause using the fault code table overleaf and first make sure that the relevant system wiring connectors are securely connected and free of corrosion – poor connections are the cause of the majority of problems. Also check the wiring itself for any obvious faults or breaks, referring to the wiring diagrams at the end of Chapter 8. Refer to Chapter 8, Section 2, for general electrical fault finding procedures and equipment. In the case of a wheel speed sensor related problem also check the sensor tip and rotor are not dirty or damaged.

10 If after a thorough check, the source of a fault has not been identified, have the system tested by a Yamaha dealer.

Fault codes (preceded by AbS)	Faulty component or system	Possible causes
11, 13, 15, 17, 25, 26, 45	Front wheel speed sensor circuit Front wheel speed sensor Front wheel sensor rotor	Faulty wiring or wiring connector Faulty sensor Damaged sensor rotor
12, 14, 16, 18, 27, 46	Rear wheel speed sensor circuit Rear wheel speed sensor Rear wheel sensor rotor	Faulty wiring or wiring connector Faulty sensor Damaged sensor rotor
21	Control unit/modulator solenoid	Faulty control unit/modulator Faulty wiring or wiring connector
22	Starter circuit	Faulty wiring or wiring connector
24	Brake light circuit	Faulty wiring or wiring connector Faulty bulb Faulty switch Faulty relay
31, 32	Control unit/modulator relay	ABS solenoid fuse Faulty wiring or wiring connector Faulty relay Faulty control unit/modulator
33, 34	Control unit/modulator motor	ABS motor fuse Faulty wiring or wiring connector Faulty relay Faulty control unit/modulator
41	Front wheel can lock	Brake drag Brake fluid or hose problem Pulse test result incorrect Faulty control unit/modulator
42, 47	Rear wheel can lock	Brake drag Brake fluid or hose problem Pulse test result incorrect Faulty control unit/modulator
43	Front wheel speed sensor signal	Incorrect sensor installation Faulty wiring or wiring connector Damaged sensor rotor
44	Rear wheel speed sensor signal	Incorrect sensor installation Faulty wiring or wiring connector Damaged sensor rotor
51 and 52	Power supply voltage high	Battery Charging system
53 and 54	Power supply voltage low	Battery Charging system Faulty wiring or wiring connector
56	Control unit/modulator power circuit	Faulty control unit/modulator
63	Front wheel speed sensor power	Faulty wiring or wiring connector Faulty control unit/modulator
64	Rear wheel speed sensor power	Faulty wiring or wiring connector Faulty control unit/modulator

ABS components

Note: *Take great care not to damage the wheel sensor head or sensor rotor surface, or use magnetic tools near them, and take care not to subject them to any sort of impact. Replace the rotor screws with new ones if removed.*

Front wheel sensor

11 Remove the air filter housing (see Chapter 4). Trace the wheel sensor wiring to the connector and disconnect it **(see illustration)**.

12 Release the sensor wiring guides and feed the wire down to the sensor, noting its routing. Undo the sensor screw and remove the sensor **(see illustration)**.

13 Make sure the tip of the sensor and its mounting surfaces are clean and show no signs of damage or distortion. Fit the sensor and tighten the screw to the torque setting specified at the beginning of the Chapter. Feed the wiring up to the connector, routing and securing it as noted on removal.

14 Install the air filter housing (see Chapter 4).

Caution – It was found that both wheel sensors were stuck fast in their mounting plates due to corrosion and it was necessary to work the sensor bolt plate back and forth to break the corrosion between it and the mounting plate – this is best done with the wheel removed (see Section 14 or 15). There was even corrosion between the surface of the sensor and its bore in the mounting plate. Once cleaned up the sensor drops into its bore easily.

Front sensor rotor

15 Remove the front wheel (see Section 14).
16 Undo the screws securing the rotor and lift it off **(see illustration)**.
17 Make sure there is no dirt or corrosion where the ring seats on the hub – if the ring does not sit flat the signals from the sensor could be distorted. Make sure the sensor rotor is clean and shows no signs of damage or distortion. Fit new screws and apply a non-permanent thread locking compound, and tighten them to the torque setting specified at the beginning of the Chapter.
18 Install the front wheel (see Section 14).

17.11 Front wheel speed sensor wiring connector (arrowed)

17.12 Undo the screw and remove the sensor

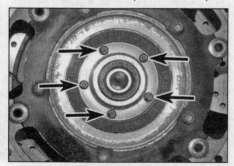

17.16 Front wheel sensor rotor screws (arrowed)

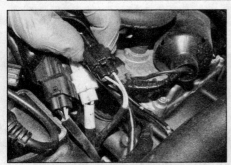

17.19 Rear wheel speed sensor wiring connector

17.20 Undo the screw and remove the sensor

17.27 ABS control unit/modulator

Rear wheel sensor

19 Raise the fuel tank (see Chapter 4). Trace the wheel sensor wiring to the connector and disconnect it **(see illustration)**.

20 Release the sensor wiring guides and feed the wire down to the sensor, noting its routing. Undo the sensor screw and remove the sensor **(see illustration)**.

21 Make sure the tip of the sensor and its mounting surfaces are clean and show no signs of damage or distortion. Fit the sensor and tighten the screw to the torque setting specified at the beginning of the Chapter. Feed the wiring up to the connector, routing and securing it as noted on removal.

22 Lower the fuel tank.

Rear sensor rotor

23 Remove the rear wheel (see Section 15).

24 Undo the screws securing the rotor and lift it off **(see illustration 17.16)**.

25 Make sure there is no dirt or corrosion where the ring seats on the hub – if the ring does not sit flat the signals from the sensor could be distorted. Make sure the sensor rotor is clean and shows no signs of damage or distortion. Fit new screws and apply a non-permanent thread locking compound, and tighten them to the torque setting specified at the beginning of the Chapter.

26 Install the rear wheel (see Section 15).

Control unit/modulator

Note: *Before removing the modulator drain all old brake fluid from the brake system, then fill with new fluid on installation (see Section 11). The modulator cannot be dismantled for overhaul, and no component parts are available. If it fails, it must be replaced with a new one.*

27 The modulator is mounted in front of the rear shock absorber **(see illustration)**.

28 Remove the rear brake pedal and the gearchange lever (see Chapter 5).

29 Remove the shock absorber and swingarm (see Chapter 5). Remove the left-hand footrest bracket assembly.

30 Remove the left-hand side panel (see Chapter 7). Remove the modulator wiring guide/connector cover **(see illustrations)**. Lift the security catch on the connector and disconnect it **(see illustration)**.

31 Cover the area around the modulator with clean rag to prevent damage to paintwork in the event that brake fluid is spilled.

32 Mark each brake pipe according to its location on the top of the modulator. Unscrew the brake pipe nuts and detach the pipes.

33 Unscrew the rear brake hose holder bolts.

34 Unscrew the two modulator mounting bracket bolts on each side **(see illustration)**. Carefully lift the bracket and modulator out. Unscrew the three nuts and the single screw to free the modulator carrier from the mounting bracket – check the condition of the rubber mountings. If required remove the screws and detach the modulator from the carrier.

35 Seal the end of each pipe and plug the holes in the modulator using rubber bungs or loosely fit M10 x 1.0 bolts to prevent dirt entering the system.

36 Installation is the reverse of removal, noting the following:

● Make sure the brake pipes are correctly aligned.
● Make sure the wiring connector is secure.
● Follow the procedure in Section 11 to refill and bleed the brake system. Check that there are no fluid leaks and test the operation of the brakes before riding the motorcycle.

18 Tyres

General information

1 The wheels fitted on all models are designed to take tubeless tyres only. Tyre sizes are given in the Specifications at the beginning of this chapter.

2 Refer to *Pre-ride checks* at the beginning

17.30a Unscrew the bolt (arrowed)...

17.30b ...and remove the cover

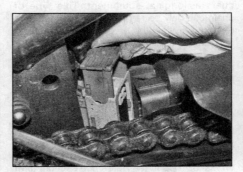

17.30c Lift the catch to release the connector

17.34 Unscrew the two bolts (arrowed) on each side

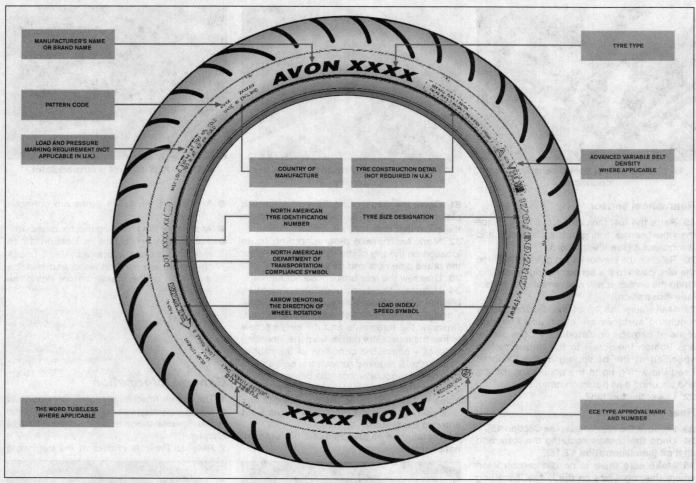

18.3 Common tyre sidewall markings

MANUFACTURER'S NAME OR BRAND NAME

PATTERN CODE

LOAD AND PRESSURE MARKING REQUIREMENT (NOT APPLICABLE IN U.K.)

THE WORD TUBELESS WHERE APPLICABLE

COUNTRY OF MANUFACTURE

NORTH AMERICAN TYRE IDENTIFICATION NUMBER

NORTH AMERICAN DEPARTMENT OF TRANSPORTATION COMPLIANCE SYMBOL

ARROW DENOTING THE DIRECTION OF WHEEL ROTATION

TYRE CONSTRUCTION DETAIL (NOT REQUIRED IN U.K.)

TYRE SIZE DESIGNATION

LOAD INDEX/ SPEED SYMBOL

TYRE TYPE

ADVANCED VARIABLE BELT DENSITY WHERE APPLICABLE

ECE TYPE APPROVAL MARK AND NUMBER

of this manual for tyre maintenance and pressures.

Fitting new tyres

3 When selecting new tyres, refer to the tyre information in the Owner's Manual. Ensure that front and rear tyre types are compatible, and of the correct size and speed rating; if necessary, seek advice from a Yamaha dealer or motorcycle tyre specialist **(see illustration)**.

4 It is recommended that tyres are fitted by a motorcycle tyre specialist and that this is not attempted in the home workshop. This is particularly relevant in the case of tubeless tyres because the force required to break the seal between the wheel rim and tyre bead is substantial, and is usually beyond the capabilities of an individual working with normal tyre levers. Additionally, the specialist will be able to balance the wheels after tyre fitting.

5 Note that punctured tubeless tyres can in some cases be repaired. Seek the advice of a Yamaha dealer or a motorcycle tyre specialist concerning tyre repairs.

19 Drive chain and sprockets

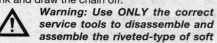

Drive chain

Removal

1 All models are fitted with an endless drive chain as original equipment. This type of chain can only be removed if the swingarm is removed. Follow the procedure in Chapter 5 and remove the swingarm.

2 If a chain with a riveted soft (joining) link has been fitted subsequently, it can be removed by splitting the soft link with a chain cutter. Such chains can be recognised by the soft link side plate's different colour, as well as by the riveted ends of the link's two pins which look as if they have been deeply centre-punched, instead of peened over as with all the other pins (see Section 8 in *Tools and Workshop Tips* in the *Reference* section) **(see illustration)**.

3 If the chain is going to be split, remove

the front sprocket cover **(see illustration 19.10)**, then slacken the chain as described in Chapter 1. Follow the procedure in *Tools and Workshop Tips* to split the soft link and draw the chain off.

⚠️ *Warning: Use ONLY the correct service tools to disassemble and assemble the riveted-type of soft link – if you do not have access to such tools or do not have the skill to operate*

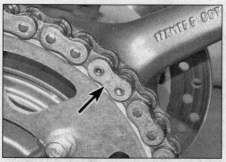

19.2 The soft link (arrowed) should be easy to identify

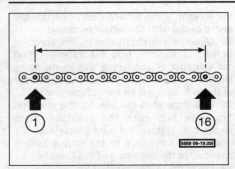

19.5 Measure chain section as shown to determine stretch

19.10 Unscrew the bolts (arrowed) and remove the cover

19.11 Slacken the bolts (arrowed) and displace the housing

them correctly, have the old chain removed and a new one fitted by a Yamaha dealer.

Chain stretch check

4 Chain condition can be determined by the amount it has stretched between a specified number of links. To assess the chain accurately, first it must be removed from the bike (see above), then follow the procedure in Chapter 1 to clean it. The chain must be free of any kinks and binding links must be loosened-up before the check is made.

5 Stretch a section of the chain across a flat surface so it is taut and measure the distance between sixteen of the pins as shown **(see illustration)**.

6 Measure the chain in several places to compensate for uneven wear along its length, then calculate the average and compare it to the limit specified at the beginning of the Chapter. If the chain stretch exceeds the service limit, the chain must be replaced with a new one.

Caution: Never fit a new chain on old sprockets, and never use the old chain if you fit new sprockets – replace the chain and sprockets as a set.

Installation

 Warning: NEVER install a drive chain which uses a clip-type master (split) link.

7 If an endless drive chain is being fitted, follow the procedure in Chapter 5 and install the chain with the swingarm. Refer to Chapter 1 and lubricate and adjust the chain.

8 If a chain with a riveted soft (joining) link is being fitted, route it over the swingarm and around the front and rear sprockets, leaving the two ends in a convenient position to work on. Follow the procedure in *Tools and Workshop Tips* to fit a new soft link. NEVER re-use old soft link components.

9 Once the chain is installed, fit the sprocket cover, then refer to Chapter 1 and lubricate and adjust the chain.

Front sprocket

10 Remove the front sprocket cover **(see illustration)**.

11 Slacken the clutch release shaft housing bolts so you can displace the housing off the engine by about 4mm **(see illustration)**.

12 Have an assistant apply the rear brake hard, then unscrew the nut and remove the washer **(see illustration)**. Note that you may need to carefully relieve the staking of the old nut using a small punch. Yamaha specify that a new nut must be used on reassembly. Adjust the chain so that it is fully slack (see Chapter 1, Section 1).

13 Draw the sprocket and chain off the transmission output shaft and slip the sprocket out of the chain **(see illustration)**. If there is not enough slack in the chain to disengage the front sprocket, slip the chain off the rear wheel sprocket. **Note:** *If the sprocket is not being replaced with a new one, mark its outside face with a dab of paint, so that it can be installed the same way round.*

14 With the sprocket removed check for signs of oil leakage from the output shaft oil

seal. To fit a new seal, lever the old one out using a seal hook **(see illustration)**. Check for any original assembly grease in the inner lip of the seal, and if there is none smear some grease into it. Slide the seal onto the shaft and press it into place, using a deep socket over its outer rim to drive it in if necessary **(see illustration)**.

15 To fit the front sprocket, first engage it with the chain, then slide it onto the transmission shaft **(see illustration 19.13)**. If removed, fit the chain on the rear sprocket. Fit the washer, then fit the **new** nut with the rimmed side facing out and tighten it finger-tight **(see illustration 19.12)**.

16 Adjust the drive chain (see Chapter 1).

17 Apply the rear brake hard and tighten the sprocket nut to the torque setting specified at the beginning of the Chapter.

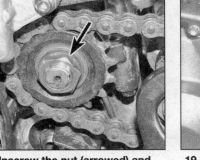

19.12 Unscrew the nut (arrowed) and remove the washer

19.13 Slide the sprocket off the shaft and remove it from the chain

19.14a Lever the old seal out...

19.14b ...and press the new one in, marked side facing out

19.17 Stake the rim of the new nut into the indent

Use a small punch to knock the rim of the nut into the indent in the end of the shaft **(see illustration)**.
18 Tighten the clutch release shaft housing bolts **(see illustration 19.11)**. Fit the front sprocket cover **(see illustration)**.

Rear sprocket

19 Remove the rear wheel (see Section 15).
Caution: Don't lay the wheel down and allow it to rest on the disc or the sprocket – they could become warped. Set the wheel on wood blocks so the wheel rim supports *the weight of the wheel. Don't operate the brake pedal with the wheel removed.*
20 Unscrew the nuts securing the sprocket to the hub assembly **(see illustration)**. Lift off the sprocket, noting which way round it fits.
Note: *The size of the sprocket (i.e. its number of teeth) is stamped on the outside face.*
21 Clean the stud threads. Fit the sprocket onto the hub with the stamped mark facing out. Tighten the nuts evenly and in a criss-cross sequence to the torque setting specified at the beginning of this Chapter.
22 Install the rear wheel (see Section 15).

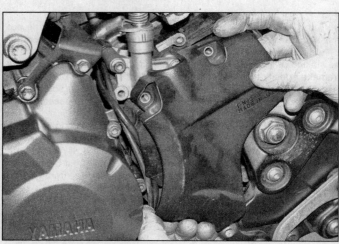

19.18 Route the wiring in the channel in the front of the cover

19.20 Rear sprocket nuts (arrowed)

Chapter 7
Bodywork

Contents

Degrees of difficulty

Easy, suitable for novice with little experience	Fairly easy, suitable for beginner with some experience	Fairly difficult, suitable for competent DIY mechanic	Difficult, suitable for experienced DIY mechanic	Very difficult, suitable for expert DIY or professional

1 General information

This Chapter covers the procedures necessary to remove and install the bodywork. Since many service and repair operations on these motorcycles require the removal of the body panels, the procedures are grouped here and referred to from other Chapters.

In the case of damage to the bodywork, it is usually necessary to remove the broken component and replace it with a new (or used) one. Note that there are however some companies that specialise in 'plastic welding' and there are a number of DIY bodywork repair kits available.

When attempting to remove any body panel, first study it closely, noting any fasteners and associated fittings, to be sure of returning everything to its correct place on installation. Once the evident fasteners have been removed, try to withdraw the panel as described but DO NOT FORCE IT – if it will not release, check that all fasteners have been removed and try again.

When installing a body panel, first study it closely, noting any fasteners and associated fittings removed with it, to be sure of returning everything to its correct place. Check that all fasteners are in good condition, including the rubber mounts; replace any faulty fasteners with new ones before the panel is reassembled. Check also that all mounting brackets are straight and repair them or replace them with new ones if necessary before attempting to install the panel.

Tighten the fasteners securely, but be careful not to overtighten any of them or the panel may break (not always immediately) due to the uneven stress.

2 XJ6-N models

Seat(s)
N model

1 Unlock the seat using the ignition key in the lock on the left-hand side – turn the key anti-clockwise (see illustration).
2 Lift the back of the seat and draw it back, noting how the tab at the front locates.
3 Installation is the reverse of removal. Make sure the tab at the front locates correctly (see illustration). Push the back of the seat down to engage the lock (see illustration).

SP model

4 To remove the passenger seat, unlock the seat using the ignition key in the lock on the

2.1 Turn the key, then lift the rear of the seat and remove it

2.3a Locate the tab in its socket...

2.3b ...and the latch in its slot

2.8a Release the trim clip (A) and undo the screw (B)...

2.8b ...then release the panel from the grommet (arrowed)

left-hand side – turn the key anti-clockwise. Lift the front of the seat and draw it forwards, noting how the tab at the back locates.

5 To remove the rider's seat first remove the passenger seat. Unscrew the two bolts, noting which holes they fit in (see Step 6), then draw

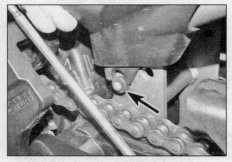

2.9 Lift the panel off the grommet (arrowed)

the seat back, noting where the tab at the front locates.

6 To adjust the height of the rider's seat, first remove it. Unscrew the two seat bracket bolts and reposition the bracket as required – there are two positions, high and low. For the high position align the bolt holes marked H with the brackets on the frame and fit the tab at the front in the higher socket; for the low position align the bolt holes marked L with the brackets on the frame and fit the tab at the front in the lower socket. When fitting the seat, for its high position use the lower two bolt holes, and for the low position use the upper two bolt holes.

7 Installation is the reverse of removal. Refer to Step 6 for the positioning of the rider's seat, and make sure the tab at the front locates correctly. Push the back of the seat down to engage the lock on the passenger seat.

Side panels

8 To remove the right-hand panel release the trim clip by pushing the centre pin in then

drawing the body out, then undo the screw (see illustration). Draw the panel forwards at an angle to release the cut-out from the grommet (see illustration).

9 To remove the left-hand panel undo the screw (see illustration 2.8a). Lift the panel slightly to release the bottom cut-out from the grommet (see illustration), then draw the panel forwards at an angle to release the top cut-out from the grommet (see illustration 2.8b).

10 Installation is the reverse of removal. Make sure the grommets are in good condition. Make sure the tabs at the front locate correctly.

Side covers

11 Undo the screws (see illustration). Carefully pull the front away to free the pegs from the grommets (see illustration).

12 Installation is the reverse of removal. Make sure all the grommets are in good condition, and those in the cover for the screws are fitted with sleeves. Make sure the pegs locate fully in their grommets – smear them with oil to

2.11a Side cover screws (arrowed)

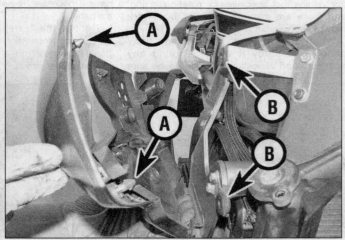

2.11b Pull the pegs (A) from the grommets (B)

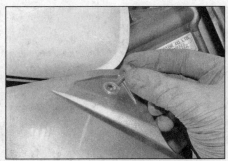

2.12 Shorter screw goes here

2.14 Grab-rail bolts (arrowed)

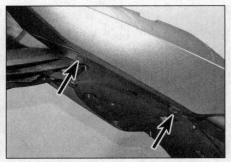

2.17 Rear cowl trim clips on underside (arrowed)

2.18 Rear cowl trim clip at forward end (arrowed)

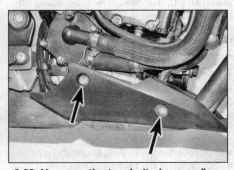

2.20 Unscrew the two bolts (arrowed) on each side

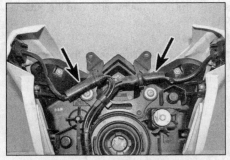

2.23 Turn signal wiring connectors are inside the boots (arrowed)

ease fitment. The shorter screw goes in the top front mount (see illustration).

Grab-rails

13 Remove the seat (passenger seat only on dual seat models).
14 Unscrew the bolts and remove the rail(s) (see illustration). Note the collars for the bolts.
15 Installation is the reverse of removal. Make sure the collars are fitted. Tighten the bolts to 16 Nm.

Rear cowls

16 Remove the seat(s) and the passenger grab-rails.
17 Release and remove the two trim clips on the underside by pushing the centre pins in then drawing the bodies out and remove the cowl (see illustration).
18 Release and remove the trim clip at

the front by unscrewing the centre pin then drawing the body out, and remove the cowl (see illustration).
19 Installation is the reverse of removal. To reset the trim clips push the centre pin out so it protrudes from the top, then fit the clip and push the centre pin in flush to secure it.

Belly pan

20 Unscrew the bolts and remove the belly pan (see illustration).
21 Installation is the reverse of removal. Make sure all the grommets are in good condition and the sleeves are fitted in them.

Headlight covers

22 Remove the headlight assembly (see Chapter 8).
23 Disconnect the turn signal wiring connectors (see illustration).

24 Undo the screws and remove the cover from the headlight (see illustration).
25 If required remove the turn signal (see Chapter 8).
26 Installation is the reverse of removal. Check the headlight, sidelight and turn signals work correctly.

Front mudguard

27 Release the brake hose from the clip on the top of the mudguard (see illustration).
28 Counter-hold the nut on the inside of each rear bolt and unscrew the bolts, noting how they secure the brake hose brackets (see illustration).
29 Unscrew the front bolt on each side.
30 Draw the mudguard forwards, taking care not to scratch it on the forks.
31 Installation is the reverse of removal. Check the condition of the grommets, and

2.24 Headlight cover screws (arrowed)

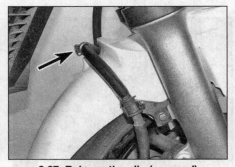

2.27 Release the clip (arrowed)

2.28 Front mudguard bolts (arrowed), right-hand side – rear bolts have nuts on the inside

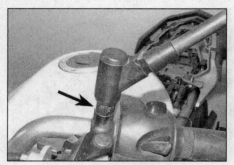

2.32 Mirror base hex (arrowed)

3.2a Undo the screws (arrowed)

3.2b Release the side tabs...

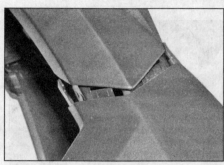

3.2c ...then the front

make sure the collars are fitted from the inner side on the front mounts and from the outside on the rear.

Mirrors

32 Unscrew the mirror using the hex at the base **(see illustration).**
33 Installation is the reverse of removal.

XJ6-S models

Seat, side panels, grab-rails, rear cowls and belly pan

1 See Section 2.

Cockpit side panels

2 Undo the cockpit side panel screws **(see**

illustration). Release the tabs along the side from the fairing side panel, then draw the panel back to release it from the cockpit centre panel **(see illustrations).**
3 Installation is the reverse of removal.

Cockpit centre panel

4 Remove the cockpit side panels.
5 Undo the cockpit centre panel screws and release the trim clips **(see illustration).** Release the tabs from the fairing on both sides, then release the top tabs on each side and remove the panel **(see illustrations).**
6 Installation is the reverse of removal.

Fairing side panels

7 Remove the cockpit side panel (Step 2).
8 Release the turn signal wiring connector cable-tie, then disconnect the wiring **(see illustration).**
9 Release the trim clip on each side by

pushing the centre pin in then drawing the body out **(see illustration).**
10 Undo the three screws securing the upper section of the panel to the fairing **(see illustration).** Carefully pull the panel away to free the pegs from the grommets, then slide it back to release the tabs from the slots

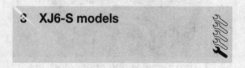

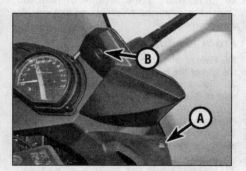

3.5a Undo the screw (A) and release the trim clip (B) on each side

3.5b Release the side tabs...

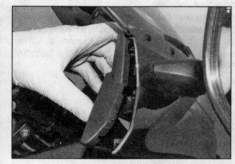

3.5c ...then the top

3.8 Release the connectors from the tie then disconnect them

3.9 Release the trim clip (arrowed) on each side

3.10a Undo the screws (arrowed)

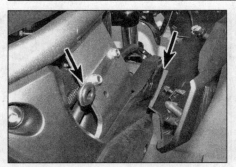

3.10b Pull the pegs from the grommets...

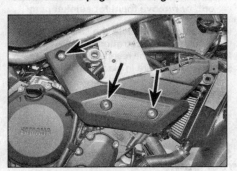

3.11 Fairing side panel lower section screws (arrowed)

and draw the front peg from the hole **(see illustrations)**.
11 Undo the screws and remove the lower section of the panel **(see illustration)**.
12 If required remove the turn signal (see Chapter 8).

3.10c ...the tabs from the slots...

13 Installation is the reverse of removal. Check the turn signals work correctly.

Fairing

14 Remove the upper sections of the fairing side panels (Steps 7 to 10).
15 Remove the cockpit side panels and centre panel.
16 Remove the mirrors (Step 26).
17 Disconnect the headlight wiring connector **(see illustration)**.
18 Release the trim clip on each side by pushing the centre pin in then drawing the body out **(see illustration)**.
19 Unscrew the two bolts on each side, then draw the fairing forwards and disconnect the sidelight wiring connector **(see illustrations)**.
20 If required remove the headlight (see Chapter 8).
21 Installation is the reverse of removal. Make sure the rubber insulator pads for the mirrors

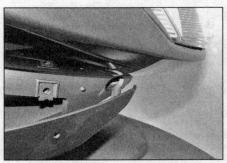

3.10d ...and the peg from the hole

are correctly in place **(see illustration)**. Make sure the grommets for the main bolts are in good condition and the collars are fitted in them **(see illustration 3.19a)**. Make sure the rear edge on each side sits on the outside of the bracket **(see illustration)**. Check the headlight, sidelight and turn signals work correctly.

Windshield

22 Undo the six screws and lift the windshield off the fairing **(see illustration 4.23)**.
23 Installation is the reverse of removal. Make sure the rubber well-nuts are in good condition and correctly in place.

Front mudguard

24 See Section 2.

Mirrors

25 Remove the cockpit side panels and centre panel.
26 Unscrew the nuts and remove the mirror

3.17 Disconnect the headlight wiring connector

3.19b Displace the fairing and disconnect the sidelight wiring

3.18 Release the trim clip on each side

3.21a Each mirror mount has a rubber pad (arrowed) on it

3.19a Unscrew the bolts (arrowed) on each side

3.21b The rear edges of the fairing seat outside the brackets

3.26a Unscrew the nuts (arrowed)...

3.26b ...and lift the mirror off

3.26c Make sure the sleeves do not drop out, or remove them for safekeeping

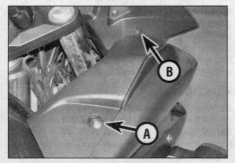

4.2a Undo the screw (A) and release the trim clip (B) on each side

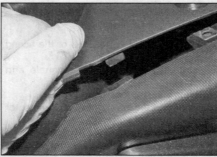

4.2b Release the back of the panel...

4.2c ...and the sides...

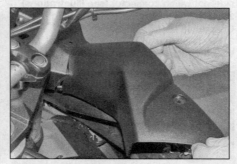

4.2d ...then the front

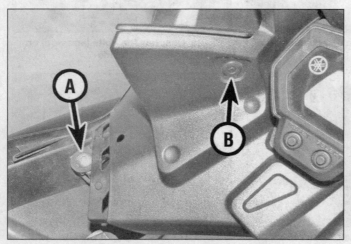

4.5a Undo the screw (A) and release the trim clip (B) on each side...

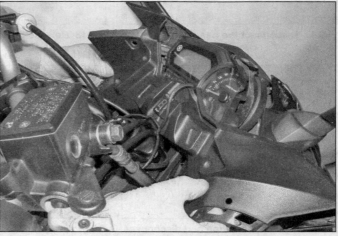

4.5b ...then release and remove the panel

(see illustrations). Note the sleeves fitted in the mounts (see illustration).

27 Installation is the reverse of removal. Make sure the sleeves are in place.

4 XJ6-F and FZ6R models

Seat, side panels, grab-rails and rear cowls

1 See Section 2.

Cockpit side panels

2 Undo the cockpit side panel screw and release the trim clip by pushing the centre pin in then drawing the body out (see illustration). Release the panel from the fairing by sliding it back, then draw the back of the panel up a bit and then back to release it from the cockpit centre panel (see illustrations).

3 Installation is the reverse of removal.

Cockpit centre panel

4 Remove the cockpit side panels.

5 Undo the cockpit centre panel screws, then release the trim clips by pushing the centre pin in then drawing the body out (see illustration). Release the panel from the fairing and remove it (see illustration).

6 Installation is the reverse of removal.

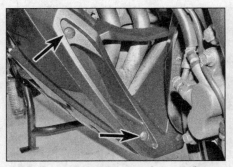

4.7 Undo the two screws (arrowed) on each side

4.8 Release the trim clip (arrowed)

4.9 Turn signal wiring connectors (arrowed)

Lower fairing panels

7 Undo the centre panel screws, then release and remove the panel (see illustration).
8 Release the trim clip joining the panels at the bottom by pushing the centre pin in then drawing the body out (see illustration).
9 Disconnect the turn signal wiring connectors (see illustration).

10 Undo the six screws, noting the washers with the three screws securing the panel to the fairing (see illustrations). Release the pegs from the frame and fairing and remove the panel (see illustration).
11 If required undo the side trim panel screw and remove the panel (see illustration).
12 If required remove the turn signal (see Chapter 8).

13 Installation is the reverse of removal. Check the turn signals work correctly.

Fairing

14 Remove the lower fairing panels (Steps 7 to 10).
15 Remove the cockpit side panels.
16 Remove the cockpit centre panel.
17 Remove the mirrors (see Section 3).

4.10a Undo the screws (arrowed)...

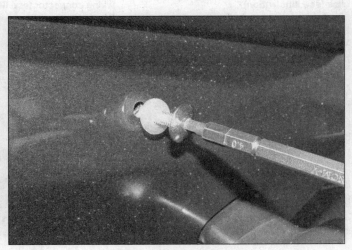

4.10b ...noting the washers

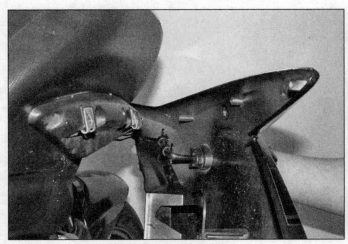

4.10c ...and remove the panel

4.11 Side trim panel screw (arrowed)

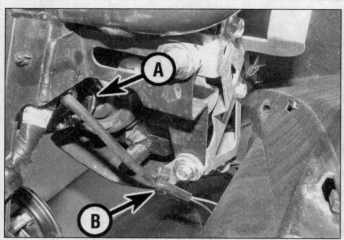

4.18 Disconnect the headlight connector (A) and release the wiring from the clip (B) on each side

4.19 Unscrew the two bolts (arrowed) on each side

18 Disconnect the headlight wiring connector and release the turn signal wiring from the clips (see illustration).
19 Unscrew the two bolts on each side (see illustration).
20 Release the peg on each side at the back from the grommet in the frame, then draw the fairing forwards and disconnect the sidelight wiring connector (see illustration and 3.19b).
21 If required remove the headlight (see Chapter 8).
22 Installation is the reverse of removal. Make sure the rubber insulator pads for the mirrors are correctly in place (see illustration 3.21a). Make sure the grommets for the main bolts are in good condition and the collars are fitted in them (see illustration 4.19). Make sure the peg on each side locates in its grommet (see illustration 4.20). Check the headlight, sidelight and turn signals work correctly.

Windshield

23 Undo the six screws and lift the windshield off the fairing (see illustration).
24 Installation is the reverse of removal. Make sure the rubber well-nuts are in good condition and correctly in place.

Front mudguard

25 See Section 2.

Mirrors

26 See Section 3.

4.20 Release the peg from the grommet on each side

4.23 Windshield screws (arrowed)

Chapter 8
Electrical system

Contents

Degrees of difficulty

| Easy, suitable for novice with little experience | Fairly easy, suitable for beginner with some experience | Fairly difficult, suitable for competent DIY mechanic | Difficult, suitable for experienced DIY mechanic | Very difficult, suitable for expert DIY or professional |

Specifications

Battery
Capacity	12V, 10Ah
Type	GT12B-4
Charge condition	
Fully charged	12.8V
Half-charged...	12.4V
Discharged	12V or less
Charging time..	Until fully charged (12.8V) (see Section 4)

Charging system
Alternator nominal output...........................	14V, 330W @ 5000 rpm
Alternator stator coil resistance	0.24 to 0.36 ohms @ 20°C
Current leakage	1mA (max)
Regulated voltage output (no load)	14.1 to 14.9V @ 5000 rpm

Oil level sensor

Resistance
   Upright (minimum level) .... 114 to 126 ohms @ 20°C
   Upside down (maximum level) .... 484 to 536 ohms @ 20°C

Speed sensor

Output voltage .... 0.6 to 4.8V recycling

Starter relay

Resistance .... 4.18 to 4.62 ohms @ 20°C

Starter circuit cut-off relay

Resistance .... 162 to 198 ohms @ 20°C

Starter motor

Brush length
   Standard .... 10 mm
   Service limit (min) .... 3.5 mm
Commutator diameter
   Standard .... 28 mm
   Service limit (min) .... 27 mm
Mica undercut .... 0.7 mm
Commutator resistance .... 0.012 to 0.022 ohms

Fuses – XJ6 models

Main 30A
IGNITION 10A
EFI (fuel injection system)....................................... 10A
HEAD (headlight) 20A
TAIL (tail light, side light, licence plate light and turn signals) 10A
SIGNAL (horn, brake light) 7.5A
FAN 20A
BACK UP 7.5A
ABS (control unit) 7.5A
ABS MTR (motor) 30A
ABS SOL (solenoid) 20A

Fuses – FZ6R models

Main 30A
IGNITION 10A
EFI (fuel injection system)....................................... 10A
HEAD (headlight) 15A
SIGNAL (horn, turn signals, brake and tail light, licence plate light) ... 15A
FAN 20A
BACK UP 10A

Bulbs

Headlight .... 60/55W halogen (H4)
Sidelight 5W
Brake/tail light 21/5W
Turn signal lights
   UK models .... 10W (amber on later models)
   US models
      Front with running light.................................. 21/5W
      Rear 21W
Licence plate light 5W
Instrument cluster illumination lights .... LED
Instrument warning lights....................................... LED

Torque wrench settings

Alternator cover bolts... 10 Nm
Alternator rotor bolt .... 75 Nm
Alternator stator screws .... 10 Nm
Neutral switch... 20 Nm
Oil level sensor bolts .... 10 Nm
Starter motor long bolts.. 3.4 Nm
Starter motor mounting bolts .... 10 Nm

1 General information

All models have a 12 volt electrical system charged by a three-phase alternator with a separate regulator/rectifier.

The regulator maintains the charging system output within the specified range to prevent overcharging, and the rectifier converts the ac (alternating current) output of the alternator to dc (direct current) to power the lights and other components and to charge the battery. The alternator rotor is mounted on the left-hand end of the crankshaft.

The starting system includes the starter motor, the battery, the relay and the various wires and switches. If the engine stop switch is in the RUN position and the ignition switch is ON, the starter relay allows the starter motor to operate only if the transmission is in neutral (neutral switch on) or, if the transmission is in gear, if the clutch lever is pulled into the handlebar and the sidestand is up. The starter motor is mounted on the top of the crankcase.

Note: *Keep in mind that electrical parts, once purchased, cannot be returned. To avoid unnecessary expense, make very sure the faulty component has been positively identified before buying a replacement part.*

2 Electrical system fault finding

⚠️ **Warning: To prevent the risk of short circuits, the battery negative (-ve) terminal should be disconnected before any of the bike's other electrical components are disturbed. Don't forget to reconnect the terminal securely once work is finished or if battery power is needed for circuit testing.**

1 A typical electrical circuit consists of an electrical component, the switches, relays, etc, related to that component and the wiring and connectors that link the component to the battery and the frame.

2 Before tackling any troublesome electrical circuit, first study the wiring diagram thoroughly to get a complete picture of what makes up that individual circuit. Trouble spots, for instance, can often be narrowed down by noting if other components related to that circuit are operating properly or not. If several components or circuits fail at one time, chances are the fault lies either in the fuse or in the common earth (ground) connection, as several circuits are often routed through the same fuse and earth (ground) connections **(see illustration)**.

3 Electrical problems often stem from simple causes, such as loose or corroded connections or a blown fuse. Prior to any electrical fault finding, always visually check the condition of the fuse, wires and connections in the problem circuit. Intermittent failures can be especially frustrating, since you can't always duplicate the failure when it's convenient to test. In such situations, a good practice is to clean all connections in the affected circuit, whether or not they appear to be good. All of the connections and wires should also be wiggled to check for looseness which can cause intermittent failure.

4 If you don't have a multimeter it is highly advisable to obtain one – they are not expensive and will enable a full range of electrical tests to be made **(see illustration)**. Go for a modern digital one with LCD display as they are easier to use. A continuity tester and/or test light are useful for certain electrical checks as an alternative, though are limited in their usefulness compared to a multimeter **(see illustrations)**.

Continuity checks

5 The term continuity describes the uninterrupted flow of electricity through an electrical circuit. Continuity can be checked with a multimeter set either to its continuity function (a beep is emitted when continuity is found), or to the resistance (ohms/Ω) function, or with a dedicated continuity tester. Both instruments are powered by an internal battery, therefore the checks are made with the ignition OFF. As a safety precaution,

2.2 Common earth point (arrowed) – remove the airbox to check it

always disconnect the battery negative (-) lead before making continuity checks, particularly if ignition system checks are being made.

6 If using a multimeter, select the continuity function if it has one, or the resistance (ohms) function. Touch the meter probes together and check that a beep is emitted or the meter reads zero, which indicates continuity. If there is no continuity there will be no beep or the meter will show infinite resistance. After using the meter, always switch it OFF to conserve its battery.

7 A continuity tester can be used in the same way – its light should come on or it should beep to indicate continuity in the switch ON position, but should be off or silent in the OFF position.

8 Note that the polarity of the test probes doesn't matter for continuity checks, although care should be taken to follow specific test procedures if a diode or solid-state component is being checked.

Switch continuity checks

9 If a switch is at fault, trace its wiring to the wiring connectors. Separate the connectors and inspect them for security and condition. A build-up of dirt or corrosion here will most likely be the cause of the problem – clean up and apply a water dispersant such as WD40, or alternatively use a dedicated contact cleaner and protection spray.

10 If using a multimeter, select the continuity function if it has one, or the resistance (ohms)

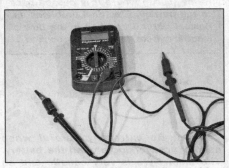

2.4a A digital multimeter can be used for all electrical tests

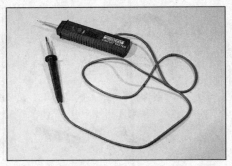

2.4b A battery-powered continuity tester

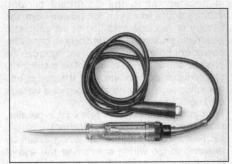

2.4c A simple test light is useful for voltage tests

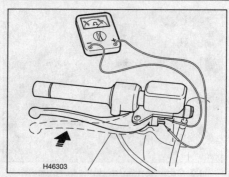

2.10 Continuity should be indicated across switch terminals when lever is operated

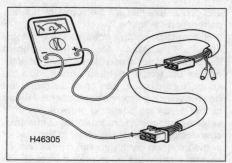

2.12 Wiring continuity check. Connect the meter probes across each end of the same wire

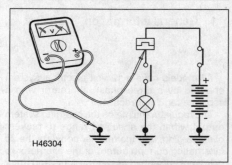

2.15 Voltage check. Connect the meter positive probe to the component and the negative probe to earth

function, and connect its probes to the terminals in the connector (see illustration). Simple ON/OFF type switches, such as brake light switches, only have two wires whereas combination switches, like the handlebar switches, have many wires. Study the wiring diagram to ensure that you are connecting to the correct pair of wires. Continuity should be indicated with the switch ON and no continuity with it OFF.

Wiring continuity checks

11 Many electrical faults are caused by damaged wiring, often due to incorrect routing or chaffing on frame components. Loose, wet or corroded wire connectors can also be the cause of electrical problems.

12 A continuity check can be made on a single length of wire by disconnecting it at each end and connecting the meter or continuity tester probes to each end of the wire (see illustration). Continuity should be indicated if the wire is good. If no continuity is shown, suspect a broken wire.

13 To check for continuity to earth in any earth wire connect one probe of your meter or tester to the earth wire terminal in the connector and the other to the frame, engine, or battery earth (-) terminal. Continuity should be indicated if the wire is good. If no continuity is shown, suspect a broken wire or corroded or loose earth point (see below).

Voltage checks

14 A voltage check can determine whether power is reaching a component. Use a multimeter set to the dc (direct current) voltage scale to check for power from the battery or regulator/rectifier, or set to the ac (alternating current) voltage scale to check for power from the alternator. A test light can be used to check for dc voltage. The test light is the cheaper component, but the meter has the advantage of being able to give a voltage reading.

15 Connect the meter or test light in parallel, i.e. across the load (see illustration).

16 First identify the relevant wiring circuit by referring to the wiring diagram at the end of this manual. If other electrical components share the same power supply (i.e. are fed from the same fuse), take note whether they are

working correctly – this is useful information in deciding where to start checking the circuit.

17 If using a meter, check first that the meter leads are plugged into the correct terminals on the meter (red to positive (+), black to negative (-)). Set the meter to the appropriate volts function (dc or ac), where necessary at a range suitable for the battery voltage – 0 to 20 vdc. Connect the meter red probe (+) to the power supply wire and the black probe to a good metal earth (ground) on the motorcycle's frame or directly to the battery negative terminal. Battery voltage, or the specified voltage, should be shown on the meter with the ignition switch, and if necessary any other relevant switch, ON.

18 If using a test light (see illustration 2.4c), connect its positive (+) probe to the power supply terminal and its negative (-) probe to a good earth (ground) on the motorcycle's frame. With the switch, and if necessary any other relevant switch, ON, the test light should illuminate.

19 If no voltage is indicated, work back towards the power source continuing to check for voltage. When you reach a point where there is voltage, you know the problem lies between that point and your last check point.

Earth (ground) checks

20 Earth connections are made either directly to the engine or frame (such as the starter motor or ignition coil which only have a positive feed) or by a separate wire into the earth circuit of the wiring harness. Alternatively a short earth wire is sometimes run from the

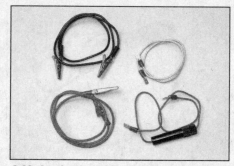

2.23 A selection of insulated jumper wires

component directly to the motorcycle's frame.

21 Corrosion is a common cause of a poor earth connection, as is a loose earth terminal fastener.

22 If total or multiple component failure is experienced, check the security of the main earth lead from the negative (-) terminal of the battery, the earth lead bolted to the engine, and the main earth point(s) on the frame (see illustration 2.2). If corroded, dismantle the connection and clean all surfaces back to bare metal. Remake the connection and prevent further corrosion from forming by smearing battery terminal grease over the connection.

23 To check the earthing of a component, use an insulated jumper wire to temporarily bypass its earth connection (see illustration) – connect one end of the jumper wire to the earth terminal or metal body of the component and the other end to the motorcycle's frame. If the circuit works with the jumper wire installed, the earth circuit is faulty.

24 To check an earth wire first check for corroded or loose connections, then check the wiring for continuity (Step 13) between each connector in the circuit in turn, and then to its earth point, to locate the break.

> **Remember that all electrical circuits are designed to conduct electricity from the battery, through the wires, switches, relays, etc. to the electrical component (light bulb, starter motor, etc). From there it is directed to the frame (earth) where it is passed back to the battery. Electrical problems are basically an interruption in the flow of electricity from the battery or back to it.**

3 Battery

Caution: Be extremely careful when handling or working around the battery. The electrolyte is very caustic and an explosive gas (hydrogen) is given off when the battery is charging.

3.2a Unhook the strap…

3.2b …and remove the cover

3.3 Disconnect the negative terminal first, then the positive terminal (arrowed)

Removal and installation

1 Remove the seat(s) (see Chapter 7).
2 Unhook the rubber strap and remove the battery cover **(see illustrations)**.
3 Unscrew the negative (-) terminal bolt first and disconnect the lead from the battery **(see illustration)**. Lift up the insulating cover to access the positive (+) terminal, then unscrew the bolt and disconnect the lead.
4 Lift the battery and its insulating shield out **(see illustration)**. If required unclip and remove the insulating shield.
5 Installation is the reverse of removal. Clean the battery terminals and lead ends with a wire brush, fine sandpaper or steel wool. Reconnect the leads, connecting the positive (+) terminal first.

Inspection and maintenance

6 The battery is of the VRLA (valve-regulated lead acid) maintenance free (sealed) type, therefore requiring no regular maintenance. However, the following checks should still be performed.
7 Check the state of charge by measuring the voltage at the battery terminals **(see illustration)**. Connect the voltmeter positive (+) probe to the battery positive (+) terminal, and the negative (-) probe to the battery negative (-) terminal. When fully charged there should be 12.8 volts present. If the voltage falls below 12 volts remove the battery (see above), and recharge it as described below in Section 4.
8 Check the battery terminals and leads are tight and free of corrosion. If corrosion is evident, clean the terminals as described in Step 5, then protect them from further corrosion.
9 Keep the battery case clean to prevent current leakage, which can discharge the battery over a period of time (especially when it sits unused). Wash the outside of the case with a solution of baking soda and water. Rinse the battery thoroughly, then dry it.
10 Look for cracks in the case and replace the battery with a new one if any are found. If acid has been spilled on the frame or battery box, neutralise it with a baking soda and water solution, then dry it thoroughly.
11 If the motorcycle sits unused for long periods of time, disconnect the leads from the battery terminals, negative (-) terminal first. Refer to Section 4 and charge the battery once every month to six weeks.

3.4 Carefully lift the battery out – it is quite heavy

4 Battery charging

Caution: Be extremely careful when handling or working around the battery. The electrolyte is very caustic and an explosive gas (hydrogen) is given off when the battery is charging.

1 Check the charger is rated for a 12V battery.
2 Remove the battery (see Section 3). If not already done, refer to Section 3, Step 7, and check the open circuit voltage of the battery. Refer to the chart **(see illustrations)** and read off the charging time required according to the voltage reading taken.

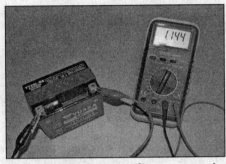

3.7 Checking battery voltage – connect the meter as shown

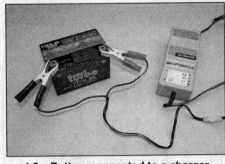

4.2a Battery connected to a charger

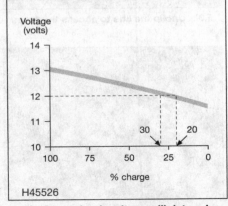

4.2b Open-circuit voltage will determine the percentage charge…

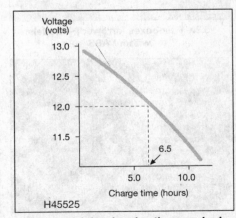

4.2c …and the charging time required

5.2a Lift the cover (arrowed) off the relay

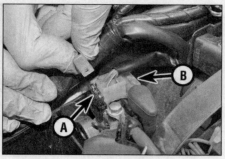

5.2b Remove the cover to access the main fuse (A) and its spare (B)

3 Connect the charger to the battery BEFORE switching the charger ON. Make sure that the positive (+) lead on the charger is connected to the positive (+) terminal on the battery, and the negative (-) lead is connected to the negative (-) terminal.
4 The battery should be charged at the rate of around 0.8 to 1.0 amp for up to 12 hours if it is completely flat, or until the voltage across the terminals reaches 12.8V – disconnect the charger and allow the battery to stabilise for 30 minutes after charging before taking a voltage reading. The actual time required depends on the initial voltage present. Exceeding this can cause the battery to overheat, buckling the plates and rendering it useless. It is best to use a dedicated motorcycle battery charger, preferably one of the 'intelligent' ones that constantly monitors the state of charge and controls its output accordingly. If a normal car type charger is used check that after a probable initial peak, the charge rate falls to a safe level consistent

with the charge rate specified on the battery. If the battery becomes hot during charging **stop**. Further charging will cause damage. Many bike-specific chargers are designed for the maintenance and recovery of heavily discharged MF batteries. They are not too expensive, and are a worthwhile investment, especially if the bike is not used over winter. Follow the manufacturer's instructions.
5 If the recharged battery discharges rapidly when left disconnected it is likely that an internal short caused by physical damage or sulphation has occurred. A new battery will be required. A sound battery will tend to lose its charge at about 1% per day.
6 Install the battery (see Section 3).
7 If the motorcycle sits unused for long periods of time, charge the battery once every month to six weeks and leave it disconnected. Note that many chargers contain a means of trickle charging the battery, allowing it to remain connected.

5 Fuses

1 The electrical system as a whole is protected by the main fuse, and individual circuits are protected by other fuses of different ratings (see Specifications). The main fuse is housed in the starter relay, which is under the rider's seat. All other fuses are housed in two fuseboxes, also under the rider's seat.
2 To access the main fuse, remove the seat(s) (see Chapter 7). Lift the terminal cover off the relay **(see illustration)**. Remove the cover from the fuse **(see illustration)**. A spare main fused is also housed in the relay.
3 To access the fusebox fuses, remove the rider's seat (see Chapter 7). Unclip the relevant fusebox lid - the identity, location and specified rating of each fuse is marked on each fusebox lid, and each fuse is marked with its rating **(see illustrations)**. A spare fuse of each rating is housed in the fusebox.
4 The fuses can be removed and checked visually. If you can't pull the fuse out with your fingertips, use a suitable pair of pliers **(see illustration)**. A blown fuse is easily identified by a break in the element **(see illustration)**, or can be tested for continuity using an ohmmeter or continuity tester – if there is no continuity, it has blown. Each fuse is clearly marked with its rating and must only be replaced by a fuse of the same rating. If a spare fuse is used, always replace it with a new one so that a spare of each rating is carried on the bike at all times.

⚠️ **Warning: Never put in a fuse of a higher rating or bridge the terminals with any other substitute, however temporary it may be. Serious damage may be done to the circuit, or a fire may start.**

5 If the new fuse blows, you need to check the relevant circuit and its components carefully for evidence of a short-circuit. Look for bare wires and chafed, melted or burned insulation.
6 Sometimes fuses blow for no specific reason, in which case replacing it with a new

5.3a Fuseboxes (arrowed) – models without ABS

5.3b Unclip the lids to access the fuses

5.3c Tail and ABS fuses on models with ABS

5.4a Use suitable pliers to remove a fuse

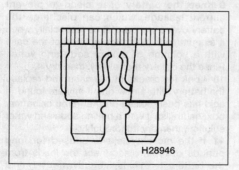

5.4b A blown fuse can be identified by a break in its element

6.5 Headlight relay (arrowed)

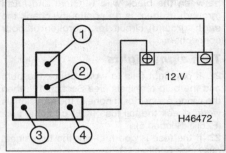

6.6 Headlight relay test terminal identification

1 Red/yellow wire terminal
2 Blue/black wire terminal
3 Yellow/black wire terminal
4 Red/yellow wire terminal

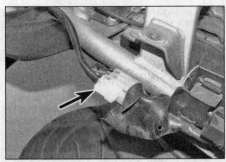

6.13 Tail light wiring connector (arrowed)

one is the only action required. Also corrosion of the fuse ends and fusebox terminals may occur and cause poor fuse contact. If this happens, remove the corrosion with a wire brush or emery paper, then spray the fuse end and terminals with electrical contact cleaner.

6 Lighting system check

Note: *If the ignition is switched ON for any checks, remember to switch it OFF again before proceeding further or removing any electrical component from the system.*
Note: *Refer to Electrical system fault finding (Section 2) and to the Wiring Diagrams at the end of the Chapter when making electrical tests on any part of the system.*
1 If a light fails first check the bulb (see relevant Section), the bulb terminals in the holder, and the wiring connector. Next check the fuse (Section 5). If none of the lights work, check battery voltage - low voltage indicates either a faulty battery or a defective charging system. Refer to Section 3 for battery checks and Section 30 for charging system tests. If there is a problem with more than one circuit at the same time, or with all circuits, it is likely to be a fault relating to a multi-function component, such as the fuse or the ignition switch. When checking for a blown filament in a bulb, it is advisable to back up a visual check with a continuity test of the filament as it is not always apparent that a bulb has blown. When testing for continuity, remember that on single terminal bulbs it is the metal body of the bulb that is the earth (ground). Refer to Section 2 for details on testing electrical circuits.

Headlight and relay

2 If the headlight fails to work, check the bulb and the bulb terminals and the wires in the connector first (see Section 7), and then check the headlight fuse (Section 5). Next check for battery voltage on the loom side of the connector with a test light or multimeter – connect the negative probe of the multimeter to earth (black wire) terminal and the positive probe to first the high beam (yellow wire) terminal and then the low beam (green wire) terminal with the ignition switch ON (see

Wiring Diagrams at the end of this Chapter. Don't forget to select either high or low beam as appropriate at the handlebar switch while conducting this test.
3 If no voltage is indicated at either terminal, check the wiring and connectors between the headlight connector, headlight relay, dimmer switch and the ignition switch, referring to *Wiring Diagrams* at the end of the chapter, then check the switches themselves.
4 If voltage is indicated, check for continuity between the black wire connector terminal and earth (ground). If there is no continuity, check the earth (ground) circuit for an open or poor connection.
5 To check the headlight relay, first remove the left-hand rear cowl (see Chapter 7). Displace the relay and disconnect the wiring connector **(see illustration)**.
6 Using a continuity tester or a multimeter set to the resistance (ohms) range, test for continuity between the No. 1 red/yellow (positive meter probe) and No. 2 blue/black (negative meter probe) wire terminals on the relay **(see illustration)**. There should be no continuity (infinite resistance). Now, using insulated jumper wires and a fully charged 12V battery, connect the battery positive (+) terminal to the No. 4 red/yellow wire terminal on the relay and the battery negative (-) terminal to the No. 3 yellow/black wire terminal. Continuity (0 ohms) should now be shown on the meter. Note that it is important to differentiate between the two red/yellow wires.
7 If the relay does not operate as described, replace it with a new one.

Sidelight (European models)

8 If the sidelight fails to work with the ignition switch either in the ON position or the P position, check the bulb and the bulb terminals and the wires in the bulbholder first (see Section 7), and then check the tail light fuse (see Section 5).
9 Next check for battery voltage at the blue/red wire terminal on the loom side of the sidelight wiring connector, with the ignition

switch first in the ON position, then in the P position.
10 If no voltage is indicated in either position, check the wiring between the sidelight, fusebox and the ignition switch, then check the switch (Section 18).
11 If voltage is indicated, check for continuity between the wiring connector terminals on the bulb side of the wiring connector and the corresponding terminals in the bulbholder; no continuity indicates a break in the circuit. If continuity is present, check for continuity between the black wire terminal and earth (ground). If there is no continuity, check the earth (ground) circuit for a broken or poor connection.
12 If the sidelight bulbs work with the ignition switch in one position (ON or P) but not the other, the switch is faulty.

Tail light

13 If the tail light fails to work, check the bulb and the bulb terminals and the wires in the bulbholder first (see Section 9), and then check the tail fuse (XJ6) or signal fuse (FZ6R). Next, remove the right-hand rear cowl (see Chapter 7) and disconnect the tail light wiring connector **(see illustration)**. Check for battery voltage at the blue wire terminal on the loom side of the connector, with the ignition switch ON.
14 If no voltage is indicated, check the wiring between the tail light, fusebox and the ignition switch, then check the switch itself.
15 If voltage is indicated, check for continuity between the black wire terminal and earth (ground). If there is no continuity, check the earth (ground) circuit for a broken or poor connection.

Brake light

16 If the brake light fails to work, check the bulb and the bulb terminals and the wires in the bulbholder first (see Section 9), and then check the signal fuse. Next, remove the right-hand rear cowl (see Chapter 7) and disconnect the tail light wiring connector **(see illustration 6.13)**. Check for battery voltage at the yellow wire terminal on the loom side of the connector, with the ignition switch ON and the brake lever or pedal applied.
17 If no voltage is indicated, check the brake light switches (see Section 14), then the wiring between the brake/tail light and the switches.

18 If voltage is indicated, check for continuity between the black wire terminal and earth (ground). If there is no continuity, check the earth (ground) circuit for a broken or poor connection.

Licence plate light

19 If the licence plate light fails to work, check the bulb and the bulb terminals and the wires in the bulbholder first (see Section 9), and then check the tail fuse (XJ6) or signal fuse (FZ6R). Next, remove the right-hand rear cowl (see Chapter 7) and disconnect the license plate light wiring connectors (**see illustration 10.6**). Check for battery voltage at the blue wire terminal on the loom side of the connector, with the ignition switch ON.

20 If no voltage is indicated, check the wiring between the tail light, fusebox and the ignition switch, then check the switch itself.

21 If voltage is indicated, check for continuity

between the black wire terminal and earth (ground). If there is no continuity, check the earth (ground) circuit for a broken or poor connection.

Turn signal lights

22 If one light fails to work, check the bulb and the bulb terminals (see Section 12), then the wiring connector. If none of the turn signals work, check the tail fuse (XJ6) or signal fuse (FZ6R) (Section 5).

23 If the fuse is good, check the turn signal relay (see Section 11).

Instrument cluster lights

24 See Section 17.

7 Headlight bulb and sidelight bulb

Caution: The headlight bulb is of the quartz-halogen type. Do not touch the bulb glass as skin acids will shorten the bulb's service life. If the bulb is accidentally touched, it should be wiped carefully when cold with a rag soaked in methylated spirit and dried before fitting.

Headlight bulb

1 On XJ6-N models, for easiest access remove the headlight (see Section 8). If the headlight is not removed, disconnect the wiring connector from the bulb (**see illustration**).

2 On XJ6-S models remove the fairing side panel on one side, and on XJ6-F and FZ6R

models remove the lower fairing panel from one side. Disconnect the wiring connector from the bulb (**see illustration**).

3 Remove the rubber cover from the back of the headlight, noting how it fits (**see illustration**).

4 Release the bulb retaining clip, noting how it fits, then remove the bulb from the back of the headlight (**see illustrations**).

5 Fit the new bulb, bearing in mind the information in the **Note** above. Make sure the tabs on the bulb flange are aligned with the slots in the back of the headlight, and secure the bulb in position with the retaining clip.

6 Fit the cover.

7 Install the headlight if removed (see Section 8), or connect the wiring connector if not. Check the operation of the headlight.

Sidelight bulb (European models)

8 On XJ6-N models remove the headlight (see Section 8).

9 On XJ6-S and XJ6-F models remove the fairing.

10 Turn the bulb holder ant-clockwise and draw it out of the back of the headlight (**see illustration**).

11 Carefully pull the bulb out of its holder (**see illustration**).

12 Align the new bulb with its socket and press it into place. Fit the bulbholder into the headlight and turn it clockwise to lock the tabs.

13 Install the headlight (see Section 8). Check the operation of the headlight and sidelight.

7.1 Disconnect the wiring connector (arrowed)

7.2 Disconnect the wiring connector (arrowed)

7.3 Remove the cover (arrowed)

7.4a Release the clip...

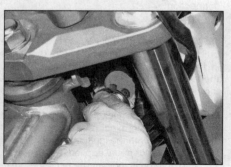
7.4b ...and remove the bulb

7.10 Release the bulbholder...

7.11 ...then pull the bulb out of the holder

8.1 Instrument cover screws (arrowed)

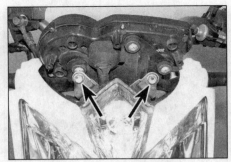

8.2a Unscrew the bolts (arrowed)...

8.2b ...and the bolt (arrowed)

8 Headlight

Removal and installation
XJ6-N models

1 Undo the instrument cover screws and remove the cover **(see illustration)**.
2 Unscrew the three headlight bolts, two on the top and one bottom left **(see illustrations)**.
3 Displace the headlight, noting how the peg on the bottom right locates in the grommet, then disconnect the headlight and sidelight/turn signal wiring connectors **(see illustrations)**.
4 If required remove the headlight covers (see Chapter 7). Remove the turn signals from the covers if required (see Section 13).

5 Installation is the reverse of removal. Check the grommet is in good condition **(see illustration 8.3a)**. Make sure all the wiring is correctly connected and secured. Check the operation of the headlight, sidelight and turn signals. Check the headlight aim.

XJ6-S, XJ6-F and FZ6R models

6 Remove the fairing (see Chapter 7).
7 Undo the headlight bracket screws and lift the assembly out of the fairing **(see illustration)**.
8 If required unscrew the headlight bracket bolts and screws and detach the brackets from the headlight .
9 Installation is the reverse of removal. Make sure all the wiring is correctly connected and secured. Check the operation of the headlight and sidelight. Check the headlight aim.

Headlight aim adjustment

Note: *An improperly adjusted headlight may cause problems for oncoming traffic or provide poor, unsafe illumination of the road ahead. Before adjusting the headlight aim, be sure to consult with local traffic laws and regulations – for UK models refer to MOT Test Checks in the Reference section.*

10 The headlight beam can adjusted both horizontally and vertically. Before making any adjustment, check that the tyre pressures are correct. Make any adjustments to the headlight aim with the machine on level ground, with the fuel tank half full and with an assistant sitting on the seat. If the bike is usually ridden with a passenger on the back, have a second assistant to do this.
11 The headlight adjusters are located on the back of the headlight, with the vertical adjuster on the lower left-hand side and the horizontal adjuster on the upper right-hand side **(see illustrations)**. You can turn the adjuster screws

8.3a Displace the peg from the grommet (arrowed)...

8.3b ...and disconnect the headlight connector...

8.3c ...and the sidelight/turn signal connector

8.7 Headlight bracket screws (arrowed)

8.11a Vertical adjuster (arrowed)

8.11b Horizontal adjuster (arrowed)

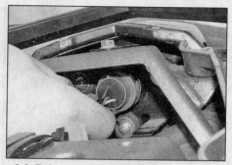

9.2 Release the bulbholder from the tail light...

9.3 ...then pull the bulb out

9.6 Undo the screws..

using a Phillips screwdriver inserted in the channel from the side, so it engages the teeth in the rim, so the headlight is easier to keep pointed straight ahead.
12 Turn the vertical adjuster clockwise to move the beam down, and anti-clockwise to move it up.
13 Turn the horizontal adjuster clockwise to move the beam to the right, and anti-clockwise to move it to the left.

9 Brake/tail light bulb and licence plate bulb

Brake/tail light bulb

Note: *It is a good idea to use a paper towel or dry cloth when handling a new bulb to prevent injury if it breaks, and to increase bulb life.*
1 Remove the seat (passenger seat only on SP models) (see Chapter 7).
2 Twist the bulbholder anti-clockwise and withdraw it from the back of the light unit **(see illustration)**.
3 Carefully pull the capless bulb out of the holder **(see illustration)**.
4 Ensure that the terminals inside the bulbholder are clean and free from corrosion.
5 Push the new bulb into the holder, then fit the bulbholder into the light and turn it clockwise until it locks into place. Check the operation of the brake/tail light.

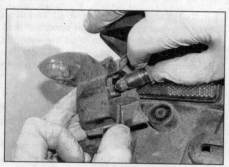

9.7a Pull the bulbholder out...

Licence plate light bulb

6 Undo the licence plate light screws and displace the light **(see illustration)**.
7 Pull the bulbholder out, then pull the capless bulb out of the holder **(see illustrations)**.
8 Align the new bulb with its holder and push it in, then push the holder into the light.
9 Fit the light – do not overtighten the screws. Check the operation of the light.
10 Installation is the reverse of removal.

10 Tail light and licence plate light

Tail light

1 Remove the rear cowls (see Chapter 7).

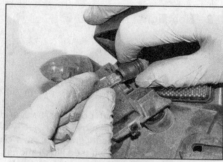

9.7b ...then pull the bulb from the holder

2 Twist the bulbholder anti-clockwise and withdraw it from the back of the light unit **(see illustration 9.2)**.
3 Undo the tail light screws and remove the light **(see illustration)**.
4 Installation is the reverse of removal. Check the operation of the tail light and brake light.

Licence plate light

5 Remove the rear cowls (see Chapter 7).
6 Disconnect the licence plate light and turn signal single bullet wiring connectors **(see illustration)**. Tag each connector pair as you disconnect them to ensure correct reconnection on installation.
7 Release the wiring guide trim clip by pushing its centre pin in then drawing the body out, and remove the guide **(see illustration)**.
8 Unscrew the four tail unit bolts **(see**

10.3 Tail light screws (arrowed)

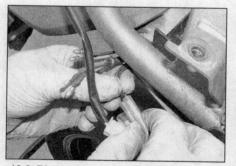

10.6 Disconnect all the bullet connectors

10.7 Release the trim clip and remove the guide

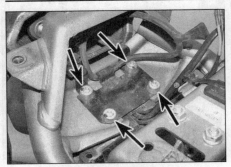

10.8a Unscrew the bolts...

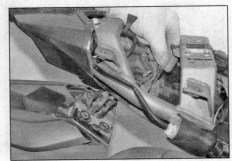

10.8b ...and remove the tail unit

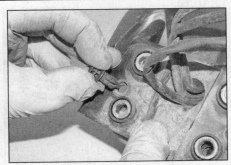

10.9a Release the trim clips...

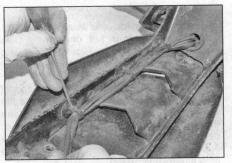

10.9b ...and the wiring guides

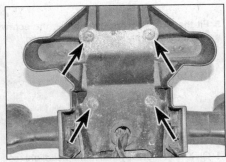

10.9c Undo the screws (arrowed) and separate the sections

10.10a Hold the bolt heads (arrowed)...

illustration). Displace the unit and carefully feed the wiring through **(see illustration).**

9 Release the two trim clips on the top of the unit **(see illustration)**. Release the wiring from the guides along the side **(see illustration)**. Undo the four screws, detach the lower section of the unit from the upper and guide the wiring through the hole **(see illustration).**

10 Hold the licence plate light bolts, unscrew the nuts and remove the light **(see illustrations)** – note the arrangement of the washers, and the sleeves in the rubber grommets.

11 Installation is the reverse of removal. Make sure that the wiring is properly routed, secured and connected. Push the trim clip centre pins out of the body before fitting them, and when fitted push the pins in flush to lock them. Check the operation of the licence plate light and turn signals before fitting the rear cowls.

11 Turn signal circuit check

1 Most turn signal problems are the result of a burned-out bulb or corroded socket. This is especially true when the turn signals function properly in one direction, but fail to flash in the other direction. First check the bulbs and the sockets (see Section 12) and the wiring connectors (Section 13). Next check the tail fuse (XJ6 models) or signal fuse (FZ6R models) (see Section 5) and the switch (see Section 19).

2 If the bulbs, sockets, connectors, fuses, switch and battery are good, remove the seat(s) (see Chapter 7) and check the turn signal relay as follows.

3 Pull the relay off the mounting bracket and disconnect the wiring connector **(see illustration).**

4 Using a voltmeter, check for battery voltage between the brown wire terminal in the

10.10b ...and unscrew the nuts (arrowed)

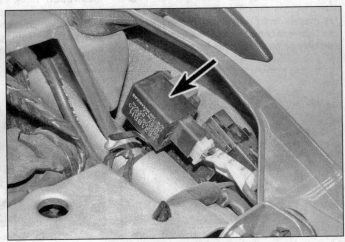

11.3 Turn signal relay (arrowed)

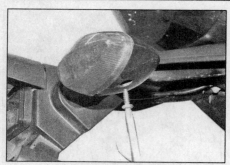

12.1a Undo the screw...

12.1b ...and remove the lens

12.2 Release and remove the bulb

connector and earth (ground) with the ignition ON. If no voltage is indicated, refer to the appropriate wiring diagram at the end of this Chapter and check the wiring between the relay and fusebox for continuity.

5 If voltage is indicated, reconnect the relay connector. Check for a fluctuating voltage between the brown/white wire terminal in the connector and earth (ground) with the ignition ON, and with the signal switch turned to either LEFT or RIGHT.

6 If no voltage is indicated, replace the relay with a new one.

7 If voltage is indicated, check the wiring between the relay, turn signal switch and turn signal lights for continuity.

12 Turn signal bulbs

1 Undo the turn signal lens screw and remove the lens **(see illustrations)**.

2 Push the bulb into the holder and twist it anti-clockwise to remove it **(see illustration)**.

3 Make sure that the terminals inside the bulbholder are clean and free from corrosion.

4 Line up the pins of the new bulb with the slots in the holder, then push the bulb in and turn it clockwise until it locks into place. **Note:** *US models fitted with front running lights use dual filament bulbs, which have offset pins and can only be fitted one way in their holders.*

5 Fit the lens - do not overtighten the screw as the lens or threads could be damaged.

13 Turn signal assemblies

Front

1 On XJ6-N models remove the headlight (see Section 8). Disconnect the wiring connectors for the turn signal being removed **(see illustration)**.

2 On XJ6-S models remove the relevant fairing side panel (see Chapter 7). On XJ6-F and FZ6R models remove the relevant lower fairing panel (see Chapter 7).

3 Unclip the mounting plate from the inner end of the turn signal stem, then draw the signal assembly out **(see illustrations)**.

4 Installation is the reverse of removal. Make sure the mounting plate is a secure fit. Check the operation of the turn signals.

Rear

5 Remove the rear cowls (see Chapter 7).

6 Disconnect the turn signal and licence plate light single bullet wiring connectors **(see illustration 10.6)**. Tag each connector pair as you disconnect them to ensure correct reconnection on installation.

7 Release the wiring guide trim clip by pushing its centre pin in then drawing the body out,

and remove the guide **(see illustration 10.7)**.

8 Unscrew the four tail unit bolts **(see illustration 10.8a)**. Displace the unit and carefully feed the wiring through **(see illustration 10.8b)**.

9 Release the two trim clips on the top of the unit **(see illustration 10.9a)**. Release the wiring from the guides along the side **(see illustration 10.9b)**. Undo the four screws, detach the lower section of the unit from the upper and guide the wiring through the hole **(see illustration 10.9c)**.

10 Unclip the mounting plate from the inner end of the turn signal stem, then draw the signal assembly out **(see illustrations 13.3a and b)**.

11 Installation is the reverse of removal. Make sure that the wiring is properly routed, secured and connected. Push the trim clip centre pins out of the body before fitting them, and when fitted push the pins in flush to lock them. Check the operation of the licence plate light and turn signals before fitting the rear cowls.

14 Brake light switches

Check

1 Before checking the switches, check the brake light circuit (see Section 6).

2 The front brake light switch is mounted on

13.1 Turn signal wiring connectors are inside the boots (arrowed)

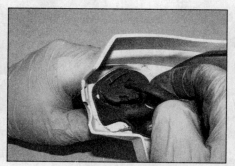

13.3a Remove the plate...

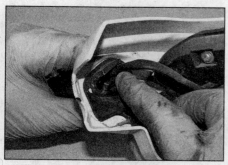

13.3b ...then push the turn signal base out

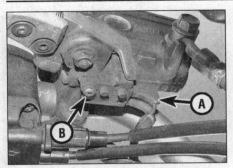

14.2 Front brake light switch wiring connectors (A) and screw (B)

14.4a Rear brake light switch (arrowed)...

14.4b ...and its wiring connector (arrowed)

the underside of the brake master cylinder. Disconnect the wiring connectors from the switch **(see illustration)**.

3 Using a continuity tester, connect its probes to the terminals of the switch. With the brake lever at rest, there should be no continuity. With the brake lever applied, there should be continuity. If the switch does not behave as described, replace it with a new one (the switch is not adjustable).

4 The rear brake light switch is mounted on the inside of the rider's right-hand footrest bracket **(see illustration)**. To access the switch wiring connector raise the fuel tank (see Chapter 4). Trace the wiring from the switch and disconnect it at the two-pin connector **(see illustration)**.

5 Using a continuity tester, connect the probes to the two terminals on the switch

side of the wiring connector. With the brake pedal at rest, there should be no continuity. With the brake pedal applied, there should be continuity. If the switch does not behave as described, replace it with a new one.

6 If the switches are good, check for voltage at the brown wire terminal on the supply side of the switch wiring connector with the ignition switch ON. If no voltage is indicated, check the wiring between the switch, fusebox and the ignition switch (see *Wiring Diagrams* at the end of this Chapter).

Removal and installation

Front brake light switch

7 Disconnect the wiring connectors from the switch **(see illustration 14.2)**.
8 Undo the switch screw and remove the switch.

9 Installation is the reverse of removal. Check the operation of the switch.

Rear brake light switch

10 Raise the fuel tank (see Chapter 4).
11 Disconnect the switch wiring connector **(see illustration 14.4b)**. Feed the wiring down to the switch, noting its routing.
12 Follow the procedure in Chapter 5, Section 3 and remove the right-hand footrest bracket assembly.
13 Detach the lower end of the switch spring from the brake pedal arm, then pull the switch out of its bracket **(see illustration)**.
14 Installation is the reverse of removal. Check the operation of the switch and adjust as necessary (see Chapter 1, Section 11).

15 Instrument removal and installation

XJ6-N models

1 Undo the instrument cover screws and remove the cover **(see illustration 8.1)**.
2 Disconnect the instrument cluster wiring connector **(see illustration)**.
3 Displace the right-hand headlight cover by undoing the two bolts **(see illustration)**.
4 Unscrew the instrument bracket bolts, noting the collars **(see illustration)**. Lift the instrument assembly off **(see illustration)**.
5 If required undo the screws securing the

14.13 Unhook the spring (arrowed) and remove the switch

15.2 Disconnect the wiring connector

15.3 Undo the screws (arrowed) and displace the cover

15.4a Unscrew the bolts (arrowed)...

15.4b ...and remove the instruments

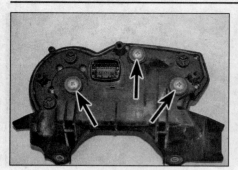

15.5 Undo the screws (arrowed) and remove the bracket

15.8a Release the hooks...

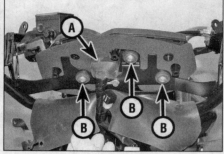

15.8b ...and displace the shield to access the wiring connector (A) and screws (B)

instrument to its bracket, noting the washers **(see illustration)**. Check the mounting bushes in the bracket – if they are worn or perished, replace them with new ones.
6 Installation is the reverse of removal. Make sure the wiring connector is secure. Check the operation of the instruments before riding the motorcycle.

XJ6-S, XJ6-F and FZ6R models

7 Remove the fairing (see Chapter 7).
8 Release and displace the rubber shield **(see illustrations)**. Disconnect the instrument cluster wiring connector.
9 Undo the screws securing the instrument to the bracket, noting the washers **(see illustration 15.8b)**. Remove the instrument and its mounting pad.
10 Installation is the reverse of removal. Make sure that the mounting pad is fitted and the wiring connector is secure. Check the operation of the instruments before riding the motorcycle.

16 Instrument check

1 If all instrument and display functions fail at the same time, check the ignition fuse and the wiring and connectors, referring to Section 15 and the *Wiring Diagrams* at the end of this Chapter.
2 The warning and indicator functions (oil level, fuel level and engine warning, neutral, high beam and turn signals) are all illuminated by LEDs (see Section 17).
3 The oil level, fuel level, coolant temperature and speedometer displays are controlled by the appropriate sensor. If a display fails or is thought to be faulty, refer to the test details for the sensor as follows:
● Oil level sensor – refer to Section 26 for test details.
● Coolant temperature sensor – refer to Chapter 3 for test details.
● Fuel level sensor – refer to Chapter 4 for test details.

● Speed sensor – refer to Chapter 4 for test details.
4 If a display is proved to be faulty, a new instrument unit will have to be fitted (see Section 15).
5 No test details are available for the tachometer.

17 Warning and indicator lights

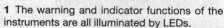

1 The warning and indicator functions of the instruments are all illuminated by LEDs.
2 The LEDs illuminate when the functions are selected by the appropriate switch or sensor. If an indicator does not illuminate, first check the switch or sensor, then test the LED as described below.
3 The oil level warning light should come on for a few seconds when the ignition is switched ON as a check of the LED, and then go off. If the light does not come on, does not go off, or starts flashing, first check the oil level (see *Pre-ride checks*). If the level is good, check the sensor (see Section 26). **Note:** *If there is a fault in the wiring circuit it will be detected by a self diagnosis function and the warning indicator will flash ten times, then go out for 2.5 seconds, and this will be repeated until the fault is repaired.*
4 The engine trouble warning light and coolant temperature warning light should come on for a few seconds when the ignition is switched ON as a check of the LED, and then go off. The same applies to the immobiliser light, where fitted.
5 On models with ABS, the ABS light should come on for a few seconds when the ignition is switched ON as a check of the LED, and go off when the bike reaches a speed of 6 mph (10 kmh). If the light does not come on, does not go off, or starts flashing, refer to Chapter 6.
6 If an LED is thought to be faulty (after checking the appropriate switch or sensor and wiring) have the instrument cluster checked by a Yamaha dealer.
7 If an LED has failed a new instrument cluster will have to be fitted.

18 Ignition switch

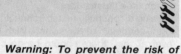

Warning: To prevent the risk of short circuits, disconnect the battery negative (–) lead before making any ignition switch checks.

Check

1 Remove the air filter housing to access the switch wiring connectors (see Chapter 4).
2 Trace the wiring back from the switch and disconnect it at the white connectors **(see illustration)**.
3 Using a multimeter or a continuity tester, make the checks on the switch side of the connector. Check the continuity of the connector terminal pairs (see *Wiring Diagrams* at the end of this Chapter). Continuity should exist between the terminals connected by a solid line on the diagram when the switch key is turned to the indicated position.
4 If the switch fails any of the tests, replace it with a new one.

Removal

5 Disconnect the battery negative (–) lead.
6 Remove the air filter housing to access the switch wiring connectors (see Chapter 4).
7 Trace the wiring back from the switch and disconnect it at the white connectors **(see illustration 18.2)**. On models with an immobiliser also disconnect the receiver

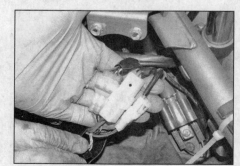

18.2 Ignition switch and immobiliser wiring connectors (arrowed)

18.8a Unscrew the instrument bracket bolt on each side

18.8b Unscrew the guide bolt (arrowed) on each side

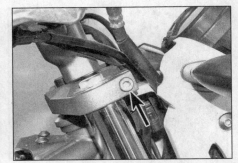

18.9a Slacken the clamp bolt (arrowed) on each side...

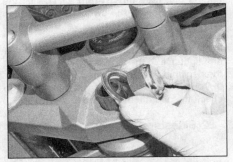

18.9b ...then unscrew the steering stem nut

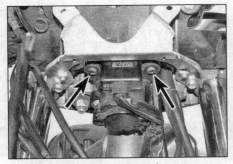

18.10 Immobiliser transceiver screws (arrowed)

18.11 Ignition switch shear-head bolt (arrowed)

wiring connector. Feed the wiring back to the switch, noting its routing.

8 On XJ6-N models unscrew the instrument bracket bolts from the underside of the top yoke **(see illustration)**. On XJ6-S, XJ6-F and FZ6R models remove the fairing (see Chapter 7), then unscrew the wiring and cable guide bolts on the underside of the yoke **(see illustration)**. Displace the handlebars from the top yoke (see Chapter 5).

9 Slacken the fork clamp bolts in the top yoke **(see illustration)**. Unscrew the steering stem nut and remove it along with its washer, then ease the top yoke up and off the fork tubes **(see illustration)**.

10 Where fitted, undo the Torx screws and remove the immobiliser transceiver, noting how it fits **(see illustration)**.

11 Two shear-head security bolts mount the ignition switch to the underside of the top yoke **(see illustration)**. The heads of the bolts must be tapped around using a suitable drift such as a cold chisel, or drilled off, before the switch can be removed. To do this, mount the yoke in a vice equipped with padded soft jaws to avoid damaging the yoke. Remove the bolts and discard them as new ones must be used on reassembly, then withdraw the switch from the top yoke.

Installation

12 Installation is the reverse of removal, noting the following:
● Obtain the correct type shear-head bolts from a Yamaha dealer – do not use another

type of bolt. Tighten the bolts until their heads shear off.
● Ensure the wiring is securely connected and correctly routed.
● Ensure all top yoke and handlebar bolts are tightened to the torque settings specified in Chapters 1 and 5.

19 Handlebar switch check

1 Generally speaking, the handlebar switch units are reliable and trouble-free. Most problems are caused by dirty or corroded contacts, but wear and breakage of internal parts is a possibility that should not be overlooked. If breakage does occur, the entire

switch unit and related wiring harness will have to be replaced with a new one, as individual parts are not available. The switches can be checked for continuity using a multimeter or a continuity tester.

2 Remove the air filter housing to access the switch wiring connectors (see Chapter 4).

3 Trace the wiring harness of the switch in question back to its connector and disconnect it **(see illustrations)**.

4 Check for continuity between the terminals of the switch harness with the switch in the various positions (i.e. switch OFF – no continuity, switch ON – continuity) – see *Wiring Diagrams* at the end of this Chapter.

5 If the continuity check indicates a problem exists, refer to Section 20 and displace the switch from the handlebar. Spray the inside of the switch with electrical contact cleaner.

19.3a Right-hand switch wiring connector

19.3b Left-hand switch wiring connector (housed in rubber boot)

20.4 Left-hand switch housing screws (arrowed)

6 If they are accessible, the contacts can be scraped clean with a penknife or polished with steel wool. If switch components or wiring connections are damaged or broken, it should be obvious when the switch is disassembled.

20 Handlebar switch removal and installation

Removal

1 If the switch unit is to be removed from the motorcycle, rather than just displaced from the handlebar, follow the procedure in Section 19 and disconnect the appropriate wiring connector **(see illustration 19.3a or b)**. Feed the wiring back to the switch, freeing it from any clips and ties and noting its routing.
2 Disconnect the wiring connector(s) from the brake light switch (if removing the right-hand switch unit) or the clutch switch (if removing the left-hand switch unit) **(see illustration 14.2 or 23.2)**.
3 Note that the right-hand switch unit incorporates the throttle twistgrip housing. Follow the procedure in Chapter 4, Section 12, to detach the throttle cables, then remove the switch unit.
4 To remove the left-hand switch unit, undo the screws, noting which fits where **(see illustration)**.
5 Separate the two halves of the switch unit and lift it off, noting how the pin on the wiring clamp locates in the hole in the underside of the handlebar.

22.2 Disconnect the switch wiring connector (arrowed)

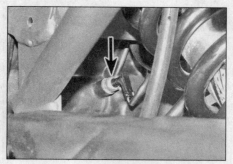

21.1 Neutral switch (arrowed)

Installation

6 Installation is the reverse of removal. Refer to Chapter 4 for installation of the throttle cables. Make sure the locating pin locates in the hole in the handlebar. Make sure the wiring is securely connected and correctly routed. Check the operation of all switches before riding the motorcycle.

21 Neutral switch

Check

1 The switch is located on the back of the engine unit **(see illustration)**. Disconnect the wiring connector from the switch. Make sure the transmission is in neutral.
2 With the connector disconnected and the ignition switch ON, the neutral light should be out. If not, the wire between the connector and instrument cluster must be earthed (grounded) at some point.
4 Check for continuity between the terminal on the switch and the crankcase – with the transmission in neutral, there should be continuity; with the transmission in gear, there should be no continuity. If there is continuity when in gear or no continuity when in neutral, remove the switch (see below), and check that the contact plunger is not damaged or seized in the switch body.
5 If the switch is good, check the wire between the connector, the starter circuit cut-off relay

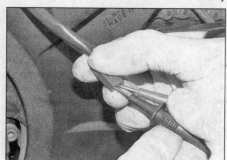

22.3 Connect the meter and test the switch as described

and the instrument cluster for continuity (see *Wiring Diagrams* at the end of this Chapter). Refer to Section 24 for details of checking the diode in the cut-off relay.
6 If the wiring is good, check the LED in the instrument cluster (see Section 17), then check the starter circuit cut-off relay (Section 24) and other components in the starter circuit as described in the relevant Sections of this Chapter. If all components are good, check the wiring between the various components (see *Wiring Diagrams* at the end of this Chapter).

Removal and installation

7 The switch is located on the back of the engine unit **(see illustration 21.1)**. Pull the wire connector off the switch terminal, then unscrew the switch. Remove the sealing washer - a new one must be used.
8 Fit the switch using a new sealing washer and tighten it to the torque setting specified at the beginning of this Chapter.
9 Connect the wire to the switch terminal and check the operation of the neutral light.

22 Sidestand switch

Check

1 The sidestand switch is mounted on the back of the sidestand bracket. The switch is part of the safety circuit, which prevents or stops the engine running if the transmission is in gear whilst the sidestand is down, and prevents the engine from starting if the transmission is in gear unless the sidestand is up and the clutch lever is pulled in.
2 To access the switch wiring connector, raise the fuel tank (see Chapter 4). Trace the wiring from the switch and disconnect it at the blue 2-pin connector, housed inside a rubber boot **(see illustration)**.
3 Check the operation of the switch using a multimeter or continuity tester. Connect the meter probes to the terminals on the switch side of the connector **(see illustration)**. With the sidestand up there should be continuity (with a low resistance) between the terminals, and with the stand down there should be no continuity (infinite resistance).
4 If the switch is good, check the starter circuit cut-off relay (Section 24) and other components in the starter circuit as described in the relevant Sections of this Chapter.
5 If all components are good, check the wiring between the various components (see *Wiring Diagrams* at the end of this Chapter).

Renewal

6 The sidestand switch is mounted on the back of the sidestand bracket.
7 To access the switch wiring connector, raise the fuel tank (see Chapter 4). Trace the wiring from the switch and disconnect it at the blue 2-pin connector, housed inside a rubber boot

22.8 Hold the screws and undo the nuts

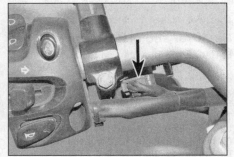

23.2 Clutch switch wiring connector (arrowed)

23.4 Clutch switch screw (arrowed)

(see illustration 22.2). Feed the wiring down to the switch, noting its routing.

8 Counter-hold the screw heads and undo the nuts, and remove the switch (see illustration).

9 Installation is the reverse of removal. Check the operation of the switch (see Step 1).

23 Clutch switch

Check

1 The clutch switch is mounted on the underside of the clutch lever bracket. The switch is part of the safety circuit, which prevents or stops the engine running if the transmission is in gear whilst the sidestand is down, and prevents the engine from starting if the transmission is up and the clutch lever is pulled in. The switch is not adjustable.

2 Disconnect the switch wiring connector (see illustration). Check the operation of the switch using a multimeter or continuity tester. Connect the meter probes to the terminals on the switch. With the lever pulled in there should be continuity (zero resistance) between the terminals, and with the lever out there should be no continuity (infinite resistance).

3 If the switch is good, check the starter circuit cut-off relay (Section 24) and other components in the starter circuit as described

in the relevant Sections of this Chapter. If all components are good, check the wiring between the various components (see Wiring Diagrams at the end of this Chapter).

Renewal

4 Disconnect the wiring connector (see illustration 23.2). Undo the screw securing the switch and remove it (see illustration).

5 Installation is the reverse of removal.

24 Starter circuit cut-off relay

1 The starter circuit cut-off relay and its associated diodes are contained within the relay assembly. They are part of the safety circuit, which prevents or stops the engine running if the transmission is in gear whilst the sidestand is down, and prevents the engine from starting if the transmission is in gear unless the sidestand is up and the clutch lever is pulled in. The relay assembly also contains the fuel injection system relay, which controls power to the fuel pump and injectors, and is covered in Chapter 4, Section 8.

2 To check the operation of the relay, remove the seat(s), and for best access the right-hand rear cowl (see Chapter 7).

3 Disconnect the battery negative (–) lead (see

Section 3). Displace the relay and disconnect the wiring connector (see illustration). Move the relay to the bench to test its operation and diodes.

4 Using a continuity tester or a multimeter set to the resistance (ohms) range, test for continuity between the No. 1 (blue/white - positive meter probe) and No. 2 (white/blue - negative meter probe) wire terminals on the relay (see illustration). There should be no continuity (infinite resistance). Now, using insulated jumper wires and a fully charged 12V battery, connect the battery positive (+) terminal to the No. 3 (red/black) wire terminal on the relay and the battery negative (-) terminal to the No. 4 (black/yellow) wire terminal. Continuity (0 ohms) should now be shown on the meter.

5 If the relay does not operate as described, replace it with a new one.

6 The diodes contained within the relay assembly can be checked by performing a continuity test – diodes should show continuity in one direction and no continuity when the meter or tester probes are reversed. Connect the multimeter (set to ohms) or continuity tester across the wire terminals for the diode being tested and perform the tests (see illustration). If any diode shows continuity in both directions it is faulty, and the relay assembly must be replaced with a new one.

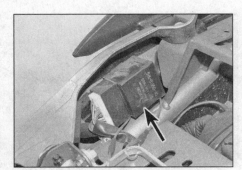

24.3 Starter circuit cut-off relay (arrowed)

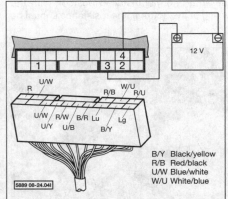

24.4 Starter circuit cut-off relay check terminal identification

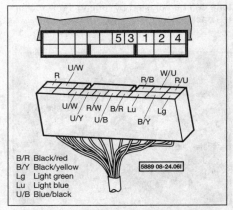

24.6 Starter circuit cut-off relay diode check terminal identification

Positive probe (+)	Negative probe (-)	Result
Light blue (1)	Black/yellow (2)	No continuity
Black/yellow (2)	Light blue (1)	Continuity
Light blue (1)	Black/red (3)	No continuity
Black/red (3)	Light blue (1)	Continuity
Light blue (1)	Light green (4)	No continuity
Light green (4)	Light blue (1)	Continuity
Blue/black (5)	Black/red (3)	No continuity
Black/red (3)	Blue/black (5)	Continuity

7 If the cut-out relay and diodes are good, but the starting system fault still exists, check all other components in the starting circuit (i.e. the neutral switch, sidestand switch, clutch switch, starter switch and starter relay) as described in the relevant Sections of this Chapter. If all components are good, check the wiring between the various components (see *Wiring Diagrams* at the end of this Chapter).

8 Installation is the reverse of removal.

25 Horn

Check

1 If the horn doesn't work, first check the signal fuse (see Section 5).

2 The horn is mounted on the bottom yoke. For best access, on XJ6-S models remove the left-hand fairing side panel, and on XJ6-F and FZ6R models remove the left-hand lower fairing panel (see Chapter 7).

3 Pull the wiring connectors off the horn terminals **(see illustration)**. Using two jumper wires and a fully charged 12V battery, apply voltage directly to the terminals on the horn. If the horn sounds, check the switch (see Section 19) and the wiring between the switch and the horn (see *Wiring Diagrams* at the end of this Chapter).

4 If the horn sounds weak or distorted, the tone can be adjusted by turning the screw on the back.

5 If the horn doesn't sound, or can't be adjusted, replace it with a new one.

Removal and installation

6 The horn is mounted on the bottom yoke. For best access, on XJ6-S models remove the left-hand fairing side panel, and on XJ6-N and FZ6R models remove the left-hand lower fairing panel (see Chapter 7).

7 Pull the wiring connectors off the horn terminals **(see illustration 25.3)**.

8 Unscrew the nut securing the horn **(see illustration 25.3)**.

9 Fit the horn and tighten the nut. Connect the wiring connectors and check the operation of the horn. If removed, install the fairing panel.

26 Oil level sensor
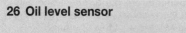

Check

1 The oil level warning light will come on for a few seconds when the ignition is switched ON as a check of the LED, and then go out. If the warning indicator does not go off or starts flashing, check the engine oil level as described in *Pre-ride checks*. If the oil level is correct, check the sensor as described below. Equally, if the warning light comes on (and/or flashes) whilst the motorcycle is being ridden, stop the engine and check the engine oil level immediately. **Note:** *If there is a fault in the wiring circuit it will be detected by a self diagnosis function and the warning indicator will flash ten times, then go out for 2.5 seconds, and this will be repeated until the fault is repaired.*

2 If the warning light does not come on when the ignition is switched ON, check the LED as described in Section 17.

3 To check the sensor, remove it from the sump (see Steps 4 to 6). Connect one probe of a multimeter set to the ohms x 100 scale to the sensor wire and the other probe to the base of the sensor. With the sensor upright (i.e. in its normal installed position with the wiring at the bottom), the resistance should be

as specified (minimum level) at the beginning of this Chapter. Turn the sensor upside down and check the resistance again – it should be as specified (maximum level). If either result is not as specified, replace the sensor with a new one.

Removal

4 Drain the engine oil (see Chapter 1).

5 Raise the fuel tank (see Chapter 4). Disconnect the sensor wiring connector **(see illustration)**.

6 Feed the wire back to the sensor, noting its routing and releasing it from the clamps - the bottom one is secured by a sump bolt, which must be unscrewed **(see illustration)**.

7 Unscrew the sensor bolts and withdraw the sensor from the sump, being prepared to catch any residual oil **(see illustration 26.6)**. Remove the O-ring and replace it with a new one.

Installation

8 Smear the new O-ring with lithium-based grease and fit it onto the sensor, then fit the sensor into the sump. Tighten the bolts to the torque setting specified at the beginning of this Chapter.

9 Feed the wiring to the connector and secure it with the clamps and sump bolt **(see illustration 26.6)**.

10 Fill the engine with the specified amount of oil (see Chapter 1) and check the operation of the sensor.

27 Starter relay
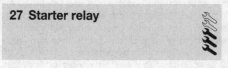

Check

1 If the starter circuit appears to be faulty, first check the main fuse and ignition fuses (see Section 5).

2 Remove the seat(s) (see Chapter 7). The starter relay is located to the rear of the battery on the right-hand side.

3 Lift the rubber covers and unscrew the bolt securing the black starter motor lead **(see**

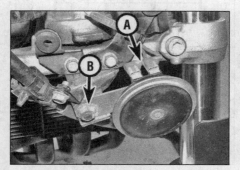

25.3 Horn wiring connectors (A) and mounting nut (B)

26.5 Oil level sensor wiring connector (arrowed)

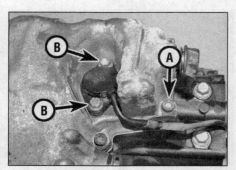

26.6 Oil level sensor wiring clamp bolt (A) and mounting bolts (B)

27.3a Lift the covers (arrowed)...

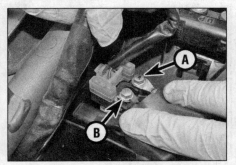

27.3b ...to access the starter motor lead terminal (A) and battery lead terminal (B)

27.12 Disconnect the wiring connector

illustrations). Position the lead away from the relay terminal.

4 With the ignition switch ON, the engine kill switch in the RUN position and the transmission in neutral, press the starter switch. The relay should be heard to click.

5 If the relay doesn't click, switch the ignition OFF, remove the relay (see Steps 10 to 12) and test it as follows.

6 Using a continuity tester or a multimeter set to the resistance (ohms) range, test for continuity between the relay's starter motor (black) and battery (red) lead terminals **(see illustration 27.3b)**. There should be no continuity (infinite resistance). Now, using insulated jumper wires and a fully charged 12V battery, connect the battery positive (+) terminal to the red/white wire terminal on the relay and the battery negative (-) terminal to the blue/white wire terminal. With voltage applied, the relay should be heard to click and continuity (0 ohms) should now be shown on the meter.

7 If the relay does not click when battery voltage is applied and indicates no continuity (infinite resistance) across its terminals, it is faulty and must be replaced with a new one.

8 The starter relay coil resistance can be checked by connecting a multimeter set to the ohms x 1 range across the red/white and blue/white terminals of the relay wire connector; the value should be as specified at the beginning of this Chapter.

9 If the relay is good, check for battery voltage at the red/white wire terminal on the loom side

of the relay wiring connector when the starter button is pressed with the ignition switched ON. If voltage is present, check the other components in the starter circuit as described in the relevant Sections of this Chapter. If no voltage is present, check the wiring between the various components (see *Wiring Diagrams* at the end of this Chapter).

Renewal

10 Remove the seat(s) (see Chapter 7). Disconnect the battery negative (-) lead.

11 Lift the rubber covers and Unscrew the starter motor and battery lead bolts and detach the leads, noting which fits where **(see illustration 27.3a and b)**.

12 Disconnect the relay wiring connector **(see illustration)**.

13 Remove the relay, and if it is being replaced with a new one remove the main fuse and its spare, and fit them into the new relay (though it may come with new ones already fitted, in which case keep the others as spares).

14 Installation is the reverse of removal. Make sure the terminal bolts are tight.

28 Starter motor removal and installation

Removal

1 The starter motor is mounted on the crankcase, behind the cylinder block.

2 Disconnect the battery negative (-) lead

(see Section 3). Drain the cooling system (see Chapter 1). Remove the throttle bodies (see Chapter 4). Remove the thermostat cover (see Chapter 3).

3 Peel back the terminal boot, unscrew the nut securing the lead to the starter motor terminal and detach the lead **(see illustration)**.

4 Unscrew the two starter motor mounting bolts **(see illustration)**. Draw the starter motor out of the crankcase **(see illustration 28.7)** - use a screwdriver to initially lever it out if required.

5 Remove the O-ring on the end of the starter motor - a new one must be used.

Installation

6 Fit a new O-ring onto the end of the starter motor, making sure it is seated in its groove, and smear it with grease **(see illustration)**.

7 Manoeuvre the motor into position and slide it into the crankcase **(see illustration)**.

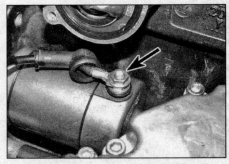

28.3 Unscrew the nut (arrowed) and detach the lead

28.4 Starter motor bolts (arrowed)

28.6 Fit a new O-ring (arrowed) and smear it with grease

28.7 Manoeuvre the motor into place as shown

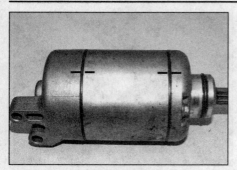

29.2 Note the alignment marks between the housing and the end covers

29.3a Unscrew the two long bolts (arrowed), noting the O-rings...

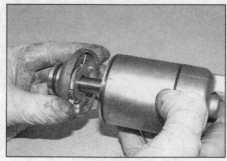

29.3b ... and remove the front cover...

29.3c ... and its tabbed washer

29.4 Slide the insulating washer (A) and shims (B) off the shaft

29.5 Draw the main housing off the armature

Make sure that the starter motor teeth mesh correctly with those of the starter idler gear.

8 Fit the mounting bolts and tighten them to the torque setting specified at the beginning of this Chapter.

9 Connect the lead to the starter motor terminal and secure it with the nut **(see illustration 28.3)**. Make sure the boot is correctly seated over the terminal.

10 Install the thermostat cover (see Chapter 3) and the throttle bodies (see Chapter 4). Fill the cooling system (see Chapter 1).

11 Connect the battery negative (–) lead.

29 Starter motor overhaul

Disassembly

1 Remove the starter motor (see Section 28).

2 Note the alignment marks between the main housing and the front and rear covers, or make your own if they are unclear **(see illustration)**.

3 Unscrew and remove the two long bolts, noting the O-rings **(see illustration)**. Remove the front cover from the motor **(see**

illustration)**. Remove the tabbed washer from inside the cover **(see illustration)**.

4 Slide the insulating washer and shim(s) from the front end of the armature, noting the order in which they are fitted **(see illustration)**.

5 Holding the armature in place, draw the main housing off, noting that the attraction of the magnets will have to be overcome. Remove the housing O-rings **(see illustration)**.

6 Remove the rear cover and brushplate assembly from the armature commutator **(see illustration)**. Remove the shim(s) from the rear end of the armature shaft **(see illustration)**.

29.6a Draw the armature out of the rear cover

29.6b Remove the shims (arrowed)

29.7 Unscrew the nut (arrowed) and remove the washers

29.8a Remove the brushplate

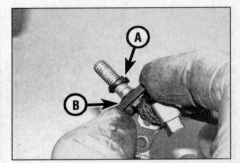

29.8b Remove the O-ring (A) and insulator (B) if required

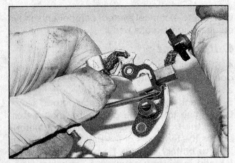

29.9 Move the spring end off the back of the brush then draw the brush out

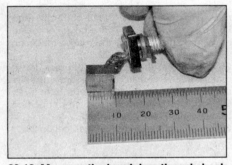

29.10 Measure the brush length and check for wear and damage

29.12 There should be continuity between the bars...

7 Noting the order in which they are fitted, unscrew the terminal nut and remove it along with its washer and insulating washers **(see illustration)**.

8 Withdraw the terminal and brushplate assembly from the rear cover **(see illustration)**. Note the O-ring and square insulator on the terminal and remove them if required **(see illustrations)**.

9 Lift the brush springs and slide the brushes out from their holders, noting that one brush is attached to the terminal and the other is attached to the brushplate **(see illustration)**.

Inspection

10 Check the general condition of all the starter motor components. The parts that are most likely to require attention are the brushes. Measure the length of the brushes and compare the results to the brush length listed in this Chapter's Specifications **(see**

illustration). If either of the brushes are worn beyond the service limit, renew the brushplate assembly. If the brushes are not worn excessively, cracked, chipped, or otherwise damaged, they may be re-used.

11 Inspect the commutator bars on the armature for scoring, scratches and discoloration. The commutator can be cleaned and polished with steel wool, but do not use sandpaper or emery paper. After cleaning, wipe away any residue with a cloth soaked in electrical system cleaner or denatured alcohol.

12 Using a multimeter or a continuity tester, check for continuity between the commutator bars **(see illustration)**. Continuity should exist (Yamaha specify 0.0012 to 0.0022 ohms) between each bar and all of the others.

13 Check for continuity between the commutator bars and the armature shaft **(see illustration)**. There should be no continuity

(infinite resistance – Yamaha specify a resistance of over 1 M-ohm); if the checks indicate otherwise, the armature is defective.

14 Check the depth of the insulating mica undercut between the commutator bars **(see illustration)** – if it is less than the amount specified at the beginning of this Chapter, scrape the mica away using a suitably shaped hacksaw blade until it is correct.

15 Measure the diameter of the commutator and replace the starter motor with a new one if it has worn below the minimum diameter specified.

16 Check the starter pinion gear for worn, cracked, chipped and broken teeth. If the gear is damaged or worn, replace the starter motor with a new one.

17 Inspect the end covers for signs of cracks or wear. Check the oil seal and needle bearing in the front cover and the bush in the rear cover for wear and damage **(see illustrations)**.

29.13 ...and no continuity between the bars and the shaft

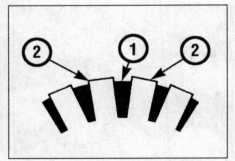

29.14 Check the commutator bars and make sure the mica (1) is below the bars (2)

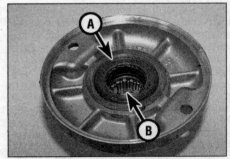

29.17a Check the front cover oil seal (A) and bearing (B)...

29.17b ...and the rear cover bush (arrowed)

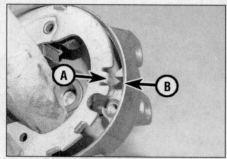

29.20a Seat the tab (A) between the lugs (B)

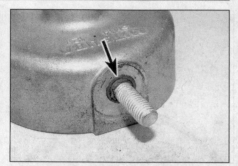

29.20b Make sure the O-ring (arrowed) fully insulates the bolt from the cover

Inspect the magnets in the main housing and the housing itself for cracks.

18 Inspect the terminal insulating washers, the O-ring and square insulating washer for signs of damage, and replace them with new ones if necessary **(see illustrations 29.7 and 29.8b)**. Check the housing O-rings and the long bolt O-rings for distortion and deterioration and replace them with new ones if necessary – note that Yamaha specify to fit new ones whatever the apparent condition of the old ones.

Reassembly

19 Slide the brushes back into their holders and place the brush spring ends onto the brushes **(see illustration 29.9)**.
20 Fit the square insulating washer and O-ring onto the terminal and fit the terminal and brushplate assembly into the rear cover **(see illustrations 29.8b and a)**. Make sure the brushplate tab sits between the tabs on the cover, and the O-ring sits between the bolt and the cover **(see illustrations)**.
21 Fit the insulating washers onto the terminal, followed by the plain washer and nut, and tighten the nut **(see illustration 29.7)**.
22 Slide the shims onto the rear end of the armature shaft **(see illustration 29.6b)**. Lubricate the shaft with a smear of grease, then insert the shaft into the rear cover, locating the brushes on the commutator as you do, taking care not to damage the brushes **(see illustration 29.6a)**. Check that each brush is securely pressed against the commutator by its spring and is free to move easily in its holder.
23 Fit the O-rings onto the main housing, then fit the housing, notched end first, over the armature and onto the rear cover, aligning the marks made on removal – hold the armature to prevent it being drawn out of the rear cover by the attraction of the magnets, and make sure you do not get your fingers caught between the housing and the rear cover as the housing is drawn on **(see illustrations 29.5 and 29.2)**.
24 Slide the shims and then the insulating washer onto the front end of the armature shaft and lubricate the shaft with a smear of grease **(see illustration 29.4)**. Apply a smear of grease to the inside of the front cover oil seal. Fit the tabbed washer into the cover,

making sure the tabs locate correctly **(see illustrations 29.3c)**. Fit the cover onto the main housing, aligning the marks made on removal **(see illustration 29.3b)**.
25 Check that the marks on the rear cover, main housing and front cover are correctly aligned, then fit the long bolts with their O-rings and tighten them to the specified torque setting **(see illustration)**.
26 Install the starter motor (see Section 28).

30 Charging system testing

1 If the performance of the charging system is suspect, the system as a whole should be checked first, followed by testing of the individual components. **Note:** *Before beginning the checks, make sure the battery is fully charged and that all system connections are clean and tight.*
2 Checking the output of the charging system and the performance of the various components within the charging system requires the use of a multimeter (with voltage, current and resistance checking facilities). If a multimeter is not available, the job of checking the charging system should be left to a Yamaha dealer or automotive electrician.
3 When making the checks, follow the procedures carefully to prevent incorrect connections or short circuits, as irreparable

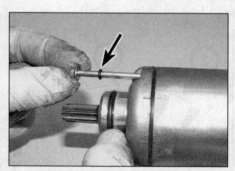

29.25 Make sure the O-ring (arrowed) is fitted with each bolt

damage to electrical system components may result if short circuits occur.

Output test

4 Start the engine and warm it up to normal operating temperature. Remove the seat(s) to access the battery terminals (see Chapter 7).
5 To check the regulated voltage output, allow the engine to idle and connect a multimeter set to the 0 to 20 volts DC scale (voltmeter) across the terminals of the battery, positive (+) lead to battery positive (+) terminal, negative (–) lead to battery negative (–) terminal **(see illustration)**. Slowly increase the engine speed to 5000 rpm and note the reading obtained.
6 The regulated voltage should be as specified at the beginning of this Chapter. If the voltage is outside these limits, check the alternator, then the regulator/rectifier (see Sections 31 and 32).
7 Stop the engine and disconnect the test meter.

Leakage test

Caution: Always connect an ammeter in series, never in parallel with the battery, otherwise it will be damaged. Do not turn the ignition ON or operate the starter motor when the ammeter is connected – a sudden surge in current will blow the meter's fuse.
8 Turn the ignition switch OFF. Remove the

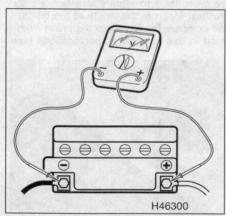

30.5 Checking the charging system output – connect the voltmeter as shown

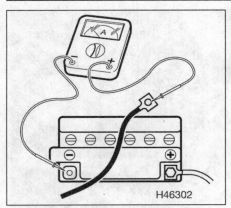

30.9 Checking the charging system leakage rate – connect the ammeter as shown

31.2 Alternator wiring connector (arrowed)

31.3 Checking stator coil resistance

seat(s) (see Chapter 7). Disconnect the lead from the battery negative (–) terminal (see Section 3).

9 Set the multimeter to the Amps function - set the meter to a high amps range initially and then bring it down to the mA (milli Amps) range; if there is a high current flow in the circuit it may blow the meter's fuse. Connect the meter negative (–) probe to the battery negative (–) terminal, and the positive (+) probe to the disconnected negative (–) lead **(see illustration)**.

10 No current flow should be indicated. If current leakage is indicated (generally greater than 1mA, but may be more if an alarm is fitted), there is a short circuit in the wiring. Using the wiring diagrams at the end of this Chapter, systematically disconnect individual electrical components, checking the meter each time until the source is identified.

11 If no leakage is indicated, disconnect the meter and connect the negative (–) lead to the battery.

31 Alternator rotor and stator

Check

1 Raise the fuel tank (see Chapter 4).

2 Trace the wiring from the top of the alternator cover on the left-hand side of the engine and disconnect it at the white connector containing the three white wires, housed inside a rubber boot **(see illustration)**.

3 Using a multimeter set to the ohms x 1 (ohmmeter) scale, measure the resistance between the centre wire and each of the other two on the alternator side of the connector, then between the outer two wires, taking a total of three readings, then check for continuity between each terminal and ground (earth) **(see illustration)**. If the stator coil windings are in good condition the resistance readings should be within the range shown in *Specifications* at the beginning of this Chapter and there should be no continuity (infinite resistance) between the terminals and ground

(earth). If not, check the fault is not due to damaged wiring between the connector and coils. If the wiring is good, the alternator stator coil assembly is at fault and should be replaced with a new one.

Removal

Special Tool: *A centre-bolt type puller is essential for removal of the alternator rotor from the crankshaft.*

4 Refer to Chapter 2, Section 14 and remove the alternator cover.

5 Withdraw the idle/reduction gear shaft from the crankcase and remove the gear **(see illustration)**.

6 To remove the rotor bolt it is necessary to stop the rotor from turning. This is best achieved using a rotor holding tool, either Yamaha Part No. 90890-01701 or YS-01880-A, or there are several commercially available types. Keep the tool strap away from any raised projections on the rotor. If a rotor holding tool is not available and the engine is still in the frame, place the transmission in gear and have an assistant apply the rear brake. Unscrew the rotor bolt and remove the washer **(see illustration)**.

31.5 Withdraw the shaft and remove the gear

31.6 Using a rotor holder while unscrewing the bolt

31.7a Fit the puller onto the rotor...

31.7b ...then hold the rotor and tighten the puller bolt

31.9 Alternator stator and wiring clamp bolts (arrowed)

31.13 Slide the rotor onto the shaft

31.14a Fit the bolt and washer...

31.14b ...and tighten the bolt to the specified torque

7 To remove the rotor from the shaft it is necessary to use a rotor puller. Yamaha make a tool (Part Nos. 90890-01362 and 90890-04089 or YU-33270 and YM-33282), or alternatively a similar tool can be obtained commercially **(see illustration)**. **Note:** *The rotor has three threaded holes designed to accept the bolts of the puller – there are many types of puller available, so if buying one make sure you get the correct type as shown.* Fit the puller, hold the rotor as before, and tighten the puller centre bolt until the rotor is displaced from the shaft **(see illustration)** – remove the starter driven gear along with the rotor **(see illustration 31.13)**.

8 If required, refer to Chapter 2, Section 14 and remove the starter driven gear and starter clutch from the back of the rotor.

9 To remove the stator from the cover, undo the screw securing the wiring clamp and the three screws securing the stator, then remove the assembly, noting how the wiring grommet locates **(see illustration)**.

Installation

10 Fit the stator, aligning the wiring grommet with the recess in the alternator cover **(see illustration 31.9)**. Clean the stator screw and clamp screw threads and apply a suitable non-permanent thread locking compound, then fit the screws and tighten them to the torque setting specified at the beginning of this Chapter.

11 Apply a suitable sealant to the wiring grommet, then press it into the recess in the cover and secure the wiring with the clamp.

12 If removed, refer to Chapter 2, Section 14 and fit the starter clutch and starter driven gear onto the back of the rotor.

13 Clean the tapered end of the crankshaft and the corresponding mating surface on the inside of the rotor with a suitable solvent. Make sure that no metal objects have attached themselves to the magnet on the inside of the rotor, then slide the rotor onto the shaft **(see illustration)**.

14 Apply some clean engine oil to the rotor bolt threads and washer, fit the washer onto the bolt and thread the bolt in **(see illustration)**. Use the method employed on removal to prevent the rotor from turning and tighten the bolt to the torque setting specified at the beginning of this Chapter **(see illustration)**.

15 Lubricate the idle/reduction gear shaft with clean engine oil. Position the gear, making sure the smaller pinion faces inwards and engages the driven gear teeth, and the teeth of the larger pinion mesh with the teeth of the starter motor shaft, then insert the gear shaft **(see illustration 31.5)**.

16 Refer to Chapter 2, Section 14 and install the alternator cover.

17 Top-up the engine with oil to the correct level (see *Pre-ride checks*).

32 Regulator/rectifier

Check

1 Yamaha provide no test specifications for the regulator/rectifier other than the charging system output test (see Section 30). If the regulator/rectifier is suspected of being faulty, first check all other components and the wiring and connectors in the charging circuit, referring to the relevant Sections in this Chapter and to the *Wiring Diagrams* at the end.

2 If all other components and the wiring are good, remove the unit (see below) and take it to a Yamaha dealer for testing. Alternatively, substitute the suspect unit with a known good one and see if the fault is cured.

Removal and installation

3 The regulator/rectifier is mounted on the front of the undertray, behind the rear shock absorber. Remove the seat(s) (see Chapter 7).

4 Disconnect the wiring connector **(see illustration)**.

5 Unscrew the two nuts, accessing the top nut from above, and remove the regulator/rectifier **(see illustration)**.

6 Check the mounting grommets on the bracket – if they are worn or perished, replace them with new ones.

7 Installation is the reverse of removal.

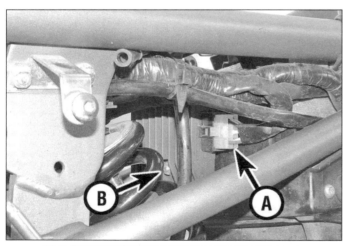

32.4 Regulator/rectifier wiring connector (A), lower mounting nut (B)...

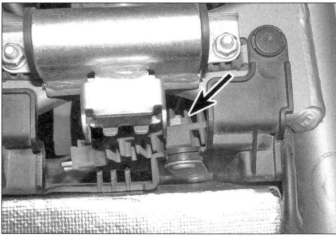

32.5 ...and upper mounting nut (arrowed)

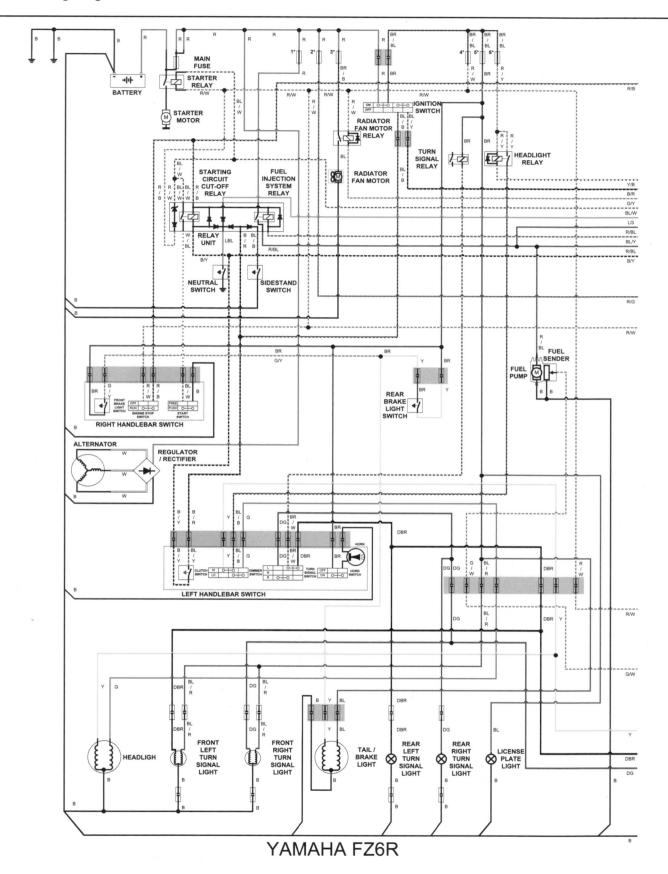

YAMAHA FZ6R

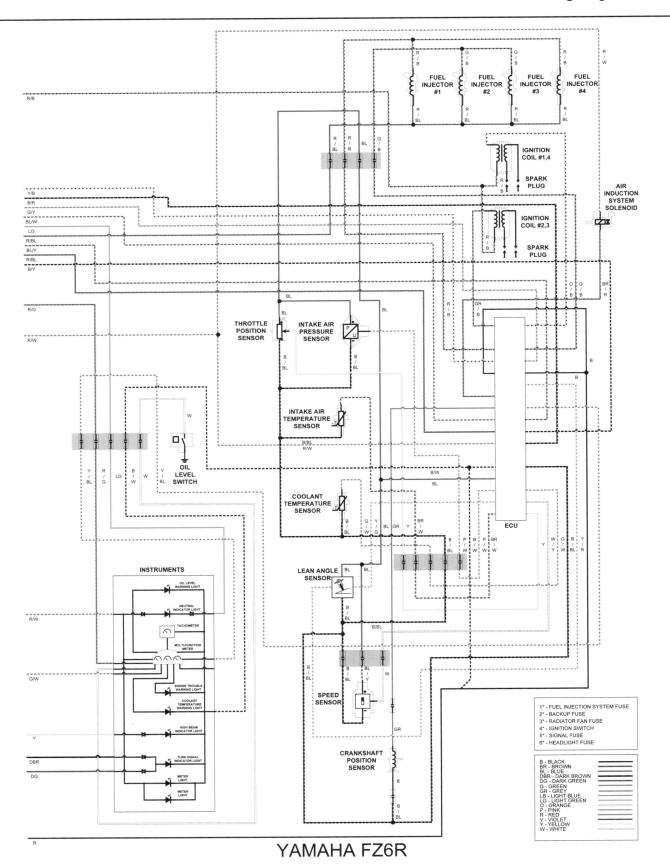

YAMAHA FZ6R

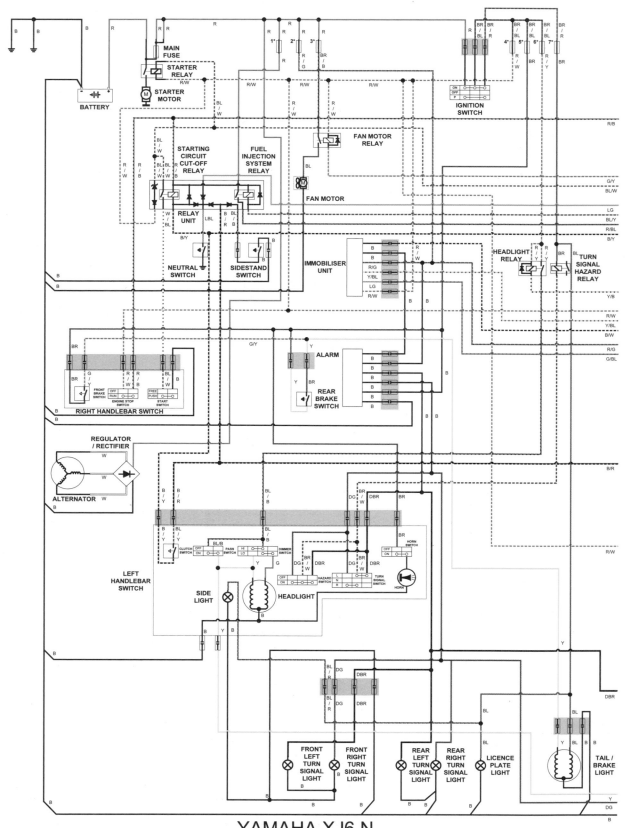

YAMAHA XJ6 N

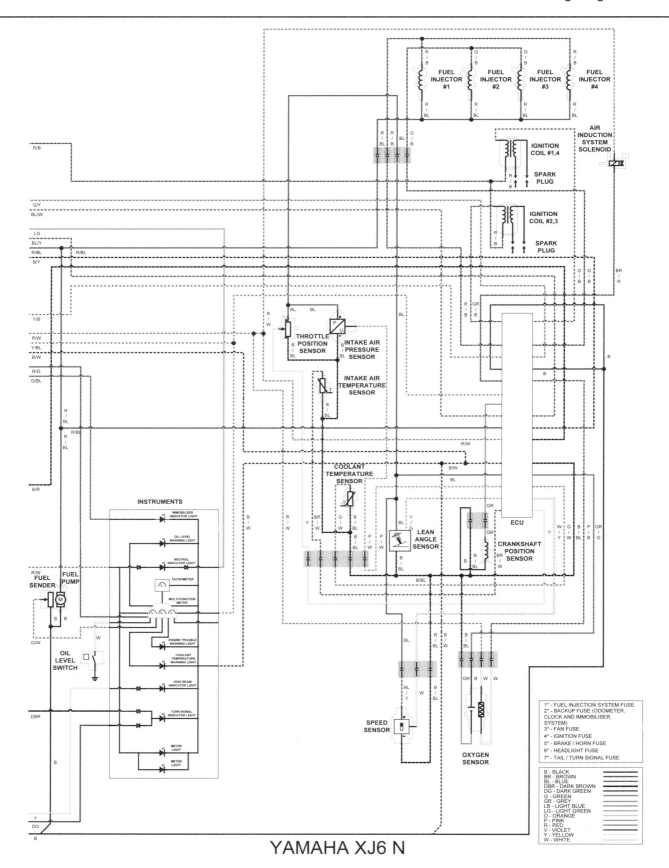

YAMAHA XJ6 N

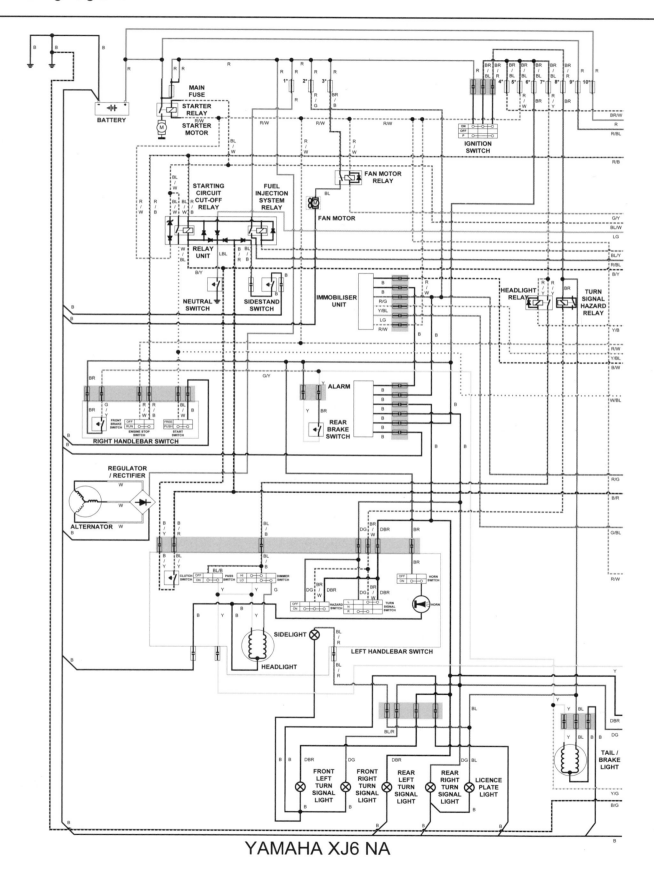

YAMAHA XJ6 NA

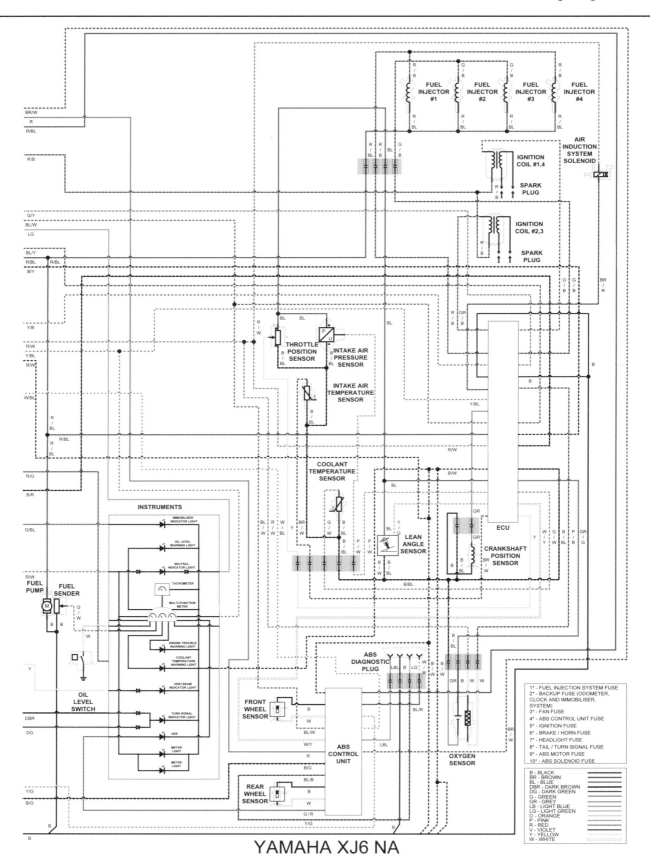

YAMAHA XJ6 NA

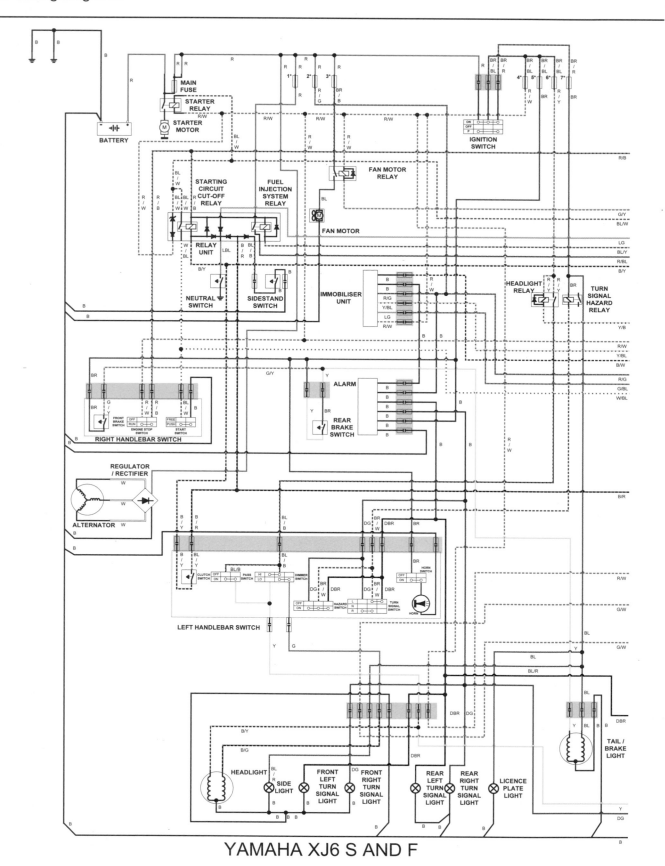

YAMAHA XJ6 S AND F

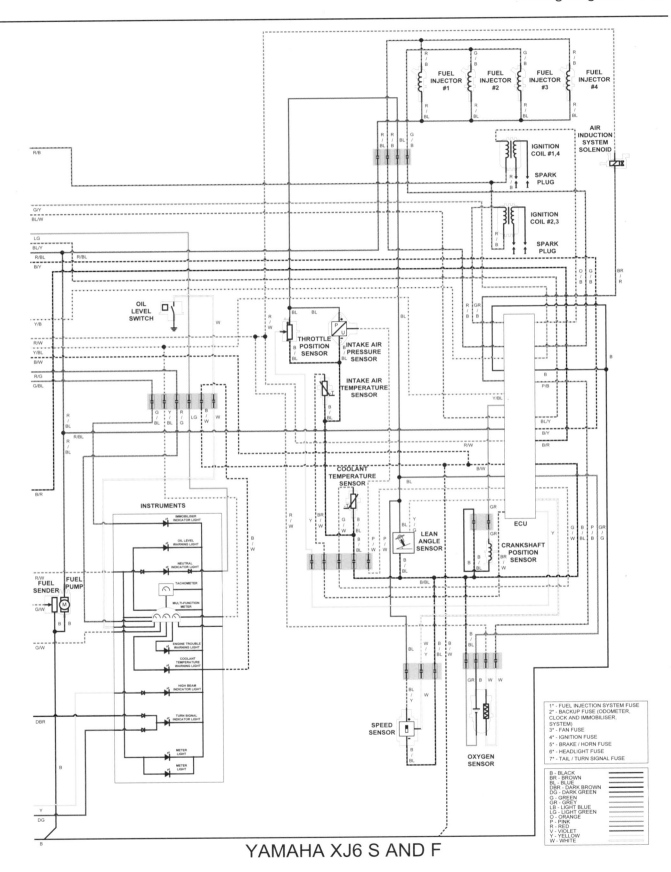

YAMAHA XJ6 S AND F

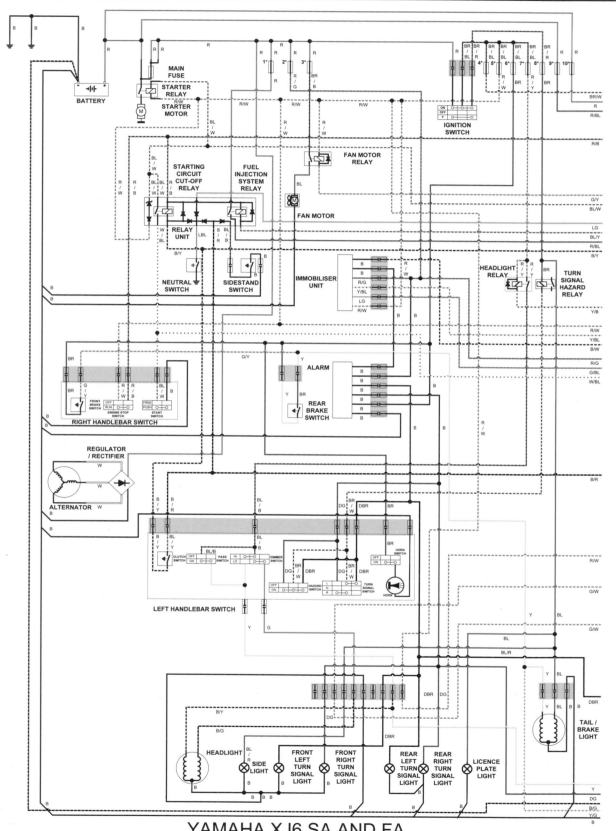

YAMAHA XJ6 SA AND FA

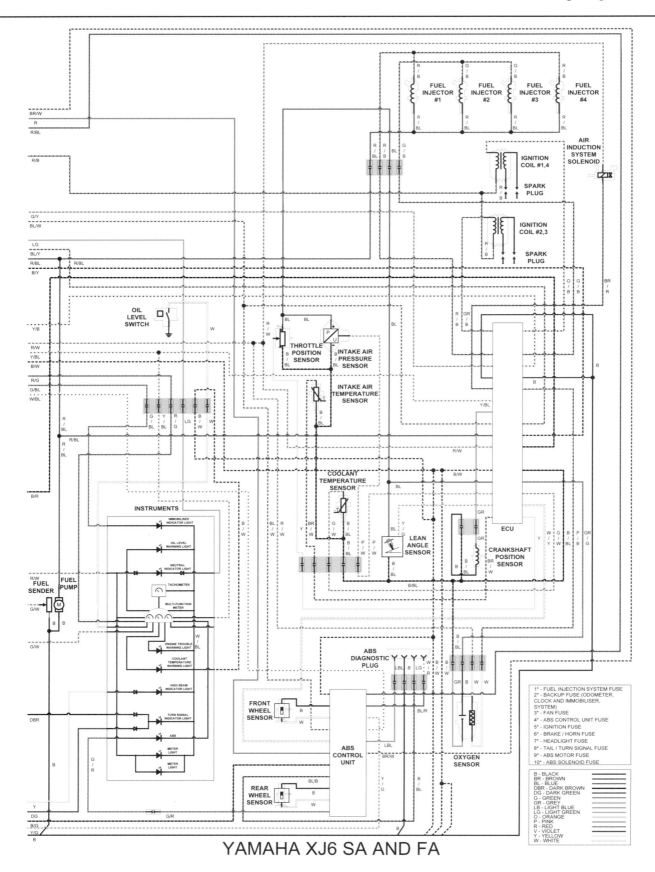

YAMAHA XJ6 SA AND FA

Notes

Reference

Tools and Workshop Tips

● Building up a tool kit and equipping your workshop ● Using tools ● Understanding bearing, seal, fastener and chain sizes and markings ● Repair techniques

Security

● Locks and chains ● U-locks ● Disc locks ● Alarms and immobilisers ● Security marking systems ● Tips on how to prevent bike theft

Lubricants and fluids

● Engine oils ● Transmission (gear) oils ● Coolant/anti-freeze ● Fork oils and suspension fluids ● Brake/clutch fluids ● Spray lubes, degreasers and solvents

Conversion Factors

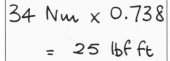

● Formulae for conversion of the metric (SI) units used throughout the manual into Imperial measures

MOT Test Checks

● A guide to the UK MOT test ● Which items are tested ● How to prepare your motorcycle for the test and perform a pre-test check

Storage

● How to prepare your motorcycle for going into storage and protect essential systems ● How to get the motorcycle back on the road

Fault Finding

● Common faults and their likely causes ● Links to main chapters for testing and repair procedures

Technical Terms Explained

● Component names, technical terms and common abbreviations explained

Index

Buying tools

A toolkit is a fundamental requirement for servicing and repairing a motorcycle. Although there will be an initial expense in building up enough tools for servicing, this will soon be offset by the savings made by doing the job yourself. As experience and confidence grow, additional tools can be added to enable the repair and overhaul of the motorcycle. Many of the specialist tools are expensive and not often used so it may be preferable to hire them, or for a group of friends or motorcycle club to join in the purchase.

As a rule, it is better to buy more expensive, good quality tools. Cheaper tools are likely to wear out faster and need to be renewed more often, nullifying the original saving.

> ⚠ **Warning: To avoid the risk of a poor quality tool breaking in use, causing injury or damage to the component being worked on, always aim to purchase tools which meet the relevant national safety standards.**

The following lists of tools do not represent the manufacturer's service tools, but serve as a guide to help the owner decide which tools are needed for this level of work. In addition, items such as an electric drill, hacksaw, files, soldering iron and a workbench equipped with a vice, may be needed. Although not classed as tools, a selection of bolts, screws, nuts, washers and pieces of tubing always come in useful.

For more information about tools, refer to the Haynes *Motorcycle Workshop Practice Techbook* (Bk. No. 3470).

Manufacturer's service tools

Inevitably certain tasks require the use of a service tool. Where possible an alternative tool or method of approach is recommended, but sometimes there is no option if personal injury or damage to the component is to be avoided. Where required, service tools are referred to in the relevant procedure.

Service tools can usually only be purchased from a motorcycle dealer and are identified by a part number. Some of the commonly-used tools, such as rotor pullers, are available in aftermarket form from mail-order motorcycle tool and accessory suppliers.

Maintenance and minor repair tools

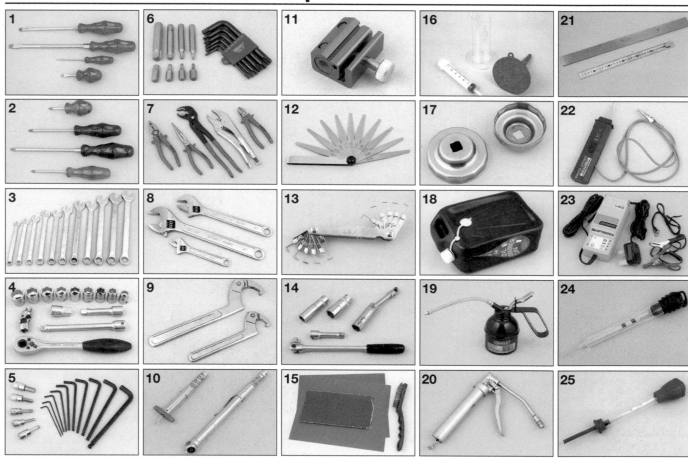

1 Set of flat-bladed screwdrivers
2 Set of Phillips head screwdrivers
3 Combination open-end and ring spanners
4 Socket set (3/8 inch or 1/2 inch drive)
5 Set of Allen keys or bits
6 Set of Torx keys or bits
7 Pliers, cutters and self-locking grips (Mole grips)
8 Adjustable spanners
9 C-spanners
10 Tread depth gauge and tyre pressure gauge
11 Cable oiler clamp
12 Feeler gauges
13 Spark plug gap measuring tool
14 Spark plug spanner or deep plug sockets
15 Wire brush and emery paper
16 Calibrated syringe, measuring vessel and funnel
17 Oil filter adapters
18 Oil drainer can or tray
19 Pump type oil can
20 Grease gun
21 Straight-edge and steel rule
22 Continuity tester
23 Battery charger
24 Hydrometer (for battery specific gravity check)
25 Anti-freeze tester (for liquid-cooled engines)

Repair and overhaul tools

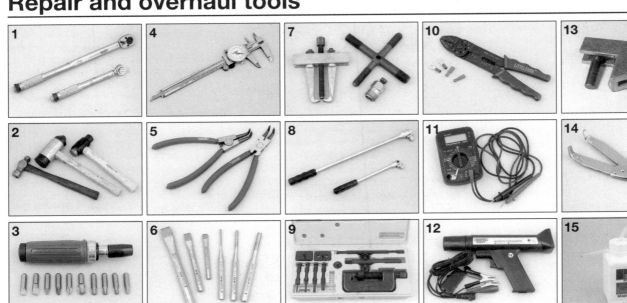

1 Torque wrench
   (small and mid-ranges)
2 Conventional, plastic or
   soft-faced hammers
3 Impact driver set

4 Vernier gauge
5 Circlip pliers (internal and
   external, or combination)
6 Set of cold chisels
   and punches

7 Selection of pullers
8 Breaker bars
9 Chain breaking/
   riveting tool set

10 Wire stripper and
    crimper tool
11 Multimeter (measures
    amps, volts and ohms)
12 Stroboscope (for
    dynamic timing checks)

13 Hose clamp
    (wingnut type shown)
14 Clutch holding tool
15 One-man brake/clutch
    bleeder kit

Specialist tools

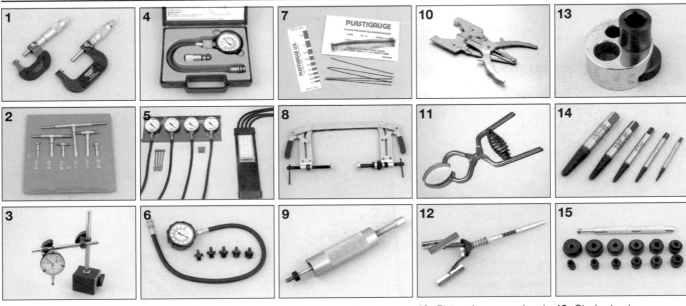

1 Micrometers
   (external type)
2 Telescoping gauges
3 Dial gauge

4 Cylinder
   compression gauge
5 Vacuum gauges (left) or
   manometer (right)
6 Oil pressure gauge

7 Plastigauge kit
8 Valve spring compressor
   (4-stroke engines)
9 Piston pin drawbolt tool

10 Piston ring removal and
    installation tool
11 Piston ring clamp
12 Cylinder bore hone
    (stone type shown)

13 Stud extractor
14 Screw extractor set
15 Bearing driver set

1 Workshop equipment and facilities

The workbench

● Work is made much easier by raising the bike up on a ramp - components are much more accessible if raised to waist level. The hydraulic or pneumatic types seen in the dealer's workshop are a sound investment if you undertake a lot of repairs or overhauls **(see illustration 1.1)**.

1.1 Hydraulic motorcycle ramp

● If raised off ground level, the bike must be supported on the ramp to avoid it falling. Most ramps incorporate a front wheel locating clamp which can be adjusted to suit different diameter wheels. When tightening the clamp, take care not to mark the wheel rim or damage the tyre - use wood blocks on each side to prevent this.
● Secure the bike to the ramp using tie-downs **(see illustration 1.2)**. If the bike has only a sidestand, and hence leans at a dangerous angle when raised, support the bike on an auxiliary stand.

1.2 Tie-downs are used around the passenger footrests to secure the bike

● Auxiliary (paddock) stands are widely available from mail order companies or motorcycle dealers and attach either to the wheel axle or swingarm pivot **(see illustration 1.3)**. If the motorcycle has a centrestand, you can support it under the crankcase to prevent it toppling whilst either wheel is removed **(see illustration 1.4)**.

1.3 This auxiliary stand attaches to the swingarm pivot

1.4 Always use a block of wood between the engine and jack head when supporting the engine in this way

Fumes and fire

● Refer to the Safety first! page at the beginning of the manual for full details. Make sure your workshop is equipped with a fire extinguisher suitable for fuel-related fires (Class B fire - flammable liquids) - it is not sufficient to have a water-filled extinguisher.
● Always ensure adequate ventilation is available. Unless an exhaust gas extraction system is available for use, ensure that the engine is run outside of the workshop.
● If working on the fuel system, make sure the workshop is ventilated to avoid a build-up of fumes. This applies equally to fume build-up when charging a battery. Do not smoke or allow anyone else to smoke in the workshop.

Fluids

● If you need to drain fuel from the tank, store it in an approved container marked as suitable for the storage of petrol (gasoline) **(see illustration 1.5)**. Do not store fuel in glass jars or bottles.

1.5 Use an approved can only for storing petrol (gasoline)

● Use proprietary engine degreasers or solvents which have a high flash-point, such as paraffin (kerosene), for cleaning off oil, grease and dirt - never use petrol (gasoline) for cleaning. Wear rubber gloves when handling solvent and engine degreaser. The fumes from certain solvents can be dangerous - always work in a well-ventilated area.

Dust, eye and hand protection

● Protect your lungs from inhalation of dust particles by wearing a filtering mask over the nose and mouth. Many frictional materials still contain asbestos which is dangerous to your health. Protect your eyes from spouts of liquid and sprung components by wearing a pair of protective goggles **(see illustration 1.6)**.

1.6 A fire extinguisher, goggles, mask and protective gloves should be at hand in the workshop

● Protect your hands from contact with solvents, fuel and oils by wearing rubber gloves. Alternatively apply a barrier cream to your hands before starting work. If handling hot components or fluids, wear suitable gloves to protect your hands from scalding and burns.

What to do with old fluids

● Old cleaning solvent, fuel, coolant and oils should not be poured down domestic drains or onto the ground. Package the fluid up in old oil containers, label it accordingly, and take it to a garage or disposal facility. Contact your local authority for location of such sites or ring the oil care hotline.

OIL CARE

Note: It is antisocial and illegal to dump oil down the drain. To find the location of your local oil recycling bank in the UK, call 03708 506 506 or visit www.oilbankline.org.uk

In the USA, note that any oil supplier must accept used oil for recycling.

2 Fasteners - screws, bolts and nuts

Fastener types and applications

Bolts and screws

● Fastener head types are either of hexagonal, Torx or splined design, with internal and external versions of each type (see illustrations 2.1 and 2.2); splined head fasteners are not in common use on motorcycles. The conventional slotted or Phillips head design is used for certain screws. Bolt or screw length is always measured from the underside of the head to the end of the item (see illustration 2.11).

2.1 Internal hexagon/Allen (A), Torx (B) and splined (C) fasteners, with corresponding bits

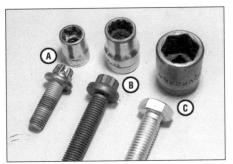

2.2 External Torx (A), splined (B) and hexagon (C) fasteners, with corresponding sockets

● Certain fasteners on the motorcycle have a tensile marking on their heads, the higher the marking the stronger the fastener. High tensile fasteners generally carry a 10 or higher marking. Never replace a high tensile fastener with one of a lower tensile strength.

Washers (see illustration 2.3)

● Plain washers are used between a fastener head and a component to prevent damage to the component or to spread the load when torque is applied. Plain washers can also be used as spacers or shims in certain assemblies. Copper or aluminium plain washers are often used as sealing washers on drain plugs.

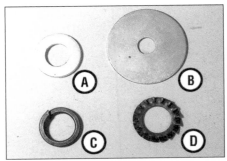

2.3 Plain washer (A), penny washer (B), spring washer (C) and serrated washer (D)

● The split-ring spring washer works by applying axial tension between the fastener head and component. If flattened, it is fatigued and must be renewed. If a plain (flat) washer is used on the fastener, position the spring washer between the fastener and the plain washer.

● Serrated star type washers dig into the fastener and component faces, preventing loosening. They are often used on electrical earth (ground) connections to the frame.

● Cone type washers (sometimes called Belleville) are conical and when tightened apply axial tension between the fastener head and component. They must be installed with the dished side against the component and often carry an OUTSIDE marking on their outer face. If flattened, they are fatigued and must be renewed.

● Tab washers are used to lock plain nuts or bolts on a shaft. A portion of the tab washer is bent up hard against one flat of the nut or bolt to prevent it loosening. Due to the tab washer being deformed in use, a new tab washer should be used every time it is disturbed.

● Wave washers are used to take up endfloat on a shaft. They provide light springing and prevent excessive side-to-side play of a component. Can be found on rocker arm shafts.

Nuts and split pins

● Conventional plain nuts are usually six-sided (see illustration 2.4). They are sized by thread diameter and pitch. High tensile nuts carry a number on one end to denote their tensile strength.

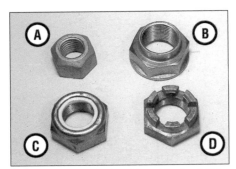

2.4 Plain nut (A), shouldered locknut (B), nylon insert nut (C) and castellated nut (D)

● Self-locking nuts either have a nylon insert, or two spring metal tabs, or a shoulder which is staked into a groove in the shaft - their advantage over conventional plain nuts is a resistance to loosening due to vibration. The nylon insert type can be used a number of times, but must be renewed when the friction of the nylon insert is reduced, ie when the nut spins freely on the shaft. The spring tab type can be reused unless the tabs are damaged. The shouldered type must be renewed every time it is disturbed.

● Split pins (cotter pins) are used to lock a castellated nut to a shaft or to prevent slackening of a plain nut. Common applications are wheel axles and brake torque arms. Because the split pin arms are deformed to lock around the nut a new split pin must always be used on installation - always fit the correct size split pin which will fit snugly in the shaft hole. Make sure the split pin arms are correctly located around the nut (see illustrations 2.5 and 2.6).

2.5 Bend split pin (cotter pin) arms as shown (arrows) to secure a castellated nut

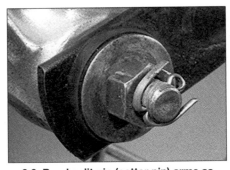

2.6 Bend split pin (cotter pin) arms as shown to secure a plain nut

Caution: If the castellated nut slots do not align with the shaft hole after tightening to the torque setting, tighten the nut until the next slot aligns with the hole - never slacken the nut to align its slot.

● R-pins (shaped like the letter R), or slip pins as they are sometimes called, are sprung and can be reused if they are otherwise in good condition. Always install R-pins with their closed end facing forwards (see illustration 2.7).

2.7 Correct fitting of R-pin. Arrow indicates forward direction

Circlips (see illustration 2.8)

● Circlips (sometimes called snap-rings) are used to retain components on a shaft or in a housing and have corresponding external or internal ears to permit removal. Parallel-sided (machined) circlips can be installed either way round in their groove, whereas stamped circlips (which have a chamfered edge on one face) must be installed with the chamfer facing away from the direction of thrust load **(see illustration 2.9)**.

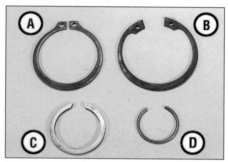

2.8 External stamped circlip (A), internal stamped circlip (B), machined circlip (C) and wire circlip (D)

● Always use circlip pliers to remove and install circlips; expand or compress them just enough to remove them. After installation, rotate the circlip in its groove to ensure it is securely seated. If installing a circlip on a splined shaft, always align its opening with a shaft channel to ensure the circlip ends are well supported and unlikely to catch **(see illustration 2.10)**.

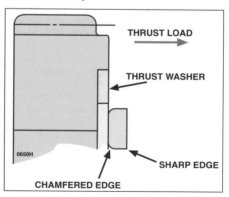

2.9 Correct fitting of a stamped circlip

THRUST LOAD

THRUST WASHER

SHARP EDGE

CHAMFERED EDGE

0650H

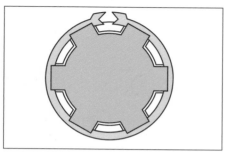

2.10 Align circlip opening with shaft channel

● Circlips can wear due to the thrust of components and become loose in their grooves, with the subsequent danger of becoming dislodged in operation. For this reason, renewal is advised every time a circlip is disturbed.
● Wire circlips are commonly used as piston pin retaining clips. If a removal tang is provided, long-nosed pliers can be used to dislodge them, otherwise careful use of a small flat-bladed screwdriver is necessary. Wire circlips should be renewed every time they are disturbed.

Thread diameter and pitch

● Diameter of a male thread (screw, bolt or stud) is the outside diameter of the threaded portion **(see illustration 2.11)**. Most motorcycle manufacturers use the ISO (International Standards Organisation) metric system expressed in millimetres, eg M6 refers to a 6 mm diameter thread. Sizing is the same for nuts, except that the thread diameter is measured across the valleys of the nut.
● Pitch is the distance between the peaks of the thread **(see illustration 2.11)**. It is expressed in millimetres, thus a common bolt size may be expressed as 6.0 x 1.0 mm (6 mm thread diameter and 1 mm pitch). Generally pitch increases in proportion to thread diameter, although there are always exceptions.
● Thread diameter and pitch are related for conventional fastener applications and the accompanying table can be used as a guide. Additionally, the AF (Across Flats), spanner or socket size dimension of the bolt or nut **(see illustration 2.11)** is linked to thread and pitch specification. Thread pitch can be measured with a thread gauge **(see illustration 2.12)**.

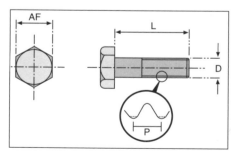

AF

L

D

P

2.11 Fastener length (L), thread diameter (D), thread pitch (P) and head size (AF)

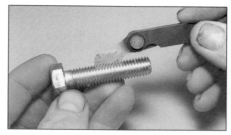

2.12 Using a thread gauge to measure pitch

AF size	Thread diameter x pitch (mm)
8 mm	M5 x 0.8
8 mm	M6 x 1.0
10 mm	M6 x 1.0
12 mm	M8 x 1.25
14 mm	M10 x 1.25
17 mm	M12 x 1.25

● The threads of most fasteners are of the right-hand type, ie they are turned clockwise to tighten and anti-clockwise to loosen. The reverse situation applies to left-hand thread fasteners, which are turned anti-clockwise to tighten and clockwise to loosen. Left-hand threads are used where rotation of a component might loosen a conventional right-hand thread fastener.

Seized fasteners

● Corrosion of external fasteners due to water or reaction between two dissimilar metals can occur over a period of time. It will build up sooner in wet conditions or in countries where salt is used on the roads during the winter. If a fastener is severely corroded it is likely that normal methods of removal will fail and result in its head being ruined. When you attempt removal, the fastener thread should be heard to crack free and unscrew easily - if it doesn't, stop there before damaging something.
● A smart tap on the head of the fastener will often succeed in breaking free corrosion which has occurred in the threads **(see illustration 2.13)**.
● An aerosol penetrating fluid (such as WD-40) applied the night beforehand may work its way down into the thread and ease removal. Depending on the location, you may be able to make up a Plasticine well around the fastener head and fill it with penetrating fluid.

2.13 A sharp tap on the head of a fastener will often break free a corroded thread

● If you are working on an engine internal component, corrosion will most likely not be a problem due to the well lubricated environment. However, components can be very tight and an impact driver is a useful tool in freeing them **(see illustration 2.14)**.

2.14 Using an impact driver to free a fastener

● Where corrosion has occurred between dissimilar metals (eg steel and aluminium alloy), the application of heat to the fastener head will create a disproportionate expansion rate between the two metals and break the seizure caused by the corrosion. Whether heat can be applied depends on the location of the fastener - any surrounding components likely to be damaged must first be removed **(see illustration 2.15)**. Heat can be applied using a paint stripper heat gun or clothes iron, or by immersing the component in boiling water - wear protective gloves to prevent scalding or burns to the hands.

2.15 Using heat to free a seized fastener

● As a last resort, it is possible to use a hammer and cold chisel to work the fastener head unscrewed **(see illustration 2.16)**. This will damage the fastener, but more importantly extreme care must be taken not to damage the surrounding component.

Caution: Remember that the component being secured is generally of more value than the bolt, nut or screw - when the fastener is freed, do not unscrew it with force, instead work the fastener back and forth when resistance is felt to prevent thread damage.

2.16 Using a hammer and chisel to free a seized fastener

Broken fasteners and damaged heads

● If the shank of a broken bolt or screw is accessible you can grip it with self-locking grips. The knurled wheel type stud extractor tool or self-gripping stud puller tool is particularly useful for removing the long studs which screw into the cylinder mouth surface of the crankcase or bolts and screws from which the head has broken off **(see illustration 2.17)**. Studs can also be removed by locking two nuts together on the threaded end of the stud and using a spanner on the lower nut **(see illustration 2.18)**.

2.17 Using a stud extractor tool to remove a broken crankcase stud

2.18 Two nuts can be locked together to unscrew a stud from a component

● A bolt or screw which has broken off below or level with the casing must be extracted using a screw extractor set. Centre punch the fastener to centralise the drill bit, then drill a hole in the fastener **(see illustration 2.19)**. Select a drill bit which is approximately half to three-quarters the diameter of the fastener

2.19 When using a screw extractor, first drill a hole in the fastener . . .

and drill to a depth which will accommodate the extractor. Use the largest size extractor possible, but avoid leaving too small a wall thickness otherwise the extractor will merely force the fastener walls outwards wedging it in the casing thread.

● If a spiral type extractor is used, thread it anti-clockwise into the fastener. As it is screwed in, it will grip the fastener and unscrew it from the casing **(see illustration 2.20)**.

2.20 . . . then thread the extractor anti-clockwise into the fastener

● If a taper type extractor is used, tap it into the fastener so that it is firmly wedged in place. Unscrew the extractor (anti-clockwise) to draw the fastener out.

⚠ *Warning: Stud extractors are very hard and may break off in the fastener if care is not taken - ask an engineer about spark erosion if this happens.*

● Alternatively, the broken bolt/screw can be drilled out and the hole retapped for an oversize bolt/screw or a diamond-section thread insert. It is essential that the drilling is carried out squarely and to the correct depth, otherwise the casing may be ruined - if in doubt, entrust the work to an engineer.

● Bolts and nuts with rounded corners cause the correct size spanner or socket to slip when force is applied. Of the types of spanner/socket available always use a six-point type rather than an eight or twelve-point type - better grip

2.21 Comparison of surface drive ring spanner (left) with 12-point type (right)

is obtained. Surface drive spanners grip the middle of the hex flats, rather than the corners, and are thus good in cases of damaged heads **(see illustration 2.21)**.

● Slotted-head or Phillips-head screws are often damaged by the use of the wrong size screwdriver. Allen-head and Torx-head screws are much less likely to sustain damage. If enough of the screw head is exposed you can use a hacksaw to cut a slot in its head and then use a conventional flat-bladed screwdriver to remove it. Alternatively use a hammer and cold chisel to tap the head of the fastener around to slacken it. Always replace damaged fasteners with new ones, preferably Torx or Allen-head type.

HAYNES
HiNT

A dab of valve grinding compound between the screw head and screwdriver tip will often give a good grip.

Thread repair

● Threads (particularly those in aluminium alloy components) can be damaged by overtightening, being assembled with dirt in the threads, or from a component working loose and vibrating. Eventually the thread will fail completely, and it will be impossible to tighten the fastener.

● If a thread is damaged or clogged with old locking compound it can be renovated with a thread repair tool (thread chaser) **(see illustrations 2.22 and 2.23)**; special thread

2.22 A thread repair tool being used to correct an internal thread

2.23 A thread repair tool being used to correct an external thread

chasers are available for spark plug hole threads. The tool will not cut a new thread, but clean and true the original thread. Make sure that you use the correct diameter and pitch tool. Similarly, external threads can be cleaned up with a die or a thread restorer file **(see illustration 2.24)**.

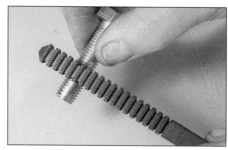

2.24 Using a thread restorer file

● It is possible to drill out the old thread and retap the component to the next thread size. This will work where there is enough surrounding material and a new bolt or screw can be obtained. Sometimes, however, this is not possible - such as where the bolt/screw passes through another component which must also be suitably modified, also in cases where a spark plug or oil drain plug cannot be obtained in a larger diameter thread size.

● The diamond-section thread insert (often known by its popular trade name of Heli-Coil) is a simple and effective method of renewing the thread and retaining the original size. A kit can be purchased which contains the tap, insert and installing tool **(see illustration 2.25)**. Drill out the damaged thread with the size drill specified **(see illustration 2.26)**. Carefully retap the thread **(see illustration 2.27)**. Install the

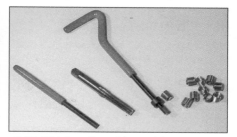

2.25 Obtain a thread insert kit to suit the thread diameter and pitch required

2.26 To install a thread insert, first drill out the original thread . . .

2.27 . . . tap a new thread . . .

2.28 . . . fit insert on the installing tool . . .

2.29 . . . and thread into the component . . .

2.30 . . . break off the tang when complete

insert on the installing tool and thread it slowly into place using a light downward pressure **(see illustrations 2.28 and 2.29)**. When positioned between a 1/4 and 1/2 turn below the surface withdraw the installing tool and use the break-off tool to press down on the tang, breaking it off **(see illustration 2.30)**.

● There are epoxy thread repair kits on the market which can rebuild stripped internal threads, although this repair should not be used on high load-bearing components.

Thread locking and sealing compounds

● Locking compounds are used in locations where the fastener is prone to loosening due to vibration or on important safety-related items which might cause loss of control of the motorcycle if they fail. It is also used where important fasteners cannot be secured by other means such as lockwashers or split pins.

● Before applying locking compound, make sure that the threads (internal and external) are clean and dry with all old compound removed. Select a compound to suit the component being secured - a non-permanent general locking and sealing type is suitable for most applications, but a high strength type is needed for permanent fixing of studs in castings. Apply a drop or two of the compound to the first few threads of the fastener, then thread it into place and tighten to the specified torque. Do not apply excessive thread locking compound otherwise the thread may be damaged on subsequent removal.

● Certain fasteners are impregnated with a dry film type coating of locking compound on their threads. Always renew this type of fastener if disturbed.

● Anti-seize compounds, such as copper-based greases, can be applied to protect threads from seizure due to extreme heat and corrosion. A common instance is spark plug threads and exhaust system fasteners.

3 Measuring tools and gauges

Feeler gauges

● Feeler gauges (or blades) are used for measuring small gaps and clearances (see illustration 3.1). They can also be used to measure endfloat (sideplay) of a component on a shaft where access is not possible with a dial gauge.

● Feeler gauge sets should be treated with care and not bent or damaged. They are etched with their size on one face. Keep them clean and very lightly oiled to prevent corrosion build-up.

3.1 Feeler gauges are used for measuring small gaps and clearances - thickness is marked on one face of gauge

● When measuring a clearance, select a gauge which is a light sliding fit between the two components. You may need to use two gauges together to measure the clearance accurately.

Micrometers

● A micrometer is a precision tool capable of measuring to 0.01 or 0.001 of a millimetre. It should always be stored in its case and not in the general toolbox. It must be kept clean and never dropped, otherwise its frame or measuring anvils could be distorted resulting in inaccurate readings.

● External micrometers are used for measuring outside diameters of components and have many more applications than internal micrometers. Micrometers are available in different size ranges, eg 0 to 25 mm, 25 to 50 mm, and upwards in 25 mm steps; some large micrometers have interchangeable anvils to allow a range of measurements to be taken. Generally the largest precision measurement you are likely to take on a motorcycle is the piston diameter.

● Internal micrometers (or bore micrometers) are used for measuring inside diameters, such as valve guides and cylinder bores. Telescoping gauges and small hole gauges are used in conjunction with an external micrometer, whereas the more expensive internal micrometers have their own measuring device.

External micrometer

Note: *The conventional analogue type instrument is described. Although much easier to read, digital micrometers are considerably more expensive.*

● Always check the calibration of the micrometer before use. With the anvils closed (0 to 25 mm type) or set over a test gauge

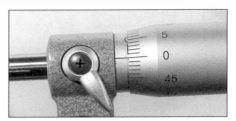

3.2 Check micrometer calibration before use

(for the larger types) the scale should read zero (see illustration 3.2); make sure that the anvils (and test piece) are clean first. Any discrepancy can be adjusted by referring to the instructions supplied with the tool. Remember that the micrometer is a precision measuring tool - don't force the anvils closed, use the ratchet (4) on the end of the micrometer to close it. In this way, a measured force is always applied.

● To use, first make sure that the item being measured is clean. Place the anvil of the micrometer (1) against the item and use the thimble (2) to bring the spindle (3) lightly into contact with the other side of the item (see illustration 3.3). Don't tighten the thimble down because this will damage the micrometer - instead use the ratchet (4) on the end of the micrometer. The ratchet mechanism applies a measured force preventing damage to the instrument.

● The micrometer is read by referring to the linear scale on the sleeve and the annular scale on the thimble. Read off the sleeve first to obtain the base measurement, then add the fine measurement from the thimble to obtain the overall reading. The linear scale on the sleeve represents the measuring range of the micrometer (eg 0 to 25 mm). The annular scale

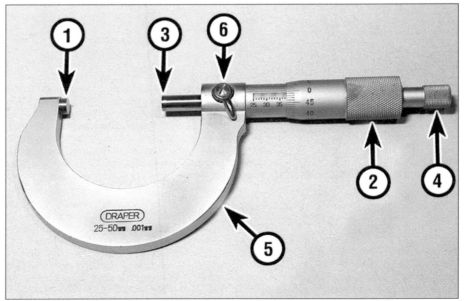

3.3 Micrometer component parts

1	Anvil	3	Spindle	5	Frame
2	Thimble	4	Ratchet	6	Locking lever

on the thimble will be in graduations of 0.01 mm (or as marked on the frame) - one full revolution of the thimble will move 0.5 mm on the linear scale. Take the reading where the datum line on the sleeve intersects the thimble's scale. Always position the eye directly above the scale otherwise an inaccurate reading will result.

In the example shown the item measures 2.95 mm (see illustration 3.4):

Linear scale	2.00 mm
Linear scale	0.50 mm
Annular scale	0.45 mm
Total figure	2.95 mm

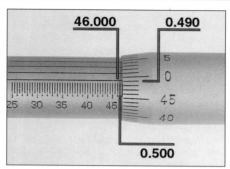

3.5 Micrometer reading of 46.99 mm on linear and annular scales . . .

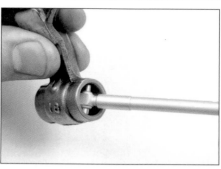

3.7 Expand the telescoping gauge in the bore, lock its position . . .

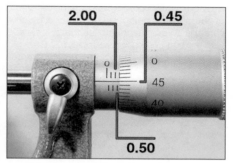

3.4 Micrometer reading of 2.95 mm

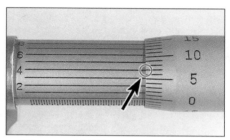

3.6 . . . and 0.004 mm on vernier scale

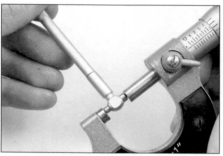

3.8 . . . then measure the gauge with a micrometer

Most micrometers have a locking lever (6) on the frame to hold the setting in place, allowing the item to be removed from the micrometer.

● Some micrometers have a vernier scale on their sleeve, providing an even finer measurement to be taken, in 0.001 increments of a millimetre. Take the sleeve and thimble measurement as described above, then check which graduation on the vernier scale aligns with that of the annular scale on the thimble **Note:** *The eye must be perpendicular to the scale when taking the vernier reading - if necessary rotate the body of the micrometer to ensure this.* Multiply the vernier scale figure by 0.001 and add it to the base and fine measurement figures.

In the example shown the item measures 46.994 mm (see illustrations 3.5 and 3.6):

Linear scale (base)	46.000 mm
Linear scale (base)	00.500 mm
Annular scale (fine)	00.490 mm
Vernier scale	00.004 mm
Total figure	46.994 mm

Internal micrometer

● Internal micrometers are available for measuring bore diameters, but are expensive and unlikely to be available for home use. It is suggested that a set of telescoping gauges and small hole gauges, both of which must be used with an external micrometer, will suffice for taking internal measurements on a motorcycle.

● Telescoping gauges can be used to measure internal diameters of components. Select a gauge with the correct size range, make sure its ends are clean and insert it into the bore. Expand the gauge, then lock its position and withdraw it from the bore (see illustration 3.7). Measure across the gauge ends with a micrometer (see illustration 3.8).

● Very small diameter bores (such as valve guides) are measured with a small hole gauge. Once adjusted to a slip-fit inside the component, its position is locked and the gauge withdrawn for measurement with a micrometer (see illustrations 3.9 and 3.10).

Vernier caliper

Note: *The conventional linear and dial gauge type instruments are described. Digital types are easier to read, but are far more expensive.*

● The vernier caliper does not provide the precision of a micrometer, but is versatile in being able to measure internal and external diameters. Some types also incorporate a depth gauge. It is ideal for measuring clutch plate friction material and spring free lengths.

● To use the conventional linear scale vernier, slacken off the vernier clamp screws (1) and set its jaws over (2), or inside (3), the item to be measured (see illustration 3.11). Slide the jaw into contact, using the thumb-wheel (4) for fine movement of the sliding scale (5) then tighten the clamp screws (1). Read off the main scale (6) where the zero on the sliding scale (5) intersects it, taking the whole number to the left of the zero; this provides the base measurement. View along the sliding scale and select the division which

3.9 Expand the small hole gauge in the bore, lock its position . . .

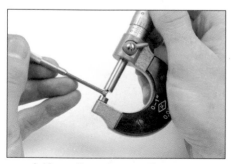

3.10 . . . then measure the gauge with a micrometer

lines up exactly with any of the divisions on the main scale, noting that the divisions usually represents 0.02 of a millimetre. Add this fine measurement to the base measurement to obtain the total reading.

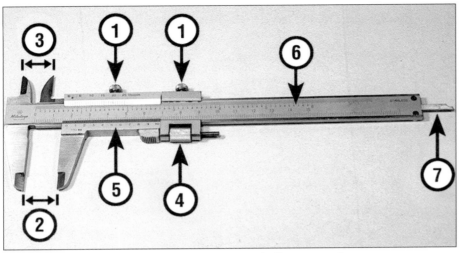

3.11 Vernier component parts (linear gauge)

1 Clamp screws	3 Internal jaws	5 Sliding scale	7 Depth gauge
2 External jaws	4 Thumbwheel	6 Main scale	

In the example shown the item measures 55.92 mm **(see illustration 3.12)**:

Base measurement	55.00 mm
Fine measurement	00.92 mm
Total figure	55.92 mm

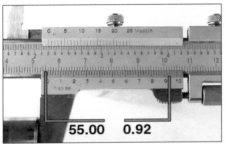

3.12 Vernier gauge reading of 55.92 mm

● Some vernier calipers are equipped with a dial gauge for fine measurement. Before use, check that the jaws are clean, then close them fully and check that the dial gauge reads zero. If necessary adjust the gauge ring accordingly. Slacken the vernier clamp screw (1) and set its jaws over (2), or inside (3), the item to be measured **(see illustration 3.13)**. Slide the jaws into contact, using the thumbwheel (4) for fine movement. Read off the main scale (5) where the edge of the sliding scale (6) intersects it, taking the whole number to the left of the zero; this provides the base measurement. Read off the needle position on the dial gauge (7) scale to provide the fine measurement; each division represents 0.05 of a millimetre. Add this fine measurement to the base measurement to obtain the total reading.

In the example shown the item measures 55.95 mm **(see illustration 3.14)**:

Base measurement	55.00 mm
Fine measurement	00.95 mm
Total figure	55.95 mm

3.14 Vernier gauge reading of 55.95 mm

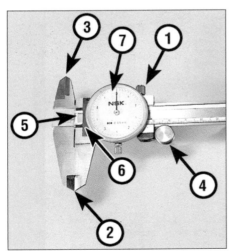

3.13 Vernier component parts (dial gauge)

1 Clamp screw	5 Main scale
2 External jaws	6 Sliding scale
3 Internal jaws	7 Dial gauge
4 Thumbwheel	

Plastigauge

● Plastigauge is a plastic material which can be compressed between two surfaces to measure the oil clearance between them. The width of the compressed Plastigauge is measured against a calibrated scale to determine the clearance.

● Common uses of Plastigauge are for measuring the clearance between crankshaft journal and main bearing inserts, between crankshaft journal and big-end bearing inserts, and between camshaft and bearing surfaces. The following example describes big-end oil clearance measurement.

● Handle the Plastigauge material carefully to prevent distortion. Using a sharp knife, cut a length which corresponds with the width of the bearing being measured and place it carefully across the journal so that it is parallel with the shaft **(see illustration 3.15)**. Carefully install both bearing shells and the connecting rod. Without rotating the rod on the journal tighten its bolts or nuts (as applicable) to the specified torque. The connecting rod and bearings are then disassembled and the crushed Plastigauge examined.

3.15 Plastigauge placed across shaft journal

● Using the scale provided in the Plastigauge kit, measure the width of the material to determine the oil clearance **(see illustration 3.16)**. Always remove all traces of Plastigauge after use using your fingernails.

Caution: Arriving at the correct clearance demands that the assembly is torqued correctly, according to the settings and sequence (where applicable) provided by the motorcycle manufacturer.

3.16 Measuring the width of the crushed Plastigauge

Dial gauge or DTI (Dial Test Indicator)

● A dial gauge can be used to accurately measure small amounts of movement. Typical uses are measuring shaft runout or shaft endfloat (sideplay) and setting piston position for ignition timing on two-strokes. A dial gauge set usually comes with a range of different probes and adapters and mounting equipment.

● The gauge needle must point to zero when at rest. Rotate the ring around its periphery to zero the gauge.

● Check that the gauge is capable of reading the extent of movement in the work. Most gauges have a small dial set in the face which records whole millimetres of movement as well as the fine scale around the face periphery which is calibrated in 0.01 mm divisions. Read off the small dial first to obtain the base measurement, then add the measurement from the fine scale to obtain the total reading.

In the example shown the gauge reads 1.48 mm (see illustration 3.17):

Base measurement	1.00 mm
Fine measurement	0.48 mm
Total figure	1.48 mm

3.17 Dial gauge reading of 1.48 mm

● If measuring shaft runout, the shaft must be supported in vee-blocks and the gauge mounted on a stand perpendicular to the shaft. Rest the tip of the gauge against the centre of the shaft and rotate the shaft slowly whilst watching the gauge reading (see illustration 3.18). Take several measurements along the length of the shaft and record the

3.18 Using a dial gauge to measure shaft runout

maximum gauge reading as the amount of runout in the shaft. **Note:** *The reading obtained will be total runout at that point - some manufacturers specify that the runout figure is halved to compare with their specified runout limit.*

● Endfloat (sideplay) measurement requires that the gauge is mounted securely to the surrounding component with its probe touching the end of the shaft. Using hand pressure, push and pull on the shaft noting the maximum endfloat recorded on the gauge **(see illustration 3.19)**.

3.19 Using a dial gauge to measure shaft endfloat

● A dial gauge with suitable adapters can be used to determine piston position BTDC on two-stroke engines for the purposes of ignition timing. The gauge, adapter and suitable length probe are installed in the place of the spark plug and the gauge zeroed at TDC. If the piston position is specified as 1.14 mm BTDC, rotate the engine back to 2.00 mm BTDC, then slowly forwards to 1.14 mm BTDC.

Cylinder compression gauges

● A compression gauge is used for measuring cylinder compression. Either the rubber-cone type or the threaded adapter type can be used. The latter is preferred to ensure a perfect seal against the cylinder head. A 0 to 300 psi (0 to 20 Bar) type gauge (for petrol/gasoline engines) will be suitable for motorcycles.

● The spark plug is removed and the gauge either held hard against the cylinder head (cone type) or the gauge adapter screwed into the cylinder head (threaded type) **(see illustration 3.20)**. Cylinder compression is measured with the engine turning over, but not running. The

3.20 Using a rubber-cone type cylinder compression gauge

gauge will hold the reading until manually released.

Oil pressure gauge

● An oil pressure gauge is used for measuring engine oil pressure. Most gauges come with a set of adapters to fit the thread of the take-off point **(see illustration 3.21)**. If the take-off point specified by the motorcycle manufacturer is an external oil pipe union, make sure that the specified replacement union is used to prevent oil starvation.

3.21 Oil pressure gauge and take-off point adapter (arrow)

● Oil pressure is measured with the engine running (at a specific rpm) and often the manufacturer will specify pressure limits for a cold and hot engine.

Straight-edge and surface plate

● If checking the gasket face of a component for warpage, place a steel rule or precision straight-edge across the gasket face and measure any gap between the straight-edge and component with feeler gauges **(see illustration 3.22)**. Check diagonally across the component and between mounting holes **(see illustration 3.23)**.

3.22 Use a straight-edge and feeler gauges to check for warpage

3.23 Check for warpage in these directions

● Checking individual components for warpage, such as clutch plain (metal) plates, requires a perfectly flat plate or piece or plate glass and feeler gauges.

4 Torque and leverage

What is torque?

● Torque describes the twisting force about a shaft. The amount of torque applied is determined by the distance from the centre of the shaft to the end of the lever and the amount of force being applied to the end of the lever; distance multiplied by force equals torque.

● The manufacturer applies a measured torque to a bolt or nut to ensure that it will not slacken in use and to hold two components securely together without movement in the joint. The actual torque setting depends on the thread size, bolt or nut material and the composition of the components being held.

● Too little torque may cause the fastener to loosen due to vibration, whereas too much torque will distort the joint faces of the component or cause the fastener to shear off. Always stick to the specified torque setting.

Using a torque wrench

● Check the calibration of the torque wrench and make sure it has a suitable range for the job. Torque wrenches are available in Nm (Newton-metres), kgf m (kilograms-force metre), lbf ft (pounds-feet), lbf in (inch-pounds). Do not confuse lbf ft with lbf in.

● Adjust the tool to the desired torque on the scale (see illustration 4.1). If your torque wrench is not calibrated in the units specified, carefully convert the figure (see Conversion Factors). A manufacturer sometimes gives a torque setting as a range (8 to 10 Nm) rather than a single figure - in this case set the tool midway between the two settings. The same torque may be expressed as 9 Nm ± 1 Nm. Some torque wrenches have a method of locking the setting so that it isn't inadvertently altered during use.

4.1 Set the torque wrench index mark to the setting required, in this case 12 Nm

● Install the bolts/nuts in their correct location and secure them lightly. Their threads must be clean and free of any old locking compound. Unless specified the threads and flange should be dry - oiled threads are necessary in certain circumstances and the manufacturer will take this into account in the specified torque figure. Similarly, the manufacturer may also specify the application of thread-locking compound.

● Tighten the fasteners in the specified sequence until the torque wrench clicks, indicating that the torque setting has been reached. Apply the torque again to double-check the setting. Where different diameter fasteners secure the component, as a rule tighten the larger diameter ones first.

● When the torque wrench has been finished with, release the lock (where applicable) and fully back off its setting to zero - do not leave the torque wrench tensioned. Also, do not use a torque wrench for slackening a fastener.

Angle-tightening

● Manufacturers often specify a figure in degrees for final tightening of a fastener. This usually follows tightening to a specific torque setting.

● A degree disc can be set and attached to the socket (see illustration 4.2) or a protractor can be used to mark the angle of movement on the bolt/nut head and the surrounding casting (see illustration 4.3).

4.2 Angle tightening can be accomplished with a torque-angle gauge . . .

4.3 . . . or by marking the angle on the surrounding component

Loosening sequences

● Where more than one bolt/nut secures a component, loosen each fastener evenly a little at a time. In this way, not all the stress of the joint is held by one fastener and the components are not likely to distort.

● If a tightening sequence is provided, work in the REVERSE of this, but if not, work from the outside in, in a criss-cross sequence (see illustration 4.4).

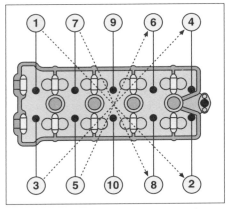

4.4 When slackening, work from the outside inwards

Tightening sequences

● If a component is held by more than one fastener it is important that the retaining bolts/nuts are tightened evenly to prevent uneven stress build-up and distortion of sealing faces. This is especially important on high-compression joints such as the cylinder head.

● A sequence is usually provided by the manufacturer, either in a diagram or actually marked in the casting. If not, always start in the centre and work outwards in a criss-cross pattern (see illustration 4.5). Start off by securing all bolts/nuts finger-tight, then set the torque wrench and tighten each fastener by a small amount in sequence until the final torque is reached. By following this practice,

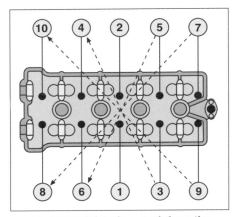

4.5 When tightening, work from the inside outwards

the joint will be held evenly and will not be distorted. Important joints, such as the cylinder head and big-end fasteners often have two- or three-stage torque settings.

Applying leverage

● Use tools at the correct angle. Position a socket wrench or spanner on the bolt/nut so that you pull it towards you when loosening. If this can't be done, push the spanner without curling your fingers around it **(see illustration 4.6)** - the spanner may slip or the fastener loosen suddenly, resulting in your fingers being crushed against a component.

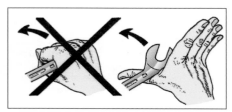

4.6 If you can't pull on the spanner to loosen a fastener, push with your hand open

● Additional leverage is gained by extending the length of the lever. The best way to do this is to use a breaker bar instead of the regular length tool, or to slip a length of tubing over the end of the spanner or socket wrench.
● If additional leverage will not work, the fastener head is either damaged or firmly corroded in place (see Fasteners).

5 Bearings

Bearing removal and installation

Drivers and sockets

● Before removing a bearing, always inspect the casing to see which way it must be driven out - some casings will have retaining plates or a cast step. Also check for any identifying markings on the bearing and if installed to a certain depth, measure this at this stage. Some roller bearings are sealed on one side - take note of the original fitted position.
● Bearings can be driven out of a casing using a bearing driver tool (with the correct size head) or a socket of the correct diameter. Select the driver head or socket so that it contacts the outer race of the bearing, not the balls/rollers or inner race. Always support the casing around the bearing housing with wood blocks, otherwise there is a risk of fracture. The bearing is driven out with a few blows on the driver or socket from a heavy mallet. Unless access is severely restricted (as with wheel bearings), a pin-punch is not recommended unless it is moved around the bearing to keep it square in its housing.

● The same equipment can be used to install bearings. Make sure the bearing housing is supported on wood blocks and line up the bearing in its housing. Fit the bearing as noted on removal - generally they are installed with their marked side facing outwards. Tap the bearing squarely into its housing using a driver or socket which bears only on the bearing's outer race - contact with the bearing balls/rollers or inner race will destroy it **(see illustrations 5.1 and 5.2)**.
● Check that the bearing inner race and balls/rollers rotate freely.

5.1 Using a bearing driver against the bearing's outer race

5.2 Using a large socket against the bearing's outer race

Pullers and slide-hammers

● Where a bearing is pressed on a shaft a puller will be required to extract it **(see illustration 5.3)**. Make sure that the puller clamp or legs fit securely behind the bearing and are unlikely to slip out. If pulling a bearing

5.3 This bearing puller clamps behind the bearing and pressure is applied to the shaft end to draw the bearing off

off a gear shaft for example, you may have to locate the puller behind a gear pinion if there is no access to the race and draw the gear pinion off the shaft as well **(see illustration 5.4)**.

> *Caution: Ensure that the puller's centre bolt locates securely against the end of the shaft and will not slip when pressure is applied. Also ensure that puller does not damage the shaft end.*

5.4 Where no access is available to the rear of the bearing, it is sometimes possible to draw off the adjacent component

● Operate the puller so that its centre bolt exerts pressure on the shaft end and draws the bearing off the shaft.
● When installing the bearing on the shaft, tap only on the bearing's inner race - contact with the balls/rollers or outer race with destroy the bearing. Use a socket or length of tubing as a drift which fits over the shaft end **(see illustration 5.5)**.

5.5 When installing a bearing on a shaft use a piece of tubing which bears only on the bearing's inner race

● Where a bearing locates in a blind hole in a casing, it cannot be driven or pulled out as described above. A slide-hammer with knife-edged bearing puller attachment will be required. The puller attachment passes through the bearing and when tightened expands to fit firmly behind the bearing **(see illustration 5.6)**. By operating the slide-hammer part of the tool the bearing is jarred out of its housing **(see illustration 5.7)**.
● It is possible, if the bearing is of reasonable weight, for it to drop out of its housing if the casing is heated as described opposite.

5.6 Expand the bearing puller so that it locks behind the bearing . . .

5.7 . . . attach the slide hammer to the bearing puller

If this method is attempted, first prepare a work surface which will enable the casing to be tapped face down to help dislodge the bearing - a wood surface is ideal since it will not damage the casing's gasket surface. Wearing protective gloves, tap the heated casing several times against the work surface to dislodge the bearing under its own weight **(see illustration 5.8)**.

5.8 Tapping a casing face down on wood blocks can often dislodge a bearing

● Bearings can be installed in blind holes using the driver or socket method described above.

Drawbolts

● Where a bearing or bush is set in the eye of a component, such as a suspension linkage arm or connecting rod small-end, removal by drift may damage the component. Furthermore, a rubber bushing in a shock absorber eye cannot successfully be driven out of position. If access is available to a engineering press, the task is straightforward. If not, a drawbolt can be fabricated to extract the bearing or bush.

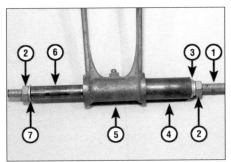

5.9 Drawbolt component parts assembled on a suspension arm

1 Bolt or length of threaded bar
2 Nuts
3 Washer (external diameter greater than tubing internal diameter)
4 Tubing (internal diameter sufficient to accommodate bearing)
5 Suspension arm with bearing
6 Tubing (external diameter slightly smaller than bearing)
7 Washer (external diameter slightly smaller than bearing)

5.10 Drawing the bearing out of the suspension arm

● To extract the bearing/bush you will need a long bolt with nut (or piece of threaded bar with two nuts), a piece of tubing which has an internal diameter larger than the bearing/bush, another piece of tubing which has an external diameter slightly smaller than the bearing/bush, and a selection of washers **(see illustrations 5.9 and 5.10)**. Note that the pieces of tubing must be of the same length, or longer, than the bearing/bush.
● The same kit (without the pieces of tubing) can be used to draw the new bearing/bush back into place **(see illustration 5.11)**.

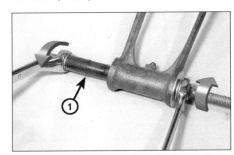

5.11 Installing a new bearing (1) in the suspension arm

Temperature change

● If the bearing's outer race is a tight fit in the casing, the aluminium casing can be heated to release its grip on the bearing. Aluminium will expand at a greater rate than the steel bearing outer race. There are several ways to do this, but avoid any localised extreme heat (such as a blow torch) - aluminium alloy has a low melting point.
● Approved methods of heating a casing are using a domestic oven (heated to 100°C) or immersing the casing in boiling water **(see illustration 5.12)**. Low temperature range localised heat sources such as a paint stripper heat gun or clothes iron can also be used **(see illustration 5.13)**. Alternatively, soak a rag in boiling water, wring it out and wrap it around the bearing housing.

> ⚠️ **Warning: All of these methods require care in use to prevent scalding and burns to the hands. Wear protective gloves when handling hot components.**

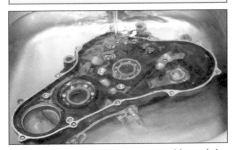

5.12 A casing can be immersed in a sink of boiling water to aid bearing removal

5.13 Using a localised heat source to aid bearing removal

● If heating the whole casing note that plastic components, such as the neutral switch, may suffer - remove them beforehand.
● After heating, remove the bearing as described above. You may find that the expansion is sufficient for the bearing to fall out of the casing under its own weight or with a light tap on the driver or socket.
● If necessary, the casing can be heated to aid bearing installation, and this is sometimes the recommended procedure if the motorcycle manufacturer has designed the housing and bearing fit with this intention.

● Installation of bearings can be eased by placing them in a freezer the night before installation. The steel bearing will contract slightly, allowing easy insertion in its housing. This is often useful when installing steering head outer races in the frame.

Bearing types and markings

● Plain shell bearings, ball bearings, needle roller bearings and tapered roller bearings will all be found on motorcycles **(see illustrations 5.14 and 5.15)**. The ball and roller types are usually caged between an inner and outer race, but uncaged variations may be found.

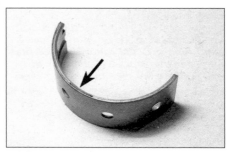

5.14 Shell bearings are either plain or grooved. They are usually identified by colour code (arrow)

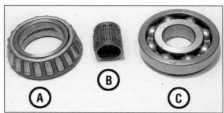

5.15 Tapered roller bearing (A), needle roller bearing (B) and ball journal bearing (C)

● Shell bearings (often called inserts) are usually found at the crankshaft main and connecting rod big-end where they are good at coping with high loads. They are made of a phosphor-bronze material and are impregnated with self-lubricating properties.

● Ball bearings and needle roller bearings consist of a steel inner and outer race with the balls or rollers between the races. They require constant lubrication by oil or grease and are good at coping with axial loads. Taper roller bearings consist of rollers set in a tapered cage set on the inner race; the outer race is separate. They are good at coping with axial loads and prevent movement along the shaft - a typical application is in the steering head.

● Bearing manufacturers produce bearings to ISO size standards and stamp one face of the bearing to indicate its internal and external diameter, load capacity and type **(see illustration 5.16)**.

● Metal bushes are usually of phosphor-bronze material. Rubber bushes are used in suspension mounting eyes. Fibre bushes have also been used in suspension pivots.

5.16 Typical bearing marking

Bearing fault finding

● If a bearing outer race has spun in its housing, the housing material will be damaged. You can use a bearing locking compound to bond the outer race in place if damage is not too severe.

● Shell bearings will fail due to damage of their working surface, as a result of lack of lubrication, corrosion or abrasive particles in the oil **(see illustration 5.17)**. Small particles of dirt in the oil may embed in the bearing material whereas larger particles will score the bearing and shaft journal. If a number of short journeys are made, insufficient heat will be generated to drive off condensation which has built up on the bearings.

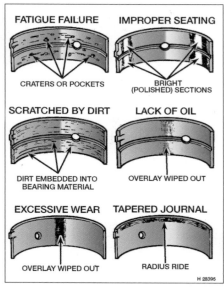

5.17 Typical bearing failures

● Ball and roller bearings will fail due to lack of lubrication or damage to the balls or rollers. Tapered-roller bearings can be damaged by overloading them. Unless the bearing is sealed on both sides, wash it in paraffin (kerosene) to remove all old grease then allow it to dry. Make a visual inspection looking to dented balls or rollers, damaged cages and worn or pitted races **(see illustration 5.18)**.

● A ball bearing can be checked for wear by listening to it when spun. Apply a film of light oil to the bearing and hold it close to the ear - hold the outer race with one hand and spin the

5.18 Example of ball journal bearing with damaged balls and cages

5.19 Hold outer race and listen to inner race when spun

inner race with the other hand **(see illustration 5.19)**. The bearing should be almost silent when spun; if it grates or rattles it is worn.

6 Oil seals

Oil seal removal and installation

● Oil seals should be renewed every time a component is dismantled. This is because the seal lips will become set to the sealing surface and will not necessarily reseal.

● Oil seals can be prised out of position using a large flat-bladed screwdriver **(see illustration 6.1)**. In the case of crankcase seals, check first that the seal is not lipped on the inside, preventing its removal with the crankcases joined.

6.1 Prise out oil seals with a large flat-bladed screwdriver

● New seals are usually installed with their marked face (containing the seal reference code) outwards and the spring side towards the fluid being retained. In certain cases, such as a two-stroke engine crankshaft seal, a double lipped seal may be used due to there being fluid or gas on each side of the joint.

• Use a bearing driver or socket which bears only on the outer hard edge of the seal to install it in the casing - tapping on the inner edge will damage the sealing lip.

Oil seal types and markings

• Oil seals are usually of the single-lipped type. Double-lipped seals are found where a liquid or gas is on both sides of the joint.

• Oil seals can harden and lose their sealing ability if the motorcycle has been in storage for a long period - renewal is the only solution.

• Oil seal manufacturers also conform to the ISO markings for seal size - these are moulded into the outer face of the seal **(see illustration 6.2)**.

6.2 These oil seal markings indicate inside diameter, outside diameter and seal thickness

7 Gaskets and sealants

Types of gasket and sealant

• Gaskets are used to seal the mating surfaces between components and keep lubricants, fluids, vacuum or pressure contained within the assembly. Aluminium gaskets are sometimes found at the cylinder joints, but most gaskets are paper-based. If the mating surfaces of the components being joined are undamaged the gasket can be installed dry, although a dab of sealant or grease will be useful to hold it in place during assembly.

• RTV (Room Temperature Vulcanising) silicone rubber sealants cure when exposed to moisture in the atmosphere. These sealants are good at filling pits or irregular gasket faces, but will tend to be forced out of the joint under very high torque. They can be used to replace a paper gasket, but first make sure that the width of the paper gasket is not essential to the shimming of internal components. RTV sealants should not be used on components containing petrol (gasoline).

• Non-hardening, semi-hardening and hard setting liquid gasket compounds can be used with a gasket or between a metal-to-metal joint. Select the sealant to suit the application: universal non-hardening sealant can be used on virtually all joints; semi-hardening on joint faces which are rough or damaged; hard setting sealant on joints which require a permanent bond and are subjected to high temperature and pressure. **Note:** *Check first if the paper gasket has a bead of sealant*

impregnated in its surface before applying additional sealant.

• When choosing a sealant, make sure it is suitable for the application, particularly if being applied in a high-temperature area or in the vicinity of fuel. Certain manufacturers produce sealants in either clear, silver or black colours to match the finish of the engine. This has a particular application on motorcycles where much of the engine is exposed.

• Do not over-apply sealant. That which is squeezed out on the outside of the joint can be wiped off, whereas an excess of sealant on the inside can break off and clog oilways.

Breaking a sealed joint

• Age, heat, pressure and the use of hard setting sealant can cause two components to stick together so tightly that they are difficult to separate using finger pressure alone. Do not resort to using levers unless there is a pry point provided for this purpose **(see illustration 7.1)** or else the gasket surfaces will be damaged.

• Use a soft-faced hammer **(see illustration 7.2)** or a wood block and conventional hammer to strike the component near the mating surface. Avoid hammering against cast extremities since they may break off. If this method fails, try using a wood wedge between the two components.

Caution: If the joint will not separate, double-check that you have removed all the fasteners.

7.1 If a pry point is provided, apply gently pressure with a flat-bladed screwdriver

7.2 Tap around the joint with a soft-faced mallet if necessary - don't strike cooling fins

Removal of old gasket and sealant

• Paper gaskets will most likely come away complete, leaving only a few traces stuck

Most components have one or two hollow locating dowels between the two gasket faces. If a dowel cannot be removed, do not resort to gripping it with pliers - it will almost certainly be distorted. Install a close-fitting socket or Phillips screwdriver into the dowel and then grip the outer edge of the dowel to free it.

on the sealing faces of the components. It is imperative that all traces are removed to ensure correct sealing of the new gasket.

• Very carefully scrape all traces of gasket away making sure that the sealing surfaces are not gouged or scored by the scraper **(see illustrations 7.3, 7.4 and 7.5)**. Stubborn deposits can be removed by spraying with an aerosol gasket remover. Final preparation of

7.3 Paper gaskets can be scraped off with a gasket scraper tool . . .

7.4 . . . a knife blade . . .

7.5 . . . or a household scraper

7.6 Fine abrasive paper is wrapped around a flat file to clean up the gasket face

7.7 A kitchen scourer can be used on stubborn deposits

the gasket surface can be made with very fine abrasive paper or a plastic kitchen scourer **(see illustrations 7.6 and 7.7)**.

● Old sealant can be scraped or peeled off components, depending on the type originally used. Note that gasket removal compounds are available to avoid scraping the components clean; make sure the gasket remover suits the type of sealant used.

8 Chains

Breaking and joining final drive chains

● Drive chains for all but small bikes are continuous and do not have a clip-type connecting link. The chain must be broken using a chain breaker tool and the new chain securely riveted together using a new soft rivet-type link. Never use a clip-type connecting link instead of a rivet-type link, except in an emergency. Various chain breaking and riveting tools are available, either as separate tools or combined as illustrated in the accompanying photographs - read the instructions supplied with the tool carefully.

> ⚠ **Warning: The need to rivet the new link pins correctly cannot be overstressed - loss of control of the motorcycle is very likely to result if the chain breaks in use.**

● Rotate the chain and look for the soft link. The soft link pins look like they have been

8.1 Tighten the chain breaker to push the pin out of the link . . .

8.2 . . . withdraw the pin, remove the tool . . .

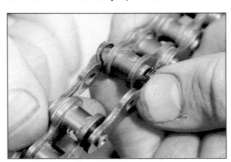

8.3 . . . and separate the chain link

deeply centre-punched instead of peened over like all the other pins **(see illustration 8.9)** and its sideplate may be a different colour. Position the soft link midway between the sprockets and assemble the chain breaker tool over one of the soft link pins **(see illustration 8.1)**. Operate the tool to push the pin out through the chain **(see illustration 8.2)**. On an O-ring chain, remove the O-rings **(see illustration 8.3)**. Carry out the same procedure on the other soft link pin.

> **Caution: Certain soft link pins (particularly on the larger chains) may require their ends to be filed or ground off before they can be pressed out using the tool.**

● Check that you have the correct size and strength (standard or heavy duty) new soft link - do not reuse the old link. Look for the size marking on the chain sideplates **(see illustration 8.10)**.

● Position the chain ends so that they are engaged over the rear sprocket. On an O-ring

8.4 Insert the new soft link, with O-rings, through the chain ends . . .

8.5 . . . install the O-rings over the pin ends . . .

8.6 . . . followed by the sideplate

chain, install a new O-ring over each pin of the link and insert the link through the two chain ends **(see illustration 8.4)**. Install a new O-ring over the end of each pin, followed by the sideplate (with the chain manufacturer's marking facing outwards) **(see illustrations 8.5 and 8.6)**. On an unsealed chain, insert the link through the two chain ends, then install the sideplate with the chain manufacturer's marking facing outwards.

● Note that it may not be possible to install the sideplate using finger pressure alone. If using a joining tool, assemble it so that the plates of the tool clamp the link and press the sideplate over the pins **(see illustration 8.7)**. Otherwise, use two small sockets placed over

8.7 Push the sideplate into position using a clamp

8.8 Assemble the chain riveting tool over one pin at a time and tighten it fully

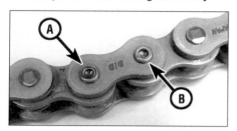

8.9 Pin end correctly riveted (A), pin end unriveted (B)

the rivet ends and two pieces of the wood between a G-clamp. Operate the clamp to press the sideplate over the pins.

● Assemble the joining tool over one pin (following the maker's instructions) and tighten the tool down to spread the pin end securely **(see illustrations 8.8 and 8.9)**. Do the same on the other pin.

> ⚠ **Warning: Check that the pin ends are secure and that there is no danger of the sideplate coming loose. If the pin ends are cracked the soft link must be renewed.**

Final drive chain sizing

● Chains are sized using a three digit number, followed by a suffix to denote the chain type **(see illustration 8.10)**. Chain type is either standard or heavy duty (thicker sideplates), and also unsealed or O-ring/X-ring type.

● The first digit of the number relates to the pitch of the chain, ie the distance from the centre of one pin to the centre of the next pin **(see illustration 8.11)**. Pitch is expressed in eighths of an inch, as follows:

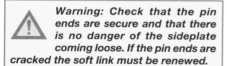

8.10 Typical chain size and type marking

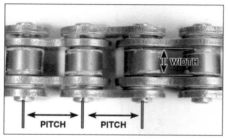

8.11 Chain dimensions

Sizes commencing with a 4 (eg 428) have a pitch of 1/2 inch (12.7 mm)
Sizes commencing with a 5 (eg 520) have a pitch of 5/8 inch (15.9 mm)
Sizes commencing with a 6 (eg 630) have a pitch of 3/4 inch (19.1 mm)

● The second and third digits of the chain size relate to the width of the rollers, again in imperial units, eg the 525 shown has 5/16 inch (7.94 mm) rollers **(see illustration 8.11)**.

9 Hoses

Clamping to prevent flow

● Small-bore flexible hoses can be clamped to prevent fluid flow whilst a component is worked on. Whichever method is used, ensure that the hose material is not permanently distorted or damaged by the clamp.

   a) A brake hose clamp available from auto accessory shops **(see illustration 9.1)**.
   b) A wingnut type hose clamp **(see illustration 9.2)**.

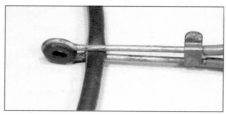

9.1 Hoses can be clamped with an automotive brake hose clamp . . .

9.2 . . . a wingnut type hose clamp . . .

   c) Two sockets placed each side of the hose and held with straight-jawed self-locking grips **(see illustration 9.3)**.
   d) Thick card each side of the hose held between straight-jawed self-locking grips **(see illustration 9.4)**.

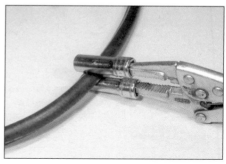

9.3 . . . two sockets and a pair of self-locking grips . . .

9.4 . . . or thick card and self-locking grips

Freeing and fitting hoses

● Always make sure the hose clamp is moved well clear of the hose end. Grip the hose with your hand and rotate it whilst pulling it off the union. If the hose has hardened due to age and will not move, slit it with a sharp knife and peel its ends off the union **(see illustration 9.5)**.

● Resist the temptation to use grease or soap on the unions to aid installation; although it helps the hose slip over the union it will equally aid the escape of fluid from the joint. It is preferable to soften the hose ends in hot water and wet the inside surface of the hose with water or a fluid which will evaporate.

9.5 Cutting a coolant hose free with a sharp knife

Introduction

In less time than it takes to read this introduction, a thief could steal your motorcycle. Returning only to find your bike has gone is one of the worst feelings in the world. Even if the motorcycle is insured against theft, once you've got over the initial shock, you will have the inconvenience of dealing with the police and your insurance company.

The motorcycle is an easy target for the professional thief and the joyrider alike and the official figures on motorcycle theft make for depressing reading; on average a motor-cycle is stolen every 16 minutes in the UK!

Motorcycle thefts fall into two categories, those stolen 'to order' and those taken by opportunists. The thief stealing to order will be on the look out for a specific make and model and will go to extraordinary lengths to obtain that motorcycle. The opportunist thief on the other hand will look for easy targets which can be stolen with the minimum of effort and risk.

Whilst it is never going to be possible to make your machine 100% secure, it is estimated that around half of all stolen motorcycles are taken by opportunist thieves. Remember that the opportunist thief is always on the look out for the easy option: if there are two similar motorcycles parked side-by-side, they will target the one with the lowest level of security. By taking a few precautions, you can reduce the chances of your motorcycle being stolen.

Security equipment

There are many specialised motorcycle security devices available and the following text summarises their applications and their good and bad points.

Once you have decided on the type of security equipment which best suits your needs, we recommended that you read one of the many equipment tests regularly carried out by the motorcycle press. These tests

Ensure the lock and chain you buy is of good quality and long enough to shackle your bike to a solid object

compare the products from all the major manufacturers and give impartial ratings on their effectiveness, value-for-money and ease of use.

No one item of security equipment can provide complete protection. It is highly recommended that two or more of the items described below are combined to increase the security of your motorcycle (a lock and chain plus an alarm system is just about ideal). The more security measures fitted to the bike, the less likely it is to be stolen.

Lock and chain

Pros: *Very flexible to use; can be used to secure the motorcycle to almost any immovable object. On some locks and chains, the lock can be used on its own as a disc lock (see below).*

Cons: *Can be very heavy and awkward to carry on the motorcycle, although some types*

will be supplied with a carry bag which can be strapped to the pillion seat.

● Heavy-duty chains and locks are an excellent security measure **(see illustration 1).** Whenever the motorcycle is parked, use the lock and chain to secure the machine to a solid, immovable object such as a post or railings. This will prevent the machine from being ridden away or being lifted into the back of a van.

● When fitting the chain, always ensure the chain is routed around the motorcycle frame or swingarm **(see illustrations 2 and 3).** Never merely pass the chain around one of the wheel rims; a thief may unbolt the wheel and lift the rest of the machine into a van, leaving you with just the wheel! Try to avoid having excess chain free, thus making it difficult to use cutting tools, and keep the chain and lock off the ground to prevent thieves attacking it with a cold chisel. Position the lock so that its lock barrel is facing downwards; this will make it harder for the thief to attack the lock mechanism.

Pass the chain through the bike's frame, rather than just through a wheel . . .

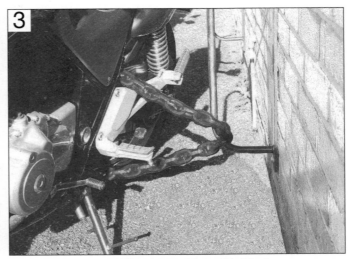

. . . and loop it around a solid object

U-locks

Pros: *Highly effective deterrent which can be used to secure the bike to a post or railings. Most U-locks come with a carrier which allows the lock to be easily carried on the bike.*

Cons: *Not as flexible to use as a lock and chain.*

● These are solid locks which are similar in use to a lock and chain. U-locks are lighter than a lock and chain but not so flexible to use. The length and shape of the lock shackle limit the objects to which the bike can be secured **(see illustration 4)**.

Disc locks

Pros: *Small, light and very easy to carry; most can be stored underneath the seat.*

Cons: *Does not prevent the motorcycle being lifted into a van. Can be very embarrassing if*

A typical disc lock attached through one of the holes in the disc

U-locks can be used to secure the bike to a solid object – ensure you purchase one which is long enough

you forget to remove the lock before attempting to ride off!

● Disc locks are designed to be attached to the front brake disc. The lock passes through one of the holes in the disc and prevents the wheel rotating by jamming against the fork/brake caliper **(see illustration 5)**. Some are equipped with an alarm siren which sounds if the disc lock is moved; this not only acts as a theft deterrent but also as a handy reminder if you try to move the bike with the lock still fitted.

● Combining the disc lock with a length of cable which can be looped around a post or railings provides an additional measure of security **(see illustration 6)**.

Alarms and immobilisers

Pros: *Once installed it is completely hassle-free to use. If the system is 'Thatcham' or 'Sold Secure-approved', insurance companies may give you a discount.*

Cons: *Can be expensive to buy and complex to install. No system will prevent the motorcycle from being lifted into a van and taken away.*

● Electronic alarms and immobilisers are available to suit a variety of budgets. There are three different types of system available: pure alarms, pure immobilisers, and the more expensive systems which are combined alarm/immobilisers **(see illustration 7)**.
● An alarm system is designed to emit an audible warning if the motorcycle is being tampered with.
● An immobiliser prevents the motorcycle being started and ridden away by disabling its electrical systems.
● When purchasing an alarm/immobiliser system, check the cost of installing the system unless you are able to do it yourself. If the motorcycle is not used regularly, another consideration is the current drain of the system. All alarm/immobiliser systems are powered by the motorcycle's battery; purchasing a system with a very low current drain could prevent the battery losing its charge whilst the motorcycle is not being used.

A disc lock combined with a security cable provides additional protection

A typical alarm/immobiliser system

Indelible markings can be applied to most areas of the bike – always apply the manufacturer's sticker to warn off thieves

Chemically-etched code numbers can be applied to main body panels . . .

. . . again, always ensure that the kit manufacturer's sticker is applied in a prominent position

Security marking kits

Pros: *Very cheap and effective deterrent. Many insurance companies will give you a discount on your insurance premium if a recognised security marking kit is used on your motorcycle.*

Cons: *Does not prevent the motorcycle being stolen by joyriders.*

● There are many different types of security marking kits available. The idea is to mark as many parts of the motorcycle as possible with a unique security number **(see illustrations 8, 9 and 10)**. A form will be included with the kit to register your personal details and those of the motorcycle with the kit manufacturer. This register is made available to the police to help them trace the rightful owner of any motorcycle or components which they recover should all other forms of identification have been removed. Always apply the warning stickers provided with the kit to deter thieves.

Ground anchors, wheel clamps and security posts

Pros: *An excellent form of security which will deter all but the most determined of thieves.*

Cons: *Awkward to install and can be expensive.*

● Whilst the motorcycle is at home, it is a good idea to attach it securely to the floor or a solid wall, even if it is kept in a securely locked garage. Various types of ground anchors, security posts and wheel clamps are available for this purpose **(see illustration 11)**. These security devices are either bolted to a solid concrete or brick structure or can be cemented into the ground.

Permanent ground anchors provide an excellent level of security when the bike is at home

Security at home

A high percentage of motorcycle thefts are from the owner's home. Here are some things to consider whenever your motorcycle is at home:
● Where possible, always keep the motorcycle in a securely locked garage. Never rely solely on the standard lock on the garage door, these are usual hopelessly inadequate. Fit an additional locking mechanism to the door and consider having the garage alarmed. A security light, activated by a movement sensor, is also a good investment.

● Always secure the motorcycle to the ground or a wall, even if it is inside a securely locked garage.
● Do not regularly leave the motorcycle outside your home, try to keep it out of sight wherever possible. If a garage is not available, fit a motorcycle cover over the bike to disguise its true identity.
● It is not uncommon for thieves to follow a motorcyclist home to find out where the bike is kept. They will then return at a later date. Be aware of this whenever you are returning

home on your motorcycle. If you suspect you are being followed, do not return home, instead ride to a garage or shop and stop as a precaution.
● When selling a motorcycle, do not provide your home address or the location where the bike is normally kept. Arrange to meet the buyer at a location away from your home. Thieves have been known to pose as potential buyers to find out where motorcycles are kept and then return later to steal them.

Security away from the home

As well as fitting security equipment to your motorcycle here are a few general rules to follow whenever you park your motorcycle.
● Park in a busy, public place.
● Use car parks which incorporate security features, such as CCTV.

● At night, park in a well-lit area, preferably directly underneath a street light.
● Engage the steering lock.
● Secure the motorcycle to a solid, immovable object such as a post or railings with an additional lock. If this is not possible,

secure the bike to a friend's motorcycle. Some public parking places provide security loops for motorcycles.
● Never leave your helmet or luggage attached to the motorcycle. Take them with you at all times.

Lubricants and fluids

A wide range of lubricants, fluids and cleaning agents is available for motor-cycles. This is a guide as to what is available, its applications and properties.

Four-stroke engine oil

● Engine oil is without doubt the most important component of any four-stroke engine. Modern motorcycle engines place a lot of demands on their oil and choosing the right type is essential. Using an unsuitable oil will lead to an increased rate of engine wear and could result in serious engine damage. Before purchasing oil, always check the recommended oil specification given by the manufacturer. The manufacturer will state a recommended 'type or classification' and also a specific 'viscosity' range for engine oil.

● The oil 'type or classification' is identified by its API (American Petroleum Institute) rating. The API rating will be in the form of two letters, e.g. SG. The S identifies the oil as being suitable for use in a petrol (gasoline) engine (S stands for spark ignition) and the second letter, ranging from A to J, identifies the oil's performance rating. The later this letter, the higher the specification of the oil; for example API SG oil exceeds the requirements of API SF oil. **Note:** *On some oils there may also be a second rating consisting of another two letters, the first letter being C, e.g. API SF/CD. This rating indicates the oil is also suitable for use in a diesel engines (the C stands for compression ignition) and is thus of no relevance for motorcycle use.*

● The 'viscosity' of the oil is identified by its SAE (Society of Automotive Engineers) rating. All modern engines require multigrade oils and the SAE rating will consist of two numbers, the first followed by a W, e.g. 10W/40. The first number indicates the viscosity rating of the oil at low temperatures (W stands for winter – tested at –20ºC) and the second number represents the viscosity of the oil at high temperatures (tested at 100ºC). The lower the number, the thinner the oil. For example an oil with an SAE 10W/40 rating will give better cold starting and running than an SAE 15W/40 oil.

● As well as ensuring the 'type' and 'viscosity' of the oil match the recommendations, another consideration to make when buying engine oil is whether to purchase a standard mineral-based oil, a semi-synthetic oil (also known as a synthetic blend or synthetic-based oil) or a fully-synthetic oil. Although all oils will have a similar rating and viscosity, their cost will vary considerably; mineral-based oils are the cheapest, the fully-synthetic oils the most expensive with the semi-synthetic oils falling somewhere in-between. This decision is very much up to the owner, but it should be noted that modern synthetic oils have far better lubricating and cleaning qualities than traditional mineral-based oils and tend to retain these properties for far longer. Bearing in mind the operating conditions inside a modern, high-revving motorcycle engine it is highly recommended that a fully synthetic oil is used. The extra expense at each service could save you money in the long term by preventing premature engine wear.

● As a final note always ensure that the oil is specifically designed for use in motorcycle engines. Engine oils designed primarily for use in car engines sometimes contain additives or friction modifiers which could cause clutch slip on a motorcycle fitted with a wet-clutch.

Two-stroke engine oil

● Modern two-stroke engines, with their high power outputs, place high demands on their oil. If engine seizure is to be avoided it is essential that a high-quality oil is used. Two-stroke oils differ hugely from four-stroke oils. The oil lubricates only the crankshaft and piston(s) (the transmission has its own lubricating oil) and is used on a total-loss basis where it is burnt completely during the combustion process.

● The Japanese have recently introduced a classification system for two-stroke oils, the JASO rating. This rating is in the form of two letters, either FA, FB or FC – FA is the lowest classification and FC the highest. Ensure the oil being used meets or exceeds the recommended rating specified by the manufacturer.

● As well as ensuring the oil rating matches the recommendation, another consideration to make when buying engine oil is whether to purchase a standard mineral-based oil, a semi-synthetic oil (also known as a synthetic blend or synthetic-based oil) or a fully-synthetic oil. The cost of each type of oil varies considerably; mineral-based oils are the cheapest, the fully-synthetic oils the most expensive with the semi-synthetic oils falling somewhere in-between. This decision is very much up to the owner, but it should be noted that modern synthetic oils have far better lubricating properties and burn cleaner than traditional mineral-based oils. It is therefore recommended that a fully synthetic oil is used. The extra expense could save you money in the long term by preventing premature engine wear, engine performance will be improved, carbon deposits and exhaust smoke will be reduced.

● Always ensure that the oil is specifically designed for use in an injector system. Many high quality two-stroke oils are designed for competition use and need to be pre-mixed with fuel. These oils are of a much higher viscosity and are not designed to flow through the injector pumps used on road-going two-stroke motorcycles.

Transmission (gear) oil

● On a two-stroke engine, the transmission and clutch are lubricated by their own separate oil bath which must be changed in accordance with the Maintenance Schedule.
● Although the engine and transmission units of most four-strokes use a common lubrication supply, there are some exceptions where the engine and gearbox have separate oil reservoirs and a dry clutch is used.
● Motorcycle manufacturers will either recommend a monograde transmission oil or a four-stroke multigrade engine oil to lubricate the transmission.
● Transmission oils, or gear oils as they are often called, are designed specifically for use in transmission systems. The viscosity of these oils is represented by an SAE number, but the scale of measurement applied is different to that used to grade engine oils. As a rough guide a SAE90 gear oil will be of the same viscosity as an SAE50 engine oil.

Shaft drive oil

● On models equipped with shaft final drive, the shaft drive gears are will have their own oil supply. The manufacturer will state a recommended 'type or classification' and also a specific 'viscosity' range in the same manner as for four-stroke engine oil.
● Gear oil classification is given by the number which follows the API GL (GL standing for gear lubricant) rating, the higher the number, the higher the specification of the oil, e.g. API GL5 oil is a higher specification than API GL4 oil. Ensure the oil meets or

exceeds the classification specified and is of the correct viscosity. The viscosity of gear oils is also represented by an SAE number but the scale of measurement used is different to that used to grade engine oils. As a rough guide an SAE90 gear oil will be of the same viscosity as an SAE50 engine oil.
● If the use of an EP (Extreme Pressure) gear oil is specified, ensure the oil purchased is suitable.

Fork oil and suspension fluid

● Conventional telescopic front forks are hydraulic and require fork oil to work. To ensure the forks function correctly, the fork oil must be changed in accordance with the Maintenance Schedule.
● Fork oil is available in a variety of viscosities, identified by their SAE rating; fork oil ratings vary from light (SAE 5) to heavy (SAE 30). When purchasing fork oil, ensure the viscosity rating matches that specified by the manufacturer.
● Some lubricant manufacturers also produce a range of high-quality suspension fluids which are very similar to fork oil but are designed mainly for competition use. These fluids may have a different viscosity rating system which is not to be confused with the SAE rating of normal fork oil. Refer to the manufacturer's instructions if in any doubt.

Brake and clutch fluid

● All disc brake systems and some clutch systems are hydraulically operated. To ensure correct operation, the hydraulic fluid must be changed in accordance with the Maintenance Schedule.
● Brake and clutch fluid is classified by its DOT rating with most motorcycle manufacturers specifying DOT 3 or 4 fluid. Both fluid types are glycol-based and can be mixed together without adverse effect; DOT 4 fluid exceeds the requirements of DOT 3

fluid. Although it is safe to use DOT 4 fluid in a system designed for use with DOT 3 fluid, never use DOT 3 fluid in a system which specifies the use of DOT 4 as this will adversely affect the system's performance. The type required for the system will be marked on the fluid reservoir cap.
● Some manufacturers also produce a DOT 5 hydraulic fluid. DOT 5 hydraulic fluid is silicone-based and is not compatible with the glycol-based DOT 3 and 4 fluids. Never mix DOT 5 fluid with DOT 3 or 4 fluid as this will seriously affect the performance of the hydraulic system.

Coolant/antifreeze

● When purchasing coolant/antifreeze, always ensure it is suitable for use in an aluminium engine and contains corrosion inhibitors to prevent possible blockages of the internal coolant passages of the system. As a general rule, most coolants are designed to be used neat and should not be diluted whereas antifreeze can be mixed with distilled water to provide  a coolant solution of the required strength. Refer to the manufacturer's instructions on the bottle.
● Ensure the coolant is changed in accordance with the Maintenance Schedule.

Chain lube

● Chain lube is an aerosol-type spray lubricant specifically designed for use on motorcycle final drive chains. Chain lube has two functions, to minimise friction between the final drive chain and sprockets and to prevent corrosion of the chain. Regular use of a good-quality chain lube will extend the life of the drive chain and sprockets and thus maximise the power being transmitted from the transmission to the rear wheel.
● When using chain lube, always allow some time for the solvents in the lube to evaporate before riding the motorcycle. This will minimise the amount of lube which will

'fling' off from the chain when the motorcycle is used. If the motorcycle is equipped with an 'O-ring' chain, ensure the chain lube is labelled as being suitable for use on 'O-ring' chains.

Degreasers and solvents

● There are many different types of solvents and degreasers available to remove the grime and grease which accumulate around the motorcycle during normal use. Degreasers and solvents are usually available as an aerosol-type spray or as a liquid which you apply with a brush. Always closely follow the manufacturer's instructions and wear eye protection during use. Be aware that many solvents are flammable and may give off noxious fumes; take adequate precautions when using them (see Safety First!).

● For general cleaning, use one of the many solvents or degreasers available from most motorcycle accessory shops. These solvents are usually applied then left for a certain time before being washed off with water.

Brake cleaner is a solvent specifically designed to remove all traces of oil, grease and dust from braking system components. Brake cleaner is designed to evaporate quickly and leaves behind no residue.

Carburettor cleaner is an aerosol-type solvent specifically designed to clear carburettor blockages and break down the hard deposits and gum often found inside carburettors during overhaul.

Contact cleaner is an aerosol-type solvent designed for cleaning electrical components. The cleaner will remove all traces of oil and dirt from components such as switch contacts or fouled spark plugs and then dry, leaving behind no residue.

Gasket remover is an aerosol-type solvent designed for removing stubborn gaskets from engine components during overhaul. Gasket remover will minimise the amount of scraping required to remove the gasket and therefore reduce the risk of damage to the mating surface.

Spray lubricants

● Aerosol-based spray lubricants are widely available and are excellent for lubricating lever pivots and exposed cables and switches. Try to use a lubricant which is of the dry-film type as the fluid evaporates, leaving behind a dry-film of lubricant. Lubricants which leave behind an oily residue will attract dust and dirt which will increase the rate of wear of the cable/lever.

● Most lubricants also act as a moisture dispersant and a penetrating fluid. This means they can also be used to 'dry out' electrical components such as wiring connectors or switches as well as helping to free seized fasteners.

Greases

● Grease is used to lubricate many of the pivot-points. A good-quality multi-purpose grease is suitable for most applications but some manufacturers will specify the use of specialist greases for use on components such as swingarm and suspension linkage bushes. These specialist greases can be purchased from most motorcycle (or car) accessory shops; commonly specified types include molybdenum disulphide grease, lithium-based grease, graphite-based grease, silicone-based grease and high-temperature copper-based grease.

Gasket sealing compounds

● Gasket sealing compounds can be used in conjunction with gaskets, to improve their sealing capabilities, or on their own to seal metal-to-metal joints. Depending on their type, sealing compounds either set hard or stay relatively soft and pliable.

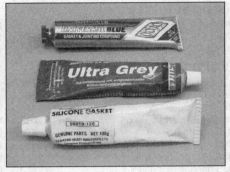

● When purchasing a gasket sealing compound, ensure that it is designed specifically for use on an internal combustion engine. General multi-purpose sealants available from DIY stores may appear visibly similar but they are not designed to withstand the extreme heat or contact with fuel and oil encountered when used on an engine (see 'Tools and Workshop Tips' for further information).

Thread locking compound

● Thread locking compounds are used to secure certain threaded fasteners in position to prevent them from loosening due to vibration. Thread locking compounds can be purchased from most motorcycle (and car) accessory shops. Ensure the threads of the both components are completely clean and dry before sparingly applying the locking compound (see 'Tools and Workshop Tips' for further information).

Fuel additives

● Fuel additives which protect and clean the fuel system components are widely available. These additives are designed to remove all traces of deposits that build up on the carburettors/injectors and prevent wear, helping the fuel system to operate more efficiently. If a fuel additive is being used, check that it is suitable for use with your motorcycle, especially if your motorcycle is equipped with a catalytic converter.

● Octane boosters are also available. These additives are designed to improve the performance of highly-tuned engines being run on normal pump-fuel and are of no real use on standard motorcycles.

Conversion factors

Length (distance)

Inches (in)	x 25.4	= Millimetres (mm)	x 0.0394	= Inches (in)	
Feet (ft)	x 0.305	= Metres (m)	x 3.281	= Feet (ft)	
Miles	x 1.609	= Kilometres (km)	x 0.621	= Miles	

Volume (capacity)

Cubic inches (cu in; in³)	x 16.387	= Cubic centimetres (cc; cm³)	x 0.061	= Cubic inches (cu in; in³)	
Imperial pints (Imp pt)	x 0.568	= Litres (l)	x 1.76	= Imperial pints (Imp pt)	
Imperial quarts (Imp qt)	x 1.137	= Litres (l)	x 0.88	= Imperial quarts (Imp qt)	
Imperial quarts (Imp qt)	x 1.201	= US quarts (US qt)	x 0.833	= Imperial quarts (Imp qt)	
US quarts (US qt)	x 0.946	= Litres (l)	x 1.057	= US quarts (US qt)	
Imperial gallons (Imp gal)	x 4.546	= Litres (l)	x 0.22	= Imperial gallons (Imp gal)	
Imperial gallons (Imp gal)	x 1.201	= US gallons (US gal)	x 0.833	= Imperial gallons (Imp gal)	
US gallons (US gal)	x 3.785	= Litres (l)	x 0.264	= US gallons (US gal)	

Mass (weight)

Ounces (oz)	x 28.35	= Grams (g)	x 0.035	= Ounces (oz)	
Pounds (lb)	x 0.454	= Kilograms (kg)	x 2.205	= Pounds (lb)	

Force

Ounces-force (ozf; oz)	x 0.278	= Newtons (N)	x 3.6	= Ounces-force (ozf; oz)	
Pounds-force (lbf; lb)	x 4.448	= Newtons (N)	x 0.225	= Pounds-force (lbf; lb)	
Newtons (N)	x 0.1	= Kilograms-force (kgf; kg)	x 9.81	= Newtons (N)	

Pressure

Pounds-force per square inch (psi; lbf/in²; lb/in²)	x 0.070	= Kilograms-force per square centimetre (kgf/cm²; kg/cm²)	x 14.223	= Pounds-force per square inch (psi; lbf/in²; lb/in²)	
Pounds-force per square inch (psi; lbf/in²; lb/in²)	x 0.068	= Atmospheres (atm)	x 14.696	= Pounds-force per square inch (psi; lbf/in²; lb/in²)	
Pounds-force per square inch (psi; lbf/in²; lb/in²)	x 0.069	= Bars	x 14.5	= Pounds-force per square inch (psi; lbf/in²; lb/in²)	
Pounds-force per square inch (psi; lbf/in²; lb/in²)	x 6.895	= Kilopascals (kPa)	x 0.145	= Pounds-force per square inch (psi; lbf/in²; lb/in²)	
Kilopascals (kPa)	x 0.01	= Kilograms-force per square centimetre (kgf/cm²; kg/cm²)	x 98.1	= Kilopascals (kPa)	
Millibar (mbar)	x 100	= Pascals (Pa)	x 0.01	= Millibar (mbar)	
Millibar (mbar)	x 0.0145	= Pounds-force per square inch (psi; lbf/in²; lb/in²)	x 68.947	= Millibar (mbar)	
Millibar (mbar)	x 0.75	= Millimetres of mercury (mmHg)	x 1.333	= Millibar (mbar)	
Millibar (mbar)	x 0.401	= Inches of water (inH₂O)	x 2.491	= Millibar (mbar)	
Millimetres of mercury (mmHg)	x 0.535	= Inches of water (inH₂O)	x 1.868	= Millimetres of mercury (mmHg)	
Inches of water (inH₂O)	x 0.036	= Pounds-force per square inch (psi; lbf/in²; lb/in²)	x 27.68	= Inches of water (inH₂O)	

Torque (moment of force)

Pounds-force inches (lbf in; lb in)	x 1.152	= Kilograms-force centimetre (kgf cm; kg cm)	x 0.868	= Pounds-force inches (lbf in; lb in)	
Pounds-force inches (lbf in; lb in)	x 0.113	= Newton metres (Nm)	x 8.85	= Pounds-force inches (lbf in; lb in)	
Pounds-force inches (lbf in; lb in)	x 0.083	= Pounds-force feet (lbf ft; lb ft)	x 12	= Pounds-force inches (lbf in; lb in)	
Pounds-force feet (lbf ft; lb ft)	x 0.138	= Kilograms-force metres (kgf m; kg m)	x 7.233	= Pounds-force feet (lbf ft; lb ft)	
Pounds-force feet (lbf ft; lb ft)	x 1.356	= Newton metres (Nm)	x 0.738	= Pounds-force feet (lbf ft; lb ft)	
Newton metres (Nm)	x 0.102	= Kilograms-force metres (kgf m; kg m)	x 9.804	= Newton metres (Nm)	

Power

Horsepower (hp)	x 745.7	= Watts (W)	x 0.0013	= Horsepower (hp)	

Velocity (speed)

Miles per hour (miles/hr; mph)	x 1.609	= Kilometres per hour (km/hr; kph)	x 0.621	= Miles per hour (miles/hr; mph)	

Fuel consumption*

Miles per gallon, Imperial (mpg)	x 0.354	= Kilometres per litre (km/l)	x 2.825	= Miles per gallon, Imperial (mpg)	
Miles per gallon, US (mpg)	x 0.425	= Kilometres per litre (km/l)	x 2.352	= Miles per gallon, US (mpg)	

Temperature

Degrees Fahrenheit = (°C x 1.8) + 32   Degrees Celsius (Degrees Centigrade; °C) = (°F - 32) x 0.56

It is common practice to convert from miles per gallon (mpg) to litres/100 kilometres (l/100km), where mpg x l/100 km = 282

About the MOT Test

In the UK, all vehicles more than three years old are subject to an annual test to ensure that they meet minimum safety requirements. A current test certificate must be issued before a machine can be used on public roads, and is required before a road fund licence can be issued. Riding without a current test certificate will also invalidate your insurance.

For most owners, the MOT test is an annual cause for anxiety, and this is largely due to owners not being sure what needs to be checked prior to submitting the motorcycle for testing. The simple answer is that a fully roadworthy motorcycle will have no difficulty in passing the test.

This is a guide to getting your motorcycle through the MOT test. Obviously it will not be possible to examine the motorcycle to the same standard as the professional MOT tester, particularly in view of the equipment required for some of the checks. However, working through the following procedures will enable you to identify any problem areas before submitting the motorcycle for the test.

It has only been possible to summarise the test requirements here, based on the regulations in force at the time of printing. Test standards are becoming increasingly stringent, although there are some exemptions for older vehicles. More information about the MOT test can be

obtained from the TSO publications, *How Safe is your Motorcycle* and *The MOT Inspection Manual for Motorcycle Testing*.

Many of the checks require that one of the wheels is raised off the ground. If the motorcycle doesn't have a centre stand, note that an auxiliary stand will be required. Additionally, the help of an assistant may prove useful.

Certain exceptions apply to machines under 50 cc, machines without a lighting system, and Classic bikes - if in doubt about any of the requirements listed below seek confirmation from an MOT tester prior to submitting the motorcycle for the test.

Check that the frame number is clearly visible.

Electrical System

Lights, turn signals, horn and reflector

● With the ignition on, check the operation of the following electrical components. **Note:** *The electrical components on certain small-capacity machines are powered by the generator, requiring that the engine is run for this check.*

a) *Headlight and tail light. Check that both illuminate in the low and high beam switch positions.*

b) *Position lights. Check that the front position (or sidelight) and tail light illuminate in this switch position.*

c) *Turn signals. Check that all flash at the correct rate, and that the warning light(s) function correctly. Check that the turn signal switch works correctly.*

d) *Hazard warning system (where fitted). Check that all four turn signals flash in this switch position.*

e) *Brake stop light. Check that the light comes on when the front and rear brakes are independently applied. Models first used on or after 1st April 1986 must have a brake light switch on each brake.*

f) *Horn. Check that the sound is continuous and of reasonable volume.*

● Check that there is a red reflector on the rear of the machine, either mounted separately or as part of the tail light lens.

● Check the condition of the headlight, tail light and turn signal lenses.

Headlight beam height

● The MOT tester will perform a headlight beam height check using specialised beam setting equipment **(see illustration 1)**. This equipment will not be available to the home mechanic, but if you suspect that the headlight is incorrectly set or may have been maladjusted in the past, you can perform a rough test as follows.

● Position the bike in a straight line facing a brick wall. The bike must be off its stand, upright and with a rider seated. Measure the height from the ground to the centre of the headlight and mark a horizontal line on the wall at this height. Position the motorcycle 3.8 metres from the wall and draw a vertical

Headlight beam height checking equipment

line up the wall central to the centreline of the motorcycle. Switch to dipped beam and check that the beam pattern falls slightly lower than the horizontal line and to the left of the vertical line **(see illustration 2)**.

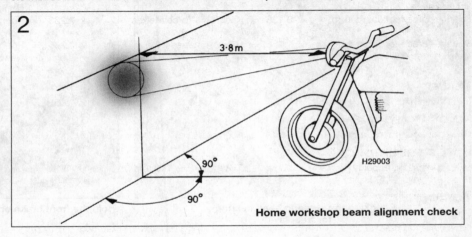

Home workshop beam alignment check

Exhaust System and Final Drive

Exhaust

● Check that the exhaust mountings are secure and that the system does not foul any of the rear suspension components.
● Start the motorcycle. When the revs are increased, check that the exhaust is neither holed nor leaking from any of its joints. On a linked system, check that the collector box is not leaking due to corrosion.

● Note that the exhaust decibel level ("loudness" of the exhaust) is assessed at the discretion of the tester. If the motorcycle was first used on or after 1st January 1985 the silencer must carry the BSAU 193 stamp, or a marking relating to its make and model, or be of OE (original equipment) manufacture. If the silencer is marked NOT FOR ROAD USE, RACING USE ONLY or similar, it will fail the MOT.

Final drive

● On chain or belt drive machines, check that the chain/belt is in good condition and does not have excessive slack. Also check that the sprocket is securely mounted on the rear wheel hub. Check that the chain/belt guard is in place.
● On shaft drive bikes, check for oil leaking from the drive unit and fouling the rear tyre.

Steering and Suspension

Steering

● With the front wheel raised off the ground, rotate the steering from lock to lock. The handlebar or switches must not contact the fuel tank or be close enough to trap the rider's hand. Problems can be caused by damaged lock stops on the lower yoke and frame, or by the fitting of non-standard handlebars.
● When performing the lock to lock check, also ensure that the steering moves freely without drag or notchiness. Steering movement can be impaired by poorly routed cables, or by overtight head bearings or worn bvearings. The tester will perform a check of the steering head bearing lower race by mounting the front wheel on a surface plate, then performing a lock to

lock check with the weight of the machine on the lower bearing (see illustration 3).
● Grasp the fork sliders (lower legs) and attempt to push and pull on the forks

3

Front wheel mounted on a surface plate for steering head bearing lower race check

(see illustration 4). Any play in the steering head bearings will be felt. Note that in extreme cases, wear of the front fork bushes can be misinterpreted for head bearing play.
● Check that the handlebars are securely mounted.
● Check that the handlebar grip rubbers are secure. They should by bonded to the bar left end and to the throttle cable pulley on the right end.

Front suspension

● With the motorcycle off the stand, hold the front brake on and pump the front forks up and down (see illustration 5). Check that they are adequately damped.

4

Checking the steering head bearings for freeplay

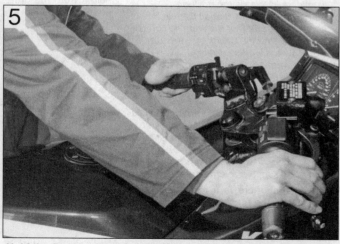

5

Hold the front brake on and pump the front forks up and down to check operation

Inspect the area around the fork dust seal for oil leakage (arrow)

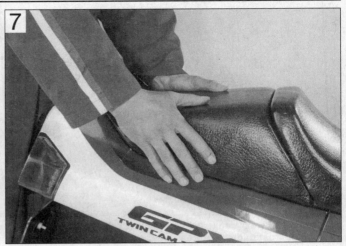

Bounce the rear of the motorcycle to check rear suspension operation

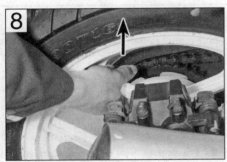

Checking for rear suspension linkage play

● Inspect the area above and around the front fork oil seals **(see illustration 6)**. There should be no sign of oil on the fork tube (stanchion) nor leaking down the slider (lower leg). On models so equipped, check that there is no oil leaking from the anti-dive units.

● On models with swingarm front suspension, check that there is no freeplay in the linkage when moved from side to side.

Rear suspension

● With the motorcycle off the stand and an assistant supporting the motorcycle by its handlebars, bounce the rear suspension **(see illustration 7)**. Check that the suspension components do not foul on any of the cycle parts and check that the shock absorber(s) provide adequate damping.

● Visually inspect the shock absorber(s) and check that there is no sign of oil leakage from its damper. This is somewhat restricted on certain single shock models due to the location of the shock absorber.

● With the rear wheel raised off the ground, grasp the wheel at the highest point and attempt to pull it up **(see illustration 8)**. Any play in the swingarm pivot or suspension linkage bearings will be felt as movement. **Note:** *Do not confuse play with actual suspension movement.* Failure to lubricate suspension linkage bearings can lead to bearing failure **(see illustration 9)**.

● With the rear wheel raised off the ground, grasp the swingarm ends and attempt to move the swingarm from side to side and forwards and backwards - any play indicates wear of the swingarm pivot bearings **(see illustration 10)**.

Worn suspension linkage pivots (arrows) are usually the cause of play in the rear suspension

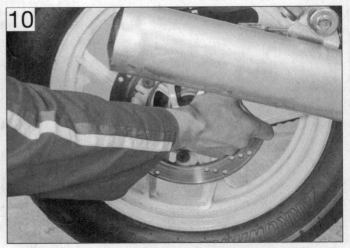

Grasp the swingarm at the ends to check for play in its pivot bearings

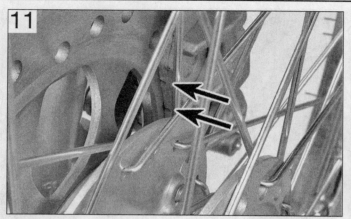

Brake pad wear can usually be viewed without removing the caliper. Most pads have wear indicator grooves (arrowed) and some also have indicator tangs or cut-outs.

On drum brakes, check the angle of the operating lever with the brake fully applied. Most drum brakes have a wear indicator pointer or scale.

Brakes, Wheels and Tyres

Brakes

● With the wheel raised off the ground, apply the brake then free it off, and check that the wheel is about to revolve freely without brake drag.
● On disc brakes, examine the disc itself. Check that it is securely mounted and not cracked.
● On disc brakes, view the pad material through the caliper mouth and check that the pads are not worn down beyond the limit **(see illustration 11)**.
● On drum brakes, check that when the brake is applied the angle between the operating lever and cable or rod is not too great **(see illustration 12)**. Check also that the operating lever doesn't foul any other components.
● On disc brakes, examine the flexible hoses

from top to bottom. Have an assistant hold the brake on so that the fluid in the hose is under pressure, and check that there is no sign of fluid leakage, bulges or cracking. If there are any metal brake pipes or unions, check that these are free from corrosion and damage. Where a brake-linked anti-dive system is fitted, check the hoses to the anti-dive in a similar manner.
● Check that the rear brake torque arm is secure and that its fasteners are secured by self-locking nuts or castellated nuts with split-pins or R-pins **(see illustration 13)**.
● On models with ABS, check that the self-check warning light in the instrument panel works.
● The MOT tester will perform a test of the motorcycle's braking efficiency based on a calculation of rider and motorcycle weight. Although this cannot be carried out at home, you can at least ensure that the braking systems are properly maintained. For hydraulic disc brakes, check the fluid level,

lever/pedal feel (bleed of air if its spongy) and pad material. For drum brakes, check adjustment, cable or rod operation and shoe lining thickness.

Wheels and tyres

● Check the wheel condition. Cast wheels should be free from cracks and if of the built-up design, all fasteners should be secure. Spoked wheels should be checked for broken, corroded, loose or bent spokes.
● With the wheel raised off the ground, spin the wheel and visually check that the tyre and wheel run true. Check that the tyre does not foul the suspension or mudguards.
● With the wheel raised off the ground, grasp the wheel and attempt to move it about the axle (spindle) **(see illustration 14)**. Any play felt here indicates wheel bearing failure.

Brake torque arm must be properly secured at both ends

Check for wheel bearing play by trying to move the wheel about the axle (spindle)

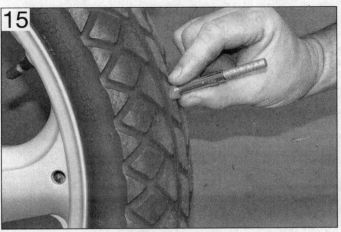

Checking the tyre tread depth

Tyre direction of rotation arrow can be found on tyre sidewall

Castellated type wheel axle (spindle) nut must be secured by a split pin or R-pin

Two straightedges are used to check wheel alignment

● Check the tyre tread depth, tread condition and sidewall condition **(see illustration 15)**.
● Check the tyre type. Front and rear tyre types must be compatible and be suitable for road use. Tyres marked NOT FOR ROAD USE, COMPETITION USE ONLY or similar, will fail the MOT.

● If the tyre sidewall carries a direction of rotation arrow, this must be pointing in the direction of normal wheel rotation **(see illustration 16)**.
● Check that the wheel axle (spindle) nuts (where applicable) are properly secured. A self-locking nut or castellated nut with a split-pin or R-pin can be used **(see illustration 17)**.
● Wheel alignment is checked with the motorcycle off the stand and a rider seated. With the front wheel pointing straight ahead, two perfectly straight lengths of metal or wood and placed against the sidewalls of both tyres **(see illustration 18)**. The gap each side of the front tyre must be equidistant on both sides. Incorrect wheel alignment may be due to a cocked rear wheel (often as the result of poor chain adjustment) or in extreme cases, a bent frame.

General checks and condition

● Check the security of all major fasteners, bodypanels, seat, fairings (where fitted) and mudguards.

● Check that the rider and pillion footrests, handlebar levers and brake pedal are securely mounted.

● Check for corrosion on the frame or any load-bearing components. If severe, this may affect the structure, particularly under stress.

Sidecars

A motorcycle fitted with a sidecar requires additional checks relating to the stability of the machine and security of attachment and swivel joints, plus specific wheel alignment (toe-in) requirements. Additionally, tyre and lighting requirements differ from conventional motorcycle use. Owners are advised to check MOT test requirements with an official test centre.

Preparing for storage

Before you start

If repairs or an overhaul is needed, see that this is carried out now rather than left until you want to ride the bike again.

Give the bike a good wash and scrub all dirt from its underside. Make sure the bike dries completely before preparing for storage.

Engine

● Remove the spark plug(s) and lubricate the cylinder bores with approximately a teaspoon of motor oil using a spout-type oil can (see illustration 1). Reinstall the spark plug(s). Crank the engine over a couple of times to coat the piston rings and bores with oil. If the bike has a kickstart, use this to turn the engine over. If not, flick the kill switch to the OFF position and crank the engine over on the starter (see illustration 2). If the nature on the ignition system prevents the starter operating with the kill switch in the OFF position, remove the spark plugs and fit them back in their caps; ensure that the plugs are earthed (grounded) against the cylinder head when the starter is operated (see illustration 3).

⚠️ **Warning:** *It is important that the plugs are earthed (grounded) away from the spark plug holes otherwise there is a risk of atomised fuel from the cylinders igniting.*

HAYNES HiNT *On a single cylinder four-stroke engine, you can seal the combustion chamber completely by positioning the piston at TDC on the compression stroke.*

● Drain the carburettor(s) otherwise there is a risk of jets becoming blocked by gum deposits from the fuel (see illustration 4).

● If the bike is going into long-term storage, consider adding a fuel stabiliser to the fuel in the tank. If the tank is drained completely, corrosion of its internal surfaces may occur if left unprotected for a long period. The tank can be treated with a rust preventative especially for this purpose. Alternatively, remove the tank and pour half a litre of motor oil into it, install the filler cap and shake the tank to coat its internals with oil before draining off the excess. The same effect can also be achieved by spraying WD40 or a similar water-dispersant around the inside of the tank via its flexible nozzle.

● Make sure the cooling system contains the correct mix of antifreeze. Antifreeze also contains important corrosion inhibitors.

● The air intakes and exhaust can be sealed off by covering or plugging the openings. Ensure that you do not seal in any condensation; run the engine until it is hot,

Squirt a drop of motor oil into each cylinder

Flick the kill switch to OFF . . .

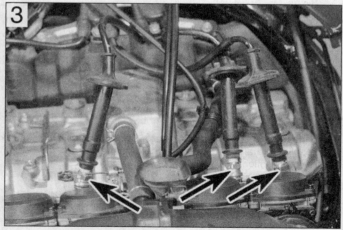

. . . and ensure that the metal bodies of the plugs (arrows) are earthed against the cylinder head

Connect a hose to the carburettor float chamber drain stub (arrow) and unscrew the drain screw

5

Exhausts can be sealed off with a plastic bag

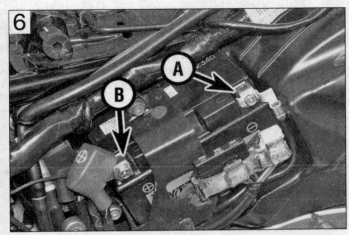

6

Disconnect the negative lead (A) first, followed by the positive lead (B)

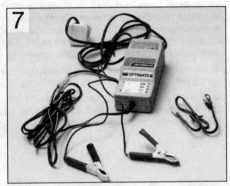

7

Use a suitable battery charger - this kit also assess battery condition

then switch off and allow to cool. Tape a piece of thick plastic over the silencer end(s) (see illustration 5). Note that some advocate pouring a tablespoon of motor oil into the silencer(s) before sealing them off.

Battery

● Remove it from the bike - in extreme cases of cold the battery may freeze and crack its case (see illustration 6).

● Check the electrolyte level and top up if necessary (conventional refillable batteries). Clean the terminals.
● Store the battery off the motorcycle and away from any sources of fire. Position a wooden block under the battery if it is to sit on the ground.
● Give the battery a trickle charge for a few hours every month (see illustration 7).

Tyres

● Place the bike on its centrestand or an auxiliary stand which will support the motorcycle in an upright position. Position wood blocks under the tyres to keep them off the ground and to provide insulation from damp. If the bike is being put into long-term storage, ideally both tyres should be off the ground; not only will this protect the tyres, but will also ensure that no load is placed on the steering head or wheel bearings.
● Deflate each tyre by 5 to 10 psi, no more or the beads may unseat from the rim, making subsequent inflation difficult on tubeless tyres.

Pivots and controls

● Lubricate all lever, pedal, stand and footrest

pivot points. If grease nipples are fitted to the rear suspension components, apply lubricant to the pivots.
● Lubricate all control cables.

Cycle components

● Apply a wax protectant to all painted and plastic components. Wipe off any excess, but don't polish to a shine. Where fitted, clean the screen with soap and water.
● Coat metal parts with Vaseline (petroleum jelly). When applying this to the fork tubes, do not compress the forks otherwise the seals will rot from contact with the Vaseline.
● Apply a vinyl cleaner to the seat.

Storage conditions

● Aim to store the bike in a shed or garage which does not leak and is free from damp.
● Drape an old blanket or bedspread over the bike to protect it from dust and direct contact with sunlight (which will fade paint). This also hides the bike from prying eyes. Beware of tight-fitting plastic covers which may allow condensation to form and settle on the bike.

Getting back on the road

Engine and transmission

● Change the oil and replace the oil filter. If this was done prior to storage, check that the oil hasn't emulsified - a thick whitish substance which occurs through condensation.
● Remove the spark plugs. Using a spout-type oil can, squirt a few drops of oil into the cylinder(s). This will provide initial lubrication as the piston rings and bores comes back into contact. Service the spark plugs, or fit new ones, and install them in the engine.

● Check that the clutch isn't stuck on. The plates can stick together if left standing for some time, preventing clutch operation. Engage a gear and try rocking the bike back and forth with the clutch lever held against the handlebar. If this doesn't work on cable-operated clutches, hold the clutch lever back against the handlebar with a strong elastic band or cable tie for a couple of hours (see illustration 8).
● If the air intakes or silencer end(s) were blocked off, remove the bung or cover used.
● If the fuel tank was coated with a rust

8

Hold clutch lever back against the handlebar with elastic bands or a cable tie

preventative, oil or a stabiliser added to the fuel, drain and flush the tank and dispose of the fuel sensibly. If no action was taken with the fuel tank prior to storage, it is advised that the old fuel is disposed of since it will go off over a period of time. Refill the fuel tank with fresh fuel.

Frame and running gear

● Oil all pivot points and cables.
● Check the tyre pressures. They will definitely need inflating if pressures were reduced for storage.
● Lubricate the final drive chain (where applicable).
● Remove any protective coating applied to the fork tubes (stanchions) since this may well destroy the fork seals. If the fork tubes weren't protected and have picked up rust spots, remove them with very fine abrasive paper and refinish with metal polish.
● Check that both brakes operate correctly. Apply each brake hard and check that it's not possible to move the motorcycle forwards, then check that the brake frees off again once released. Brake caliper pistons can stick due to corrosion around the piston head, or on the sliding caliper types, due to corrosion of the slider pins. If the brake doesn't free after repeated operation, take the caliper off for examination. Similarly drum brakes can stick

due to a seized operating cam, cable or rod linkage.
● If the motorcycle has been in long-term storage, renew the brake fluid and clutch fluid (where applicable).
● Depending on where the bike has been stored, the wiring, cables and hoses may have been nibbled by rodents. Make a visual check and investigate disturbed wiring loom tape.

Battery

● If the battery has been previously removal and given top up charges it can simply be reconnected. Remember to connect the positive cable first and the negative cable last.
● On conventional refillable batteries, if the battery has not received any attention, remove it from the motorcycle and check its electrolyte level. Top up if necessary then charge the battery. If the battery fails to hold a charge and a visual checks show heavy white sulphation of the plates, the battery is probably defective and must be renewed. This is particularly likely if the battery is old. Confirm battery condition with a specific gravity check.
● On sealed (MF) batteries, if the battery has not received any attention, remove it from the motorcycle and charge it according to the information on the battery case - if the battery fails to hold a charge it must be renewed.

Starting procedure

● If a kickstart is fitted, turn the engine over a couple of times with the ignition OFF to distribute oil around the engine. If no kickstart is fitted, flick the engine kill switch OFF and the ignition ON and crank the engine over a couple of times to work oil around the upper cylinder components. If the nature of the ignition system is such that the starter won't work with the kill switch OFF, remove the spark plugs, fit them back into their caps and earth (ground) their bodies on the cylinder head. Reinstall the spark plugs afterwards.
● Switch the kill switch to RUN, operate the choke and start the engine. If the engine won't start don't continue cranking the engine - not only will this flatten the battery, but the starter motor will overheat. Switch the ignition off and try again later. If the engine refuses to start, go through the fault finding procedures in this manual. **Note:** *If the bike has been in storage for a long time, old fuel or a carburettor blockage may be the problem. Gum deposits in carburettors can block jets - if a carburettor cleaner doesn't prove successful the carburettors must be dismantled for cleaning.*
● Once the engine has started, check that the lights, turn signals and horn work properly.
● Treat the bike gently for the first ride and check all fluid levels on completion. Settle the bike back into the maintenance schedule.

This Section provides an easy reference-guide to the more common faults that are likely to afflict your machine. Obviously, the opportunities are almost limitless for faults to occur as a result of obscure failures, and to try and cover all eventualities would require a book. Indeed, a number have been written on the subject.

Successful troubleshooting is not a mysterious 'black art' but the application of a bit of knowledge combined with a systematic and logical approach to the problem. Approach any troubleshooting by first accurately identifying the symptom and then checking through the list of possible causes, starting with the simplest or most obvious and progressing in stages to the most complex.

Take nothing for granted, but above all apply liberal quantities of common sense.

The main symptom of a fault is given in the text as a major heading below which are listed the various systems or areas which may contain the fault. Details of each possible cause for a fault and the remedial action to be taken are given, in brief, in the paragraphs below each heading. Further information should be sought in the relevant Chapter.

1 Engine doesn't start or is difficult to start

- [ ] Starter motor doesn't rotate
- [ ] Starter motor rotates but engine does not turn over
- [ ] Starter works but engine won't turn over (seized)
- [ ] No fuel flow
- [ ] Engine flooded
- [ ] No spark or weak spark
- [ ] Compression low
- [ ] Stalls after starting
- [ ] Rough idle

2 Poor running at low speed

- [ ] Spark weak
- [ ] Fuel/air mixture incorrect
- [ ] Compression low
- [ ] Poor acceleration

3 Poor running or no power at high speed

- [ ] Firing incorrect
- [ ] Fuel/air mixture incorrect
- [ ] Compression low
- [ ] Knocking or pinking
- [ ] Miscellaneous causes

4 Overheating

- [ ] Engine overheats
- [ ] Firing incorrect
- [ ] Fuel/air mixture incorrect
- [ ] Compression too high
- [ ] Engine load excessive
- [ ] Lubrication inadequate
- [ ] Miscellaneous causes

5 Clutch problems

- [ ] Clutch slipping
- [ ] Clutch not disengaging completely

6 Gearchanging problems

- [ ] Doesn't go into gear, or lever doesn't return
- [ ] Jumps out of gear
- [ ] Overselects

7 Abnormal engine noise

- [ ] Knocking or pinking
- [ ] Piston slap or rattling
- [ ] Valve noise
- [ ] Other noise

8 Abnormal driveline noise

- [ ] Clutch noise
- [ ] Transmission noise
- [ ] Final drive noise

9 Abnormal frame and suspension noise

- [ ] Front end noise
- [ ] Shock absorber noise
- [ ] Brake noise

10 Oil level warning light comes on

- [ ] Engine lubrication system
- [ ] Electrical system

11 Excessive exhaust smoke

- [ ] White smoke
- [ ] Black smoke
- [ ] Brown smoke

12 Poor handling or stability

- [ ] Handlebar hard to turn
- [ ] Handlebar shakes or vibrates excessively
- [ ] Handlebar pulls to one side
- [ ] Poor shock absorbing qualities

13 Braking problems

- [ ] Brakes are spongy, don't hold
- [ ] Brake lever or pedal pulsates
- [ ] Brakes drag
- [ ] ABS system (where fitted)

14 Electrical problems

- [ ] Battery dead or weak
- [ ] Battery overcharged

1 Engine doesn't start or is difficult to start

Starter motor doesn't rotate

- [ ] Engine kill switch OFF.
- [ ] Fuse blown. Check main fuse, ignition fuse and EFI fuse (Chapter 8).
- [ ] Battery voltage low. Check battery condition and recharge or replace battery (Chapter 8).
- [ ] Loose or corroded battery connections/terminals. Tighten or clean connections.
- [ ] Starter motor defective. Make sure the wiring to the starter is secure and free of corrosion. Replace or repair the motor if defective (Chapter 8).
- [ ] Starter relay defective. Make sure the wiring to relay is secure and free of corrosion. Test the operation of the relay, internal corrosion or arcing can cause the relay to not pass sufficient current to the starter motor even if it clicks when the start button is operated (Chapter 8).
- [ ] Starter switch not contacting. The contacts could be wet, corroded or dirty. Disassemble and clean the switch (Chapter 8).
- [ ] Wiring open or shorted. Check all wiring connections and harnesses to make sure that they are dry, tight and not corroded. Also check for broken or frayed wires that can cause a short to ground (earth) (see *Wiring diagrams*, Chapter 8).
- [ ] Ignition or kill switch defective. This is usually caused by water, corrosion, damage or excessive wear. The switches can be disassembled and cleaned with electrical contact cleaner. If cleaning does not help, replace the switches (Chapter 8).
- [ ] Faulty neutral switch, sidestand switch or clutch switch. Check the wiring to each switch and the switch itself (see Chapter 8).
- [ ] Faulty starter circuit cut-off relay or diode (Chapter 8).
- [ ] Fuel injection system shutdown due to system fault (Chapter 4).

Starter motor rotates but engine does not turn over

- [ ] Starter clutch defective. Inspect and repair or replace with a new one (see Chapter 2).
- [ ] Damaged idler or starter gears. Inspect and replace the damaged parts (see Chapter 2).

Starter works but engine won't turn over (seized)

- [ ] Seized engine caused by one or more internally damaged components. Failure due to wear, abuse or lack of lubrication. Damage can include seized valves, followers, camshafts, pistons, crankshaft, connecting rod bearings, or transmission gears or bearings. Refer to Chapter 2 for engine disassembly.

No fuel flow

- [ ] No fuel in tank.
- [ ] Fuel tank breather hose obstructed.
- [ ] Faulty fuel injection system relay. Check the relay (see Chapter 4).
- [ ] Fuel pump or pressure regulator faulty, or the pump's internal filter is blocked (see Chapter 4).
- [ ] Engine control unit (ECU) defective (Chapter 4).
- [ ] Ignition key not recognised by immobiliser system (where fitted).
- [ ] Fuel hose kinked. Fit a new hose.
- [ ] Fuel rail or injector clogged. For all of the injectors to be clogged, either a very bad batch of fuel with an unusual additive has been used, or some other foreign material has entered the tank. Check the fuel pump. In some cases, if a machine has been unused for several months, the fuel turns to a varnish-like liquid which can cause an injector needle to stick to its seat. Drain the tank and fuel system, ultrasonically clean or replace fuel injectors (Chapter 4).

Engine flooded

- [ ] Injector needle valve worn or stuck open. A piece of dirt, rust or other debris can cause the needle to seat improperly, causing excess fuel to be admitted to the throttle body. In this case, the injector should be cleaned and the needle and seat inspected (see Chapter 4). If the needle and seat are worn, then the leaking will persist and the parts should be renewed.
- [ ] Starting technique incorrect. Under normal circumstances (i.e. if all the components of the fuel injection system are good) the machine should start with the throttle closed.

No spark or weak spark

- [ ] Ignition switch OFF.
- [ ] Engine kill switch turned to the OFF position.
- [ ] Ignition or kill switch shorted. This is usually caused by water, corrosion, damage or excessive wear. The switches can be disassembled and cleaned with electrical contact cleaner. If cleaning does not help, replace the switches (see Chapter 8).
- [ ] Battery voltage low. Check battery condition and recharge or replace battery (Chapter 8).
- [ ] Spark plug cap not making good contact. Make sure that the caps are pushed fully onto the spark plugs.
- [ ] Spark plugs dirty, defective or worn out. Locate reason for fouled plugs using spark plug condition chart on the inside back cover and follow the plug maintenance procedures (see Chapter 1).
- [ ] Incorrect spark plugs. Wrong type or heat range. Check and install correct plugs (see Chapter 1).
- [ ] Ignition coil defective. Check the coils (Chapter 4).
- [ ] Fuel injection system shutdown due to system fault (Chapter 4).
- [ ] Crankshaft position (CKP) sensor defective (see Chapter 4).
- [ ] Faulty fuel injection relay or tip-over sensor (Chapter 4).
- [ ] Engine control unit (ECU) defective (see Chapter 4).
- [ ] Wiring shorted or broken between:
  - a) Ignition (main) switch and engine kill switch (or blown fuse)
  - b) ECU and engine kill switch
  - c) ECU and ignition coils
  - d) ECU and CKP sensor
- [ ] Make sure that all wiring connections are clean, dry and tight. Look for chafed and broken wires (see Chapters 4 and 8).

Compression low

- [ ] Spark plugs loose. Remove the plugs and inspect their threads. Reinstall and tighten securely (see Chapter 1).
- [ ] Cylinder head not sufficiently tightened down. If a cylinder head is suspected of being loose, then there's a chance that the gasket or head is damaged if the problem has persisted for any length of time. The head bolts should be tightened to the proper torque and in the correct sequence (Chapter 2).
- [ ] Improper valve clearance. This means that the valve is not closing completely and compression pressure is leaking past the valve. Check and adjust the valve clearances (Chapter 1).
- [ ] Cylinder and/or piston worn. Excessive wear will cause compression pressure to leak past the rings. This is usually accompanied by worn rings as well. A top-end overhaul is necessary (Chapter 2).
- [ ] Piston rings worn, weak, broken, or sticking. Broken or sticking piston rings usually indicate a lubrication or fuelling problem that causes excess carbon deposits to form on the pistons and rings. Top-end overhaul is necessary (Chapter 2).
- [ ] Piston ring-to-groove clearance excessive. This is caused by excessive wear of the piston ring lands. Piston renewal is necessary (Chapter 2).
- [ ] Cylinder head gasket damaged. If a head is allowed to become loose, or if excessive carbon build-up on the piston crown and combustion chamber causes extremely high compression, the head gasket may leak. Retorquing the head is not always sufficient to restore the seal, so a new gasket is necessary (Chapter 2).
- [ ] Cylinder head warped. This is caused by overheating or improperly tightened head bolts. Machine shop resurfacing or head renewal is necessary (Chapter 2).
- [ ] Valve spring broken or weak. Caused by component failure or wear; the springs must be renewed (Chapter 2).
- [ ] Valve not seating properly. This is caused by a bent valve (from over-revving or improper valve adjustment), burned valve or seat (incorrect air/fuel mixture) or an accumulation of carbon deposits on the seat. The valves must be cleaned and/or renewed and the seats lapped (Chapter 2).

1 Engine doesn't start or is difficult to start (continued)

Stalls after starting

- ☐ Faulty idle control system. Check the operation of the fast idle unit (see Chapter 4).
- ☐ Engine idle speed incorrect. Turn idle adjusting screw until the engine idles at the specified rpm (Chapter 1).
- ☐ Ignition malfunction (see Chapter 4).
- ☐ Fuel injection system malfunction (see Chapter 4).
- ☐ Fuel contaminated. The fuel can be contaminated with either dirt or water, or can change chemically if the machine has been unused for several months. Drain the tank and fuel system (Chapter 4).
- ☐ Intake air leak. Check for loose throttle body-to-intake manifold connections, loose or damaged AIS vacuum hose or throttle body synchronising hose plug (Chapter 4).

Rough idle

- ☐ Idle speed incorrect (see Chapter 1).
- ☐ Ignition fault (see Chapter 4).
- ☐ Throttle bodies out of balance. Synchronise them as described in Chapter 1.
- ☐ Vacuum take off plug or screw missing. Vacuum hose damaged.
- ☐ Fuel injection system malfunction (see Chapter 4).
- ☐ Fuel contaminated. The fuel can be contaminated with either dirt or water, or can change chemically if the machine has been unused for several months. Drain the tank and the fuel system (Chapter 4).
- ☐ Intake air leak. Check for loose throttle body-to-intake manifold connections, loose or damaged AIS vacuum hose or throttle body vacuum hoses (Chapter 4).
- ☐ Air filter clogged. Renew the filter and clean its housing (Chapter 1).

2 Poor running at low speeds

Spark weak

- ☐ Battery voltage low. Check battery condition and recharge or replace battery (Chapter 8).
- ☐ Spark plug caps not making good contact. Make sure that the caps are pushed fully onto the spark plugs.
- ☐ Spark plugs dirty, defective or worn out. Locate reason for fouled plugs using spark plug condition chart on the inside back cover and follow the plug maintenance procedures (see Chapter 1).
- ☐ Incorrect spark plugs. Wrong type or heat range. Check and install correct plugs (see Chapter 1).
- ☐ Ignition coil, HT lead or spark plug cap defective. Test and renew if necessary (Chapter 4).
- ☐ Loose or corroded connections on low tension side of coil. Check security and clean connections.

Fuel/air mixture incorrect

- ☐ Fuel tank breather hose obstructed.
- ☐ Fuel pump or pressure regulator faulty, or the pump's internal filter is blocked (see Chapter 4).
- ☐ Fuel hose kinked. Replace the fuel hose.
- ☐ Fuel rail or injector clogged. For all of the injectors to be clogged, either a very bad batch of fuel with an unusual additive has been used, or some other foreign material has entered the tank. Check the fuel pump. In some cases, if a machine has been unused for several months, the fuel turns to a varnish-like liquid which can cause an injector needle to stick to its seat. Drain the tank and fuel system, ultrasonically clean or replace fuel injectors (Chapter 4).
- ☐ Intake air leak. Check for loose throttle body-to-intake manifold connections, loose or damaged AIS vacuum hose or throttle body synchronising hose plug (Chapter 4).
- ☐ Air filter clogged. Renew the filter and clean its housing (Chapter 1).

Compression low

Check by performing a compression test (see Chapter 2).

- ☐ Spark plugs loose. Remove the plugs and inspect their threads. Reinstall and tighten securely (see Chapter 1).
- ☐ Cylinder head not sufficiently tightened down. If a cylinder head is suspected of being loose, then there's a chance that the gasket or head is damaged if the problem has persisted for any length of time. The head bolts should be tightened to the proper torque and in the correct sequence (Chapter 2).

- ☐ Improper valve clearance. This means that the valve is not closing completely and compression pressure is leaking past the valve. Check and adjust the valve clearances (Chapter 1).
- ☐ Cylinder and/or piston worn. Excessive wear will cause compression pressure to leak past the rings. This is usually accompanied by worn rings as well. A top-end overhaul is necessary (Chapter 2).
- ☐ Piston rings worn, weak, broken, or sticking. Broken or sticking piston rings usually indicate a lubrication or fuelling problem that causes excess carbon deposits to form on the pistons and rings. Top-end overhaul is necessary (Chapter 2).
- ☐ Piston ring-to-groove clearance excessive. This is caused by excessive wear of the piston ring lands. Piston renewal is necessary (Chapter 2).
- ☐ Cylinder head gasket damaged. If the head is allowed to become loose, or if excessive carbon build-up on the piston crown and combustion chamber causes extremely high compression, the head gasket may leak. Retorquing the head is not always sufficient to restore the seal, so a new gasket is necessary (Chapter 2).
- ☐ Cylinder head warped. This is caused by overheating or improperly tightened head bolts. Machine shop resurfacing or head renewal is necessary (Chapter 2).
- ☐ Valve spring broken or weak. Caused by component failure or wear; the springs must be renewed (Chapter 2).
- ☐ Valve not seating properly. This is caused by a bent valve (from over-revving or improper valve adjustment), burned valve or seat (improper fuelling) or an accumulation of carbon deposits on the seat (from fuelling or lubrication problems). The valves must be cleaned and/or renewed and the seats lapped (Chapter 2).

Poor acceleration

- ☐ Timing not advancing. The crankshaft position sensor (CKP) or the engine control unit (ECU) may be defective (see Chapter 4). If so, they must be renewed.
- ☐ Engine oil viscosity too high. Using a heavier oil than that recommended in Chapter 1 can damage the oil pump or lubrication system and cause drag on the engine.
- ☐ Brakes dragging. Usually caused by corrosion behind dust seals, ingestion of dirt past a deteriorated seal or from a warped disc or bent axle (Chapter 6).

3 Poor running or no power at high speed

Firing incorrect

☐ Spark plug caps not making good contact. Make sure that the caps are pushed fully onto the spark plugs.

☐ Spark plugs dirty, defective or worn out. Locate reason for fouled plugs using spark plug condition chart on the inside back cover and follow the plug maintenance procedures (see Chapter 1).

☐ Incorrect spark plugs. Wrong type or heat range. Check and install correct plugs (see Chapter 1).

☐ Wrongly connected ignition coil wiring or plug leads.

☐ Ignition coil defective. Test and renew if necessary (see Chapter 4).

☐ Faulty ECU (engine control unit) (see Chapter 4).

Fuel/air mixture incorrect

☐ Fuel tank breather hose obstructed.

☐ Fuel pump faulty or blocked pump internal filter. Inspect and replace if necessary (Chapter 4).

☐ Fuel hose kinked. Replace the fuel hose.

☐ Fuel rail or injector clogged. For all of the injectors to be clogged, either a very bad batch of fuel with an unusual additive has been used, or some other foreign material has entered the tank. Check the fuel pump. In some cases, if a machine has been unused for several months, the fuel turns to a varnish-like liquid which can cause an injector needle to stick to its seat. Drain the tank and fuel system, ultrasonically clean or replace fuel injectors (Chapter 4).

☐ Intake air leak. Check for loose throttle body-to-intake manifold connections, loose or damaged AIS vacuum hose or throttle body synchronising hose plug (Chapter 4).

☐ Air filter clogged. Renew the filter and clean its housing (Chapter 1).

Compression low

Check by performing a compression test (see Chapter 2).

☐ Spark plugs loose. Remove the plugs and inspect their threads. Reinstall and tighten securely (see Chapter 1).

☐ Cylinder head not sufficiently tightened down. If a cylinder head is suspected of being loose, then there's a chance that the gasket or head is damaged if the problem has persisted for any length of time. The head bolts should be tightened to the proper torque and in the correct sequence (Chapter 2).

☐ Improper valve clearance. This means that the valve is not closing completely and compression pressure is leaking past the valve. Check and adjust the valve clearances (Chapter 1).

☐ Cylinder and/or piston worn. Excessive wear will cause compression pressure to leak past the rings. This is usually accompanied by worn rings as well. A top-end overhaul is necessary (Chapter 2).

☐ Piston rings worn, weak, broken, or sticking. Broken or sticking piston rings usually indicate a lubrication or fuelling problem that causes excess carbon deposits to form on the pistons and rings. Top-end overhaul is necessary (Chapter 2).

☐ Piston ring-to-groove clearance excessive. This is caused by excessive wear of the piston ring lands. Piston renewal is necessary (Chapter 2).

☐ Cylinder head gasket damaged. If a head is allowed to become loose, or if excessive carbon build-up on the piston crown and combustion chamber causes extremely high compression, the head gasket may leak. Retorquing the head is not always sufficient to restore the seal, so a new gasket is necessary (Chapter 2).

☐ Cylinder head warped. This is caused by overheating or improperly tightened head bolts. Machine shop resurfacing or head renewal is necessary (Chapter 2).

☐ Valve spring broken or weak. Caused by component failure or wear; the springs must be replaced with new ones (Chapter 2).

☐ Valve not seating properly. This is caused by a bent valve (from over-revving or improper valve adjustment), burned valve or seat (improper fuelling) or an accumulation of carbon deposits on the seat (from fuelling or lubrication problems). The valves must be cleaned and/or renewed and the seats serviced (Chapter 2).

Knocking or pinking

☐ Carbon build-up in combustion chamber. Use of a fuel additive that will dissolve the adhesive bonding the carbon particles to the piston crown and chamber is the easiest way to remove the build-up. Otherwise, the cylinder head will have to be removed and decarbonised (Chapter 2).

☐ Incorrect or poor quality fuel. Old or improper grades of fuel can cause detonation. This causes the pistons to rattle, thus the knocking or pinking sound. Drain old fuel and always use the recommended fuel grade.

☐ Spark plug heat range incorrect. Uncontrolled detonation indicates the plug heat range is too hot. The plug in effect becomes a glow plug, raising cylinder temperatures. Install the proper heat range plug (Chapter 1).

☐ Improper air/fuel mixture. This will cause the cylinders to run hot, which leads to detonation. A blockage in the fuel system or an air leak can cause this imbalance (see Chapter 4).

Miscellaneous causes

☐ Throttle valve doesn't open fully. Adjust the throttle cable freeplay (see Chapter 1).

☐ Clutch slipping due loose or worn clutch components (see Chapter 2).

☐ Timing not advancing. The crankshaft position sensor (CKP) or the engine control unit (ECU) may be defective (see Chapter 4). If so, they must be replaced with new ones.

☐ Engine oil viscosity too high. Using a heavier oil than the one recommended in Chapter 1 can damage the oil pump or lubrication system and cause drag on the engine.

☐ Brakes dragging. Usually caused by corrosion behind dust seals, ingestion of dirt past a deteriorated seal or from a warped disc or bent axle (Chapter 6).

4 Overheating

Engine overheats

- [ ] Coolant level low. Check and add coolant (see *Pre-ride checks*).
- [ ] Leak in cooling system. Check cooling system hoses and radiator for leaks and other damage. Repair or renew parts as necessary (see Chapter 3).
- [ ] Faulty thermostat. Check and renew as described in Chapter 3.
- [ ] Faulty radiator cap. Remove the cap and have it pressure tested.
- [ ] Coolant passages clogged. Drain, flush and refill with fresh coolant (Chapter 1).
- [ ] Water pump defective. Remove the pump and check the components (see Chapter 3).
- [ ] Clogged or damaged radiator fins (see Chapter 1).
- [ ] Faulty cooling fan, relay or coolant temperature sensor (see Chapter 3).

Firing incorrect

- [ ] Wrongly connected ignition coil wiring.
- [ ] Spark plugs dirty, defective or worn out. Locate reason for fouled plugs using spark plug condition chart on the inside back cover and follow the plug maintenance procedures (see Chapter 1).
- [ ] Incorrect spark plugs. Wrong type or heat range. Check and install correct plugs (see Chapter 1).
- [ ] Ignition coil defective. Test and replace with a new one if necessary (see Chapter 4).
- [ ] Faulty engine control unit (ECU) (see Chapter 4).

Fuel/air mixture incorrect

- [ ] Fuel tank breather hose obstructed.
- [ ] Fuel pump faulty or blocked internal filter. Inspect the pump and renew if necessary (Chapter 4).
- [ ] Fuel hose kinked. Replace the fuel hose.
- [ ] Fuel rail or injector clogged. For all of the injectors to be clogged, either a very bad batch of fuel with an unusual additive has been used, or some other foreign material has entered the tank. Check the fuel pump. In some cases, if a machine has been unused for several months, the fuel turns to a varnish-like liquid which can cause an injector needle to stick to its seat. Drain the tank and fuel system, ultrasonically clean or replace fuel injectors (Chapter 4).
- [ ] Intake air leak. Check for loose throttle body-to-intake manifold connections, loose or damaged AIS vacuum hose or throttle body synchronising hose plug (Chapter 4).

- [ ] Air filter clogged. Renew the filter and clean its housing (Chapter 1).

Compression too high

Check by performing a compression test (see Chapter 2).

- [ ] Carbon build-up in combustion chamber. Use of a fuel additive that will dissolve the adhesive bonding the carbon particles to the piston crown and chamber is the easiest way to remove the build-up. Otherwise, the cylinder head will have to be removed and decarbonised (Chapter 2).

Engine load excessive

- [ ] Clutch slipping due loose or worn clutch components (see Chapter 2).
- [ ] Engine oil level too high. Too much oil will cause pressurisation of the crankcase and inefficient engine operation. Check Specifications and drain to proper level (Chapter 1 and *Pre-ride checks*).
- [ ] Engine oil viscosity too high. Using a heavier oil than the one recommended in Chapter 1 can damage the oil pump or lubrication system as well as cause drag on the engine.
- [ ] Brakes dragging. Usually caused by corrosion behind dust seals, ingestion of dirt past deteriorated seal or from a warped disc or bent axle (Chapter 6).

Lubrication inadequate

- [ ] Engine oil level too low. Friction caused by intermittent lack of lubrication or from oil that is overworked can cause overheating. The oil provides a definite cooling function in the engine. Check the oil level (see *Pre-ride checks*).
- [ ] Low engine oil pressure. Check the pressure (see Chapter 2).
- [ ] Blocked oil filter or oil cooler (see Chapter 2).

Miscellaneous causes

- [ ] Modification to exhaust system. Most aftermarket exhaust systems cause the engine to run leaner, which make them run hotter. When installing an accessory exhaust system, always check with the manufacturer/supplier as to whether the fuel system requires adjustment.

5 Clutch problems

Clutch slipping

- [ ] Insufficient clutch cable freeplay. Check and adjust (see Chapter 1).
- [ ] Clutch plates worn or warped. Overhaul the clutch assembly (see Chapter 2).
- [ ] Clutch springs broken or weak. Old or heat-damaged (from slipping clutch) springs should be renewed (Chapter 2).
- [ ] Clutch release mechanism faulty or clutch adjusted (see Chapter 2).
- [ ] Clutch centre or housing unevenly worn. This causes improper engagement of the plates. Replace the damaged or worn parts (see Chapter 2).
- [ ] Incorrect oil used in engine. Oils designed for car engines often contain friction modifiers, which if used in an engine with a wet clutch can promote clutch slip. Always use the correct oil designed for motorcycle engines (see *Pre-ride checks*).

Clutch not disengaging completely

- [ ] Excessive clutch cable freeplay. Check and adjust (see Chapter 1).
- [ ] Clutch release mechanism faulty or wrongly adjusted (see Chapter 2).

- [ ] Clutch plates warped or damaged. This will cause clutch drag, which in turn will cause the machine to creep. Overhaul the clutch assembly (see Chapter 2).
- [ ] Clutch springs fatigued or broken. Check and renew the springs (see Chapter 2).
- [ ] Engine oil deteriorated. Old, thin oil will not provide proper lubrication for the plates, causing the clutch to drag. Renew the oil and filter (see Chapter 1).
- [ ] Engine oil viscosity too high. Using a heavier oil than recommended in Chapter 1 can cause the plates to stick together. Change to the correct weight oil.
- [ ] Clutch housing bearing seized on the transmission input shaft. Lack of lubrication, severe wear or damage can cause the bearing to seize. Overhaul of the clutch, and perhaps transmission, may be necessary to repair the damage (see Chapter 2).
- [ ] Loose clutch centre nut. Causes housing and centre misalignment putting a drag on the engine. Engagement adjustment continually varies. Overhaul the clutch assembly (see Chapter 2).

6 Gearchanging problems

Doesn't go into gear or lever doesn't return

- ☐ Clutch not disengaging (see above).
- ☐ Gearchange mechanism stopper arm spring weak or broken, or arm roller broken or worn. Replace the spring or arm with a new one (see Chapter 2).
- ☐ Selector fork(s) bent, worn or seized. Overhaul the transmission (see Chapter 2).
- ☐ Gear(s) stuck on shaft. Most often caused by a lack of lubrication or excessive wear in transmission bearings and bushes. Overhaul the transmission (see Chapter 2).
- ☐ Selector drum binding. Caused by lubrication failure or excessive wear. Replace the drum and/or its bearing with a new one (see Chapter 2).
- ☐ Gearchange mechanism return spring weak or broken (see Chapter 2).

- ☐ Gearchange linkage arm broken. Splines stripped out of arm or shaft, caused by a loose linkage arm pinch bolt or from dropping the bike (see Chapter 2).

Jumps out of gear

- ☐ Selector fork(s) worn (see Chapter 2).
- ☐ Selector fork groove(s) in selector drum worn (see Chapter 2).
- ☐ Gear pinion dogs or dog slots worn or damaged. The gear pinions should be inspected and renewed. No attempt should be made to repair the worn parts.

Overselects

- ☐ Gearchange mechanism stopper arm spring weak or broken, or arm roller broken or worn. Renew the spring or arm (see Chapter 2).
- ☐ Gearchange mechanism return spring weak or broken (see Chapter 2).

7 Abnormal engine noise

Knocking or pinking

- ☐ Carbon build-up in combustion chamber. Use of a fuel additive that will dissolve the adhesive bonding the carbon particles to the piston crown and chamber is the easiest way to remove the build-up. Otherwise, the cylinder head will have to be removed and decarbonised (Chapter 2).
- ☐ Incorrect or poor quality fuel. Old or improper grades of fuel can cause detonation. This causes the pistons to rattle, thus the knocking or pinking sound. Drain old fuel and always use the recommended fuel grade.
- ☐ Spark plug heat range incorrect. Uncontrolled detonation indicates the plug heat range is too hot. The plug in effect becomes a glow plug, raising cylinder temperatures. Install the proper heat range plug (Chapter 1).
- ☐ Improper air/fuel mixture. This will cause the cylinders to run hot, which leads to detonation. A blockage in the fuel system or an air leak can cause this imbalance (see Chapter 4).

Piston slap or rattling

- ☐ Cylinder-to-piston clearance excessive. Cylinder and/or piston worn, usually accompanied by worn rings as well. A top-end overhaul is necessary (see Chapter 2).
- ☐ Piston ring(s) worn, broken or sticking. Overhaul the top-end (see Chapter 2).
- ☐ Piston pin, piston pin bore or connecting rod small-end worn from high mileage or seized due to lack of lubrication (see Chapter 2).
- ☐ Piston seizure damage. Usually from lack of lubrication or overheating. Replace the pistons and upper crankcase, as necessary (see Chapter 2).
- ☐ Connecting rod big-end clearance excessive. Caused by excessive wear or lack of lubrication. Replace worn parts.

- ☐ Connecting rod bent. Caused by over-revving, trying to start a badly flooded engine or from ingesting a foreign object into the combustion chamber. Replace the damaged parts (Chapter 2).

Valve noise

- ☐ Incorrect valve clearances – check and adjust (see Chapter 1).
- ☐ Valve spring broken or weak. Check and replace weak valve springs with new ones (see Chapter 2).
- ☐ Camshaft or camshaft journals in the cylinder head worn or damaged. Lubrication failure at high rpm is usually the cause of damage due to insufficient oil or failure to change the oil at the recommended intervals. Since there are no replaceable bearings in the head, the head and camshaft holders will have to be renewed (see Chapter 2).

Other noise

- ☐ Cylinder head gasket leaking. Check around the joint for blowing with the engine running.
- ☐ Exhaust pipe leaking at cylinder head connection. Caused by incorrect fit of pipe(s), loose exhaust flange or damaged gasket. All exhaust system fasteners should be tightened evenly and carefully to avoid leaks (see Chapter 4).
- ☐ Crankshaft runout excessive. Caused by a bent crankshaft (from over-revving) or damage from an upper cylinder component failure. Can also be attributed to dropping the machine on either of the crankshaft ends.
- ☐ Engine mounting bolts loose – ensure all the bolts are tightened to the specified torque settings (see Chapter 2).
- ☐ Crankshaft bearings worn (see Chapter 2).
- ☐ Cam chain rattle, due to worn chain or defective tensioner. Also worn chain tensioner/guide blades (see Chapter 2).

8 Abnormal driveline noise

Clutch noise

☐ Clutch housing/friction plate clearance excessive (Chapter 2).
☐ Wear between the clutch housing splines and input shaft splines (Chapter 2).
☐ Worn release bearing (Chapter 2).

Transmission noise

☐ Bearings worn. Also includes the possibility that the shafts are worn. Overhaul the transmission (Chapter 2).
☐ Gears worn or chipped (Chapter 2).
☐ Metal chips jammed in gear teeth. Probably pieces from a broken clutch, gear or selector mechanism that were picked up by the gears. This will cause early bearing failure (Chapter 2).

☐ Engine oil level too low. Causes a howl from transmission. Also affects engine power and clutch operation (Pre-ride checks).

Final drive noise

☐ Drive chain excessively loose/worn or drive sprockets excessively worn. Adjust chain or replace chain and sprockets as a set (Chapters 1 and 6).
☐ Front or rear sprocket loose. Tighten fasteners (Chapter 6).
☐ Sprockets and/or chain worn. Fit new sprockets and chain (Chapter 6).
☐ Rear sprocket warped. Fit a new sprocket (Chapter 6).
☐ Rubber dampers in rear wheel worn (Chapter 6).

9 Abnormal frame and suspension noise

Front end noise

☐ Low fluid level or improper viscosity oil in forks. This can sound like spurting and is usually accompanied by irregular fork action (Chapter 5).
☐ Spring weak or broken. Makes a clicking or scraping sound. Fork oil, when drained, will have a lot of metal particles in it (Chapter 5).
☐ Steering head bearings loose or damaged. Clicks when braking. Check and adjust or replace with new ones as necessary (Chapters 1 and 5).
☐ Fork yoke clamp bolts loose – ensure all the bolts are tightened to the specified torque (Chapter 6).
☐ Forks bent. Good possibility if machine has been dropped. Replace the inner tubes with new ones as required (Chapter 5).
☐ Front axle or axle pinch bolt loose. Tighten them to the specified torque (Chapter 6).
☐ Loose or worn wheel bearings. Check and replace with new ones as needed (Chapters 1 and 6).

Rear end noise

☐ Shock absorber fluid level incorrect. Indicates a leak caused by defective seal. Shock will be covered with oil. Replace shock with a new one or seek advice on repair from a suspension specialist (Chapter 5).
☐ Defective shock absorber with internal damage. This is in the body of the shock and can't be remedied. The shock must be replaced with a new one or rebuilt (Chapter 5).
☐ Bent or damaged shock body. Replace the shock with a new one (Chapter 5).

☐ Loose or worn swingarm bearings. Check and replace with new ones as necessary (Chapter 5).
☐ Loose or worn wheel bearings/sprocket bearing. Check and replace with new ones as needed (Chapters 1 and 6).

Brake noise

☐ Squeal caused by pad shim not installed or positioned correctly (where fitted) (Chapter 6).
☐ Squeal caused by dust on brake pads. Usually found in combination with glazed pads. Clean using brake cleaning solvent (Chapter 6).
☐ Pads glazed. Caused by excessive heat from prolonged hard use or from contamination. DO NOT use sandpaper, emery cloth, carborundum cloth or any other abrasive to roughen the pad surfaces as abrasives will stay in the pad material and damage the disc. A very fine flat file can be used, but new pads is the best remedy (Chapter 6).
☐ Contamination of brake pads. Oil or brake fluid can cause the brake pads to chatter or squeal. Fit new pads. Identify the cause of the contamination, especially check the caliper piston seals for leaking fluid. Clean disc thoroughly with brake system cleaner (Chapter 6).
☐ Disc warped. Can cause a chattering, clicking or intermittent squeal. Usually accompanied by a pulsating lever and uneven braking. Replace the disc with new one (Chapter 6).
☐ Loose or worn wheel bearings. Check and replace with new ones as needed (Chapters 1 and 6).
☐ Forks incorrectly aligned on front wheel axle causing caliper or mounting to contact disc. Loosen front axle pinch bolt and re-align.

10 Oil level warning light comes on

Engine lubrication system

☐ Engine oil level low. Inspect for leak or other problem causing low oil level and add recommended oil (see Pre-ride checks).
☐ Engine oil pump defective, blocked oil strainer gauze or failed pressure relief valve. Carry out an oil pressure check (Chapter 2).
☐ Engine oil viscosity too low. Very old, thin oil or an improper weight of oil used in the engine. Change to correct oil (Chapter 1).
☐ Camshaft or crankshaft journals worn. Excessive wear causing drop in oil pressure. Abnormal wear could be caused by oil

starvation at high rpm from low oil level or improper weight or type of oil (Chapter 1).

Electrical system

☐ Oil level switch defective. Check the switch according to the procedure in Chapter 8. Replace it with a new one it if it is defective.
☐ Oil level warning LED defective. Check for pinched, shorted, disconnected or damaged wiring (Chapter 8).

11 Excessive exhaust smoke

White smoke

☐ Piston rings worn or broken, causing oil from the crankcase to be pulled past the piston into the combustion chamber. Replace the rings with new ones (Chapter 2).

☐ Cylinders worn or scored. Caused by overheating or oil starvation. Install a new upper crankcase and new pistons (Chapter 2).

☐ Valve stem oil seal damaged or worn. Replace the oil seals with new ones (Chapter 2).

☐ Valve guide worn. Perform a complete valve job (Chapter 2).

☐ Engine oil level too high, which causes the oil to be forced past the rings. Drain oil to the proper level (see Chapter 1 and *Pre-ride checks*).

☐ Head gasket broken between oil return and cylinder. Causes oil to be pulled into the combustion chamber. Replace the head gasket with a new one and check the head for warpage (Chapter 2).

☐ Abnormal crankcase pressurisation which forces oil past the rings, usually caused by a clogged breather.

Black smoke

☐ Air filter clogged. Clean the air filter element or replace it with a new one (Chapter 1).

☐ Fuel injection system malfunction (Chapter 4).

Brown smoke

☐ Air filter poorly sealed or not installed (Chapter 1).

☐ Fuel injection system malfunction (Chapter 4).

12 Poor handling or stability

Handlebars hard to turn

☐ Steering head bearing adjuster nut too tight. Check adjustment as described in Chapter 1.

☐ Bearings damaged. Roughness can be felt as the bars are turned from side-to-side. Replace the bearings with new ones (Chapter 5).

☐ Races dented or worn. Denting results from wear in only one position (e.g., straight ahead), from a collision or hitting a pothole or from dropping the machine. Replace the bearings with new ones (Chapter 5).

☐ Steering stem lubrication inadequate. Causes are grease getting hard from age or being washed out by high pressure car washes. Disassemble steering head and repack bearings (Chapter 5).

☐ Steering stem bent. Caused by a collision, hitting a pothole or by dropping the machine. Replace damaged part. Don't try to straighten the steering stem (Chapter 5).

☐ Front tyre air pressure too low (*Pre-ride checks*).

Handlebar shakes or vibrates excessively

☐ Tyres worn or out of balance.

☐ Swingarm bearings worn. Replace the bearings with new ones (Chapter 5).

☐ Wheel rim(s) warped or damaged. Inspect wheels for runout (Chapter 6).

☐ Wheel bearings worn. Worn front or rear wheel bearings can cause poor tracking. Worn front bearings will cause wobble (Chapters 1 and 6).

☐ Fork yoke clamp bolts or handlebar clamp bolts loose. Tighten them to the specified torque (Chapter 5).

☐ Engine mounting bolts loose. Will cause excessive vibration with increased engine rpm – ensure all the bolts are tightened to the specified torque settings (see Chapter 2).

Machine pulls to one side

☐ Frame bent. Definitely suspect this if the machine has been dropped. May or may not be accompanied by cracking near the steering head, swingarm mountings or engine mountings. Replace the frame with a new one (Chapter 5).

☐ Wheels out of alignment. Caused by improper location of axle spacers or from bent steering stem or frame (Chapter 5).

☐ Forks bent. Disassemble the forks and replace the damaged parts (Chapter 5).

☐ Swingarm bent or twisted. Replace the swingarm with a new one (Chapter 5).

☐ Fork oil level uneven. Check and add or drain as necessary (Chapter 5).

Poor shock absorbing qualities

☐ Too hard:
  a) Front fork oil level excessive (Chapter 5).
  b) Front fork oil viscosity too high. Use the correct oil (see the Specifications in Chapter 5).
  c) Front fork tube bent. Causes a harsh, sticking feeling (Chapter 5).
  d) Front fork internal damage (Chapter 5).
  e) Rear shock pre-load too high (Chapter 5).
  f) Rear shock shaft or body bent or damaged, or shock internal failure (Chapter 5).
  g) Tyre pressure too high (*Pre-ride checks*).

☐ Too soft:
  a) Front fork oil level too low (Chapter 5).
  b) Front fork oil viscosity too light (Chapter 5).
  c) Front fork springs weak or broken (Chapter 5).
  d) Front fork oil leaking. Strip fork and renew seals (Chapter 5).
  e) Rear shock pre-load too low for weight load (Chapter 5).
  f) Rear shock oil leaking or internal damage (Chapter 5).

13 Braking problems

Brakes are spongy, don't hold

☐ Low brake fluid level (see *Pre-ride checks*).
☐ Air in hydraulic system. Caused by inattention to master cylinder fluid level or by leakage. Locate problem and bleed brakes (Chapter 6).
☐ Pads worn. Renew pads (Chapters 1 and 6).
☐ Disc worn. Measure disc thickness and renew if necessary (Chapter 6).
☐ Contaminated pads. Caused by contamination with oil, grease, brake fluid, etc. Fit new pads. Identify the cause of the contamination, especially check the caliper piston seals for leaking fluid. Clean disc thoroughly with brake system cleaner (Chapter 6).
☐ Brake fluid deteriorated. Fluid is old or contaminated. Drain system, replenish with new fluid and bleed the system (Chapter 6).
☐ Master cylinder internal seals worn or damaged causing fluid to bypass (Chapter 6).
☐ Master cylinder bore scratched by foreign material or broken spring. Fit a new master cylinder (Chapter 6).
☐ Disc warped. Replace disc with new one (Chapter 6)

Brake lever or pedal pulsates

☐ Disc warped. Replace disc with new one (Chapter 6).
☐ Axle bent. Replace axle with new one (Chapter 6).

☐ Brake caliper bolts loose – tighten the bolts to the specified torque (Chapter 6).
☐ Wheel warped or otherwise damaged (Chapter 6).
☐ Wheel bearings damaged or worn (Chapters 1 and 6).

Brakes drag

☐ Brake caliper piston seized in bore. Caused by corrosion behind dust seals or ingestion of dirt past deteriorated seal (Chapter 6).
☐ Brake caliper slider pins sticking or corroded, preventing full movement of caliper (Chapter 6).
☐ Brake pad damaged. Pad material separated from backing plate. Usually caused by faulty manufacturing process or from contact with chemicals. Fit new pads (Chapter 6).
☐ Pads improperly installed (Chapter 6).
☐ Brake caliper incorrectly installed (Chapter 6).
☐ Master cylinder piston seized. Caused by wear or damage to piston or cylinder bore (Chapter 6).
☐ Lever balky or stuck. Check pivot and lubricate (Chapter 6).
☐ Forks incorrectly aligned on front wheel axle. Loosen front axle pinch bolts and re-align.

ABS system (where fitted)

☐ System fault indicated by indicator light coming on while the machine is being ridden. Download the fault code to identify the problem (Chapter 6).

14 Electrical problems

Battery dead or weak

☐ Battery faulty. Caused by sulphated plates which are shorted through sedimentation. Confirm by terminal voltage check (Chapter 8).
☐ Broken battery terminal making only occasional contact.
☐ Battery leads making poor contact (Chapter 8).
☐ Load excessive. Caused by addition of high wattage lights or other electrical accessories.
☐ Ignition switch defective. Switch either grounds (earths) internally or fails to shut off system. Renew the switch (Chapter 8).
☐ Regulator/rectifier defective (Chapter 8).
☐ Alternator stator coil open or shorted (Chapter 8).

☐ Electrical system fault. Check for excessive current leakage (Chapter 8).
☐ Wiring faulty. Wiring grounded (earthed) or connections loose in ignition, charging or lighting circuits (Chapter 8).

Battery overcharged

☐ Regulator/rectifier defective. Overcharging is noticed when battery gets excessively warm (Chapter 8).
☐ Battery faulty. Confirm with battery terminal voltage check (Chapter 8).
☐ Battery amperage too low, wrong type or size of battery. Install manufacturer's specified amp-hour battery to handle charging load (Chapter 8).

A

ABS (Anti-lock braking system) A system, usually electronically controlled, that senses incipient wheel lockup during braking and relieves hydraulic pressure at wheel which is about to skid.

Aftermarket Components suitable for the motorcycle, but not produced by the motorcycle manufacturer.

Allen key A hexagonal wrench which fits into a recessed hexagonal hole.

Alternating current (ac) Current produced by an alternator. Requires converting to direct current by a rectifier for charging purposes.

Alternator Converts mechanical energy from the engine into electrical energy to charge the battery and power the electrical system.

Ampere (amp) A unit of measurement for the flow of electrical current. Current = Volts ÷ Ohms.

Ampere-hour (Ah) Measure of battery capacity.

Angle-tightening A torque expressed in degrees. Often follows a conventional tightening torque for cylinder head or main bearing fasteners **(see illustration)**.

Angle-tightening con-rod bolts

Antifreeze A substance (usually ethylene glycol) mixed with water, and added to the cooling system, to prevent freezing of the coolant in winter. Antifreeze also contains chemicals to inhibit corrosion and the formation of rust and other deposits that would tend to clog the radiator and coolant passages and reduce cooling efficiency.

Anti-dive System attached to the fork lower leg (slider) to prevent fork dive when braking hard.

Anti-seize compound A coating that reduces the risk of seizing on fasteners that are subjected to high temperatures, such as exhaust clamp bolts and nuts.

API American Petroleum Institute. A quality standard for 4-stroke motor oils.

Asbestos A natural fibrous mineral with great heat resistance, commonly used in the composition of brake friction materials. Asbestos is a health hazard and the dust created by brake systems should never be inhaled or ingested.

ATF Automatic Transmission Fluid. Often used in front forks.

ATU Automatic Timing Unit. Mechanical device for advancing the ignition timing on early engines.

ATV All Terrain Vehicle. Often called a Quad.

Axial play Side-to-side movement.

Axle A shaft on which a wheel revolves. Also known as a spindle.

B

Backlash The amount of movement between meshed components when one component is held still. Usually applies to gear teeth.

Ball bearing A bearing consisting of a hardened inner and outer race with hardened steel balls between the two races.

Bearings Used between two working surfaces to prevent wear of the components and a build-up of heat. Four types of bearing are commonly used on motorcycles: plain shell bearings, ball bearings, tapered roller bearings and needle roller bearings.

Bevel gears Used to turn the drive through 90°. Typical applications are shaft final drive and camshaft drive **(see illustration)**.

Bevel gears are used to turn the drive through 90°

BHP Brake Horsepower. The British measurement for engine power output. Power output is now usually expressed in kilowatts (kW).

Bias-belted tyre Similar construction to radial tyre, but with outer belt running at an angle to the wheel rim.

Big-end bearing The bearing in the end of the connecting rod that's attached to the crankshaft.

Bleeding The process of removing air from an hydraulic system via a bleed nipple or bleed screw.

Bottom-end A description of an engine's crankcase components and all components contained there-in.

BTDC Before Top Dead Centre in terms of piston position. Ignition timing is often expressed in terms of degrees or millimetres BTDC.

Bush A cylindrical metal or rubber component used between two moving parts.

Burr Rough edge left on a component after machining or as a result of excessive wear.

C

Cam chain The chain which takes drive from the crankshaft to the camshaft(s).

Canister The main component in an evaporative emission control system (California market only); contains activated charcoal granules to trap vapours from the fuel system rather than allowing them to vent to the atmosphere.

Castellated Resembling the parapets along the top of a castle wall. For example, a castellated wheel axle or spindle nut.

Catalytic converter A device in the exhaust system of some machines which converts certain pollutants in the exhaust gases into less harmful substances.

Charging system Description of the components which charge the battery, ie the alternator, rectifier and regulator.

Circlip A ring-shaped clip used to prevent endwise movement of cylindrical parts and shafts. An internal circlip is installed in a groove in a housing; an external circlip fits into a groove on the outside of a cylindrical piece such as a shaft. Also known as a snap-ring.

Clearance The amount of space between two parts. For example, between a piston and a cylinder, between a bearing and a journal, etc.

Coil spring A spiral of elastic steel found in various sizes throughout a vehicle, for example as a springing medium in the suspension and in the valve train.

Compression Reduction in volume, and increase in pressure and temperature, of a gas, caused by squeezing it into a smaller space.

Compression damping Controls the speed the suspension compresses when hitting a bump.

Compression ratio The relationship between cylinder volume when the piston is at top dead centre and cylinder volume when the piston is at bottom dead centre.

Continuity The uninterrupted path in the flow of electricity. Little or no measurable resistance.

Continuity tester Self-powered bleeper or test light which indicates continuity.

Cp Candlepower. Bulb rating commonly found on US motorcycles.

Crossply tyre Tyre plies arranged in a criss-cross pattern. Usually four or six plies used, hence 4PR or 6PR in tyre size codes.

Cush drive Rubber damper segments fitted between the rear wheel and final drive sprocket to absorb transmission shocks **(see illustration)**.

Cush drive rubbers dampen out transmission shocks

D

Decarbonisation The process of removing carbon deposits - typically from the combustion chamber, valves and exhaust port/system.

Degree disc Calibrated disc for measuring piston position. Expressed in degrees.

Detonation Destructive and damaging explosion of fuel/air mixture in combustion chamber instead of controlled burning.

Dial gauge Clock-type gauge with adapters for measuring runout and piston position. Expressed in mm or inches.

Diaphragm The rubber membrane in a master cylinder or carburettor which seals the upper chamber.

Diaphragm spring A single sprung plate often used in clutches.

Direct current (dc) Current produced by a dc generator.

Diode An electrical valve which only allows current to flow in one direction. Commonly used in rectifiers and starter interlock systems.

Disc valve (or rotary valve) A induction system used on some two-stroke engines.

Double-overhead camshaft (DOHC) An engine that uses two overhead camshafts, one for the intake valves and one for the exhaust valves.

Drivebelt A toothed belt used to transmit drive to the rear wheel on some motorcycles. A drivebelt has also been used to drive the camshafts. Drivebelts are usually made of Kevlar.

Driveshaft Any shaft used to transmit motion. Commonly used when referring to the final driveshaft on shaft drive motorcycles.

E

Earth return The return path of an electrical circuit, utilising the motorcycle's frame.

ECU (Electronic Control Unit) A computer which controls (for instance) an ignition system, or an anti-lock braking system.

EGO Exhaust Gas Oxygen sensor. Sometimes called a Lambda sensor.

Electrolyte The fluid in a lead-acid battery.

EMS (Engine Management System) A computer controlled system which manages the fuel injection and the ignition systems in an integrated fashion.

Endfloat The amount of lengthways movement between two parts. As applied to a crankshaft, the distance that the crankshaft can move side-to-side in the crankcase.

Endless chain A chain having no joining link. Common use for cam chains and final drive chains.

EP (Extreme Pressure) Oil type used in locations where high loads are applied, such as between gear teeth.

Evaporative emission control system Describes a charcoal filled canister which stores fuel vapours from the tank rather than allowing them to vent to the atmosphere. Usually only fitted to California models and referred to as an EVAP system.

Expansion chamber Section of two-stroke engine exhaust system so designed to improve engine efficiency and boost power.

F

Feeler blade or gauge A thin strip or blade of hardened steel, ground to an exact thickness, used to check or measure clearances between parts.

Final drive Description of the drive from the transmission to the rear wheel. Usually by chain or shaft, but sometimes by belt.

Firing order The order in which the engine cylinders fire, or deliver their power strokes, beginning with the number one cylinder.

Flooding Term used to describe a high fuel level in the carburettor float chambers, leading to fuel overflow. Also refers to excess fuel in the combustion chamber due to incorrect starting technique.

Free length The no-load state of a component when measured. Clutch, valve and fork spring lengths are measured at rest, without any preload.

Freeplay The amount of travel before any action takes place. The looseness in a linkage, or an assembly of parts, between the initial application of force and actual movement. For example, the distance the rear brake pedal moves before the rear brake is actuated.

Fuel injection The fuel/air mixture is metered electronically and directed into the engine intake ports (indirect injection) or into the cylinders (direct injection). Sensors supply information on engine speed and conditions.

Fuel/air mixture The charge of fuel and air going into the engine. See Stoichiometric ratio.

Fuse An electrical device which protects a circuit against accidental overload. The typical fuse contains a soft piece of metal which is calibrated to melt at a predetermined current flow (expressed as amps) and break the circuit.

G

Gap The distance the spark must travel in jumping from the centre electrode to the side electrode in a spark plug. Also refers to the distance between the ignition rotor and the pickup coil in an electronic ignition system.

Gasket Any thin, soft material - usually cork, cardboard, asbestos or soft metal - installed between two metal surfaces to ensure a good seal. For instance, the cylinder head gasket seals the joint between the block and the cylinder head.

Gauge An instrument panel display used to monitor engine conditions. A gauge with a movable pointer on a dial or a fixed scale is an analogue gauge. A gauge with a numerical readout is called a digital gauge.

Gear ratios The drive ratio of a pair of gears in a gearbox, calculated on their number of teeth.

Glaze-busting see **Honing**

Grinding Process for renovating the valve face and valve seat contact area in the cylinder head.

Gudgeon pin The shaft which connects the connecting rod small-end with the piston. Often called a piston pin or wrist pin.

H

Helical gears Gear teeth are slightly curved and produce less gear noise that straight-cut gears. Often used for primary drives.

Helicoil A thread insert repair system. Commonly used as a repair for stripped spark plug threads **(see illustration)**.

Installing a Helicoil thread insert

Honing A process used to break down the glaze on a cylinder bore (also called glaze-busting). Can also be carried out to roughen a rebored cylinder to aid ring bedding-in.

HT (High Tension) Description of the electrical circuit from the secondary winding of the ignition coil to the spark plug.

Hydraulic A liquid filled system used to transmit pressure from one component to another. Common uses on motorcycles are brakes and clutches.

Hydrometer An instrument for measuring the specific gravity of a lead-acid battery.

Hygroscopic Water absorbing. In motorcycle applications, braking efficiency will be reduced if DOT 3 or 4 hydraulic fluid absorbs water from the air - care must be taken to keep new brake fluid in tightly sealed containers.

I

lbf ft Pounds-force feet. An imperial unit of torque. Sometimes written as ft-lbs.

lbf in Pound-force inch. An imperial unit of torque, applied to components where a very low torque is required. Sometimes written as in-lbs.

IC Abbreviation for Integrated Circuit.

Ignition advance Means of increasing the timing of the spark at higher engine speeds. Done by mechanical means (ATU) on early engines or electronically by the ignition control unit on later engines.

Ignition timing The moment at which the spark plug fires, expressed in the number of crankshaft degrees before the piston reaches the top of its stroke, or in the number of millimetres before the piston reaches the top of its stroke.

Infinity (∞) Description of an open-circuit electrical state, where no continuity exists.

Inverted forks (upside down forks) The sliders or lower legs are held in the yokes and the fork tubes or stanchions are connected to the wheel axle (spindle). Less unsprung weight and stiffer construction than conventional forks.

J

JASO Quality standard for 2-stroke oils.

Joule The unit of electrical energy.

Journal The bearing surface of a shaft.

K

Kickstart Mechanical means of turning the engine over for starting purposes. Only usually fitted to mopeds, small capacity motorcycles and off-road motorcycles.

Kill switch Handebar-mounted switch for emergency ignition cut-out. Cuts the ignition circuit on all models, and additionally prevent starter motor operation on others.

km Symbol for kilometre.

kmh Abbreviation for kilometres per hour.

L

Lambda (λ) sensor A sensor fitted in the exhaust system to measure the exhaust gas oxygen content (excess air factor).

Lapping see Grinding.

LCD Abbreviation for Liquid Crystal Display.

LED Abbreviation for Light Emitting Diode.

Liner A steel cylinder liner inserted in a aluminium alloy cylinder block.

Locknut A nut used to lock an adjustment nut, or other threaded component, in place.

Lockstops The lugs on the lower triple clamp (yoke) which abut those on the frame, preventing handlebar-to-fuel tank contact.

Lockwasher A form of washer designed to prevent an attaching nut from working loose.

LT Low Tension Description of the electrical circuit from the power supply to the primary winding of the ignition coil.

M

Main bearings The bearings between the crankshaft and crankcase.

Maintenance-free (MF) battery A sealed battery which cannot be topped up.

Manometer Mercury-filled calibrated tubes used to measure intake tract vacuum. Used to synchronise carburettors on multi-cylinder engines.

Micrometer A precision measuring instrument that measures component outside diameters **(see illustration)**.

Tappet shims are measured with a micrometer

MON (Motor Octane Number) A measure of a fuel's resistance to knock.

Monograde oil An oil with a single viscosity, eg SAE80W.

Monoshock A single suspension unit linking the swingarm or suspension linkage to the frame.

mph Abbreviation for miles per hour.

Multigrade oil Having a wide viscosity range (eg 10W40). The W stands for Winter, thus the viscosity ranges from SAE10 when cold to SAE40 when hot.

Multimeter An electrical test instrument with the capability to measure voltage, current and resistance. Some meters also incorporate a continuity tester and buzzer.

N

Needle roller bearing Inner race of caged needle rollers and hardened outer race. Examples of uncaged needle rollers can be found on some engines. Commonly used in rear suspension applications and in two-stroke engines.

Nm Newton metres.

NOx Oxides of Nitrogen. A common toxic pollutant emitted by petrol engines at higher temperatures.

O

Octane The measure of a fuel's resistance to knock.

OE (Original Equipment) Relates to components fitted to a motorcycle as standard or replacement parts supplied by the motorcycle manufacturer.

Ohm The unit of electrical resistance. Ohms = Volts ÷ Current.

Ohmmeter An instrument for measuring electrical resistance.

Oil cooler System for diverting engine oil outside of the engine to a radiator for cooling purposes.

Oil injection A system of two-stroke engine lubrication where oil is pump-fed to the engine in accordance with throttle position.

Open-circuit An electrical condition where there is a break in the flow of electricity - no continuity (high resistance).

O-ring A type of sealing ring made of a special rubber-like material; in use, the O-ring is compressed into a groove to provide the sealing action.

Oversize (OS) Term used for piston and ring size options fitted to a rebored cylinder.

Overhead cam (sohc) engine An engine with single camshaft located on top of the cylinder head.

Overhead valve (ohv) engine An engine with the valves located in the cylinder head, but with the camshaft located in the engine block or crankcase.

Oxygen sensor A device installed in the exhaust system which senses the oxygen content in the exhaust and converts this information into an electric current. Also called a Lambda sensor.

P

Plastigauge A thin strip of plastic thread, available in different sizes, used for measuring clearances. For example, a strip of Plastigauge is laid across a bearing journal. The parts are assembled and dismantled; the width of the crushed strip indicates the clearance between journal and bearing.

Polarity Either negative or positive earth (ground), determined by which battery lead is connected to the frame (earth return). Modern motorcycles are usually negative earth.

Pre-ignition A situation where the fuel/air mixture ignites before the spark plug fires. Often due to a hot spot in the combustion chamber caused by carbon build-up. Engine has a tendency to 'run-on'.

Pre-load (suspension) The amount a spring is compressed when in the unloaded state. Preload can be applied by gas, spacer or mechanical adjuster.

Premix The method of engine lubrication on older two-stroke engines. Engine oil is mixed with the petrol in the fuel tank in a specific ratio. The fuel/oil mix is sometimes referred to as "petroil".

Primary drive Description of the drive from the crankshaft to the clutch. Usually by gear or chain.

PS Pfedestärke - a German interpretation of BHP.

PSI Pounds-force per square inch. Imperial measurement of tyre pressure and cylinder pressure measurement.

PTFE Polytetrafluroethylene. A low friction substance.

Pulse secondary air injection system A process of promoting the burning of excess fuel present in the exhaust gases by routing fresh air into the exhaust ports.

Q

Quartz halogen bulb Tungsten filament surrounded by a halogen gas. Typically used for the headlight **(see illustration)**.

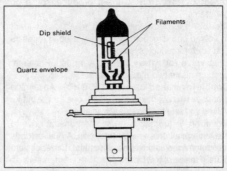

Quartz halogen headlight bulb construction

R

Rack-and-pinion A pinion gear on the end of a shaft that mates with a rack (think of a geared wheel opened up and laid flat). Sometimes used in clutch operating systems.

Radial play Up and down movement about a shaft.

Radial ply tyres Tyre plies run across the tyre (from bead to bead) and around the circumference of the tyre. Less resistant to tread distortion than other tyre types.

Radiator A liquid-to-air heat transfer device designed to reduce the temperature of the coolant in a liquid cooled engine.

Rake A feature of steering geometry - the angle of the steering head in relation to the vertical **(see illustration)**.

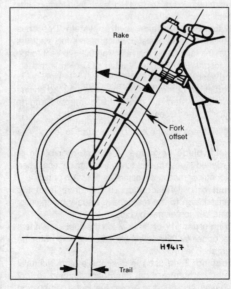

Steering geometry

Rebore Providing a new working surface to the cylinder bore by boring out the old surface. Necessitates the use of oversize piston and rings.

Rebound damping A means of controlling the oscillation of a suspension unit spring after it has been compressed. Resists the spring's natural tendency to bounce back after being compressed.

Rectifier Device for converting the ac output of an alternator into dc for battery charging.

Reed valve An induction system commonly used on two-stroke engines.

Regulator Device for maintaining the charging voltage from the generator or alternator within a specified range.

Relay A electrical device used to switch heavy current on and off by using a low current auxiliary circuit.

Resistance Measured in ohms. An electrical component's ability to pass electrical current.

RON (Research Octane Number) A measure of a fuel's resistance to knock.

rpm revolutions per minute.

Runout The amount of wobble (in-and-out movement) of a wheel or shaft as it's rotated. The amount a shaft rotates 'out-of-true'. The out-of-round condition of a rotating part.

S

SAE (Society of Automotive Engineers) A standard for the viscosity of a fluid.

Sealant A liquid or paste used to prevent leakage at a joint. Sometimes used in conjunction with a gasket.

Service limit Term for the point where a component is no longer useable and must be renewed.

Shaft drive A method of transmitting drive from the transmission to the rear wheel.

Shell bearings Plain bearings consisting of two shell halves. Most often used as big-end and main bearings in a four-stroke engine. Often called bearing inserts.

Shim Thin spacer, commonly used to adjust the clearance or relative positions between two parts. For example, shims inserted into or under tappets or followers to control valve clearances. Clearance is adjusted by changing the thickness of the shim.

Short-circuit An electrical condition where current shorts to earth (ground) bypassing the circuit components.

Skimming Process to correct warpage or repair a damaged surface, eg on brake discs or drums.

Slide-hammer A special puller that screws into or hooks onto a component such as a shaft or bearing; a heavy sliding handle on the shaft bottoms against the end of the shaft to knock the component free.

Small-end bearing The bearing in the upper end of the connecting rod at its joint with the gudgeon pin.

Spalling Damage to camshaft lobes or bearing journals shown as pitting of the working surface.

Specific gravity (SG) The state of charge of the electrolyte in a lead-acid battery. A measure of the electrolyte's density compared with water.

Straight-cut gears Common type gear used on gearbox shafts and for oil pump and water pump drives.

Stanchion The inner sliding part of the front forks, held by the yokes. Often called a fork tube.

Stoichiometric ratio The optimum chemical air/fuel ratio for a petrol engine, said to be 14.7 parts of air to 1 part of fuel.

Sulphuric acid The liquid (electrolyte) used in a lead-acid battery. Poisonous and extremely corrosive.

Surface grinding (lapping) Process to correct a warped gasket face, commonly used on cylinder heads.

T

Tapered-roller bearing Tapered inner race of caged needle rollers and separate tapered outer race. Examples of taper roller bearings can be found on steering heads.

Tappet A cylindrical component which transmits motion from the cam to the valve stem, either directly or via a pushrod and rocker arm. Also called a cam follower.

TCS Traction Control System. An electronically-controlled system which senses wheel spin and reduces engine speed accordingly.

TDC Top Dead Centre denotes that the piston is at its highest point in the cylinder.

Thread-locking compound Solution applied to fastener threads to prevent slackening. Select type to suit application.

Thrust washer A washer positioned between two moving components on a shaft. For example, between gear pinions on gearshaft.

Timing chain See **Cam Chain**.

Timing light Stroboscopic lamp for carrying out ignition timing checks with the engine running.

Top-end A description of an engine's cylinder block, head and valve gear components.

Torque Turning or twisting force about a shaft.

Torque setting A prescribed tightness specified by the motorcycle manufacturer to ensure that the bolt or nut is secured correctly. Undertightening can result in the bolt or nut coming loose or a surface not being sealed. Overtightening can result in stripped threads, distortion or damage to the component being retained.

Torx key A six-point wrench.

Tracer A stripe of a second colour applied to a wire insulator to distinguish that wire from another one with the same colour insulator. For example, Br/W is often used to denote a brown insulator with a white tracer.

Trail A feature of steering geometry. Distance from the steering head axis to the tyre's central contact point.

Triple clamps The cast components which extend from the steering head and support the fork stanchions or tubes. Often called fork yokes.

Turbocharger A centrifugal device, driven by exhaust gases, that pressurises the intake air. Normally used to increase the power output from a given engine displacement.

TWI Abbreviation for Tyre Wear Indicator. Indicates the location of the tread depth indicator bars on tyres.

U

Universal joint or U-joint (UJ) A double-pivoted connection for transmitting power from a driving to a driven shaft through an angle. Typically found in shaft drive assemblies.

Unsprung weight Anything not supported by the bike's suspension (ie the wheel, tyres, brakes, final drive and bottom (moving) part of the suspension).

V

Vacuum gauges Clock-type gauges for measuring intake tract vacuum. Used for carburettor synchronisation on multi-cylinder engines.

Valve A device through which the flow of liquid, gas or vacuum may be stopped, started or regulated by a moveable part that opens, shuts or partially obstructs one or more ports or passageways. The intake and exhaust valves in the cylinder head are of the poppet type.

Valve clearance The clearance between the valve tip (the end of the valve stem) and the rocker arm or tappet/follower. The valve clearance is measured when the valve is closed. The correct clearance is important - if too small the valve won't close fully and will burn out, whereas if too large noisy operation will result.

Valve lift The amount a valve is lifted off its seat by the camshaft lobe.

Valve timing The exact setting for the opening and closing of the valves in relation to piston position.

Vernier caliper A precision measuring instrument that measures inside and outside dimensions. Not quite as accurate as a micrometer, but more convenient.

Wet liner arrangement

VIN Vehicle Identification Number. Term for the bike's engine and frame numbers.

Viscosity The thickness of a liquid or its resistance to flow.

Volt A unit for expressing electrical "pressure" in a circuit. Volts = current x ohms.

W

Water pump A mechanically-driven device for moving coolant around the engine.

Watt A unit for expressing electrical power. Watts = volts x current.

Wear limit see **Service limit**

Wet liner A liquid-cooled engine design where the pistons run in liners which are directly surrounded by coolant **(see illustration)**.

Wheelbase Distance from the centre of the front wheel to the centre of the rear wheel.

Wiring harness or loom Describes the electrical wires running the length of the motorcycle and enclosed in tape or plastic sheathing. Wiring coming off the main harness is usually referred to as a sub harness.

Woodruff key A key of semi-circular or square section used to locate a gear to a shaft. Often used to locate the alternator rotor on the crankshaft.

Wrist pin Another name for gudgeon or piston pin.

Note: *References throughout this index are in the form - "Chapter number" • "Page number"*

Haynes Motorcycle Manuals – The Complete List

Title		Book No
APRILIA RS50 (99 – 06) & RS125 (93 – 06)		4298
Aprilia RSV1000 Mille (98 – 03)	♦	4255
Aprilia SR50		4755
BMW 2-valve Twins (70 -96)	♦	0249
BMW F650	♦	4761
BMW K100 & 75 2-valve models (83 - 96)	♦	1373
BMW F800 (F650) Twins (06 – 10)	♦	4872
BMW R850, 1100 & 1150 4-valve Twins (93 – 06)	♦	3466
BMW R1200 (04 – 09)	♦	4598
BMW R1200 dohc Twins (10 – 12)	♦	4925
BSA Bantam (48 – 71)		0117
BSA Unit Singles (58 – 72)		0127
BSA Pre-unit Singles (54 – 61)		0326
BSA A7 & A10 Twins (47 – 62)		0121
BSA A50 & A65 Twins (62 – 73)		0155
CHINESE, Taiwanese & Korean Scooters		4768
Chinese, Taiwanese & Korean 125cc motorcyles		4781
DUCATI 600, 620, 750 & 900 2-valve V-twins (91 – 05)	♦	3290
Ducati Mk III & Desmo singles (69 – 76)	◊	0445
Ducati 748, 916 & 996 4-valve V-twins (94 – 01)	♦	3756
GILERA Runner, DNA, Ice & SKP/Stalker (97 – 11)		4163
HARLEY-DAVIDSON Sportsters (70 – 10)	♦	2534
Harley-Davidson Shovelhead & Evolution Big Twins (70 -99)	♦	2536
Harley-Davidson Twin Cam 88, 96 & 103 models (99 – 10)	♦	2478
HONDA NB, ND, NP & NS50 Melody (81 -85)	◊	0622
Honda NE/NB50 Vision & SA50 Vision Met-in (85-95)	◊	1278
Honda MB, MBX, MT & MTX50 (80 – 93)		0731
Honda C50, C70 & C90 (67 – 03)		0324
Honda XR50/70/80/100R & CRF50/70/80/100F (85 – 07)		2218
Honda XL/XR 80, 100, 125, 185 & 200 2-valve models (78 – 87)		0566
Honda H100 & H100S Singles (80 – 92)	◊	0734
Honda 125 Scooters (00 – 09)		4873
Honda ANF125 Innova Scooters (03 -12)	♦	4926
Honda CB/CD125T & CM125C Twins (77 – 88)	◊	0571
Honda CBF125 (09 – 12)	♦	5540
Honda CG125 (76 – 07)	◊	0433
Honda NS125 (86 – 93)	◊	3056
Honda CBR125R (04 – 10)		4620
Honda MBX/MTX125 & MTX200 (83 – 93)	◊	1132
Honda XL125V & VT125C (99 – 11)		4899
Honda CD/CM185 200T & CM250C 2-valve Twins (77 – 85)		0572
Honda CMX250 Rebel & CB250 Nighthawk Twins (85 – 09)	◊	2756
Honda XL/XR 250 & 500 (78 – 84)		0567
Honda XR250L, XR250R & XR400R (86 – 03)		2219
Honda CB250 & CB400N Super Dreams (78 – 84)	◊	0540
Honda CR Motocross Bikes (86 – 07)		2222
Honda CRF250 & CRF450 (02 – 06)		2630
Honda CBR400RR Fours (88 – 99)	◊♦	3552
Honda VFR400 (NC30) & RVF400 (NC35) V-Fours (89 – 98)	◊♦	3496
Honda CB500 (93 – 02) & CBF500 (03 – 08)	◊	3753
Honda CB400 & CB550 Fours (73 – 77)		0262
Honda CX/GL500 & 650 V-Twins (78 – 86)		0442
Honda CBX550 Four (82 – 86)	◊	0940
Honda XL600R & XR600R (83 – 08)	♦	2183
Honda XL600/650V Transalp & XRV750 Africa Twin (87 – 07)	♦	3919
Honda CB600 Hornet, CBF600 & CBR600F (07 – 12)	♦	5572
Honda CBR600F1 & 1000F Fours (87 – 96)	♦	1730
Honda CBR600F2 & F3 Fours (91 – 98)	♦	2070
Honda CBR600F4 (99 – 06)	♦	3911
Honda CB600F Hornet & CBF600 (98 – 06)	◊♦	3915
Honda CBR600RR (03 – 06)	♦	4590
Honda CBR600RR (07 -12)	♦	4795
Honda CB650 sohc Fours (78 – 84)		0665
Honda NTV600 Revere, NTV650 & NT650V Deauville (88 – 05)	◊♦	3243
Honda Shadow VT600 & 750 (USA) (88 – 09)		2312
Honda NT700V Deauville & XL700V Transalp (06 -13)	♦	5541
Honda CB750 sohc Four (69 – 79)		0131
Honda V45/65 Sabre & Magna (82 – 88)		0820
Honda VFR750 & 700 V-Fours (86 – 97)	♦	2101
Honda VFR800 V-Fours (97 – 01)	♦	3703
Honda VFR800 V-Tec V-Fours (02 – 09)	♦	4196
Honda CB750 & CB900 dohc Fours (78 – 84)		0535
Honda CBF1000 (06 -10) & CB1000R (08 – 11)	♦	4927
Honda VTR1000 Firestorm, Super Hawk & XL1000V Varadero (97 – 08)	♦	3744
Honda CBR900RR Fireblade (92 – 99)	♦	2161
Honda CBR900RR Fireblade (00 – 03)	♦	4060
Honda CBR1000RR Fireblade (04 – 07)	♦	4604
Honda CBR1100XX Super Blackbird (97 – 07)	♦	3901
Honda ST1100 Pan European V-Fours (90 – 02)	♦	3384
Honda ST1300 Pan European (02 -11)	♦	4908

Title		Book No
Honda Shadow VT1100 (USA) (85 – 07)		2313
Honda GL1000 Gold Wing (75 – 79)		0309
Honda GL1100 Gold Wing (79 – 81)		0669
Honda Gold Wing 1200 (USA) (84 - 87)		2199
Honda Gold Wing 1500 (USA) (88 – 00)		2225
Honda Goldwing GL1800	♦	2787
KAWASAKI AE/AR 50 & 80 (81 – 95)		1007
Kawasaki KC, KE & KH100 (75 – 99)		1371
Kawasaki KMX125 & 200 (86 – 02)	◊	3046
Kawasaki 250, 350 & 400 Triples (72 – 79)		0134
Kawasaki 400 & 440 Twins (74 – 81)		0281
Kawasaki 400, 500 & 550 Fours (79 – 91)		0910
Kawasaki EN450 & 500 Twins (Ltd/Vulcan) (85 – 07)		2053
Kawasaki ER-6F & ER-6N (06 -10)	♦	4874
Kawasaki EX500 (GPZ500S) & ER500 (ER-5) (87 – 08)	♦	2052
Kawasaki ZX600 (ZZ-R600 & Ninja ZX-6) (90 – 06)	♦	2146
Kawasaki ZX-6R Ninja Fours (95 – 02)	♦	3451
Kawasaki ZX-6R (03 – 06)	♦	4742
Kawasaki ZX600 (GPZ600R, GPX600R, Ninja 600R & RX) & ZX750 (GPX750R, Ninja 750R) (85 – 97)	♦	1780
Kawasaki 650 Four (76 – 78)		0373
Kawasaki Vulcan 700/750 & 800 (85 – 04)	♦	2457
Kawasaki Vulcan 1500 & 1600 (87 – 08)	♦	4913
Kawasaki 750 Air-cooled Fours		0574
Kawasaki ZR550 & 750 Zephyr Fours (90 – 97)	♦	3382
Kawasaki Z750 & Z1000 (03 – 08)	♦	4762
Kawasaki ZX750 (Ninja ZX-7 & ZXR750) Fours (89 – 96)	♦	2054
Kawasaki Ninja ZX-7R & ZX-9R (94 – 04)	♦	3721
Kawasaki 900 & 1000 Fours (73 – 77)		0222
Kawasaki ZX900, 1000 & 1100 Liquid-cooled Fours (83 – 97)	♦	1681
KTM EXC Enduro & SX Motocross (00 – 07)	♦	4629
LAMBRETTA Scooters (58 – 00)	♦	5573
MOTO GUZZI 750, 850 & 1000 V-Twins (74 – 78)		0339
MZ ETZ models (81 – 95)	◊	1680
NORTON 500, 600, 650 & 750 Twins (57 – 70)		0187
Norton Commando (68 – 77)		0125
PEUGEOT Speedfight, Trekker & Vivacity Scooters (96 – 08)	◊	3920
PIAGGIO (Vespa) Scooters (91 – 09)	◊	3492
SUZUKI GT, ZR & TS50 (77 – 90)	◊	0799
Suzuki TS50X (84 – 00)	◊	1599
Suzuki 100, 125, 185 & 250 Air-cooled Trail bikes (79 – 89)		0797
Suzuki GP100 & 125 Singles (78 – 93)	◊	0576
Suzuki GS, GN, GZ & DR125 Singles (82 – 05)	◊	0888
Suzuki Burgman 250 & 400 (98 – 11)	♦	4909
Suzuki GSX-R600/750 (06 – 09)	♦	4790
Suzuki 250 & 350 Twins (68 – 78)		0120
Suzuki GT250X7, GT200X5 & SB200 Twins (78 – 83)	◊	0469
Suzuki DR-Z400 (00 – 10)	♦	2933
Suzuki GS/GSX250, 400 & 450 Twins (79 – 85)		0736
Suzuki GS500 Twin (89 – 08)	♦	3238
Suzuki GS550 (77 – 82) & GS750 Fours (76 – 79)		0363
Suzuki GS/GSX550 4-valve Fours (83 – 88)		1133
Suzuki SV650 & SV650S (99 – 08)	♦	3912
Suzuki GSX-R600 & 750 (96 – 00)	♦	3553
Suzuki GSX-R600 (01 – 03), GSX-R750 (00 – 03) & GSX-R1000 (01 – 02)	♦	3986
Suzuki GSX-R600/750 (04 – 05) & GSX-R1000 (03 – 06)	♦	4382
Suzuki GSF600, 650 & 1200 Bandit Fours (95 – 06)	♦	3367
Suzuki Intruder, Marauder, Volusia & Boulevard (85 – 09)	♦	2618
Suzuki GS850 Fours (78 – 88)		0536
Suzuki GS1000 Four (77 – 79)		0484
Suzuki GSX-R750, GSX-R1100 (85 – 92) GSX600F, GSX750F, GSX1100F (Katana) Fours (88 – 96)	♦	2055
Suzuki GSX600/750F & GSX750 (98 – 02)	♦	3987
Suzuki GS/GSX1000, 1100 & 1150 4-valve Fours (79 – 88)		0737
Suzuki TL1000S/R & DL V-Strom (97 – 04)	♦	4083
Suzuki GSF650/1250 (07 – 09)	♦	4798
Suzuki GSX1300R Hayabusa (99 – 04)	♦	4184
Suzuki GSX1400 (02 – 08)	♦	4758
TRIUMPH Tiger Cub & Terrier (52 – 68)		0414
Triumph 350 & 500 Unit Twins (58 – 73)		0137
Triumph Pre-Unit Twins (47 – 62)		0251
Triumph 650 & 750 2-valve Unit Twins (63 – 83)		0122
Triumph 675 (06 – 10)	♦	4876
Triumph 1050 Sprint, Speed Triple & Tiger (05 -13)	♦	4796
Triumph Trident & BSA Rocket 3 (69 – 75)		0136
Triumph Bonneville (01 – 12)	♦	4364
Triumph Daytona, Speed Triple, Sprint & Tiger (97 – 05)	♦	3755
Triumph Triples & Fours (carburetor engines) (91 – 04)	♦	2162
VESPA P/PX125, 150 & 200 Scooters (78 – 12)		0707
Vespa GTS125, 250 & 300 (05 – 10)		4898

Title		Book No
Vespa Scooters (59 – 78)		0126
YAMAHA DT50 & 80 Trail Bikes (78 – 95)	◊	0800
Yamaha T50 & 80 Townmate (83 – 95)	◊	1247
Yamaha YB100 Singles (73 – 91)	◊	0474
Yamaha RS/RXS 100 & 125 Singles (74 – 95)		0331
Yamaha RD & DT125LC (82 – 87)	◊	0887
Yamaha TZR125 (87 – 93) & DT125R (88 – 07)	◊	1655
Yamaha TY50, 80, 125 & 175 (74 – 84)	◊	0464
Yamaha XT & SR125 (82 – 03)	◊	1021
Yamaha YBR125 & XT125R/X (05 – 13)		4797
Yamaha YZF-R125 (08 – 11)	♦	5543
Yamaha Trail Bikes (81 – 00)		2350
Yamaha 2-stroke Motocross Bikes (86 – 06)		2662
Yamaha YZ & WR 4-stroke Motorcross Bikes (98 – 08)		2689
Yamaha 250 & 350 Twins (70 – 79)		0040
Yamaha XS250, 360 & 400 sohc Twins (75 – 84)		0378
Yamaha RD250 & 350LC Twins (80 – 82)		0803
Yamaha RD350 YPVS Twins (83 – 95)		1158
Yamaha RD400 Twin (75 – 79)		0333
Yamaha XT, TT & SR500 Singles (75 – 83)		0342
Yamaha XZ550 Vision V-Twins (82 – 85)		0821
Yamaha FJ, FX, XY & YX600 Radian (84 – 92)		2100
Yamaha XT660 & MT-03 (04 – 11)	♦	4910
Yamaha XJ600S (Diversion, Seca II) & XJ600N Fours (92 – 03)	♦	2145
Yamaha YZF600R Thundercat & FZS600 Fazer (96 – 03)	♦	3702
Yamaha FZ-6 Fazer (04 – 08)	♦	4751
Yamaha YZF-R6 (99 – 02)	♦	3900
Yamaha YZF-R6 (03 – 05)	♦	4601
Yamaha YZF-R6 (06 – 13)	♦	5544
Yamaha 650 Twins (70 – 83)		0341
Yamaha XJ650 & 750 Fours (80 – 84)		0738
Yamaha XS750 & 850 Triples (76 – 85)		0340
Yamaha TDM850, TRX850 & XTZ750 (89 – 99)	◊♦	3450
Yamaha YZF750R & YZF1000R Thunderace (93 – 00)	♦	3720
Yamaha FZR600, 750 & 1000 Fours (87 – 96)	♦	2056
Yamaha XV (Virago) V-Twins (81 – 03)	♦	0802
Yamaha XVS650 & 1100 Drag Star/V-Star (97 – 05)	♦	4195
Yamaha XJ900F Fours (83 – 94)	♦	3239
Yamaha XJ900S Diversion (94 – 01)	♦	3739
Yamaha YZF-R1 (98 – 03)	♦	3754
Yamaha YZF-R1 (04 – 06)	♦	4605
Yamaha FZS1000 Fazer (01 – 05)	♦	4287
Yamaha FJ1100 & 1200 Fours (84 – 96)	♦	2057
Yamaha XJR1200 & 1300 (95 – 06)	♦	3981
Yamaha V-Max (85 – 03)	♦	4072
ATV's		
Honda ATC 70, 90, 110, 185 & 200 (71 – on)		0565
Honda Rancher, Recon & TRX250EX ATVs		2553
Honda TRX300 Shaft Drive ATVs (88 – 00)		2125
Honda Foreman (95 – 11)		2465
Honda TRX300EX, TRX400EX & TRX450R/ER ATVs (93 – 06)		2318
Kawasaki Bayou 220/250/300 & Prairie 300 ATVs (86 – 03)		2351
Polaris ATVs (85 – 97)		2302
Polaris ATVs (98 – 07)		2508
Suzuki/Kawasaki/Artic Cat ATVs (03 – 09)		2910
Yamaha YFS200 Blaster ATV (88 – 06)		2317
Yamaha YFM350 & YFM400 (ER & Big Bear) ATVs (87 – 09)		2126
Yamaha YFZ450 & YFZ450R (04 – 10)		2899
Yamaha Banshee and Warrior ATVs (87 – 10)		2314
Yamaha Kodiak and Grizzly ATVs (93 – 05)		2567
ATV Basics		10450
TECHBOOK SERIES		
Twist and Go (automatic transmission) Scooters Service and Repair Manual		4082
Motorcycle Basics Techbook (2nd edition)		3515
Motorcycle Electrical Techbook (3rd edition)		3471
Motorcycle Fuel Systems Techbook		3514
Motorcycle Maintenance Techbook		4071
Motorcycle Modifying		4272
Motorcycle Workshop Practice Techbook (2nd edition)		3470

◊ = not available in the USA ♦ = Superbike

The manuals on this page are available through good motorcycle dealers and accessory shops.
In case of difficulty, contact: **Haynes Publishing**
(UK) **+44 1963 442030** (USA) **+1 805 498 6703**
(SV) **+46 18 124016**
(Australia/New Zealand) **+61 2 8713 1400**

MCL 30.09.13

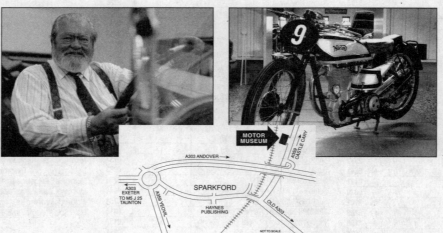